Managerial Control of American Workers

ALSO BY MEL VAN ELTEREN

*Labor and the American Left:
An Analytical History* (McFarland, 2011)

*Americanism and Americanization: A Critical History
of Domestic and Global Influence* (McFarland, 2006)

Managerial Control of American Workers

Methods and Technology from the 1880s to Today

Mel van Elteren

McFarland & Company, Inc., Publishers
Jefferson, North Carolina

LIBRARY OF CONGRESS CATALOGUING-IN-PUBLICATION DATA

Names: Elteren, Mel van, author.
Title: Managerial control of American workers : methods and technology from the 1880s to today / Mel van Elteren.
Description: Jefferson, North Carolina : McFarland & Company, Inc., Publishers, [2017] | Includes bibliographical references and index.
Identifiers: LCCN 2016059862 | ISBN 9781476664996 (softcover : acid free paper) ∞
Subjects: LCSH: Industrial management—United States—History. | Industrial relations—United States—History. | Organization—History.
Classification: LCC HD70.U5 E45 2017 | DDC 658.3/15—dc23
LC record available at https://lccn.loc.gov/2016059862

BRITISH LIBRARY CATALOGUING DATA ARE AVAILABLE

ISBN (print) 978-1-4766-6499-6
ISBN (ebook) 978-1-4766-2727-4

© 2017 Mel van Elteren. All rights reserved

No part of this book may be reproduced or transmitted in any form or by any means, electronic or mechanical, including photocopying or recording, or by any information storage and retrieval system, without permission in writing from the publisher.

Front cover image © 2017 peshkov/iStock

Printed in the United States of America

*McFarland & Company, Inc., Publishers
Box 611, Jefferson, North Carolina 28640
www.mcfarlandpub.com*

To Vera and Edmund

Table of Contents

Acknowledgments   ix

Introduction   1

1. The Rise of the Factory System and the Origins of Systematic Management   19
2. Taylorism and Fordism and Their Early Impact on Manufacturing and Service Work   35
3. Welfare Capitalism and Human Relations as Additional Means of Managerial Control   56
4. Taylorization During World War II and the Postwar Automation Movement   88
5. The "New Nonunion Model" and the Great Risk Shift   98
6. Renewal of "Flexible Mass Production" Through a Japanese Filter   110
7. Industrial Rationalization of Retail and Service Work Intensified   133
8. Enhanced Top-Down Management Systems in Manufacturing and Office Work   144
9. Enterprise Resource Planning: Business Process Reengineering Taken to the Next Level   171
10. Twists and Turns of High-Tech Jobs and the Reengineering of Skilled White-Collar Work   183
11. Technology-First Automation and the Double-Edged Sword of Decision-Support Systems   209

12	The Extensive and Intrusive Reach of Computer Business Systems	224
13	Robots: Cooperating with or Replacing Human Workers?	236
14	Digital Information Technologies and the Nikefication of Production and Work Organization	244

Conclusion   253
Chapter Notes   267
Bibliography   299
Index   313

Acknowledgments

My interest in managerial control strategies concerning workers and labor processes in U.S. industrial firms dates back to the early 1980s, when I did research for my doctoral dissertation, *Staal en Arbeid* (1986), an historical study of management policies regarding "industrial accommodation processes" of workers in the Dutch steel industry. I then traced and analyzed (among other things) the reception of U.S.–originated management practices by this company during the postwar years. These imports included not only interventions in the workplace, such as scientific management (in relation to work organization, job classifications and work rules, wage incentive schemes), "human relations" and Training Within Industry programs, but also corporate paternalism in the form of welfare programs "outside the gate." I am still grateful to the people who supported me in bringing that research to fruition, especially the late Harry van den Eerenbeemt, professor emeritus of history at Tilburg University, and Henk Pirovano, former head of Hoogovens Central Archive.

Subsequently, I examined the broader influx of applied psychology and sociology of work from America and their appropriation by Dutch firms over the course of time. Partly in relation to this, I also made an in-depth study of the development of Kurt Lewin's social psychology of work both before and after his refuge from Germany to America. Today I remain thankful to my former fellow members of Cheiron (European Society for the History of the Behavioral & Social Sciences), Ian Lubek, Helmut Lück, Jaap van Ginneken and Pieter van Strien, for the interest they showed in these projects and resulting publications.

These studies were also one source of inspiration for the writing of my book, *Americanism and Americanization* (2006); the other major source was my later research of various forms of American (popular) culture and their reception in Europe.

With respect to the present book, which can be seen partly as a complement to my previous book, *Labor and the American Left* (2011), I want to thank Francis Shor, professor emeritus of history at Wayne State University, and Tom Discenna, Midwest PCA/ACA area chair on labor, work, and culture, for offering me the opportunity to discuss some of my ideas at conferences.

Finally, I am deeply indebted to my loving wife, Nancy A. Schaefer, a poet and scholar, for her very helpful criticism and editing.

Introduction

Control, the power to influence or direct people's behavior or the course of events, is a quintessential component of the history of humankind. Control issues are central to a variety of basic institutions that form a society, from the spheres of family, kinship, and education to the economy, political order, and culture (including religion, science and art). Likewise control issues are at the heart of both traditional and modern modes of management. This book focuses on managerial control practices regarding workers and labor processes in a variety of work settings in the U.S. from the late 19th century up until today. It looks at management strategies with regard to both blue-collar and white-collar workers over this entire period, as well as high-tech and other skilled knowledge workers over the past few decades. In taking this investigative journey through the past, the primary aim is to develop a deeper understanding and appreciation of recent developments in American working life.[1]

A labor process (sometimes loosely termed "work organization") is a means by which objects, people, tools, knowledge and tasks are organized so that they are transformed into objects or services that have some value for others. The basic components of a labor process are threefold: first, the work itself, a purposive productive activity; second, the object(s) on which that work is performed, and third, the instruments and technologies that facilitate the process of work. The combination of job designs and technologies affects where and how people work. The introduction of new technology, for instance, often combines tasks previously performed by various skill categories of workers, making some workers redundant while requiring new skills for other workers. Thus, occupations, careers, and individual well-being are intricately related to the particular labor processes people are involved in.[2] What should be apparent too, is that what happens in the workplace is also influenced by "human resources" practices and industrial relations (including the effects of labor legislation) and more indirectly by welfare programs to the extent that those are provided by the employer. Moreover, to fully grasp all the moving parts, these need to be situated within the broader context of the surrounding community, and the political-economic conditions at the local, state, and federal levels in the American case.

Managerial control is a major theme in the labor process literature that takes as its point of departure Harry Braverman's influential book, *Labor and Monopoly Capital* (1974), which builds on Marx's writing about the labor process in volume 1 of *Capital*. The focus of Braverman's book is on the processes allegedly leading to the degradation of work in the 20th century. He argues that capitalism contains an inherent logic of deskilling preeminently manifested in scientific management as espoused by Frederick W. Taylor. Following Taylor's basic principles, in factory work, each step of the production process is broken down into its simplest elements; management determines the most efficient method of performing the task and provides detailed instructions which workers are expected to follow without question. Taylor anticipated considerable increases in productivity through the simplification of production in specialized tasks, in tandem with management's suppression of "systematic soldiering" (or output restriction—in effect, when workers consciously slowed down) that he believed accompanied attempts at workers' control.

Principally, Braverman suggested that the never-ending drive toward efficient production is also a drive for the control of workers by management. Managerial control is achieved through monopolizing judgment, knowledge and the conceptual side of work, while at the same time excluding workers from control and ownership of knowledge and skill acquisition. The addition of new technology, the introduction of new work rules, changes in the wage formulas as well as the level of direct supervision all result from management's persistent effort to control the physical and mental effort of employees.

For Braverman, then, the expansion of capitalist work in the 20th century was one of work degradation, as knowledge was systematically removed from direct producers and concentrated into the hands of management and their agents. This led to the impoverishment and debasement of the quality and experience of labor, both for manual and mental workers who were condemned to execute only the routine and conceptually depleted tasks in the service of capital.[3]

Braverman's historical benchmark was the craft worker, who epitomized the unity of manual and mental work, and he noted that the initial opposition to Taylorism was not directed at the time study feature of this system but rather at its efforts to strip the craft workers of their knowledge and autonomy. Braverman assumed that control over labor was exerted above all by the separation of conception and execution of the production process. This increased the power of managers to control the simplified task performance of workers. Similarly, the introduction of machinery entailed the unobtrusive control over the pace of work, and therefore it too furthered the interests of capital rather than labor. Thus, Taylorism transferred a worker's knowledge and control of work processes to managers, and technology transferred a worker's skill and control to the machinery owned by capital.[4]

The effects of scientific management reverberated far beyond the male craftsmen when it was introduced into office work during the first decades of the 20th century. As Braverman asserted, office and retail work were reorganized on the basis of the same principles as Taylorized factory work, with the same results, namely increased output to the benefit of capital and reduced skill to the detriment of labor. He acknowledged that in expanding industries there are increased opportunities for a few workers to move into planning and supervisory positions, but he insisted that such a short-term trend does not counteract the longer-term progression of deskilling.

Although Braverman's contribution to the debate about deskilling is widely considered by experts as seminal, it has nonetheless met with serious criticism. He has been accused of romanticizing the pre-modern skilled manual worker; in this regard his work is characterized by a Proudhonian rather than a Marxist view.[5] For Pierre-Joseph Proudhon, the printer-philosopher and utopian socialist who dominated the French socialist movement until 1900, craft knowledge was the touchstone of human work. He argued that training in a craft should form the core of all public education, and that the craft workshop offered the model for rebuilding society. Thus, "the Workshop Republic would be constituted from the mini-republics of craft workshops."[6] This is not unlike the ideal of the craftsman inherent to 19th-century working-class republicanism and producerist notions about a workers' commonwealth in America that lingered until the early 20th century.[7]

This line of criticism is more than a matter of idealizing the past. It concerns the empirical question of the representativeness of the craft worker prior to the rise of scientific management and mechanization in America from about 1900 onward. On this crucial issue, Braverman implied that craft workers were central to all production processes in the 19th century, which distorts their numerical importance. It has been noted that the majority of the pre-industrial capitalist labor force were farm-laborers and domestic servants, not coppersmiths, masons, cabinet makers and the like, or farriers or thatchers. And industrialization also created dozens of new occupations—boilermakers, machinery fitters, locomotive drivers, electricians, etc.—whose work was at least as skilled as that of the longstanding traditional crafts. In the 20th century, some of the skilled occupations created by the Industrial Revolution began to contract as products and the pattern of demand changed. These changes were exacerbated in several cases by rationalization, scientific management, and a managerial quest for control of exactly the kind Braverman depicted.[8] It must also be remembered that among craft workers, there were clear variations regarding the extent to which they yielded to managerial power and were therefore able to resist deskilling.

Braverman's tendency to idealize craft work also pertained to non-manual workers. He likened clerical work to a craft and contrasted the "small and privileged clerical stratum of the past" with the enlarged Taylorized and mechanized, and therefore deskilled, clerical class of his time.[9] However, research in Britain and the U.S. has shown that Braverman's highly skilled clerical workers were a small minority (5 to 10 percent) of 19th-century clerks; the majority then did work of a routine and repetitious kind.[10] Concerning the development of data-processing work during the mid–20th century, Braverman admitted that for a short time it "displayed the characteristics of a craft."[11] However, along with the computer, a new division of labor was introduced, and the destruction of the craft greatly accelerated. At the upper echelons of the computer work hierarchy, a small number of technical specialists were indeed retained, but further down the hierarchy a mass of operators undertook work that had been "simplified, routinized, and measured," ensuring the increasing similarity between work in an electronic office and a factory.[12]

Braverman underestimated the extent of upskilling in an attempt to counter the prevailing conventional wisdom (at the time of his writing) that there had been a general upgrading of work, especially with regard to clerical workers. Although he was aware of the unevenness of the deskilling process as a result of social changes in the organization and mechanization of production which created new crafts and skills and technical specialists, he considered such possibilities as temporary.[13] Regarding the increased demand for maintenance workers and technical specialists, such as engineers, who were responsible for the conceptualization and planning of production, Braverman responded in a similar fashion. He argued that there was a tendency for their work to be "standardized in much the same fashion as that of the production worker," due in large part to the introduction of computers and numerical control instrumentation.[14] He did admit that the computerization of clerical work created the "exception of a specialized minority, whose technical and 'systems' skills are expanded."[15] But he did not consider this exception to the overall deskilling tendency (inherent to industrial capitalism) a threat to his thesis since the jobs of the majority of new technical specialists would be rationalized in due course, degraded by the twin forces of Taylorism and mechanization.

Braverman has also been criticized for portraying managers as all-powerful and workers as impotent, and therefore overestimated the extent to which capitalists were able and willing to implement Taylorism while underestimating the degree to which workers, especially craft workers, resisted the deskilling impact of Taylorization and mechanization, both individually and collectively.[16] Crucial for us here is Braverman's omission not only of the recalcitrance of individual workers against managerial attempts to control them, but also the involvement of the entire trade-union movement. Thus he ignored the differential reception of scientific management in industries—in certain places labor had even successfully evaded the attempts at control of scientific managers.[17]

Space does not permit going into more detail about the pros and cons of Braverman's work.[18] Importantly, several reformulations of labor process theory from a Marxist perspective soon followed in the "second wave" of analysis, which are relevant for the framework of this book. Braverman's belief that scientific management was the sole form of control in capitalism was criticized as simplistic by representatives of this second wave. Andrew Friedman agreed that employees could be subject to forms of direct control such as Taylorism, but argued that there were limitations to direct control that could be partially counteracted by introducing policies of what he called "responsible autonomy" for sections of the workforce. *Responsible autonomy* involved giving workers leeway and encouraging "them to adapt to changing situations in a manner beneficial to the firm."[19] To do so, top managers give workers status, authority, and responsibility. Top managers try to win their loyalty, and co-opt their organization ideologically to the firm's principal goals. *Direct control*, on the contrary, is based on coercive threats, close supervision and limiting the scope of labor power by minimizing individual workers' responsibility.

Friedman argued that the two major types of strategies for exercising authority over labor power co-exist in industrial firms. In explaining the rationale behind responsible autonomy, he suggested that skilled workers generally disciplined themselves and did not respond strongly to financial incentives. This managerial strategy "took advantage of the much deeper attitude of craftsmen towards their work which characterized simple commodity production—self-respect, pride in certain standards of workmanship and customary rewards for different grades of skill."[20] Friedman, however, criticized this strategy, suggesting that responsible autonomy was an impossible ideal given the contradiction between employee needs and the goals of the organization: "Responsible autonomy does not remove alienation and exploitation; it simply softens their operation or draws workers' attention away from them."[21] He claimed that worker alienation and exploitation became more apparent as business conditions required organizations "to cut back on loyalty or satisfaction payments."[22]

In summarizing the basic features of the two strategies, Friedman suggested that both involve contradictions which result in a persistent, fundamental tension in the workplace:

> To treat workers as though they were machines, assuming they can be forced by financial circumstances or close supervision to give up direct control over what they do for most of their waking hours; or to treat workers as though they were not alienated from their labour power by trying to convince them that the aim of top managers are their own, both of these types of strategies involve a contradiction. People do have independent and often hostile wills which cannot be destroyed, and the aim of top managers ultimately is to make steady and high profits, rather than to tend to their workers' needs.[23]

Friedman argued that as long as people were employed, the contradictions could hardly be avoided. The task for employers was to use appropriate methods to support their preferred means of control. Direct control required well-defined lines of authority and a high proportion of white-collar staff, while responsible autonomy required an elaborate ideological apparatus for co-opting workers as well as relative employment security. The effectiveness of the ideology in question depended ultimately on inculcating appropriate beliefs, attitudes, and feelings in the workers.

In *Contested Terrain*, an historical account of the ways in which employers in the U.S. have attempted to control the work of their employees, Richard Edwards identified a secular trend in control strategies, from the *simple control* characteristic of small workplaces to *technical control* in which management sought to use the capabilities of machinery and technological innovations such as assembly lines, to the *bureaucratic control* found in the long career ladders and elaborate rule books of large corporations. Edwards claimed that each form of control had emerged at a definite historical moment, reflecting the needs of capital for novel control techniques following the growth of organizations and changing occupational structures.

In what Edwards called the "entrepreneurial firm, ... the personal power and authority of the capitalist constituted the primary mechanism for control."[24] The employer, with the possible assistance of a few managers, watched over the entire operations of the firm and supervised worker activities directly. This simple control was "direct, arbitrary and personal" and typical of small businesses in the 19th century operating in highly competitive markets.[25] However, as firms grew in size and became geographically dispersed, direct personal control was increasingly difficult. The increased visibility and arbitrariness of the unequal power relations between the employers and their hierarchy of "hired bosses" and workers evoked opposition and challenges to the power of employers. Simple control came to be seen as increasingly problematic as a means of controlling the labor process in large organizations.

In the early part of the 20th century, a tendency emerged to exert control less directly, removing the stress in personal relations and the antagonistic class-imagery experience of simple control created in the minds of those exposed to it. This new technique focused on exploiting the potentialities of technology as a control mechanism. Employers commissioned production-engineering specialists to design production lines and machinery that would operate in such a way as to force workers to keep pace with them. Tension with foremen was reduced because "the track is boss" as workers sometimes said in such plants. The assembly line provides probably the most important single step in achieving this kind of control.

However, technical control did not eliminate management's need to discipline and reward workers in conventional ways. Technical control has also the tendency to create more homogeneous, and more easily unionized workforces, whose strikes and other forms of collective action gain considerable strength from the integrated nature of the technology. In light of labor disputes in the 1930s and 1970s, Edwards concluded that "technical control can never again *by itself* constitute an adequate control system for the core firms' main industrial labor force."[26]

Finally, technical and white-collar grades of labor expanded, partly reflecting the spread of technical control. These employees, having a longer formal education, do not respond well to harsh management methods. Instead, they have been controlled by the subtle pressures of bureaucratic rules and procedures. In the case of bureaucratic control, impersonal rules and procedures provide for the direction, monitoring and disciplining of the workforce. The large numbers of different job categories and other differentials divide the workforce and undermine the basis for collective action. The differentials also make possible the use of promotion in the internal labor market of the firm as an important means of reward. Because one of its main incentives for employees is the provision of job security, however, the use of "bureaucratic" means of control introduces a considerable measure of inflexibility into the utilization of labor by the firm. To make employees redundant would be to threaten the basis of control, yet even large corporations cannot be sure that this will never be necessary.[27]

Edwards recognized the workers' will to resist employers' efforts to control them. But he exaggerated the extent of co-optation of unions in claiming that unions have always been readily tamed by tough or seductive managers, while ignoring the frequency with which individual groups of workers may well continue to resist control pressures by covert means. Nor has labor been divided simply as a result of employers' action. One has to be aware that in some circumstances the labor movement becomes disunited through internal tensions that have nothing to do with employer action. It is also questionable whether employers always welcome the friction that arises between occupational and skill groups, as Edwards suggested. Indeed, the prerogatives that craft workers established made it altogether more difficult for production managers to meet targets. This is a major reason why in the 1980s and afterward there were employer drives to establish single-status employment systems, which abolish occupational distinctions and encourage "flexibility" in job and task allocation.[28]

Both Friedman and Edwards saw the changing forms of control they identified arising from conflict between management and labor. However, as Michael Burawoy—another "second wave" contributor to labor process theory—noted, this could not account for the prevalence of cooperation in most workplaces much of the time. Consent, Burawoy argued, arises from the organization of activities in workplaces in such a way that workers perceive themselves as having choices. "It is participation in choosing that generates consent."[29] From this premise, Burawoy developed his analysis of shop floor games, activities which deflect workers' attention away from (in Marxist terms) the "expropriation of surplus value" by employers, towards activities designed to "beat" the employers in matters such as incentive payments. He was struck by the ability of the piece-workers at the factory he studied to convert the tedious challenge of "making out"—reaching an output target necessary to earn a bonus—into an exciting game. The interaction between workers promoted by these output games was increased by other forms of horseplay and by joking rituals.

However, the institutional context of Burawoy's ethnographic study in a Chicago machine shop must be recognized here. It concerned working life inside a large modern, unionized corporation where winning workers' consent was required, *not* managing through coercion. In his book, *The Politics of Production* (1985), Burawoy looked at the conditions under which consent and coercion are produced.[30] Consent was strong at firms like Geer/Allied—his case study company for *Manufacturing Consent* (1979)—because these were unionized factories with strong internal labor markets, collective bargaining and an "internal state" of consent and compromise between labor and capital that were located in a wider American economy of dominant monopoly capital. Such conditions created "hegemonic production politics" with workers' activity producing the conditions for their continued economic oppression through shop floor games. This was contrasted with "despotic regimes," such as in communist Hungary with its command economy, where welfare (like those of welfare capitalist firms in America), unions, and internal labor markets were absent.

As Michael Rose has rightly pointed out, the fact that workers may voluntarily comply with managerial goals does not by definition mean that such workers become committed to these goals or integrated into the firm as a social system, even though some may. Workers may very well dispute the level of effort expected of them at any one time by managers. Yet, most do not dispute the existence of an effort *bargain*, which implies a moral obligation on their part to carry out the labor tasks in question. Thus, workers can have a normative rapport with the employer, which may be fragile: "it is merely an agreement about how to proceed, and what action is, for the time being, fair and reasonable. But the relationship is not a purely, or even primarily coercive, manipulative, or calculative one."[31] Conflict over underlying interests, which may remain latent, is coupled with cooperation. In some cases, situations emerge in which a genuine trust relationship prevails.[32] It should be remembered, however, that historically a low-trust, low-discretion system has been characteristic of American industry in comparison to international standards.[33]

Emphasizing the need to broaden the analytical perspective, Rose asserted that it is crucial to recognize at least five dimensions to the concept of control of the labor process in industrial capitalism: (1) the employment contract, which lays down what rewards, beyond wages, an employee can expect: their personal degree of job security, fringe benefits, holidays, opportunities for additional training, pensions; (2) operations and organization: specification in detail, for each employee, of his/her tasks and how any worker's tasks are integrated into the overall work organization; (3) the supervision system, which makes workers responsible to foremen, inspectors, or managers, who check how well work is done and who are sometimes skilled in building a sense of "social integration" in the workplace; (4) an employee representation arrangement—either by agreement with a union or by creating a "captive" company union, to allow workers' grievances to reach higher levels of management through representatives elected by the workforce; (5) frameworks of interpretation held by personnel, which are to a degree provided by management through techniques that attempt to influence the meanings, values, and sentiments attributed to work by workers. This dimension concerns employer efforts to shape employee behavior through altering the interpretative frames employees have of the employment relationship, management action and so forth. It points to the importance of ideology and moral aspects of control structures, in which psychosocial intervention practices based on the deployment of applied behavioral and social sciences play a crucial role.[34]

The fifth dimension of control involves deliberate managerial concern with organizational culture, and with employees' "hearts and minds" in particular, in seeking a form of control that Amitai Etzioni refers to as *normative control*.[35] Normative control can be defined as "the attempt to elicit and direct the required efforts of [a work organization's] members by controlling the underlying experiences, thoughts, and feelings that guide their actions."[36] It should be clear that this often entails a significant amount of *ideological control*. It was especially in the context of the management-led corporate culture movement of the 1980s and beyond, that normative control as an explicit managerial goal gained popularity. In the most general terms, shaping the employees' selves into the corporate image was then thought to be necessary in order to facilitate the management, and increase the efficiency, of large-scale bureaucratic enterprises faced with "turbulent environments," rapid technological change, intense competition, and a demanding and unpredictable labor force. But attempts to implement normative control in corporate settings were nothing new then. This tendency already played a significant role in the historical evolution of management practices designed to facilitate the incorporation of the worker into an "industrial community." It included various arrangements that welfare capitalist firms adopted from the 1900s to the 1920s, and became especially pronounced during the heyday of "human relations in industry" in mid–20th century America.

Workers on their part may deploy various strategies for establishing and retaining control over their activities on the job. These strategies can be classified as follows: worker-imposed job structures; formal and informal responses to management innovations; workers' counter-power regarding the following areas: rationalization, division of labor, technology, time study, supervision, hierarchy and job ladders, forms of payment, hiring, training, welfare programs, unions, external institutions of control, ideologies and values. This means that in order to do full justice to the dialectics of control over the labor process, workers' recalcitrance and attempts at control in all of these areas should be taken into account as well.

Here the workers' bargaining power in various domains is an important area of interest. Useful for differentiating types of workers' bargaining power is Erik Olin Wright's distinction between *associational* and *structural* power. Associational power consists of "the various forms of power that result from the formation of collective organization of workers" (most importantly, trade unions and political parties).[37] Structural power consists of the power that workers derive "simply from their location ... in the economic system."[38] Structural power can further be divided into two subtypes. The first subtype, which Beverly Silver calls *marketplace bargaining power*, is the power that "results directly from tight labor markets."[39] The second subtype of structural power, which Silver calls *workplace bargaining power*, is the power that results "from the strategic location of a particular group of workers within a key industrial sector."[40]

Marketplace bargaining power can take several forms including (1) the possession of scarce skills that are in demand by employers, (2) low levels of general unemployment, and (3) the ability of workers to pull out of the labor market entirely and survive on nonwage sources of income. Workplace bargaining, on the other hand, falls to workers who are deeply involved in tightly integrated production processes, where a localized work stoppage in a key connection point can cause disruptions on a much wider scale than the stoppage itself. Such bargaining power has manifested itself when entire assembly lines have been shut down by a stoppage in one segment of the line, and when entire corporations relying on the just-in-time delivery of parts have been brought to a standstill by railway workers' strikes.[41]

Further, the framework needs to be expanded to also include the higher-skilled white-collar, professional and managerial workers, in order to examine their changing positions in the corporate world and the forms of control they are subjected to. Compared with lower-level industrial and clerical (= routine white-collar) work, their tasks traditionally involved more discretion, less predictability, and less possibility of routinization, and evaluation, and were thus harder to monitor and supervise directly. Groups of relatively autonomous, skilled and professional workers cannot, will not or do not need to be tightly controlled. Rigid control is expensive and can be counter-productive. Appeals to professional values, creativity, career, good will or trust are deemed more appropriate methods of translating the capacity of skilled and professional workers into labor effort and value.[42] It is also true, however, that during the past thirty years or so industrial rationalization, with the help of modern information and communication technologies, has played an increasingly important role in their case too. This tendency involves a greater emphasis on technical-organizational control (as compared to normative control) regarding these higher-skilled and professional workers.

Bureaucratization of Employment and Managerial Control

Finally, the shift toward "bureaucratized employment"—which is central to a major part of this book's account—needs to be theorized here. The explanations for the shift vary. One strain of social theorists see the bureaucratic features of employment as an inevitable and automatic result of the technical imperatives of size and efficiency as imposed by large and complex organizations.[43] Both Weberian and Marxist critics take issue with this view, however, seeing bureaucratic devices such as calculable rules and career ladders as mechanisms of control over the work force. From this perspective, bureaucracy is calculative rationality shaped to serve the employer's interest.[44]

The first point of view does not provide an accurate guide to historical developments in the U.S. The historical record of American firms shows that size mattered but, contrary to modern organization theory, there was no one-to-one correspondence between the size of a company and the organization of its employment system. Giant manufacturing firms were common in the industrial landscape by 1890, but blue-collar employment did not acquire bureaucratic characteristics (in the sense meant here) until four or five decades later. Moreover, it was medium-sized firms that were often among the first to abandon the traditional system of factory labor administration. Managements of these firms employed bureaucracy to solve a variety of problems, many of them having nothing to do with size.[45]

What about the second view (that sees bureaucracy as calculative rationality in the employer's interest)? The first extensive analysis of "bureaucracy" was offered by Max Weber, who used it to refer to the manifestation of rational-legal authority in the sphere of administration. In Weber's view, the defining features of the ideal type of bureaucracy are: a hierarchy of offices with clear delineation of authority; a division of labor based on training and expertise; a system of rules and records; a separation between person and office; impersonality in the performance of duties; and graded, salaried careers for officials.[46] This notion of bureaucracy is embedded within a general theory of power relations or "domination." The focus is on a special instance of power, namely, legitimate power; this is based on the beliefs about the legitimacy of power that are shared by the ruler and the ruled. In contrast to Marx's position, Weber's theory of domination does not depend on economic mechanisms of control. Instead, the compliance of subordinates rests upon their perceptions of, and attitudes towards, the nature of the control relationship.

For "modern sociologists" of bureaucracy, both the need for and the mechanisms of normative control are built into the very structure of bureaucracy. As Reinhard Bendix has suggested in his book, *Work and Authority in Industry*, "Beyond what commands can effect and supervision can control, beyond what incentives can induce and penalties prevent, there exists an exercise of discretion which managers of economic enterprises seek to enlist for the achievement of managerial ends."[47] Consequently, as Robert Merton has pointed out, effective control requires that "ideal patterns of action are buttressed by strong sentiments which entail devotion to one's duties, a keen sense of the limitations of one's authority and competence, and methodical performance of routine activities."[48] In this view, the relationship of discretion and control is particularly pronounced in the case of the rapidly expanding white-collar force and regarding the types of work, technologies, and labor processes characteristic of what Daniel Bell has referred to as the "post-industrial society."[49]

Management theorists present a similar argument but cast it as the solution to a practical managerial problem. This perspective was formulated most clearly by Chester Barnard, one of the most influential of the early management theorists. In his classic book, *The Functions of the Executive*, Barnard says that in order to elicit the willing and predictable contributions of effort required by a large-scale organization, traditional economic inducements must be supplemented by an effort to change the "states of mind" that govern the willingness to contribute. This includes the "inculcation of motives," which means shaping not only work behaviors and activities but also the self-definitions of members as social actors, their world views, and, most crucially, their emotional responses to their condition. In Barnard's view, this requires "a process of deliberate education of the young, and propaganda for the adults."[50]

Marxist scholars add a critical twist to the same argument. Richard Edwards, for example, has claimed that bureaucracy leads to the need for and the use of increasingly sophisticated forms of control. As noted earlier, he identified three basic forms of control: simple control is manifested in face-to-face coercion; technical control occurs through mechanical control of the labor process; and bureaucratic control embeds control in the social structure of the workplace. Edwards suggested that contradictions and conflicts inherent in each form of capitalist control cause a new form of control to emerge gradually. The new forms of control are manifested in the more innovative industrial sectors of the time, while earlier forms are still found in other sectors. Bureaucratic control, the impersonal rule of company law and policy is coupled with a growing tendency to enforce not only obedience to the rules but also an internalization of the rules and identification with the company.[51]

Generally, the point of view that American employers used bureaucracy as a means to control their workers holds a big granule of truth. But one should be wary of a functionalist way of reasoning that assumes employers were always merely driven by a self-interested, calculative rationality in developing a firm's technological and organizational structures. That would mean falling into the trap of a "made-to-measure view," which simply "argues that the production technology [or bureaucracy] used by capitalists is in essence a set of inventions customized to their control needs."[52] Moreover, managers were not the only ones to use bureaucracy, in order to benefit from it. Through their unions (or other employee representations) workers sought to bureaucratize employment in order to enhance their bargaining power, protect themselves against turbulent competition, and ensure managerial consistency and fairness. On the other hand, managers in some companies resisted or delayed bureaucratization even as their employers promoted it. These managers were afraid that structure and rules would hinder their discretion, although in the case of nonunion firms they were sometimes willing to accept such organization and regulation in order to forestall unionization. Management also tended to be internally divided regarding the control strategies to be used.

Bureaucratic employment practices can best be seen as the outcome of a protracted struggle to overcome the insecurity and inequities produced by a market-oriented employment system, as Sanford Jacoby has suggested. The struggle was waged within management and between management and other groups.[53] In a larger context, this struggle was part of what Karl Polanyi called the "double movement" of two great organizing principles in society. One was the principle of economic liberalism, which took recourse to laissez-faire and the method of contract; the other was the principle of social protection, which relied on protective legislation, restrictive associations, and other methods of market intervention.[54]

In most of the world's major industrial nations, regulation and stabilization of the labor market were achieved through bargaining by workers organized into trade unions, and through legislation supported by middle-class reformers and labor parties. To some extent this also happened in the U.S., except that due to the absence of an effective labor party, a greater emphasis came to lie on middle-class reform activity.[55] In addition, American management had much more leeway to handle its employment policies on its own, given the relative weakness prior to the 1930s both of government regulation and of trade unionism.

Thus, between 1900 and 1945, two forces contended within American manufacturing firms. On one side were foremen, production managers, and plant superintendents—all committed to the existing employment system for both economic and ideological reasons. They were first and foremost preoccupied with getting the product out as rapidly and cheaply as possible. In administering employment, they sought quick results and maximum flexibility. The work force was to be adjusted to changes in technology and to fluctuations in output, never the other way around. Consequently, they preferred strict discipline for the worker and freedom from the restraint of rules and commitments for themselves. They also shared a set of beliefs about the industrial worker—that he was lazy, greedy, and untrustworthy—and about their responsibility to him—which was that they had none beyond paying the going wage rate.

On the other side was a heterogeneous group of trade unionists, social reformers, and personnel managers, pressing for change. Each was attempting to make the employment relationship more orderly and stable, but for different reasons. Unions aimed to give industrial labor some of the security, dignity, and status rights associated with white-collar occupations. Social reformers were sympathetic to these goals, if not always to organized labor, both because of humanitarian inclinations and fears of more radical upheaval from below. They criticized the existing employment practices as backward, crude, and wasteful. They did not reject industrial capitalism per se; they wanted rather to make it more rational and viable. These middle-class professionals also had interests of their own. They pressed for the proliferation of bureaucracy and top-down reform because these were likely to give themselves greater job opportunities and a more directive role in public and private affairs.

Within management, the conflict between the traditional and bureaucratic approach to employment manifested itself especially in clashes between the production division and the new personnel departments that began to arrive on the scene after 1910. The personnel manager's point of view differed from that of most line managers, partly because of the personnel management's function in the managerial hierarchy. The creation of a personnel department signaled a decisive change of employment policy; from now on this policy would be treated as an end in itself rather than as a means to the production division's ends. One of the personnel manager's major responsibilities was to stabilize labor relations, which required trading off short-term efficiency for the sake of achieving high employee morale over the longer run. In practice, this meant preempting many of the union's attempts at controlling employment policy and placing stringent checks on line managers, especially foremen. Because it originated in various Progressive reform movements, personnel management attracted to its ranks educators, social workers, and even former socialists. It was influenced by new middle-class beliefs in the necessity of market intervention, the positive effects of rational administration, and the power of the educated expert to mediate and mitigate social conflict. Many early personnel managers saw themselves as neutral professionals, whose task it was to reconcile opposing industrial interests and make employment practices more scientific and humane.

Personnel management and the new bureaucratic approach to employment did not gradually get a footing in an ever-growing number of firms; instead, there were big growth spurts of adoption during two periods of crisis for the traditional system of employment: World War I and the Great Depression. During these periods the unions gained strength, social experimentation was popular, and the government intervened in the labor market on behalf of workers. As this uneven growth indicates, many companies did not immediately see the benefits of a bureaucratic employment system. Top managers in these firms tended either to pay little attention to employment, which they deemed relatively unimportant, or were committed to the production manager's world view. Abolishing traditional employment practices required a change in managerial values as well as external pressure from government and unions.

From 1945 through the 1970s (with the New Deal order disintegrating later in the decade), the bureaucratic system of employment remained largely in place. During the 1980s and afterward, however, there was again a rumbling of Polyani's double movement, this time with the forces of economic liberalism (in the classic European sense) on the rise. In politics, deregulation and privatization took hold; in equity markets, a strong form of shareholder sovereignty reasserted itself against a broader stakeholder orientation that had gained some influence but never achieved dominance. And in labor markets, unions were shrinking, jobs became less secure, and employers were less willing to shield employees from risk.[56]

By the early 21st century, the economic security and social welfare functions formerly provided by American corporations had become severely strained. The value of most labor to employers had been undermined by automation and substantial changes in the organization of production, coupled with innovative new means of outsourcing/offshoring. The latter involved not only manufacturing and distribution but also, increasingly, a variety of high-skilled knowledge work.

Structure of the Book

The opening chapter begins with a description of the organization and management practices of workshops and domestic industry, and the rise of the factory system in the 19th century. It then looks at the shift to centralized managerial control between 1880 and 1920, which crystallized into the systematic management movement from which Taylorism emerged. Chapter 2 gives an overview of the principles and practices of Taylorism, as well as a characterization of Fordism, which incorporated some of Taylor's organizational innovations. This is followed by a characterization of "Sloanism" or "flexible mass production." The chapter concludes with an outline of the early implementation of Taylorism in retail and office work.

Chapter 3 presents two additional means of managerial control: welfare capitalism and "human relations." It describes welfare capitalism's origins, its creators' beliefs and intentions, as well as the programs the companies in question provided in the early decades of the 20th century. The chapter subsequently depicts the origins of the human relations approach and analyzes its basic tenets and practices, as well as the fundamental critiques it drew in the 1940s and 1950s. Next it elaborates Kurt Lewin's social psychology of industry (which gained influence somewhat later) and situates this within the U.S. tradition of "democratic social engineering." The chapter ends with two influential social criticisms of work in corporate America at mid-century: C. Wright Mills's critical analysis of the alienation of members of the new salaried middle class, and William H. Whyte's critique of a prevailing "social ethic" in big corporations.

Chapter 4 offers a brief overview of the expansion of scientific management during and after World War II, along with the further mechanization and automation of the military and industry. It also looks at the ramifications of those changes for the quality of work and skill requirements of workers. It sets the stage for what comes later regarding the technological and organizational transformations in manufacturing and large retail. Chapter 5 focuses on modern welfare capitalism in the 1960s and its increased expansion in the 1970s, coinciding with the rise of neoliberalism and the "new nonunion model." A comparison is made with unionized firms, which did not meet the challenges posed by the needs and desires of younger, higher educated, white-collar workers. This chapter further describes the short-lived Quality of Working Life Movement, as well as welfare capitalism's downturn and the "great risk shift" from the employer to the employee, beginning in the 1980s.

Chapter 6 describes the historical background and basic features of the flexible manufacturing techniques of Japanese lean production in the automobile industry. It then assesses the implications for managerial control and the effects on work organization, the quality of work, and the skill requirements for workers involved. Chapter 7 examines the ways the principles and practices of lean production—and just-in-time techniques in particular—were adopted in retail and the interactive service sector, in the latter case building on the industrial rationalization known as "McDonaldization." Chapter 8 focuses on the more openly top-down systems of management and measurement of work that were introduced in the 1990s, beginning with Total Quality Management (TQM) programs and their strained relationship to the management rhetoric of trust, commitment, and loyalty. Also scrutinized is the management practice of Business Process Reengineering (BPR), which was introduced at about the same time. This is followed by a closer look at the consequences of the combined implementation of TQM and BPR for workers and labor processes in manufacturing and office work respectively.

In Chapter 9 the attention turns to Enterprise Resource Planning (ERP), a more intensified form of reengineering, which came into vogue in the late 1990s. Next an in-depth analysis is given of call center work as the prototypical example of "digital assembly line" work, embedded in the larger reengineered business system. Chapter 10 shines light on the push by America's business and political leaders in the 1990s towards high-tech jobs in relation to the promises of the "knowledge economy." Changes in the nature of IT jobs are discussed, with a section devoted to "no-collar," new media workers, and other young entrepreneurial people in the high-tech, finance, and new professional services who were much celebrated at the time. The chapter next examines the new set of work relations for skilled office workers and professionals that emerged around the turn of the new century. It then zooms in on the further spread of just-in-time production and service-providing processes and their upward reach to higher skill levels. In addition, the ramifications of increased automation of skilled professional work for managerial control, quality of work, and skill requirements are described with regard to the medical sector.

Chapter 11 discusses the major cognitive errors that may handicap users of digital decision-support systems in reaching conclusions based on computer-generated analyses or diagnoses of particular problems (including illnesses in the case of medicine). It also explains why these issues have become especially acute in the case of the prevailing technology-first approach of automation. The chapter further traces the impact of the increasing deployment of digital expert systems on professional jobs and skill requirements in a variety of areas. It then considers the opportunities and limitations of a particularly advanced system such as IBM's supercomputer Watson for highly-skilled professional work.

Chapter 12 looks at the current state of affairs regarding the all-encompassing and far-reaching information technology known as Computer Business Systems—adopted by large corporations across the American economy—which takes reengineering to a whole new level. The implications for the quality of work and top managerial control of employees are then outlined. Chapter 13 explores the consequences of the enhanced use of robots for the employment and skill requirements of human workers in manufacturing, retail, and consumer goods logistics in recent years, and as predicted for the near future. This is followed in Chapter 14 by an analysis of the current political-economic context that co-determines the variegated impact that digital information technologies have on employment and the quality of the remaining work in the U.S. The chapter hones in on the decline of the traditional U.S. public corporation, which coincided with the emergence of "Nikefication," a new business model for production, distribution, and work organization that instigated alternative legal and fiscal forms better suited to it. The Conclusion takes stock of what has happened over the last 130 years or so, with special attention to the past 40 years. It retraces the most significant developments of the management control strategies that were involved, along with their effects on working life in America.

1

The Rise of the Factory System and the Origins of Systematic Management

In the early 19th century, most commodities in the United States were produced either in the workshops of craftsmen or at home. Skilled tradesmen—carpenters, cobblers, potters etc.—made their wares in small shops, owned by merchants or master craftsmen, which had not yet been significantly impacted by machine methods. While goods made at home were usually consumed there, in urban areas the putting-out system (sometimes called "proto-industry") was common. Merchants gave raw materials and tools to household workers, who then fabricated the goods in question (e.g., they wove the cloth or made the shoes) and returned the finished product to the merchants for distribution and sale. Workers were paid on the basis of their output and consequently had the opportunity to decide for themselves how many hours to work and when to work. Reportedly, they also had the opportunity to "embezzle wool or silk, exchange poor quality for good, conceal imperfections or devise ways to make the finished material heavier."[1] The factory system gradually replaced domestic industry in an effort by employers to increase their control over the production process. By the end of the century, most commodities were manufactured in factories, which were large agglomerations of machinery and men.

America's first factories were New England's textile mills, which replaced home methods of production over a fifty-year period, from 1790 to 1840. These early mills shared a number of features that distinguished the factory system from other modes of production, including a reliance on power-driven machinery; the integration of different production processes at a single site; an elaborate division of labor; new methods of administration based on the overseer or foreman. The overseer was the key figure in the early New England mills. Large mills employed a number of them, each in charge of a room full of machinery and workers. Although there was an agent who dealt with the mill's owners, the overseer did most of the work of maintaining mechanical and human order. In addition to tending machines, he selected the workers, assigned them to their tasks and made sure that they worked diligently. Indeed, a major managerial advantage of the textile factories was that they permitted more effective labor supervision than was previously possible. Under the putting-out system, merchants could manipulate only the piece prices they paid; workers themselves controlled their effort and could take anywhere from two days to two weeks to turn in their goods. In the factory, workers had less discretion over their work pace and methods.

Until the 1840s, the factory system was limited mainly to the textile industry. But by 1880 it had become the dominant production mode in most manufacturing industries. Then at least four-fifths of the nearly three million of people employed in these industries in the U.S., were working under the factory system. Examples of this system other than textiles then included the manufacture of boots and shoes, watches, musical instruments, clothing, agricultural implements, metal goods generally, firearms, carriages and wagons, wood goods, rubber goods, and even the slaughtering of hogs.[2]

Within the factories, employees worked more regular and longer hours, product quality could be more closely monitored and production costs could be minimized. Compliant behavior was assured through the enclosure of the factory (workers were controlled from the time they entered the factory until their departure) and constant surveillance, as well as through a series of disciplinary procedures including fines and imprisonment.[3]

However, the factory did not immediately displace other older organizational forms. In the iron and steel industry, rural forges and small foundries coexisted during the 1860s and 1870s with big rail mills employing more than a thousand workers. (These mills were one direct beneficiary of the expansion of the railroad system after the Civil War.) Likewise, certain types of women's shoes and slippers were manufactured on a putting-out basis until the end of the century, even though steam-powered machinery was the driving factor to establish shoe factories in the 1850s.[4]

Moreover, many of the industries that changed over to the factory system after 1850 continued to depend on techniques from the earlier period. In these industries, the factory was often no more than an aggregation of artisanal workshops which had been mechanized and enlarged. A steady input of craft skills was still required, particularly when the factory turned out small batches of a nonstandardized product. Consequently, owners of these firms allowed their foremen and skilled workers to make most of the decisions about the timing and manner of production. At one extreme, this practice took the form of internal contracting, which amounted to a ceding of managerial control to the contractor. The contractor, who was a highly skilled foreman, arranged with the firm's owner to deliver the product within a specified time at a specified cost. The owner provided the contractor with floor space, tools, materials, and money, and then left him in charge of production. The contractor hired and supervised a group of skilled workers, who in turn might hire their own unskilled helpers. Full-fledged internal contract systems tended to be confined to the more traditional industrial areas in the New England and Mid-Atlantic states, which were influenced by European, especially British, traditions. The extent of internal contract systems also depended on the type of industry. These systems were most common in metalworking industries—sewing machinery, locomotives, guns and so forth—where a high degree of skill was required to process component parts to rigorous tolerances—the allowable deviations from a standard in machining a piece. They further existed in the iron and steel industry (puddlers and rollers being the contractors), foundries, coal industry, potteries, glass industry, clothing.[5]

At the other extreme one could find industries that left production decisions entirely to the skilled workers, with no foreman or contractor involved. For example, at the Columbus Iron Works during the early 1870s, workers negotiated with the firm's owners on a tonnage rate for each rolling job undertaken by the firm. The crew members decided collectively how to pay themselves, how to allocate assignments, whom to hire, and how to train helpers.[6]

These two alternative practices were not very common, however. In most 19th-century factories, salaried foremen and skilled workers shared responsibility for administering production. Although the salaried foreman occupied a position lower in rank than that of the internal contractor, he nevertheless had authority to make most of the decisions about how a production task was to be accomplished, including work methods, technical processes, and work organization. The foreman exercised his power within limits set by the skilled workers who defended their autonomy in production through a multitude of working rules that governed methods of shop organization, and through the craftsman's moral code. This code included output quotas set by the workers to protect themselves from overexertion, as well as an ethos of manly defiance to any foreman who tried to undermine traditional shop rules.[7]

Foremen had their own moral code, which owed a great deal to the skilled workers' shop culture. They tended to be arrogant, proud, conservative men, well aware of their coveted position. Despite their former status as skilled workers, most foremen were fervently anti-union. They were well aware that their authority depended on severing ties to their past; and therefore they distanced themselves from the skilled worker positions they had ascended from.

By the 1880s, the power of foremen and skilled workers over production management began to erode. The new industries, such as electrical machinery and chemicals, were based on technologies that had little continuity with artisanal techniques. The older industries, like iron and steel, had mechanized to the point where craft skills were no longer essential to production. After the introduction of continuous flow methods in steel manufacturing, the foreman was left with little authority. Most production decisions were now made by engineers and metallurgists. Among skilled steelworkers—who once had been strong, even arrogant in their indispensability—the strong sense of independence disappeared. In machine-paced industries, like textiles, the overseer was forced to share authority with an increasing number of specialists equal or superior in rank. Other than making occasional repairs or carrying out quality control inspections of goods, the overseer had increasingly fewer responsibilities in production. In textiles, as in steel and other industries, most of the foremen's tasks were related to employing and supervising labor. Here the methods of the 1850s continued to be deployed, with few changes.

But while the foreman's degree of control over production varied by industry, his authority in employment matters remained uniform across industries. Whether in the machine shop, on the assembly line or in some other form of manufacturing, the foreman was given plenty of leeway in hiring, paying and supervising workers, at least until World War I. To the workers, the foreman was a despot—seldom benevolent—who made and interpreted employment policy as he saw fit. Any checks on the foreman's power stemmed from the workers he supervised, not from the company owner.[8]

Trade unionism helped to restrain the foreman's arbitrary exercise of power and gave skilled workers some control over the terms of their employment. The trade union aimed to ensure that strict rules and equitable procedures would govern decisions about task allocations to workers. It is noteworthy that while the larger internal contractors typically were staunch opponents of unions, smaller contractors with their dual status as managers and skilled workers founded many of the pioneer American Federation of Labor (AFL) unions; they constituted dominant groups within these craft unions. However, the union density in the U.S. was low, about six percent of all the possible manufacturing workers in 1900 and twelve percent in 1915. Major parts of the pottery, iron, foundry and glass industries, etc., remained unorganized, despite the bargaining power of the craftsmen-contractors. Unions admitted internal contractors in order to control wage levels and to maintain influence wherever the employer was anti-union. The contractors in turn used trade unions as a means for developing sets of rules for limiting competition among themselves, restricting entry to the trade—especially of helpers and unskilled assistants—and maintaining job jurisdiction.[9]

While only a minority of all workers belonged to unions, these unions were a constant reminder that the employer's authority, and that of his agents, could be circumscribed through "legislation" which governed wages and working conditions for union members. Enforcement depended upon members refusing—under threat of punishment by the union—to obey any order that breached the union's rules. As the unions and their national organizations grew more powerful after 1880, the status of their rules changed from unilateral group codes to contractual and bargained restrictions on the employer and his foremen. These contracts strictly regulated work methods and effort norms as well as such issues as apprenticeship standards and wage scales.

When by the turn of the century the apprenticeship system was fading away in many occupations, and an ever finer division of labor reduced the demand for versatile craftsmen who knew all the ins and outs of a particular trade, the unions had other ways to bolster their control. One crucial mechanism was the closed or preferential shop, which restricted the foreman's discretion as to whom he could hire, and enhanced the demand for union labor. This protected union members against discrimination in hiring and guaranteed that vacancies would be filled by them. It also enabled the union to exert countervailing power against the foremen (and by extension, the employer) in some other respects, such as wage determination, rules regulating manning levels and working hours, as well as output quotas (in order to reduce unemployment) and lastly, restrictions on the foreman's power to discipline and discharge.[10]

At the national level, the continuing striving of the skilled contractors to maintain their organizational and occupational position was a significant factor in the limited scope of the early American labor unions, which were built on craft and status exclusivity. The influence of the skilled contractors in shaping union policies and the policies of the AFL consequently prevented the unionization of the many unskilled and semiskilled groups.[11]

Unskilled workers dissatisfied with their jobs had few options. They could complain to higher functionaries, but the latter invariably supported the foremen in any dispute. Occasionally, the unskilled were able to establish their own workplace organization, which regulated employment in much the same way as the craft-based unions did. During the 1880s, the Knights of Labor included local assemblies made up of less-skilled workers who teamed up to press for higher wages and to protect themselves from arbitrary foremen. Some of the locals even achieved the closed shop and a seniority-based layoff system.

But unskilled workers had little bargaining power and were rarely able to sustain sizable, stable organizations; they remained largely unorganized until the New Deal era, when, in 1935, the Congress of Industrial Organizations (CIO) was founded. The absence of union organization, however, did not prevent them from engaging in militant action. In steel, for example, battles were fought in Cleveland (1899), East Chicago (1905), McKees Rocks (1909), and Bethlehem (1910), with the unskilled, immigrant work force on one side and the militia and police on the other. But these strikes, while spectacular, were sporadic and seldom successful. Limitation of output in the form of stints or slowdowns was a somewhat more effective way of checking the foreman. Yet lacking the discipline provided by a union, and fragmented by ethnic conflicts and language barriers that stymied cooperation, unskilled workers had less success with this method than did their skilled counterparts.

Given the large reservoir of immigrant labor, at least until World War I, employers hesitated to tamper with the foreman's coercive "drive system" as applied to the mass of semiskilled workers. The drive system entailed a policy of obtaining efficiency by pressuring workers to turn out a large output. It was predicated on the fear of job loss to ensure obedience, and the fact that employers did not hesitate to sack workers as they saw fit. Workers dissatisfied with their work had hardly any other alternative than to seek their fortunes on the open market. High turnover rates contributed to the overall instability of the workplace while recurring bouts of unemployment were a fact of life.[12]

But the drive system also brought costs with it. First, it entailed administrative costs that could be reduced by more bureaucratic methods of coordination and control. From around 1880 onward, employers began to overhaul the organization of their increasingly larger enterprises, turning to professional engineers for assistance. These industrial engineers applied their expertise to production problems, setting up rationalized manufacturing systems and focusing their managerial skills on the foreman's autonomous domain.

Second, other costs involved the worker's response to the drive system, including frequent labor unrest, erratic working habits, and radical political inclinations. A growing number of employers believed that they would have to take more positive steps than strikebreaking and dismissals to deal with these problems if they were to win the worker's cooperation and loyalty. After 1900, driven by a variety of motivations, employers manifested a greater willingness to experiment with "welfare work," a range of paternalistic techniques designed to make workers more industrious, sober, and loyal.

Both industrial engineering and company welfarism had a major impact on the way that American industry administered its employment policies and conceived its labor problems. Although these approaches differed drastically, they paved together the way for the proliferation of personnel departments during World War I and the rise of bureaucratized employment.[13]

Employer Hostility Toward Organized Labor

The most distinctive feature of the American system of capital-labor relations in comparison to that of other industrialized countries was not the weaker class-consciousness of workers compared with the purportedly more radical and class-conscious workers in Europe and Latin America, or more generally the "failure of American socialism," but the hostility that employers have demonstrated toward both the regulatory state and virtually all systems of worker representation.[14] One must recognize, though, that the unusually great repression by major employers was partly a product of the political opportunities that resulted from greater state repression than in many other countries.[15]

Violence by federal and state troops and private police forces suppressed strikes on many occasions, and court injunctions defeated many other strike actions in the 19th and early 20th centuries. To be sure, repression does not necessarily weaken radical movements, however, and may even strengthen them under particular circumstances. This even applies to non-radical movements and organizations in some cases. Repression, except for extermination, raises the costs of resistance but increases the sense of grievance. It may heighten a sense of injustice within a group that was previously quiescent. Most likely it will reinforce solidarity within a targeted movement. Repression may also make clear to the larger society the merits of a particular cause, or at least, the drawbacks of coercion as a response to it. Radicals may aim to provoke authorities to attack them in hopes of bringing sympathetic attention to their cause—what in political history is known as a Blanquist response to repression, seeking to galvanize broader support from all those intent on defending civil rights and free speech.[16] For example, prior to World War I, the Industrial Workers of the World (IWW) would bring hundreds of supporters to openly challenge authorities in communities that denied their right to organize. The aim was to wear down the willingness of towns to enforce anti–IWW ordinances by overwhelming the system through congregating in such numbers that the financial and other burdens would be too heavy to arrest them, feed them while in prison, and then try them in court.[17] On the other hand, however, repression may impose too many burdens on activists and movement participants. It may stymie a radical movement by harming or threatening to harm its supporters (who also lack income during their actions or imprisonment). By denying freedom of expression or freedom of association, repression may prevent the recruitment of new adherents for a movement.[18]

As Robin Archer has pointed out, in the case of the American labor movement, (inclusive) industrial unions suffered much more from court repression than (exclusive) craft unions, which dominated the American Federation of Labor. Court repression prompted the AFL to take recourse to political action, initially in pursuit of positive goals, but in the early 20th century it turned to more limited, negative goals in order to survive. In the 1890s, the AFL still sought to realize positive goals such as the eight-hour day and legislation of factory working conditions. In the early 20th century, however, it came to focus on a more narrowly-defined set of negative goals such as anti-conspiracy and anti-injunction legislation. This strategy became fully entrenched by 1914 when the AFL ruled out political action in pursuit of a general, eight-hour day through legislation.[19]

In-depth comparisons have shown that during the 1870–1914 period state repression proved more effective against organized labor in the U.S. than in other non-totalitarian states.[20] Generally speaking, the extent of repression in the U.S. was greater than in Western Europe.[21] But it was also stronger than in other settler countries like Australia, New Zealand and Canada. Notwithstanding some instances of severe anti-labor repression, these three countries were generally far more hospitable to early union movements than the U.S. was.[22]

However, while the attitude of business firms was generally adversarial toward the formation of unions, it was never monolithic, at least as far as mainstream, bread-and-butter unionism was concerned. From 1897 some of the largest finance capitalists and industrial trust-makers in America allied with advocates of "ameliorative" labor politics (including Samuel Gompers of the AFL) to establish the Chicago Civic Federation. Under this organization's auspices—and, from 1900, those of the National Civic Federation (NCF)—Ralph Easly and his colleagues in corporate business supported the voluntary arbitration of industrial disputes and the creation of trade agreements between unions and employers. But this "era of good feeling" lasted only a brief period; it was shattered by the "open shop" movement that gained momentum after 1902. This movement, which originated among smaller firms represented by locally organized Citizens' Industrial Alliances and later by the National Association of Manufacturers, eventually comprised many of the corporate trusts represented in the councils of the NCF. By 1909, when U.S. Steel denied the remnants of the once influential Amalgamated Association of Iron, Steel and Tin Workers the right to organize its workers, hardly any distinction in principle or practice remained between large and small firms with regard to labor relations.[23]

At least until the 1935 passage of the National Labor Relations Act (or Wagner Act)—with the notable exception of World War I, when the American Federation of Labor attained, temporarily, substantial influence on labor relations and employment conditions—the American labor movement was subject to virtually constant and massive political repression. This was often the result of government inactivity in the face of employer resistance; union organization depended on the constitutional freedoms of speech, press, and assembly, but employers consistently abridged these rights. Management's reliance on espionage, blacklisting, strikebreakers, private police, and ultimately, armed violence, nullified the Bill of Rights for those workers who had the nerve to stand up against their employers' unilateral exercise of power. While certain of these employer activities were illegal (though rarely punished), many successful tactics were quite legal. Two of the main legal tactics of this kind were the yellow-dog contract (a hiring agreement in which a worker disavowed membership of, and pledged never to join, a labor union in order to get a job) and (easily obtained) court injunctions that made unions responsible for a whole range of indistinct damages.[24]

From Industrial Cities to Industrial Suburbs

The late 19th century was the age of the industrial city. It corresponded to the demands of mass production capitalism in two main ways: it offered proximity to consumer markets and thereby facilitated large-scale production; and it offered a relatively large reserve army of labor. While manufacturing employment increased as fast or faster in midsized towns relative to large urban centers until the end of the Civil War, by 1870 industrial production was concentrating in a few major cities such as Chicago, Cleveland, and New York. Between 1860 and 1900, the ten largest industrial areas' share of national value added produced in manufacturing increased from 25 to 40 percent.[25]

Industrial capitalists concentrated manufacturing capacity in the big cities because large urban space offered them more opportunities to wield power over labor than midsized towns did, where workers enjoyed more community support during labor disputes. In the smaller cities, industrial capitalists were challenged by preindustrial social classes whose worldviews were markedly different from those of the industrialists; middle strata in these towns often supported workers against industrial capital.[26] In bigger cities, industrial capital had more success in winning over middle strata, whose fortunes were more closely tied to the new capitalist order. Here the labor pool of industrial workers tended to be larger, and ethnic divisions within the working class stronger to boot. Consequently, the balance of class power in the big cities initially favored capital over labor.

Yet the industrial city generated some crucial problems for industrial capitalists. Huge numbers of industrial workers were concentrated in ever-larger production units. These larger production units were located in growing cities, whose share of the U.S. population tripled between 1850 and 1910, accelerating sharply in the last two decades of that period.[27] The number of strikes in the U.S. more than tripled between 1881–1885 and 1901–1905, and the geographical spread of strike activity now included the Midwest as well as the Northeast.[28]

By the turn of the 20th century, rising labor unrest in the big cities induced capitalists to relocate their factories to surrounding suburbs. Between 1899 and 1909, central city manufacturing employment increased by 41 percent, while employment in industrial suburbs more than doubled, a whopping 98 percent.[29] The upshot was that "Once installed at a sufficient distance from the center of labor agitation, these firms achieved a measure of insulation from the epidemics of central-city strike activity to which they had previously been vulnerable."[30] At first employers experimented with company towns, but the 1894 Pullman strike made many of them abandon this option.[31] Increasingly, industrial capitalists moved their factories to production sites just outside big city limits. Between 1899 and 1905, new suburban manufacturing towns were built "in open space like move sets."[32] Gary, Indiana, constructed from 1905 to 1908, is the best example of this. In these industrial suburbs, employers could reassert both economic and political control.[33]

A crucial precondition for this move from the cities to the new industrial suburbs was the growing concentration of capital, especially the 1898–1902 merger wave.[34] The concentration of capital occurred throughout the capitalist world, but it was most advanced in the U.S.[35] The merger wave put far more capital into the hands of industrial capitalists, thus increasing their capacity to move production sites away from areas with strong labor militancy.[36] Industrial consolidation and workers' struggles were closely intertwined as is evidenced by the list of companies hit by strikes around the turn of the century, that can likewise be read as a list of consolidations: the railroads, McCormick, Carnegie Steel (owner of Homestead Steelworks), Pullman, General Electric, U.S. Steel and International Harvester.[37] Relocations to industrial suburbs dovetailed with a renewed employers' offensive, taking the form of a vigorous open-shop drive by manufacturers' organizations.[38] A good example is the Detroit area, which was an attractive location for industrial growth in part because the Employers' Association of Detroit had by 1912 "virtually obliterated the local labor movement outside the building trades."[39]

The Systematic Management Movement

Independent management was a relatively new concept in the late 19th century. Oddly enough, "modern management" was more frequently practiced on large slave plantations than in early industrial shops.[40] It was when manufacturing firms became large, and extensive functional divisions between owners, financiers, and managers emerged, that they commonly adopted independent management. The economic imperative of owners was to risk their capital by putting it to productive use. The financiers acted as intermediaries seeking lucrative opportunities for owners and furnishing the credit that managers needed to run their businesses. This tripartite relationship became necessary as growth made it both impossible and undesirable for owners to personally supervise their enterprises.[41]

This development coincided with the rise of the public corporation. Before the turn of the 20th century, there were only a few public corporations; nearly all were railroads or utilities. In 1890, fewer than a dozen manufacturers listed their shares on the stock market, and the largest manufacturer, Carnegie Steel, was a private partnership. However, by 1905, in the wake of the merger wave engineered by Wall Street that consolidated regional firms into national oligopolies in nearly every major industry, the large-scale modern corporation was born.[42]

Railroads were most responsible for developing the management techniques for multi-division industries. Railroads had to develop a structure to coordinate construction, maintenance, and operations including, among other things, safety rules. This was a crucial issue because railroads were notoriously dangerous for workers. All of this required the development of a "management science" that not only planned, supervised, and coordinated business activity, but also developed mechanisms to ensure that management itself was effective. The development of efficient management hierarchies that put authority and accountability for the various aspects of business under direct control of the appropriate managers took much trial and error. Before the arrival of Taylorism, however, labor management was given lower priority than other aspects of supervision.[43]

During the period 1880–1920, several factors facilitated the shift to centralized managerial control within industrial firms; the most important was the systematic management movement. The term "systematic management" refers to all attempts by large industrial corporations to master a complex of simultaneously emerging technical and administrative problems: planning, getting, and retaining manpower and resources; time wasting; inadequate coordination of production processes and logistic operations; failing control by overburdened and incompetent foremen (acting rather on rule of thumb than on managerial procedures); and cost accounting methods based on mere guesswork.[44]

Systematic management emerged in part out of the increasing specialization in American industry. This specialization was of two types—product specialization and process specialization. After the end of the Civil War product specialization, whereby a firm sharply reduced the range and variety of its products, proceeded very rapidly in America. This was paralleled by increasing labor specialization and fragmentation combined with specialized machinery and technology. The increasing division of labor led to systematic management in two ways. First, in order to accomplish an extensive division of labor, sophisticated job analysis was needed. Second, the increasing division of labor intensified problems of integration and coordination.

In general there were three social sources for the systematic management movement: (1) the formal organization theorists, primarily based on the railroads, (2) the shop management movement, based primarily on metalworking shops and centered on the mechanical engineers; and (3) cost-accounting, which is more difficult to locate socially since it was more widespread and diffuse.[45] These disparate origins meant that there was a certain vagueness about the meaning and use of the term "systematic management." This is not very surprising; most ideologies have a force beyond their practical impact, and systematic management was as much ideology as technique in the U.S. of the 1890s and early 1900s.

Three points deserve closer attention here. First, production control systems were developed and elaborated in order to solve the problems of workflow coordination. Within less than a fifteen-year period in the late 19th century, production control systems became progressively more detailed in specifying the schedule and methods of work. Consequently, the meticulously detailed "paper replica of production" gradually took shape, going from a single piece for each customer order, to a piece of paper for each part of a product on a customer order, to finally, a separate written order for each operation performed in making each part of a product.[46]

Second, there was a major effort to transform cost accounting from an historical record of past performance presented yearly or quarterly, to a current cost-management tool. This improved data-gathering systems and provided the basis for centralized managerial control.[47] It is important to realize that one of the advantages of the contract system was that it standardized labor costs. Part of the burden of fluctuating costs was thereby shifted onto the contractors, and management had only to keep track of material costs in order to be able to quote, for example, machinery prices. Therefore the demise of contracting necessitated the development of effective cost accounting.

Third, systematic management involved the creation of specialized, central staff departments which took over many of the powers of the old, traditional foremen and the internal contractors. Frequently, the foremen were initially responsible for the operation of some new administrative system, either because they insisted on retaining control, or because management felt it was easier and cheaper to do this. But after some time, the responsibilities and decision-making power migrated to administrative staff such as production control clerks and so forth.[48] Overall, systematic management with its development of production control systems linked to new cost-accounting procedures and the creation of centralized staff departments can be regarded as the beginning of the bureaucratization of the managerial function.[49]

Why did the systematic management movement catch fire in the United States? The answer is related essentially to the American labor market circumstances, the product market, and the organizational context including the relation of industrial capital and financial capital. Important factors at the background of American industrialization were the successive waves of immigration, the rapid job mobility, and in many cases the transient links to the work organization. The high rates of inter-firm mobility were possible because of the expanding job opportunities and recurring labor shortages, especially of skilled craftsmen. The relative lack of skilled workers combined with the massive influx of immigrants significantly prompted the development of systematic management and the widespread use of "automatic machinery."

The shortages of craftsmen led to high wages for skilled workers, which in turn led to an increasing division of labor according to skill. Jobs were analyzed in terms of skill content and high-priced workers were customarily restricted to important work, whereas all surrounding tasks were assigned to cheaper unskilled or semiskilled workers, many of them immigrants. Thus the increasing fragmentation and specialization in American industry provided an essential dynamic for the rise of systematic management. For the system of subdivided work to be successful, moreover, new means of integration and coordination became necessary.

Furthermore, the U.S. economy created a large, potential market for mass-produced goods. This, combined with the rapid rise of the American population between 1880 and 1900, constituted the economic context for the early development of large corporations. These corporations dominated the mass-production, mass-distribution industries, and were also important in transport and communication.[50] By the 1890s, large-scale enterprises had grown common. Individual firms in steel, oil, and especially several of the larger railroads, employed over or near 100,000 workers.[51] This process was further enhanced by two important merger waves in the American economy, from 1895 to 1904 and from 1919 to 1929. The first merger wave was in many respects the most important. It transformed many industries that had previously been characterized by small and medium-sized clusters of firms, and it laid the foundations for the oligopolistic structure which marked most of American industry in the 20th century. The development of large corporations was reflected at plant level. In 1870 a factory with 500 employees was still considered to be a large plant, and only a few of those existed. However, by 1900 more than 1,500 plants exceeded this size and nearly a third employed more than 1,000 people. Then there were seventy factories employing more than 2,000, and fourteen employing more than 6,000. By the 1920s, plants' sizes had increased by another order of magnitude, ranging from 20,000 to over 60,000 with Ford's River Rouge plant being the largest with 75,000 employees by 1927.[52]

The American railroads in particular were an important institutional base for the systematizers. The most important group to become organized in American industry at this time was the engineers (mechanical, mining and metallurgical, electrical, and chemical engineers), and they rapidly assumed managerial as well as technical responsibilities. Between 1880 and 1920 the engineering profession in the U.S. increased from 7,000 to 136,000 members. The ability of American engineers to move out of a technical enclave meant that they were the occupational group which captured and dominated systematic management rather than the accountants. The profession of industrial engineer attained a prominent position here. Fredrick W. Taylor, who earned a degree in mechanical engineering, is considered to be the father of industrial engineering. His books, *Shop Management* and *The Principles of Scientific Management*, which were published in the early 1900s, were the beginning of industrial engineering.

The power of the engineers to diagnose an ineffectual system or a flawed method in existing management structures was enhanced by the nature of the links between industrial capital and finance capital. American financiers such as J.P. Morgan and John D. Rockefeller played leading roles in the turn-of-the-century American merger wave. The activist role of American financial institutions in industry resulted in the early emergence of the management consultancy role in the U.S. Management consultants were preeminently outside experts whom financiers could use to push through certain policies, such as calling for the early retirement of an executive or the promotion of others. Many early American consultants were engineers and this meant that the systematizers within management ranks could frequently draw support and encouragement from outside forces. Thus, systematic management, as both ideology and a set of techniques, was sustained and advanced by two emergent and overlapping groups—professional engineers and management consultants.[53]

Scientific Management's Roots in the "Racialization" of Labor Systems

In the early 20th century, employers preferred a labor force divided by race and national origins and they structured workplaces and labor markets along those lines. Specific national origins were likewise connected to specific job classifications. Work gangs segregated by nationality could be made to compete against each other as part of a strategy in the long run to undermine labor unity and depress wages but also to foster rivalry and productivity on a daily basis. The simple pitting of workers by nationality against each other coexisted quite comfortably with new Taylorist systems of scientific management. At other times, the preferred policy was to divide each work group along racial lines.[54]

Elizabeth Esch and David Roediger have shown that the systematized management of labor in the U.S. originates in the particularities of a society that "racialized its labor systems"—slave and free—and thus made "racial knowledge" central to managerial knowledge. During the first decades of the 20th century, scientific management relied on experts to determine and develop racial categories appropriate to particular work settings, not only for the purpose of accumulating capital but also for the organization of modern production. Interestingly, the intertwinement of "race" management and management science matured in U.S. managerial practice outside the country before it became highly elaborated in factories at home. In the twenty-five years after 1890, U.S. mining engineers (technically well-trained) replaced European experts in Asian, South American, Mexican, Australian and African mines due partly to the knowledge they had acquired at the intersection of race and management. These engineers often gained their knowledge and experience in Western U.S. mines where varying decisions regarding which "races" could be in the "white man's camp" were central to management. The term "races" in this context referred to differences of European nationality as well as broad "color" divisions. The central figure (and poster boy) in this celebrated wave of U.S. engineering was the future U.S. President Herbert Hoover. His press agents effectively promoted him as the nation's "highest-paid professional" for his work as a transnational engineer whose most spectacular adventure-capitalist exploits abroad brought such "ideas of efficiency" to South Africa, China and isolated areas in Australia.[55]

"Racial" divisions at the time often referred to what would now be called ethnic divisions among new immigrants from Europe, next to divisions between whites and blacks, and other people of color. During industrial conflicts, fostering such divisions could be expediently deployed in a strategy that played groups of workers against one another and thus weakened labor solidarity. The government provided statistics, however inaccurate, breaking down the proclivity toward unionism of various races. And employers were of course interested in these figures. On the other hand, management also introduced broader hiring and promotion distinctions that were based on pan-national and racial categories. For example in some places and areas, the blast furnace in the steel industry was a pan–Slavic "hunky" job and in others a "Mexican" one. In some industrial sectors and areas (such as lumbering and mining in the South and West) divisions between workers were further reinforced though separate camps, neighborhoods or towns in company housing that segregated workers along racial and/or national (or transnational) lines. Needless to say, this ability to hire, place, and "handle" workers for the mentioned purposes provided an important source of power for managers during the influx of new immigrants in the first decades of the 20th century.[56]

2

Taylorism and Fordism and Their Early Impact on Manufacturing and Service Work

Taylorism grew out of the systematic management movement in the U.S. during the 1880s and 1890s. Taylor was much influenced by the systematizers and accepted their definitions of the problem context: lack of work-flow coordination, rudimentary cost controls, and the "labor problem." Taylor was an active participant in the American Society of Mechanical Engineers (ASME) discussions and in 1905 became its president.

Like some of the other early management reformers, only more fervently, Taylor believed in the original sin and the original stupidity of the worker. For him, the natural inclination of men is to take it easy, which he called "natural soldiering." Moreover, any man phlegmatic enough to do manual work was by definition too stupid to develop the best way, the "scientific way" of doing a job. Thus the role of the workman was a passive one. According to Taylor, workmen should "do what they are told to do promptly and without asking questions or making suggestions."[1] This managerialist view of labor stands in sharp contrast to the populist view held by laborers themselves. Under 19th-century modes of work control in the U.S., many workers saw themselves as the sole creative factor in production.[2] Taylorism and the rationalization movement generally undermined this producerist view and replaced it with a concept of labor as a passive factor of production, a mere appendage of the machine.[3]

Taylor identified major problems in the way work was normally organized. More than anything else, he believed that owners had relinquished too much control over the labor processes in their plants to skilled workers. His primary concern was to give management the ability to improve labor productivity. Taylor found management's techniques too imprecise. By vesting total authority in their plant bosses, owners failed to define exactly what was expected of workers to earn a "fair day's pay." Regarding the method of pay, particularly the piece rate, Taylor argued that it was a source of antagonism between the workers and the employer because the mutual confidence that needed to exist between the employer and his workers—the understanding that they were all working for the same end and would share in the results—was absent.[4]

To reduce reliance upon skilled workers, management should therefore monopolize knowledge of production. Scientific managers had to be able to tell workers the best way to do their jobs. As things stood, Taylor believed that workers seldom worked to their full capacity. Taylor called it "systematic soldiering" when peer pressure was used to discourage anyone who worked too hard. Workers intentionally concealed their capabilities, and consequently Taylor advocated precise "scientific" studies of the work process, in which each of the body's movements involved in a particular task was timed using a stopwatch, and the best combination of movements to accomplish the task was determined by efficiency experts. In this way management deconstructed the work of the skilled worker. Craft "mysteries" were reduced to a set of directions through which management dictated workers' operations and pace on the shop floor.

In order to secure worker compliance to the new system, Taylor proposed a dual payment scheme involving piece rates plus bonuses for beating designated quotas, thus seeking to shore up the worker's interests to the employer's. It was a wage plan designed to encourage a high quality and intensity of work. Under the old piece-rate system, when workers complied by demonstrating how much they could work, management lowered piece rates until workers no longer earned more than before. Taylor opposed this system, urging management to share the gains from their increased output by giving large bonuses to workers who exceeded their quotas. Because the increases could be paid for out of higher productivity of plant machinery, Taylor believed that management could and would stick to its commitment.[5]

Taylorism as a set of managerial practices can best be analyzed in terms of three levels of structuration which Craig Littler put forward in his book, *The Development of the Labour Process in Capitalist Society* (1982): job design, the structure of control over task performance, and the implicit employment relationship. Taylorism, then, involves systematic analysis of the labor process and the division of labor, followed by their deconstruction in accordance with several principles.[6] The systematic analysis of work was done in order to develop a "science of work"; and this systematic job analysis forms the basis for the calculation of production costs, the establishment of standard times for every task and the associated incentive payment system. The deconstruction is based on the following principles:

1. *A general principle of maximum fragmentation.* This prescribes that, after analysis of work into its simplest constituent elements, management should seek to limit an individual job to a single task as far as possible.
2. *The divorce of planning and doing.* This principle in particular is based on the idea that the worker is too stupid to understand his own job.
3. *The divorce of "direct" and "indirect" labor.* This principle is an essential component of intensified work. It entails progressively suppressing that part of the worker's activity that consists of preparing and organizing the work in his own way. All preparation and servicing tasks are stripped away to be performed by unskilled—and cheaper—workers to the extent possible.
4. *Minimization of skill requirements and job-learning time.*
5. *Reduction of material handling to a minimum.*[7]

These five principles basically constitute a dynamic of deskilling. Taylor had developed a system for taking labor (i.e., job roles) apart. In general, then, Taylorism involves a tendency of deskilling, though one should not think that it was the only cause of an increasing division of labor. Taylorism was both a consequence and a cause of deskilling and the corresponding coordination problems. Earlier management theorists such as Charles Babbage had no clear idea about the problems, and the means, of reintegration of the fragmented job roles. Systematic management emerged from the intensified problems of the integration of the new division of labor. These had been created by larger factories, more specialized machines and job roles prior to Taylor, and the failure of traditional modes of management under changed conditions.

Taylorism's Structure of Control

The second major aspect of Taylorism is the new structure of control, or integration, that it offered. This had several aspects:

(a) The principle of task control. What it means in practice is a "planning department" which plans and coordinates the entire manufacturing process. It concerns the coupling of "science" and the workman, a crucial aspect of which is the prescribing of uniform practices and operating procedures. The planning department was envisioned as the firm's production control center, housing a variety of staff positions related to cost analysis, time study, process innovation, and standardization. It represented a historical shift towards a new level of control over the labor process. In practice, however, the idea of a

planning department with its ensemble of functions envisioned by Taylor at the apex of the organization was rarely realized.[8] The principle of task control meant that craft knowledge was to be transferred to those who organized production and to machines that were designed by engineers, who in effect became technical adjuncts of management. Craftsmen began to lose their design function, except for the modifications required to adapt machines to specific production requirements. The crafts were progressively reduced to making tools and maintaining or fixing the machinery designed by the engineers.[9] Thus, the job roles of these craft workers were subject to specialization, which narrowed skill to a smaller range of tasks but still retained some discretionary content. Yet the process of specialization could lead to job fragmentation/deskilling in the longer run.[10]

Only those workers whose jobs inherently resisted routinization and fragmentation—managers, designers, engineers and other "conceptual" workers—were permitted in Taylor's "planning department." The rest were supposed to check their brains in at the door.[11] However, in practice the "American System" of production would always rely on pragmatic and shifting combinations of direct and indirect control, of rationalized work and "relative autonomy." The latter was reserved chiefly but not exclusively for engineers, designers and managerial workers.[12]

Complete task control could not be achieved simply by a planning department and standardization. Other mechanisms were necessary in Taylor's conception.

(b) Functional organization. This principle is usually overlooked because it was rarely put directly into practice. Even Taylor's early disciples had reservations about functional organization. Nevertheless, it is important as a prescription because it represents the idea of a division of management; a movement away from a single hierarchy. For Taylor, the role of the foreman and the gang boss was not clearly circumscribed; it was both too broad and too powerful. This role needed to be subdivided and deskilled, as much as the roles of the workmen. Taylor advocated dividing the shop floor foremen into four categories (setting-up boss, speed boss, quality inspector and repair boss), and placing them all under the control of the planning department. Like workers, foremen would then become subject to the rule of clerks, a clear attack on craft autonomy. But because of Taylor's emphasis on the need to subdivide managerial roles, his "functional organization" had an historical significance in relation to "over-powerful" foremen and internal contractors as much as it did to craft deskilling. What happened to the Taylorite model in practice was a shift to staff-line organization. Taylor's "planning department" became a series of departments strapped onto the side of the existing authority structure.

(c) Time study and the creation of a monitoring system. The institutionalization of time study and scheduling represents the creation of a separate monitoring system over subordinate activities. The time study and scheduling system depends upon the workers filling in (or punching) job cards and/or time sheets which constitute feedback (flowback of information) to the planning departments, enabling them to determine effort levels and compare performance. The upshot is that this flow of information largely bypasses the foremen, or more generally, the existing hierarchy.

The reduced "observability" in large, complex organizations—due to the increased physical separation and growing divergence between superior and subordinate skills—led to upper levels of management becoming progressively more isolated from knowledge about the details of task performances. Thus as one moves from specialization to fragmentation of labor, new types of problems are created which must be solved at the level of the structure of control, especially if the dynamic of deskilling is to continue.[13] (It is apparent that this situation has changed dramatically with the arrival of modern information and communication technology and the introduction of all-pervasive monitoring systems that permit continuous detailed overview of a production system/labor process and its constituent task performances, about which more later.)

(d) New social mechanisms for constituting effort standards in the wage/effort exchange system. Taylor himself argued that his system of management could be applied under any payment system, and concluded that a variety of systems could be used in the same factory depending on circumstances. Some payment systems, such as simple piece work, make the relation of effort to earnings transparent—both supervisors and workers are fully aware of the effort involved for each task—while other systems obscure the effort/wage relationship. On closer inspection, the Taylorite payment schemes made the wage/effort relationship more opaque than simple piece work in order to provide a built-in rate-cutting factor. This was done by obscuring the relationship between the output rate and the wage scale through the introduction of a third intermediary scale, namely an "effort scale," onto which the output rate was just mapped. This scale was usually derived from some output target or "standard job time," and provided an obvious arithmetic rationale for the wage scale.

Importantly, it is the way in which formal effort standards are set rather than a mere shift to incentive wages which is the crucial element in classic Taylorism in relation to wage/effort exchange. A traditional, normative basis to levels of work effort must be socially constituted. Standard norms were built into the occupation or skill over the course of time. Thus, based upon traditional notions of a "fair day's pay for a fair day's work," for example, the shop culture of skilled machinists in the formative years of the emerging auto industry controlled and regulated production through various output quotas and restrictions on the amount of effort exerted or output manufactured.

Taylorism represents the historical shift from traditional effort norms to the creation of new social mechanisms for determining effort standards within an accelerated dynamic of deskilling. In the case of work study based on ongoing systems whereby the work study practitioner was concerned with minor method or product changes, he could rely on prevailing notions of the right level of effort. But in situations of more radical job changes, a situation of accelerating division of labor and associated technological change, there were no pre-existing notions of effort levels. This meant that in practice the work study engineer was more actively involved in establishing the standard effort levels than Taylorism's objectivist image suggests.[14]

(e) Work group strategy. The conventional interpretation of Taylorism maintains that Taylor knew little about work groups, and their relevance for the organization. According to this reading, Taylor adopted an economistic view of working-class motivations; the only point of contact between managers and workers was the pay envelope. This is a superficial reading of Taylorism, however. Taylor knew much about work groups; for instance, he was well aware of the significance of solidary work groups in regulating output, the phenomenon he called "systematic soldiering." The Taylorite managerial tactic in this regard is to try and break the power of the work teams and work groups by pressure, and by appeal to individual ambition, to atomize the workforce. This in contrast to a "human relations" approach, which seeks to foster work-group solidarity, in conjunction with workers' commitment to the values of the formal organization. "Human relations" represents a form of normative control, which was practiced in many American corporations in the 1940s and 1950s. This approach also played an important role in Japan's corporate paternalism, whereby ideological control was achieved by a form of work organization called *shudan-shugi* (meaning "groupism") and the ideologies of familialism and nationalism.[15]

Taylorism in Relation to Bureaucracy

The third aspect of Taylorism concerns the way Taylorite work organization relates to bureaucracy. The characteristic features of the employment relations embodied in Taylorism are that of a "minimum interaction model."[16] This entails a minimal connection between the individual and the organization in terms of skill, training, involvement and the complexity of his/her contribution, in return for maximum flexibility and independence on the part of the organization in using its workforce. In other words, the organization aims for maximum inter-changeability of personnel (with minimum training) to reduce its dependence on the availability, ability or motivation of individuals.

This points to the concept of labor substitutability, the ability of employers to substitute employees. It concerns routinization of jobs that maximizes interchangeability of employees to the effect that individuals, work groups, and even entire departments can be replaced more easily. In practical terms this means that any modern personnel department keeps track of the replacement time for each grade of labor, composed of two elements: recruitment time and training time. Recruitment time varies with the pool of unemployment and training time with the extent of deskilling. Thus Taylorite routinization of jobs is a push towards *minimum interaction* employment relations and an intensified commodification of labor.[17]

In practice there are limits to minimum interaction and hire and fire policies. These limits were clearly recognized by Henry Ford. By the time that he started his car manufacturing business, Taylorism had begun to affect the U.S. engineering industries. Consequently, Ford adopted some of the essential aspects of Taylorism (the separation of conception and execution, the fragmentation of jobs, each task allotted a specific time etc.), but he also went further by adding two further principles: the flow-line principle and a new method of labor control.

The new method of labor control revolved around the "Five Dollar Day." A significant effect of the implementation of Taylorism and flow-line principles at Ford's automobile plants (about which more later) was the enormous turnover of workers. For example, in 1913 Ford required about 13,000 workers to run his plants at any one time, while over 50,000 workers quit that year.[18] The minimum interaction principle of Taylorism proved to be too expensive, and the answer that Ford came up with was the Five Dollar Day. This was a wage package which guaranteed relatively high rates of pay. However, for the Five Dollar Day only those who met stringent criteria qualified: six months' continuous employment, over age 21, satisfactory personal habits at home and work (cleanliness and prudency) and complete abstention from alcohol and tobacco. Everything was checked by Ford's newly established "Sociological Department." This aspect of Fordism clearly demonstrates how Taylorism relates to paternalism.[19]

Paternalism essentially involves a diffuse employer/employee relationship, whereby the employer shows concern for the non-work life of the employee. The nature of this employment relationship is related to the degree of employment security.[20] As noted earlier, Taylorism is commonly associated with casualized employment and a minimum interaction relationship; indeed, Taylor and his close associates did not care what became of the worker after he left the factory at night, so long as he was able to show up the next morning in a fit condition for "a hard day's toil."[21] For Taylor, welfare schemes and paternalistic modes of management were objects of ridicule. Fordism, with its paternalistic repressiveness and the attempt to stabilize high rates of turnover by the Five Dollar Day was, so to speak, two steps up from Taylorism in terms of the degree of employment security and diffuseness of the employer/employee relationship. Other types of paternalism, such as that of Cadbury in Britain in 1914, Krupp in Germany in 1900 and Japanese corporate paternalism as it had emerged in the late 1920s and early 1930s showed increasingly higher degrees of employment security and employer's concern for the welfare of employees outside the workplace.[22]

Finally, it is helpful to relate Taylorism to the Weberian concept of bureaucracy. Looking back at the results of the analysis above, Taylorism represents the bureaucratization of the structure of control, but not the employment relations. Taylorism does not involve (nor imply) either a career system or fixed salaries. Instead it involves what has been called a minimum interaction relationship between individual and organization. With regard to the structure of control aspects of the bureaucratic model, Taylorism takes continuity and hierarchy for granted. In addition, the Taylorites sought to introduce a systematic division of labor, work performance governed by rules based on "science," and a system of written instruction and communication. The idea of a planning office was an attempt to achieve a unified system of control, but with a functional system of organization, therefore it was not strictly monocratic. The major characteristic of a Taylorized work organization is the lack of any notion of a career system. It is this which distinguishes it from other available models of organization at the turn of the 20th century; for example, those based on the public service organizations such as the police, the railways and the post office in Britain.[23]

Thus, Taylorism as a management package affected all three levels of structuration of the labor processes that Littler distinguished: work design, the structure of control, and the employment relationship. In contrast, the structural implications of welfarism and human relations—two other major managerial ideologies and practices, to be discussed in the next chapter—do not reach down to the level of work design.

The Influence of Taylorism in the United States

It should be recognized that there were different forms of Taylorism, and that Taylorism in its initial form probably failed in the sense of a widespread implementation of a standard body of techniques. But this did not prevent Taylorism on an ideological level from being crucial to the bureaucratization of American industry. There was the influence and demonstration effect of the Taylor system as contracting and traditional modes of control were overturned. Although Taylorism was rarely transplanted onto factory floors as a complete system, the overall principles and many of the specific techniques were in fact widely diffused. One must also keep in mind that systems, such as the Bedaux system, represented later forms of Taylorism. These were probably the means by which the effect of Taylorism became profound and enduring in the U.S.[24]

The fact that some managers were reluctant to embrace Taylorism has been attributed to three major factors. First, it has been suggested that they were unconvinced about the value of Taylorism.[25] This was in part because it had been shown that implementing whole-scale scientific management methods could take between two and four years; furthermore Taylorized piece-rate schemes did not eliminate the problem of workers deceiving managers and continuing to restrict output.[26] Second, managers were concerned that the introduction of scientific management might provoke conflict in the form of strikes in the short run and jeopardize co-operation in the longer term.[27] Lastly, managers realized that their authority—hence their own position—could be threatened by the new efficiency engineers who might be more interested in productivity than profit. Senior managers demurred, tending to raise all kinds of objections to the Taylor system, because, if taken seriously, they would have to defer to the authority of the engineer at the time the methods or scientific management were installed. And from the moment the Taylor system was in operation, top management would no longer be involved in directing the day-to-day activities of lower echelons. Unsurprisingly, the implementation of the system was quite often accompanied by a power struggle between top management and (lower and middle management) engineers.[28]

Foremen and supervisors constituted a major source of resistance to the new forms of managerial control. They objected particularly to Taylor's minute systematization (versus their rule-of-thumb methods) and to the erosion of their decision-making powers. Given the recurring instances of supervisory skepticism and obstruction, there were systematic employer efforts to integrate foremen into the new managerial structures. For example, American steel companies, having abolished the contract system, gave their foremen special training courses in order to make them an integral part of management. From the employer point of view it was necessary to ensure that the new foremen did not identify with their subordinate work teams. This form of formal supervisory training became widespread throughout American industry.[29]

Worker opposition to skill-breaking machinery and Taylorite techniques was particularly widespread during the early attempts to implement Taylorism in the U.S. There were highly publicized strikes, such as the one at Watertown Arsenal in Massachusetts, which led to the 1912 House of Representatives investigation of the relationship between scientific management and labor, resulting in the 1915 Hoxie Report. From 1911 to 1915, there were long-drawn out and violent strikes on the Illinois Central and Union Pacific Railroads over the introduction of Taylorite schemes of control.[30] The skilled workers in particular felt themselves threatened by the new managerial methods and union leaders such as John P. Frey protested vehemently against the development of "fractional mechanics, who could work effectively only under the groups of functional foremen and superforemen, provided for by the system."[31] Harry Braverman's pivotal craft workers (discussed in the introduction) were often successful in defending their control of the labor process, and hence their status as skilled workers, via a combination of local and national collective action.[32]

This current of opposition reached a peak during World War I, when there was considerable resistance against skill dilution, the use of the stopwatch, and new payment systems. The American Federation of Labor (AFL) won, temporarily, an unprecedented degree of societal influence. Its leaders served as representatives on various governmental boards and agencies where they rubbed shoulders with professional "dollar-a-year" men.[33] This led to a brief love affair between Progressive reformers and organized labor and a more lasting relationship between the AFL and the liberal intellectuals within the Taylor Society, the industrial research organization and institutional home of scientific management.

After the war, when organized labor faced increasing employer and government hostility, the AFL wished to demonstrate that the trade unions were "constructive." In a spirit of cooperation the AFL then repeatedly called for an end to waste in industry, and supported the installation and extension of machinery, the linkage of wages to productivity increases, and union-management cooperation. These were significant departures from its earlier policies, which opposed or called for restrictions on technological change and backed bargaining for the sake of obtaining the maximum wage.[34]

Importantly, the Taylor Society had gradually changed its stance toward organized labor after Frederick W. Taylor's death in 1915, which brought about a reconciliation between the AFL and the Taylor Society. The latter's shift in attitude reflected a growing tolerance of trade unions by Progressive intellectuals and reformers during and after World War I; in effect, it was a crucial departure from Taylor's uncompromising attitude towards union participation in rationalization schemes.[35] The central figure in the Taylor's Society rapprochement with organized labor was Morris L. Cooke, who was Taylor's favored disciple and whom he recommended as a consultant to a number of his major clients. Twice (in 1921 and 1929) Cooke called for a new coalition of science (that is, the technical intelligentsia) and organized labor. The idea of such a coalition had a certain resemblance to Thorstein Veblen's idea about a "Soviet of Technicians," which would lead the masses to prosperity.[36] Veblen and his followers had ideologically drifted close to the Taylor Society in the early 1920s. Yet Veblen's idea also touched upon an old technocratic theme in Taylorism: that social and technological change should be left in the capable hands of experts. The new twist was that the Taylorists would now put themselves at the disposal of organized labor. But as with Taylor's original schema, it was never entirely clear precisely where the technician would stand regarding the management-labor relationship.[37] The eventual outcome of AFL's temporary alliance with the Taylor Society was a trade-off between union interest in controlling job opportunities and employer desires to bureaucratize the structure of control. The AFL unions accepted changes in the structure of managerial control over task performance in return for formalization of employment and promotion procedures. This collaboration was helped along by the fact that many of the earlier generation of craft workers found their way into the realms of supervision, design and even management.

In relation to the unskilled workers, the opposition to Taylorism and the increasing subdivision of work was dampened by new waves of workers (immigrants and women) taking over the deskilled, tightly-controlled jobs. For them, such jobs represented promotion. The Industrial Workers of the World (IWW), founded in 1905, was the only labor organization representing unskilled workers which opposed scientific management; this resulted in a minor strike wave between 1909 and 1913. However, no linkage was achieved between the IWW strikes and the pre–1914 opposition of the craft workers in the AFL. On the contrary, in some plants the AFL workers gave employers the names of suspected IWW sympathizers. Moreover, the majority of the unskilled remained outside the labor unions until the New Deal era, when the CIO was founded. Consequently, most protests of these workers were isolated and sporadic.[38]

Spatial and Technical Reorganization of the Shop Floor

Systematic management dovetailed neatly with changes in the geography of the factory and shop floor. A major element of industrial capitalists' strategy was to take advantage of shifts in the broader social division of labor to reconstruct the scale of the shop floor. The "era of scientific management" shaped and was shaped by the emergence of a new factory form. Although factories existed before the 1870s (as noted earlier), it was only after the Civil War that the modern industrial plant emerged as an "identifiable architectural form" in the U.S.[39] This was made possible by technological innovations in structural steel and reinforced concrete, but especially by advances in electrical power. By the late 1880s, engineers had pioneered the industrial application of electrical power, which fueled two developments. First, industry was no longer strongly dependent on rivers for power, which would have profound implications for industrial capital's mobility in the ensuing decades. Second, the existence of a "central generating source" fostered new factory designs, including decentralization and the spread of work areas and assembly lines.[40] Factories were increasingly a matter of deliberate planning—they were no longer merely a "place to store machinery." Factory planners now considered not just the general type of production, but "the flow of work between departments."[41]

Thus, technical-organizational control was increasingly articulated in factory design. Rather than allowing workers to consciously organize the cooperation necessary for production, industrial capitalists had factories remade to ensure that managers could now assume the coordinating function and use this power to fragment the workforce at the point of production. This became especially evident by the early 20th century, when industrialists began building larger plants away from the epicenters of industrial conflicts in the big cities:

> As plants grew larger, firms gradually abandoned the classic 19th-century model of the single open shed. A number of important technical innovations, such as reinforced concrete for construction and electric power for traveling cranes, railroads and other handling equipment, permitted more flexible plant design. After 1895–1900 ... most modern factories consisted of a series of interrelated buildings rather than a single large structure. For example, foundries were located in separate structures, isolated from the main assembly areas. Even within the general flow of assembly production, plant activities were fragmented among disparate shops and structures.[42]

Crucially, the new spatial organization of the factory and its attendant workplace fragmentation reflected the rise of managerial control at the expense of skilled workers' control. To put it bluntly, while before 1900 work revolved around the skilled craftsman, after the turn of the century it was the workers who revolved around the production process.[43]

Fordism as a Distinct Type of Labor Process

In the auto industry, even before the advent of the assembly line, Henry Ford had reorganized the shop floor into a "progressive layout" system, which was roughly structured as follows. In the machine-tool shops, operators were confined to a single machine, and the machines were clustered together. "Unnecessary" movements were eliminated, as operators were restricted to a single workstation, which could include two or more of the same type of machine. As a result, direct supervision became much easier. Most significantly, "progressive layout" ensured a rapid, continuous flow of work past operators. As such it was a crucial precondition for assembly-line production.[44]

Ford had taken the skilled work of carriage makers and machinists and turned most of it into semiskilled or unskilled work. In doing so, Ford combined the organizational innovations of Taylorism, namely the separation of conception from execution and associated task fragmentation and simplification,[45] with the introduction of special or single-purpose machine tools, which made standardized and therefore interchangeable parts. And Ford then developed a sequential layout of the detailed tasks and special machines leading to progressive or continuous flow production in the form of a moving assembly line derived from meatpacking. This assembly line was the culmination of many mechanical conveyor and transfer devices introduced between 1910 and 1914.

The first moving assembly line was introduced in 1913 in the subassembly section where flywheel magnetos were produced, and extended to other areas of production until an endless and highly synchronized chain conveyor for final assembly was achieved the following year.[46] The flow production principle was basically an organizational innovation which required changes to the layout of work processes and saved time by restricting workers to their positions on the line. In the constant search for the most efficient production method, a stopwatch was often used to calculate how much time a worker spent walking to collect materials and tools, and how much time he spent working. Ford also automated processes such as riveting the crank-case arms to a crank-case, which once automated was operated by one worker instead of twelve. These innovations increased productivity and profits dramatically.[47]

The new automotive production technology would be the dominant industrial technology for most of the 20th century. In a relatively brief time span, from World War I through the 1920s, Fordism became the global model for efficient and profitable production. (After World War I, Ford officials and managers improved and refined the Highland Park methods further and constructed the River Rouge plant, which located and concentrated all phases of automobile production within one huge industrial facility.) As the reputable management expert Peter Drucker, who had studied General Motors under Alfred P. Sloan, already proclaimed at mid-century, "The automobile industry stands for modern industry all over the globe. It is to the 20th century what the Lancashire cotton mills were to the 19th century: the industry of industries."[48]

Since the reorganization of work and the adoption of the new technologies removed skill from ordinary work tasks and routines, the establishment of work discipline and the control of workers became a priority of the modern system of mass production. Ford managers and engineers achieved the new forms of control through the stricter supervision of workers, the design of new machine tools, and the major innovation of line production. Under traditional craft production, the skilled craftsman often supervised himself and the helpers and laborers who worked with him. The years of apprenticeship and pride in craft reinforced the self-discipline and self-supervision regarding the amount of effort to be exerted and the quality of the product to be achieved. And craft notions of equity in the amounts of effort and pay might hamper management expectations for excessive overwork. In contrast, at the Highland Park factory, a large contingent of foremen, "straw bosses" (assistants to foremen), inspectors, and clerks directly supervised and monitored Ford workers and their output. Foremen and straw bosses continuously exhorted the men to hurry up and work faster. The inspectors and clerks also assured that the quality and amount of work met supervisory expectations.

Because industrial managers and engineers arranged both machines and assembly tasks in operational sequence, they could readily monitor, supervise, and control the workers on the shop floor. At the machines, the operators passed the finished work from their work station to the next. The worker with too many unfinished pieces at his work station attracted the foreman's (or the straw boss's) attention and received calls and admonitions to work faster. On the assembly lines the situation was similar. And where the assembly line moved, the pressure to maintain a specific pace of work was even greater. In this case, the line speed (like the predetermined cycle of the machine) controlled the pace of the assembler's work.

Many industrial engineers, journalists and other observers at the time noted the managerial advantages of these forms of organizational and technical control over the workforce. However, the most compelling means to control the Ford workforce was probably the famous Five Dollar Day incentive, especially when connected to the welfare programs of the Ford Sociological Department and the Ford English School. A unique experiment in industrial paternalism, the Five Dollar Day was not a simple wage increase, but a profit-sharing scheme to transform the social and cultural lives of immigrant workers (who were mainly unskilled and preindustrial) and to instill the lifestyle, personal habits, and social discipline required for modern factory life. The Five Dollar Day was divided into two parts: a worker's wages (about $2.40 per day for an unskilled worker) and a worker's profits (about $2.60 per day). All workers received their profits only if they were "worthy," or demonstrated the appropriate habits and lifestyle and lived in properly kept homes. The counseling of "sociological investigators," the publication of pamphlets, the lessons of the Ford English School, all advised and taught immigrant auto workers what Ford officials deemed the proper American values, living conditions, and work habits. Though short-lived, the Ford profit-sharing plan was a unique experiment in the social engineering of immigrant auto workers to inculcate the personal habits and work discipline desired for assembly line production.[49]

The Rise of "Sloanism" and Flexible Mass Production

In light of discussions about the innovative character of "flexible specialization" among management experts in the 1980s and beyond, it is noteworthy that William S. Knudsen's working out of "flexible mass production" at General Motors in the mid– and late 1920s already showed how resilient the mass production model could be in the face of changing consumer demands. Knudsen was a former production engineer at Ford who joined General Motors in 1921 and was appointed general manager by Alfred P. Sloan at Chevrolet in 1924. Contrary to Henry Ford, Knudsen understood that the consumer's changing desires had to be met. To this end, Knudsen pioneered methods of flexible mass production that both accommodated the consumer and also kept the workforce still largely subjected to the rules of scientific management. These technical innovations (outlined below) later became known as "Sloanism."

Ford had accomplished his mission to provide an affordable car for the masses by 1923, when 74 percent of American families owned a car (compared to less than half a percent in 1910).[50] Market saturation next required a new strategy, one that involved selling cars to those who already owned one. While Ford held on to his limited automobile range (i.e., different body styles) of one low-priced, though not unchanging car, General Motors introduced a far wider choice. It consisted of "five basic price classes by car makes and several subclasses of models" that covered a wider price range (from the lowly Chevrolet to the high-priced Cadillac).[51] It also developed the idea of annual models, which showed that the "mass production of automobiles could be reconciled with product variation"; in short "a car for every purse and purpose."[52] With stylish automobiles, Sloan hoped to attract women as new purchasers and to introduce an early notion of planned obsolescence, whereby owners would want to possess the very latest model. By the late 1920s, Sloan's strategy for all of GM was not simply to restyle its cars every year, but also to introduce a completely new model every third year.

In order to achieve this degree of model diversification, Knudson moved beyond the hyperspecialization of Ford's Highland Park plant, where most machines were assigned to the production of just one model. He devised a more flexible mass production system that facilitated frequent model changes with minimal delays in production. It involved the development of a "new middle-range machine" that had a "standard tool base, easy for the tool builders to manufacture," but also had a superstructure that could be altered to accommodate the change specifications of any new model.[53] This kind of machine "used the unskilled labor of the Ford single-purpose machine and contained some of the flexibility of the general purpose ones."[54] Such a semi-special machine required a skilled setup man to readjust and to reset its parts or components for changes in design.

Importantly, the semi-specialized machines did not alter the subordinate relationship of the worker to the machinery and the moving assembly line, since the skill was still built into the technology and the work still involved limited tasks and monotonous routines. The machine operator who worked in a sequentially-arranged machine shop did not see any significant change in the character of work tasks and routines. For assembly line workers, the annual model change meant several days or weeks of fussing and fumbling until they adjusted to the new routines and rhythms of their work.

It is also noteworthy that this innovation did not require any significant change to the workforce of mass production common to both Ford and General Motors. Only the reconfiguration of the machine's superstructure entailed skilled work, which was performed by a small indirect workforce of skilled workers, that in both companies represented only somewhere between 10 and 15 percent of the total workforce. While the required adjustments of Knudsen's machines were done by the small number of setup men, the routines of the assemblers and machine operators remained as they had been at Highland Park. In short, despite its flexible nature, the Sloanist system of production still rested on the foundation of Fordist principles of mass production.[55]

Scientific Management in the Retail Sector

Early on, Taylorism was also applied to service work, beginning with retailing. More specifically self service was first introduced in restaurants in the U.S. during the 1890s and subsequently adopted in food shops by the Lutey brothers in 1912 and by the Piggly Wiggly stores in 1916.[56] Self-service shops were based on the production line principle that centered around the moving customer rather than the moving assembly line. Standardized pre-packaged goods were delivered at one end of the shop, stacked on aisles ready to be selected by customers who transported them to the checkout counter and exited at the other end of the shop. In full-service shops knowledgeable shop workers could advise on prices and products, locate them, measure out the required amount, bag them, calculate the total costs, take payment, and arrange delivery if required. In contrast, self-service customers made their own judgments about their needs in terms of price, quantity, quality, and appropriateness of products, collected and unloaded them at the checkout, bagged them, and carried them away. The organization of the shop ensured that customers had to pass all the products in every aisle in order to reach the cashier near the exit, which had the benefit for the shop-owner of encouraging impulse buying. In doing most of the work of shopping without assistance, including acquiring knowledge about products prior to entering the shop, the customer saved in the form of lower-priced standard goods and time. One could say that, in effect, the shop worker became deskilled while the customer became upskilled.[57] Employers gained from the unpaid labor of customers and the lower wages of an increasingly deskilled retail labor force that consisted ever more of women, especially the checkout worker who no longer wasted time waiting for a customer. This assembly-line system of service provision was very successful in terms of reducing costs and increasing profits and has since spread to most services, including department stores, gas stations, and restaurants. The technology used in self-service shops initially was quite limited, consisting of such contrivances as one-way turnstiles and checkout counters. Over the course of time, more complex machines were also introduced, including cash registers which eliminated the need for workers to perform mental calculations. In sum, the specialized personal service retailing process was industrialized with the customer doing most of the work, organized on assembly-line principles.

Fordist self-service retailing was adopted on a larger scale domestically from the 1950s onward. The primary driving factor for an assembly line self-service system was to reduce costs through lower staffing levels, lesser skilled workers, and a higher proportion of part-time workers. Shelf-stocker and checkout operator became the main jobs in self-service retailing, both of which require little skill and therefore training, are poorly paid, and monotonous.[58] The fact that female workers were not considered bread winners was used to justify their low wages, which were generally lower than those of men in comparable jobs—a gender gap that has persisted up until today.

In the process of eroding the craft-like knowledge and skills of the sales clerk, the expansion of self-service retailing was accompanied by a more detailed division of unskilled labor, as outlined by Braverman in 1974 with regard to retail food trading:

> the all-around grocery clerk, fruiterer and vegetable dealer, dairyman, butcher, and so forth, has long ago been replaced by a configuration in the supermarkets which calls for truck unloaders, shelf stockers, checkout clerks, meat wrappers, and meatcutters; of these, only the last retain any semblance of skill, and none require any general knowledge of retail sale.[59]

He then also signaled the coming introduction of computerized semi-automatic checkout systems (including the use of the new bar code system) in supermarkets and in various other fields of retail trade as well. The eventual effects of this system on inventory control, quick and general price changes, and sales reporting to a central point were obvious. The checkout counter would now adopt as its own the assembly line or factory pace in the most complete form.[60]

Scientific Management in the Office

There was also a growing movement that aimed to implement the principles of Taylorism in office management. Taylor's disciple, William Henry Leffingwell (1876–1934)—whose name, contrary to Frederick Winslow Taylor's, is now almost forgotten—took the lead in finding out how the principles of scientific management could be applied to labor processes/activities in the service industries, to the routines of banks, accounting firms, insurance companies, and mail-order houses. In his books, *Office Management: Principles and Practice*, *Textbook of Office Management*, and *Better Office Management*, he described in great detail how the practices pioneered by Taylor and Ford could be used to improve the productivity of American clerks, messengers, and typists.

Leffingwell benefited from the gap of a generation that separated him from Taylor. At the turn of the century, Taylor had struggled to apply the methods of scientific management to metalworking industries still strongly influenced by the craft tradition. Leffingwell's followed some twenty years later, in the eleven-year period marked by the end of World War I in 1918 and the Wall Street crash in October 1929. It was during those years that the craft worker, along with the small and medium-sized plants in which he worked, was in stark retreat before the advance of the giant, mass production plant, epitomized by Ford's Detroit factories at Highland Park and River Rouge.

In his voluminous work, *Office Management*, Leffingwell summed up the central aim of his new conception of office management in one word: "simplification." The overarching purpose of his approach was to fill the clerical workday with activities that were linked to a concrete task and eliminate time spent on coordination and communication.[61] This was manifested most prominently in Leffingwell's detailed discussions of the physical arrangement of the office and his views on the organization, flow, planning, measurement, and control of office work.[62]

While Taylor's experiments had been focused on the routines of the Pennsylvania machine shops, Leffingwell's were concentrated on the operations of mail-order driven business. Leffingwell's case histories therefore describe work rationalization in companies such as Montgomery Ward and Curtis Publishing. The thousands of orders received each day by the mail-order houses set off a business process that required the dispatch of goods to the customer. This process presented problems of coordination and control that the methods of scientific management were able to resolve. As with Taylor, Leffingwell's routines ranged from the extremely trivial—how best to open an envelope—to the lengthy and complex, how best to fulfill a customer's order. Yet all of these lesser routines had their places in a hierarchy of routines that, for a mail-order house, together encompassed the "business process" of order fulfillment. Thus, opening the envelope was part of the task of receiving an order, while the latter, along with operations such as credit checking and dispatch, was part of the overall process of order fulfillment.

Leffingwell's fanatical attention to detail fully matches Taylor's second-by-second analysis of the shoveling of sand and clay in the backyards of the Bethlehem Steel Company. For example, in the opening of mail, a core microprocess of the mail-order business, Leffingwell reduced the necessary motions from thirteen to six and increased the output of letter opening by one clerk from 100 to 200 times an hour. Further refinements in the methods drove the rate up to 250 an hour, then to 300 an hour, and ultimately to 500 an hour.[63] He used the same methods, with comparable results, in over five hundred other clerical operations.

However, the processes of Leffingwell's mail-order houses differed in an important way from those of Taylor's machine shops. Leffingwell's processes had to adapt themselves to the customer's whims in a way that Taylor's did not. The customer orders that the mail-order house received each day could not be anticipated and classified with the same precision as the metal components that filled Taylor's machine shops. Leffingwell tackled this problem (regarding the diversity of work) by applying what he called the "exception principle," the process of weeding out "difficult" cases and sending them to an expert or team of experts who solely concentrated their attention on exceptional cases.

A significant aspect of the exception principle was that employees were sometimes required to make decisions about what should be done with particular orders: Was the order difficult, requiring the eye of an expert (such as the credit man) or was it routine and under the remit of an ordinary clerk? But any mention of decision making by workers, however trivial the decisions to be made were, was a sensitive matter for Leffingwell. Like all scientific managers, he believed it was imperative that decisions should, wherever possible, be made by managers, and not by workers. In his discussion of the exception principle, Leffingwell therefore did everything he could to assure his clients that the decision making left to the worker would be so narrowed and simplified that it would not disturb the even flow of production along the clerical assembly line, nor require any elaborate worker training. The clerk's decisions would "always be upon principles determined by management" and would "not demand profound original thought on the part of the worker."[64] Training for the work itself was brief and intensive: "Every motion is taught precisely, and the teacher is constantly at the side of the worker during the entire period of training." Although it might seem to the "casual observer that this method is expensive," it was in fact the cheapest possible method because "a worker becomes highly productive in a very short time," which, for Leffingwell, amounted to between two and three weeks.[65]

Sometimes it was necessary to supplement this on-the-job training with elementary education so that employees would have the proper literacy and numeracy to read and understand worksheets or customers' orders. In 1917 Leffingwell noted that a large number of corporations had already included such elementary education in their training schools. Leffingwell, like Taylor, had no use for the apprentice system, in which a young worker was employed by a business and spent up to three years learning a substantive, craft skill. Under what Leffingwell considered an old-fashioned system, the apprentice would work at low wages, and then be allowed "to dabble a little at a time in some of the higher-priced [i.e., skilled] work." Leffingwell noted with disapproval that, with this system, it "often took years for an employee to become worthwhile."[66]

For Leffingwell (like Taylor), the efficient running of a business required an almost exclusive concentration of power in the hands of management. In the Leffingwellian office, management was personified by the office manager, supported by his planning staff. It was the office manager's and his staff's task to work out the precise routine that the clerical workforce had to follow throughout its working day, including the amount of time each routine should take.

The office manager and his staff were responsible for training each worker so that he or she could do the work in the allotted time. It was also for the office manager to assign the work and, assisted by his foremen, closely monitor the performance of the workforce to ensure that it achieved its planned output.

Finally, it was the responsibility of the office manager to find ways of making the routines more efficient—that is, speeding them up. For Leffingwell, as for Taylor, optimal efficiency was best reached when the scope for independent decision making by employees was reduced to a minimum.[67] In his *Textbook of Office Management*, Leffingwell writes that this "human element" was "notoriously variable and unreliable," when the human element in question was that of workers, not managers. Wherever possible this element was to be "eliminated, or if not, minimized to the smallest possible degree."[68]

Leffingwell's project of applying Taylorist methods to the service industries endured. By mid-century, numerous periodicals were focused on the subject, including *The Office, Office Management, Office Control and Management, Paperwork Simplification, Office Economist,* and *Office Equipment Digest*. Founded in 1951, the Methods, Timing, Measurement Association (MTM) carried on Leffingwell's work of applying time-and motion studies to clerical work. And in the late 1950s, handbooks of scientific management such as *Manual of Standard Time Data for the Office,* relied on movie cameras to refine Leffingwell's methods.[69] Coupled with the continued industrialization of white-collar work came speed-up and growing workers' discontent. In 1960, the International Labour Organization (ILO), a United Nations agency, published a lengthy study on mechanization and automation in the office. The study found that "clerical workers often complained of muscular fatigue, backache and other such ills as a result of the unaccustomed strain of operating machines."[70] Moreover, it found that the psychological strains generated by the new forms of office work took a toll on these workers and were an even greater threat to their health than the physical exertion.

From a managerial control perspective, a more basic problem with white-collar Taylorism was that much white-collar work resisted the rigorous standardization and measurement of scientific management. Measurement efforts engulfed the lowest paid and most clericalized jobs, but it tended to bypass higher-paid jobs completely. These were jobs that continued to absorb, however weakly, both interpersonal and intellective aspects carved out of the managerial function that could not be rationalized.[71]

3

Welfare Capitalism and Human Relations as Additional Means of Managerial Control

Some companies also pursued a "softer," albeit not necessarily less, manipulative approach than Taylorism to keep labor in check. From the 1880s onward, several paternalistic, anti-union American firms introduced forms of welfare capitalism, which entailed a managerially-driven effort to generate a harmonious, union-free setting within a single work site or company. Such firms had far greater managerial resources than most of their counterparts elsewhere to develop programs for employee welfare and personnel management.

Companies throughout Europe, including Krupp, Le Creusot, Cadbury, and the textile firms of Lancashire, all had elaborate welfare schemes. But company welfarism was more pervasive in the U.S. than elsewhere, initially appearing in companies controlled by their founders. These men hoped to undo the impersonal character of their firms (that had grown large) through social provisions which were intended to reproduce the close ties that had existed when they knew each of their employees personally. They also saw what was then commonly called "welfare work" (a confusing term to modern ears) as a way of responsibly sharing their wealth and fulfilling their moral obligations as they understood them. These motives were often reinforced by religious beliefs. Quaker businessmen as well as employers influenced by mainline Protestantism's Social Gospel, initiated some of the earliest welfare schemes. Their ethical impulse, however, was closely intertwined with a great measure of self-interest. The company bonds created by the company's welfare provisions undermined trade unionism and dampened public criticisms of concentrated wealth.[1]

Between 1886 and 1889, a period of considerable labor unrest, some forty companies launched profit-sharing programs for their employees and, at the same time began to provide various provisions like lunchrooms and landscaped grounds. This marked the start of America's welfare capitalist movement. Like scientific management, company welfarism aimed to prevent strikes and to improve production, though its methods were more indirect, focusing on the workers' conditions outside the shop. It originated in the belief that the worker himself—stereotypically seen as the immoderate, lazy worker or the ignorant immigrant, susceptible to radical panaceas—was directly responsible for labor unrest, social tension, and the decline of the work ethic. To quash these tendencies, employers experimented with programs ranging from thrift clubs, compulsory religious services, and citizenship instruction to company housing, outings, and contests.

The diffusion of systematic and scientific management was accompanied by the further spread of welfare capitalism to many large corporations between 1900 and World War I. By 1914, the National Civic Federation comprised 2,500 firms pursuing an array of welfare provisions, ranging from cafeterias, gardens, and profit-sharing plans to company housing, magazines, and athletic facilities. A leading expert of modern welfare capitalism, Sanford Jacoby, calls such firms "modern manors" because in some ways they resembled the feudal baronies of a much earlier age that offered security and identity in return for deference and loyalty.[2] As firms grew larger their owners often found it possible to take the long view. Where previously the focus was first of all on labor costs to maintain competitiveness, managers of the giant survivors of corporate consolidations saw value in redirecting some of their investments towards their employees. Not only did they think this was a good way to halt the advancing thrusts of organized labor, they also saw it as an efficient alternative to market individualism in that training would be cheaper and productivity higher if employees spent their working lives within a single firm instead of trying to make a living by maneuvering on the open market. Managers reasoned that relatively small investments on labor sometimes prevented huge losses from labor turnover or unrest. A moral impulse played a role too among some self-made business owners who felt a sense of stewardship and paternal obligation to their employees. But such virtue was conveniently intertwined with strategic considerations, as these businessmen were convinced that the deployment of welfare capitalism was the best defense of "freedom" against laborism and statism.[3]

Organized labor saw in corporate welfarism a return to patriarchal habits that undermined the gains of the previous century. Union leaders argued that if workers were paid a good wage, they could make their own decisions about the housing, medical care, and personal consumption they needed. Unions in the AFL believed it was their job, not the employers, to provide those benefits for their members.[4]

Welfare work chiefly focused on employees' lives outside the workplace; inside the plant, employment policies often remained primitive. Between 1900 and 1920, however, some employers began to develop stable, structured employment systems, at first for their skilled workers. These systems entailed a combination of policies pursued by craft unions, such as seniority rules, with benefits offered to salaried employees mainly existing of deferred compensation in the form of pensions and stock bonuses. The railroads led the way in this regard, followed by large industrial companies such as U.S. Steel, Baldwin Locomotive, and International Harvester. An intended effect was a raise of the cost of engaging in union activity for workers, since the benefits could not be enjoyed if a worker was forced to leave the company.[5]

By binding skilled workers to the firm, employers sought to weaken craft union traditions, speed up the pace of work, and hasten the introduction of new technologies. Regarding the latter, they also strategically deployed piece-rates and other incentive wage devices, especially in the metalworking industries, where Taylorist ideas were popular. However, employers came to realize that incentive pay sometimes led to undesirable results, because it made workers reluctant to accept technical innovations or job transfers, which both might cause a decline in earnings. Therefore other, more career-based workplace policies—promotion ladders, seniority rules, and dismissal restraint—were introduced next to incentive wage systems. These policies were administered by new employment departments whose task was to monitor foremen and other line managers. Gradually the drive system gave way to more enduring work relationships, intertwined with welfare services provided by the employer outside the workplace.[6]

Major Characteristics of Early Company Welfarism

Welfare work flourished during the Progressive Era, a time of juvenile justice reform, domestic science, settlement work, and other well-intentioned but paternalistic attempts to remake the working-class family in a middle-class mold—thus uplifting the worker, "bettering" him, and making his family life more "wholesome" according to prevailing norms. Its practitioners and publicists came from the "helping professions"—social workers, settlement workers, educators—who sought to protect the working-class family from the exigencies of industrial life, even while questioning the family's ability to function properly without expert assistance.[7]

This work was frequently manipulative and condescending. Its champions hoped that welfare activities would transform allegedly intemperate, lazy workers or ignorant immigrants into productive middle-class citizens. The most paternalistic programs were directed at immigrants from Eastern and Southern Europe and at women. Skilled workers—virtually always men, either native-born or from Northwestern Europe—tended to be offered more straightforward economic incentives for loyalty, including wage bonuses, deferred compensation, and profit-sharing plans.

Welfare workers gave a lot of attention to the family, assuming that many of the worker's individual shortcomings were due to an improper home life. At many firms they regularly went to workers' homes to check on living conditions, family relationships, and illnesses. The role of welfare worker, like that of social worker, accorded with the stereotype of the woman as empathetic and nurturing. Not surprisingly, then, the welfare workers were disproportionately women (many former social workers). Social workers, and by extension welfare workers, were encouraged to befriend their clients, visit people in their homes and provide advice on proper living.[8] The home visit was often used to give a patronizing pep talk, advising employees on such matters as marital choice, furniture arrangement, and even personal appearance in the case of female workers. Because of their frequent contact with employees, welfare workers could also serve as a source of information regarding the workers' union proclivities and living habits.

Company welfarism also attempted to create a sense of family life within the firm itself. Realizing that firms had grown too large and impersonal, employers tried to reproduce the close personal ties of the 19th-century workplace. This nostalgic approach derived from a belief that labor relations had been less adversarial in the entrepreneurial firm, when owners knew all of their employees by name. Among the methods used to promote the image of the corporate family and boost its "team spirit" were company picnics, company athletics, company songs, company contests, and company magazines filled with tidbits about these activities.

Another aspect of company welfarism was its effort to steer skilled workers away from the unions by means of material incentives such as profit-sharing, pension benefits, and home ownership plans. These plans proliferated during times of labor unrest; often introduced when a strike seemed imminent, they usually included a clause restricting benefits to those who had remained loyal to the firm. These pecuniary welfare programs also undermined workers' collective efforts at self-improvement. Providing insurance in case of illness or death was an important function of the trade unions and of the Friendly Societies (mutual associations for the purposes of insurance, pensions, savings or cooperative banking) which flourished during the 19th century. By contrast, company welfare programs encouraged individuals to protect their interests not by mutualism but by showing loyalty to their employers. Because these plans were intended to deter strikes and unions—which usually did not involve the unskilled—most of them excluded unskilled workers either directly or by limiting eligibility to long-service employees who had made contributions to the plan. Their focus on skilled workers also reflected the motive to retain skilled labor. While plenty of unskilled workers were on tap during the period of unrestricted immigration, skilled craftsmen were oftentimes harder to find and keep. Through housing programs employers attempted to deal with both of these problems simultaneously. The prospect of home ownership was attractive to most workers, who were unlikely to quit a company that had enabled them to buy a house at below-market prices. At the same time, a worker who lost his job, might lose his home, which was a powerful disincentive to union activity.[9]

Company welfarism was also common in geographically isolated industries like mining, lumbering, and textiles throughout America. Here company towns were established in which the employer provided provisions for the workers from housing to schools, churches, and recreation. The welfare programs in these communities originated out of the economic necessity of attracting labor to undeveloped areas. The company town also served as a form of social control. It came close to a feudal system in which the employer controlled virtually all aspects of the workers' lives. Similar to preindustrial master-servant relations, in the worker-employer relations deference was combined with paternal obligation and prerogative. Because the company owned the town and wrote its laws, large demonstrations were usually prohibited, and union organizers could be forcibly removed from the area.[10]

Welfare Capitalism and Rising Workers' Expectations in the 1920s

By the early 1920s, when welfare capitalism reached its peak, millions of workers in America had come under the influence of this managerial strategy. Its corporate core then was the Special Conference Committee (SCC), which was founded in 1919 by executives from ten of America's leading companies to coordinate their labor relations and personnel policies. The SCC adopted a set of principles revolving around the central belief that the social glue that bound together all those in the same business establishment was the only "natural solidarity" in industry. Corporatist cohesion should supersede all other forms of collective solidarity: workers were expected to eschew trade unionism and instead identify with their company. In return, they could count on steady jobs and welfare benefits.

The SCC approach was relatively more "enlightened" than the unbridled repression of the open-shop policy of the American Plan—a coordinated employer campaign to break the AFL unions at the local level launched in January 1921 by members of employers' associations from twenty-two states.[11] It was called the American Plan because post–World War I employers held that the open, or nonunion, shop was an important American freedom. But in fact most employers were more interested in freedom from unions than freedom for workers. These employers hoped that under the American Plan they could win employee loyalty and cooperation by incorporating many of the tenets of welfare capitalism. One feature of the American Plan was workers' councils, or shop committees. These were basically company unions, designed to hear grievances and foster cooperation. After World War I, 317 companies—including Youngstown Sheet & Tube, International Harvester, and Goodyear Rubber—had workers' councils. Many of these councils supposedly focused on work grievances about company policy, but spent most of their time solving production problems; workers participated in them but on terms framed by management.

Employers who joined the American Plan paid membership dues. In return they had access to labor spies, strikebreaking services, and blacklists of labor organizers. The services were supplied by private agencies that hired out armed thugs as strikebreakers and security guards. Union busting was big business; in 1920 the annual income of the three largest agencies providing these services was estimated at sixty-five million dollars.[12] This counter offensive to break militant unions also involved joint coordination by state and federal officials to monitor and repress left-wing agitation.[13]

Although SCC companies did not completely abstain from repression during the 1920s, it played only a secondary role in their policies. At the heart of the SCC approach was employee representation. Company unions were supposed to offer a platform for cooperative problem-solving and ventilation of grievances. Because many worker complaints concerned supervision, foremen were fiercely against employee representation, experiencing a dwindling of their authority and loss of their disciplinary power. Unwilling to give up existing disciplinary regimes, the two most conservative members of the SCC—General Motors and U.S. Steel—did not introduce company unions in the 1920s. Internal Harvester adopted a works council plan in 1919, but under persistent complaints from foremen and the fading union threat later in the decade, Harvester left its councils without any serious influence. At DuPont, management simply began ignoring its councils, and by the early 1930s these agencies were dissolved.

Many company unions had a bad name among workers and trade unionists, but there were some that had the support from both management and employees. These included medium-sized innovators like AT&T, Goodyear, General Electric, and Jersey Standard (short for Standard Oil of New Jersey). Their company unions dealt with issues ranging from time-study standards and job transfers to plant safety and sanitation. A far cry from the drive system, they diminished, to some extent, the gap between managers and employees and proved capable of solving a variety of local problems. Moreover, company unions at firms such as Jersey Standard and General Electric included immigrants from diverse ethnic backgrounds as well as African Americans and women, groups that were neglected by most AFL unions. For this reason, among other things, some labor liberals concluded in the (politically conservative) 1920s that company unions were preferable to the AFL or at least a realistic alternative to having no representation whatsoever.[14]

Given the prominence of the SCC companies and their control of organizations such as the American Management Association,[15] the SCC approach also had significant influence on industrial relations conducted at other large firms.[16] Exemplary here are the industrial relations programs that Chicago's major manufacturers were implementing at this time, which Lizabeth Cohen has examined in detail.[17] Although these programs differed in subtle ways (with differential implications for their long-term relations with employees), generally speaking U.S. Steel, International Harvester, Swift, Armour, and Western Electric all established comprehensive welfare capitalist plans involving five kinds of activity: restructuring interpersonal relations at the plant, rewarding workers through wages and promotions, experimenting with "industrial democracy," instituting welfare programs, and assuming social responsibilities in the local community.

Top management sought to secure employees' loyalty to the company by changing the way they related both to peers and to supervisors. Until 1919, local employers (such as the steel mills of South Chicago and a meat packing plant such as Swift, for example), had assumed that the best way to keep their semiskilled workers from organizing was to divide them ethnically, each group doing a particular kind of work supervised by a foreign-speaking (or at least foreign language-understanding) foreman. But once the massive strikes of 1919 made clear that cohesive ethnic communities could actually nurture cohesive militancy within their own ranks, managers changed their strategy. To break down subversive ethnic subcultures, International Harvester and all other Chicago's large manufacturers introduced or stepped up their Americanization and naturalization programs revolving around English and civics classes. In addition, supervisors set out to isolate individual workers by breaking up ethnic and racial communities on the shop floor. Thus they hoped to force out competitors for workers' loyalties and basically individualize the relationship between management and labor.

Employers also hired blacks and Mexicans to break up ethnic solidarity among their other workers, which contributed to the increasing presence of these two groups within Chicago's factories. For large Chicago plants (except Western Electric, which recruited women to do the cleaner, electric assembly work at low wages) African Americans and Mexicans were the cheap new labor force of the 1920s, taking the place of Southern and Eastern Europeans who had been barred by immigration restriction quotas. Employers also tended to pit blacks and Mexicans against each other to ensure neither group monopolized those jobs reserved especially for them. Nevertheless, although usually assigned to the dirty, dangerous, and low-paying common laborer jobs, some from these groups, especially in steel and meatpacking, managed to rise to semi-skilled and skilled work because supervisors wanted to spread them around their plants as "strike insurance."

Furthermore, top management also recognized the need to improve the way employees experienced company authority day to day on the shop floor. Employers took authority away from foremen and turned it over to "experts" in employee management, within newly created personnel and industrial relations departments. These new departments centralized hiring and firing, standardized jobs and wages, encouraged internal promotion, and administered company welfare programs—all at the expense of the foreman's power. Meanwhile, foremen were also losing control over production matters to expanding engineering and planning staffs. Thus deprived of much of their traditional authority, foremen were subjected to special training programs designed to improve their skills in handling workers on the shop floor. During the 1920s, large employers everywhere began to offer foremanship courses.

At the same time, manufacturers turned to wages and promotions as additional methods to tie men and women to the firm. For example, many large Chicago manufacturers established wage incentive plans designed to maximize workers' efficiency by individualizing earnings. They replaced straight time or piecemeal remuneration by incentive pay systems. With the help of time-and-motion studies, fatigue tests, and other measurements, company job raters set a standard for a particular job that they expected the average worker to achieve. Whatever workers produced above the set rate was the "bonus," which, at least in the Chicago case, usually was divided 75 percent (to the employee) and 25 percent (to management for its role in providing adequate machinery and materials). It was assumed that because wage payment was calculated on an individual basis, workers would be freed from peer pressure to restrict output, a strategy previously practiced to protect jobs or to set a comfortable pace of work for the group. Needless to say, these new wage incentive plans reinforced employers' other efforts at driving a wedge between individual workers.

By differentiating jobs more systematically through the assignment of different rates, employers created yet another way of dividing their workers. Increasingly complex job ladders promised that the make-up of work groups would constantly change, and while together, members would view each other as rivals rather than colleagues for management's favor. Even when mechanization of factory work lessened the difference between one job and another, companies still shifted workers around the plant with dubious assurances such as suggesting there were real opportunities to rise from the bottom to top job positions.

Moreover, employers hoped that through offering wage incentives and job ladders the opportunity to earn more money and enjoy more job security would serve to discipline workers, help to curtail absenteeism and tardiness, and encourage cost-saving job retention. This would ultimately reduce high job turnover that had long troubled American manufacturers, with factory workers constantly quitting over grievances or because they felt they could find a better job elsewhere.[18]

To counter labor militancy, as demonstrated during the strike wave of 1919, several large employers in the Chicago area too implemented what came to be called "industrial democracy" in their plants. As noted earlier, under different names—employee representation plans, works councils, conference boards, and company unions—and structured in diverse ways, the idea everywhere involved bringing worker and management representatives together to set company policies and respond to employee grievances. In return, these employers expected the pressure for unions to subside.

Hundreds of employers instituted such plans between 1919 and the late 1920s, and rhetorically promised that company decision making would truly be shared, that no issue was too remote to be exempt from joint deliberation. Not surprisingly, the reality in most plants was quite different. Managements protected their prerogatives through loopholes and exercised firm control over council activities. What gave employee representation continuing appeal to "progressive" employers was that it helped them to accomplish their other important goals: the restriction of the foreman's authority and the individualization of employee-employer relations. By making the works council meeting the hub of management-worker interaction, employers further diminished the importance of what happened on the factory floor, the foreman's domain. The actions of foremen, moreover, were now subject to review by council committees and assemblies. Employee representation plans further advanced management's other goal of isolating workers as individuals by redressing grievances on an individual rather than collective basis. While individuals might appeal inequitable wage ratings, unfair layoffs, or inadequate sanitation facilities, these grievances were viewed as requests for special dispensation within existing policy guidelines, not challenges to those policies themselves with consequences for other workers.[19]

The aforementioned welfare capitalist strategies—breaking up ethnic communities in the factory, restraining foremen, rewarding workers with wage incentives and promotions, and "democratizing" plant government—were complemented by benefit programs offering workers such perks as sickness pay, pensions, and paid vacations. Managers hoped these welfare programs would mitigate workers' complaints and encourage them to stick with the company. Employers sought to encourage company loyalty all the more by awarding benefits according to a worker's tenure; the longer an employee stayed with the company, the greater the benefits.

Employee stock ownership plans were intended to yoke the futures of manager and worker through a shared investment in capitalism. Employers justified the selling of their stock to workers at below the market price as a way of raising capital and giving employees a greater voice, even though workers held too small a share to make these goals very realistic. Enlightened businessmen prided themselves that by making the men and women who labored in factories co-owners/capitalists, they had found a way of both avoiding paternalism and getting employees themselves to provide an important bulwark against Bolshevism.

Employers also used welfare programs to dismantle ethnic solidarity. They explicitly designed welfare programs to compete with ethnic services outside the plant. Employers were cognizant that if a worker could depend on an ethnic mutual benefit society (in tough times) or an ethnic building and loan association (in better times), he felt less need to be loyal to his job/company. Employers also recalled what they had learned in 1919 about how ethnic organizations encouraged labor militancy. Western Electric founded its own building and loan association, most companies offered sickness benefits, and some (among whom Western Electric, Swift, Armour, and U.S. Steel in Chicago) developed group life insurance plans. Likewise, companies paid new attention to leisure activities, providing a variety of company programs (including sports, social events, hobby clubs and popular entertainment) to workers in their spare time, to compete with ethnic recreation. In addition, employers experimented with bringing mass-popular cultural forms into the factory (for example, weekly sessions of group singing, which brought a movable piano and song leaders into a different department of the Hawthorne Works of Western Electric everyday), not simply to compete with ethnic communities but also to unify a diverse work force. Departmental and companywide sports also aimed at developing an *esprit de corps* that transcended differences in ethnicity, age, and rank. In all of this the "happy family," sharing a common cultural life but still respectful of those in authority, provided the ideal. Large manufacturers promoted a "family feeling" as well by distributing company magazines to all employees.[20]

Welfare capitalism, although not living up to its promises during the 1920s, apparently set an agenda that raised expectations among workers who carried those into the 1930s. By introducing the policy of bringing workers together in the workplace, mixing them ethnically and encouraging their collaboration in work groups, it helped enable them to collectively challenge their employers some years later.[21] It also legitimized standards that workers sought to institutionalize in the 1930s, whereby job security, high wages, advancement opportunity, decent working conditions and generous benefits would no longer seem illusive to them.[22]

Persistent Belief in "Moral Capitalism" Among Industrial Workers

There is evidence that, before the Great Depression, industrial workers responded positively to welfare capitalism. As Cohen points out, survey data for the 1930s showed that the majority of workers, even in the midst of the Great Depression, were not inclined to reject capitalism. "It is easy to look at the nature of workers' demands and conclude that industrial workers in the 1930s had only non-ideological, 'bread-and-butter' concerns as they fought for a union," she writes, adding "what that view misses, and the larger context of welfare capitalism helps establish, however, is that workers were very much ideological in their goals; they were just not anti-capitalist."[23] They could perhaps best be called "moral capitalists":

> They looked to the state and the union to create a more just society within a system that still respected private property and many managerial prerogatives. Although workers showed their strength on the shop floor, they did not demand a fundamental redistribution of power such as a role in hiring, firing, work and wage assignments, and production decisions.[24]

Among labor historians, both David Brody and Lizbeth Cohen assert that welfare capitalism was thriving in the 1920s and might well have become the norm in American industry had it not been for the devastating effects of the Depression.[25] It was because workers took welfare capitalism to heart that they were sorely disappointed when their employers failed to keep their promises and left them in the cold when the Depression struck by slashing wages, resorting to massive layoffs, and ending most of their welfare programs. As Robert and Helen Lynd already suggested at the time (based on their interviews with blue-collar workers in the medium-sized Midwestern industrial town Muncie, Indiana), it was the individual worker's sense of betrayal and injustice "and not a thing generalized by him into a 'class' experience" that provided a rallying point for America's bread-and-butter unions.[26] These workers searched for alternatives to safeguard their security. They voted for Franklin Delano Roosevelt/the Democratic Party, supported the New Deal, and enthusiastically joined unions in large numbers. Unions promised to protect the individual worker's "property rights in the job" (to borrow labor economist Selig Perlman's phrase), an entitlement that had been nurtured by welfare capitalism in the 1920s.

When workers joined labor protest in the 1930s, according to Lizabeth Cohen, this was not against the class structure so much as against what they saw as the shortcomings in welfare capitalism. Workers still believed in welfare capitalist values. Notwithstanding their frustrations with program failures, workers considered some employers to be better welfare capitalists than others. They made those judgments by means of criteria derived from welfare capitalist ideals. Even as workers looked for other alternatives and turned to national unions and to government for security, they continued to believe in the potential for a "moral capitalism, born out of the promise of employers' welfarism in the twenties."[27] But this interpretation does not distinguish between vanguard and laggard employers. The worst layoffs and cuts in welfare programs occurred outside the vanguard—at cyclically vulnerable, durable-goods companies that had long been ambivalent toward welfare capitalism. These included companies such as U.S. Steel and Ford (mentioned by Brody as examples of firms that abandoned welfare capitalism by the early 1930s) which were lagging behind in the 1920s, and several of the Chicago firms studied by Cohen.[28] On the other hand, employees of large nonunion companies who saw their job opportunities growing during the 1930s while most companies in the surrounding region were held back (as happened at Thompson Products in Cleveland, Ohio), experienced a sense of separation from the Depression-based "culture of unity" that elsewhere helped to unite diverse workers and to give the CIO its vitality. In contrast to the horizontal solidarity of the labor movement, these companies forged a vertical (corporate) culture of unity.[29]

Silent Transformation into Modern Welfare Capitalism

Welfare capitalism did not die in the 1930s but left the public limelight, where it would transform itself in response to a new industrial-political climate in which company unions were unlawful, collective bargaining was public policy, and an emerging welfare state promised to offer workers safeguards against the vagaries of industrial life. It must be remembered, however, that the federal governmental policies that resulted from the New Deal social legislation were largely beneficial only to male whites—by now including first and second-generation "new immigrants"—and excluded blacks, Mexican Americans and other U.S. citizens of color; most of the welfare programs offered few benefits to (white) women indeed.

Welfare capitalism gradually was modernized by a group of corporate businesses, including vanguard firms in this regard, such as AT&T, DuPont, IBM, Procter & Gamble, Standard Oil of New Jersey, Eastman Kodak, Sears Roebuck and Thompson Products, that had not experienced unionization and had been spared the ravages of the Depression. It was easier for these companies to avoid layoffs, maintain welfare programs, and deter national unions. Each made major contributions to welfare capitalism's modernization between the 1930s and 1960s, the heyday in the U.S. of labor activism and government interventions regarding work regulations and welfare arrangements.[30]

In their attempts to build "modern manors," the vanguard firms retained many elements of earlier welfare capitalism, but gave them a modern twist. They still provided relatively generous welfare plans, but now the benefits took the form of supplements to Social Security and other public programs. And the management of each company still asserted that theirs was a cohesive corporate community that stood in opposition to the occupational and industrial solidarity of the labor movement. The circumstances of the 1930s forced employers to take more seriously the idea that workers were part of the corporate community. Modern welfare capitalism responded positively to the demands of its workers to attain more of the privileges that previously had been reserved for salaried employees by becoming less tolerant of the coercive drive system that had characterized the earlier form of welfare capitalism. Paternalism was redefined during those years. Companies still focused attention on their lord of the manor—the CEO—but they also sought to routinize paternalism by offering insurance instead of discretionary benefits and by educating managers about human relations (to be discussed later), With modern welfare capitalism, then, the emphasis shifted to a kinder, gentler form of paternalism (at least when compared to its predecessor), in which consent, and therefore managerial normative control, played a greater role. An important factor was the Wagner Act, which in tandem with labor's newfound power, made it much harder for employers to come down hard on workers when subject to an organizing campaign. Coercion (hard power) did not disappear altogether, but large nonunion companies had to rely more on persuasion (soft power) to get things done.[31] To justify coercion, company managers adopted the rhetoric of corporate relationships in terms of *Gemeinschaft*; unions were labeled as outsiders and their supporters were supposedly harming the enterprise community. Nonunion firms after all were planned communities that hardly allowed for dissent.[32] The greater emphasis on persuasion also reflected changes at the point of production, where the career job system was displacing the close supervision system. Thus, modern welfare capitalism was an intricate amalgam: "controlling yet consensual, coldly efficient yet cozily humane."[33]

Another characteristic of modern welfare capitalism was the absence of an armory and of the use of violence more generally to resist or repress militant labor. With very few exceptions, the era of tear gas, guns, strikebreakers, militias, or other physical threats had passed. The companies' managements were well aware that such actions had become a losing strategy in resisting unionism. Not only would violence provoke unwanted scrutiny from government agencies, it would also harden attitudes at work as well as in the community. There was an overall consensus among these managers that attitudes—of employees, government officials, and the public—were the key to maintaining control. In order to gain and maintain employee loyalty, companies used every possible means from attitude surveys and nondirective interviewing to sociometry (a quantitative method for measuring social relationships) and new methods of mass communication. These firms also employed staff specialists who counseled employees about problems in the workplace, while secretly identifying potential troublemakers. Social conformity was further encouraged by the insular atmosphere of these companies, whose managements closed themselves off from the outside world, refusing to discuss employee relations with outsiders.[34]

Human Relations in Industry

The human relations approach that came into vogue within welfare capitalist firms, focused on how the beliefs and feelings of workers affected productivity. In this approach—in contrast to scientific management—work was seen not just as a physical process and motivation was about more than money. The human relations management technique did not replace scientific management; it complemented it. This approach to management emphasized the importance of the relationship between supervisor and workers and the dynamics of the groups formed by workers. Managers (in practice mostly low-level managers) had to learn how to understand workers, and most important, they needed to know how to talk and listen to them.[35] Special training programs would help those managers to become better at this.

Sanford Jacoby uses the term "authoritarian Mayoism" in reference to the work of the group of Harvard Business School professors under Elton Mayo, renowned for their experiments aimed at identifying factory conditions most conducive to worker productivity. These experiments were carried out at Western Electric's Hawthorne plant outside Chicago during the 1920s and early 1930s. At the time, Western Electric, a subsidiary of American Telephone and Telegraph (AT&T), was Chicagoland's largest employer with a workforce between 25,000 and 30,000 employees. Rather than instituting employee representation as several other welfare capitalist companies there did, Western Electric adopted a human relations approach that shared many of the same goals. In 1928, F.W. Willard, the personnel director of Western Electric, explained why the company had chosen this different path. While acknowledging that employee representation had its merits, he argued that it was based on a conflict of interest. In that regard it did not differ in principle from the trade union relationship. Western Electric aimed to avoid conflict entirely: "To do this ... [management] must really know what the employee thinks ... what are the worker's satisfactions and aspirations, and ... set up management policies that will synchronize with the worker's viewpoint and compel thereby his cooperation."[36] This conception would lead to an extensive interviewing program that the Hawthorne plant instituted toward the end of the decade "to find out what the worker thinks." Originally developed in tandem with foremen training to identify common complaints workers had on the shop floor about their supervisors, the program soon became an end in itself. Industrial relations experts determined that by talking privately with every hourly worker at least once a year (a task carried out by Western Electric's personnel counseling section), they could keep employee grievances individual as well as foster an alliance between workers and top management that kept lower-level supervisors in check.[37]

The Hawthorne experiments purportedly demonstrated that workers found personal recognition and a sense of community even more important than high wages or easy work. The lessons drawn from these experiments, culminating in the publication of *Management and the Worker*,[38] influenced a generation of managers who sought to produce a permanent "Hawthorne effect," a social-psychological environment in the workplace that motivates workers and links their aspirations to those of the company.[39] Instrumental in this shift in managerial style was an approach to industrial behavior called "human relations in industry," which was two-pronged. The first prong concerned the work group in the organization. Behavior, particular productivity or cooperativeness with management, was thought to be shaped and constrained by the worker's role and status in a group. Other informal sets of relationships might emerge within the formal organization as a whole, modifying or overriding the official social structure of the plant, which was based on purely technical criteria such as the division of labor. The second prong involved society as a whole. Sometimes explicitly, but more usually implicitly, industrial society was seen as a precarious fabric, whose scale, diversity, and constant change supposedly frustrated a basic desire for intimacy, consistency, and predictability in social life. Lacking this wider social certainly, workers presumably would try to create it at the workplace by means of informal organization.[40]

Mayo believed that large-scale social organisms—such as corporations and labor unions—led indirectly to irresponsible social behavior. Deprived of the human experiences of community and group that might foster some notion of social responsibility, individuals developed habits of interaction and personality characteristics dangerous to a democratic society. From the perspective of labor-capital relations, it is noteworthy that in Mayo's view conflict between workers and management was unrelated to any fundamental or objective difference, class or otherwise. Animosities existed, but they were "irrational," the natural product of a decline in "spontaneous collaboration" due to the artificial collaborative forms (i.e., unions) established during the Industrial Revolution and its aftermath. According to Mayo, labor unions were *not* evidence of substantive differences between capital and labor; they were essentially social clubs designed to meet psychological and social needs. The decline in spontaneous collaboration, though deeply rooted in history, could be quashed, hatred eliminated, and business efficiency increased. The mechanism for this turnaround was the development of a healthy group process and the associated reestablishment of spontaneous unconscious collaboration.[41]

Rather than accepted at face value, the findings of the Hawthorne studies were much debated at the time. One of the severest critics was Mary B. Gilson, a co-researcher of Mayo, who was later dropped from the Western Electric studies. In her review of Roethlisberger and Dickson's book *Management and the Worker*, she wrote that the most provocative question about the conclusions of the Hawthorne studies was, "Why does big business fund social research?"[42] She pointed out that between 1933 and 1936 the Western Electric Company also paid nearly $26,000 for espionage in its plants. Gilson wrote: "We know of no instance where spies have been employees without some fear of unionism on the part of management."[43] She also found it questionable that Mayo and his researchers interviewed 20,000 workers and none criticized the company or mentioned unions. In the 1920s, many large companies required employees to sign yellow-dog contracts, stating that they would not join a union. Under these agreements, then, joining a union was considered a breach of contract. And even though employees had a right to strike, they did not have a right to instigate a strike. Given this labor-unfriendly situation, it is understandable that employees did not bring up unions in the interviews, or if they did, that some researchers did not report it. Gilson wondered aloud whether Mayo and Roethlisberger had been used by Western Electric, suggesting that their research simply told the company what it wanted to hear. One of her most scathing comments about their research was that perhaps someone ought to do a study on "Research in the Obvious Financed by Big Business." She accused Mayo and Roethlisberger of not raising questions about power, authority, class, and workers' rights. Gilson went further, pointing out that the Hawthorne studies ignored other relevant research and left out important facts. This especially concerned the plight of women workers, on whom Gilson had done extensive work herself. Gilson found Mayo and Roethlisberger's explanation for why women did not talk about job advancement as much as men in the interviews ridiculous. The authors failed to mention that women were not allowed to advance in the company in the first place. And the researchers assumed that women did not work to support families; they only worked for "pin money," a view commonly shared by mainstream society at that time. Gilson countered with a contemporary Department of Labor study, which showed that most women who worked for wages outside the house supported their parents' family or their own family, or were widows. In effect, their wages were crucial, not incidental, to the support not only of themselves but also their families.[44]

A Broader Wave of Applied Behavioral Sciences

"Human relations" was part of a broader wave of applied behavioral sciences, which became highly influential in American business and industry during the 1940s and afterward. During World War II, government agencies—especially the army—hired thousands of psychologists and other behavioral scientists. After the war, those behavioral scientists found ready employment in private industry, which was eager to apply the techniques that helped the military win the war. These experts found jobs as independent consultants, corporate staff specialists, and university-based researchers, which led to an intricate network linking corporations to academia and the military. The nexus of ties among government, corporations, and behavioral scientists resembled similar networks developing in the 1950s around other technologies such as nuclear energy, electronics, and aeronautics. This proliferation of the applied behavioral sciences can be seen as yet another technological offshoot of the Cold War, a "soft" component of the military-industrial complex. Thus it was part of what has been called "military Keynesianism."[45]

Before the war, industrial psychology had remained narrowly focused on hiring methods and supervisory training. Despite John Dewey's belief in psychology's liberating potential, its industrial practitioners adopted a highly mechanistic approach, which sought to apply the concepts and methodology of engineering to the problems of human organization. But after 1940 the applied behavioral sciences became more dynamic as a result of infusions from social psychology, anthropology, psychiatry, and other fields. Mayo's studies of group behavior at Western Electric's Hawthorne plant were partly responsible for this change, leading to a common practice to use the terms "human relations" and "behavioral science" interchangeably.

At the center of the human relations movement were large nonunion companies like Sears, whose personnel research department was highly visible in the academic community. During the 1940s and early 1950s, Sears was the corporate hub of this movement, a position previously held by Western Electric. Generous profit-sharing formed "golden handcuffs" that tied many full-time male employees to the company, while a vigorous program of employee attitude surveys and interviews provided management with much intelligence about their employees, who were offered a cathartic experience designed to relieve "emotional stress" through counseling. The Sears survey annex counseling program was manipulative in that it changed—or at least aimed to change—an employee's behavior without his/her knowledge or consent. It was also deceptive (employees were never informed about the survey's labor relations objectives) and consistently reinforced a managerial perspective on workplace relations, as in its definition of "morale" and its deliberate design to ward off unions. By the 1970s, such union avoidance techniques had even become a standard industrial model guiding many executives and human resource officers who sought to boost productivity and keep both the government and unions at bay.[46]

Human relations techniques did not easily take root in the more polarized management-labor relations of unionized firms. There was also a causal relationship between the behavioral sciences and the nonunion status of firms. Leading companies deployed the new techniques to build employee loyalty and identify union supporters. This was the very reason why labor economists, sociologists and others sympathetic to organized labor condemned industry's use of the behavioral sciences. They saw open expression of conflict—

especially as channeled through collective bargaining—as healthier and more democratic than the integrative methods of human relations that obscured social hierarchy and for the most part amounted to manipulative social engineering.[47]

Fundamental Criticism of Human Relations in Industry

In 1948, the sociologist C. Wright Mills published his critical analysis of the contribution of American sociologists engaged in applied research on industrial relations, and specifically his indictment of the Mayo school. It predates subsequent attacks by other critics and is also more radical in its disclosure of the managerial elitist bias and ideology of manipulation held by these human relation practitioners.[48] Exemplary of the latter tendency is Daniel Bell's accusation, in 1956, that Mayo and the other Hawthorne researchers took the goals of production as a given and viewed themselves as social engineers who managed a social system—not people—in an effort to "adjust" workers to their jobs. According to Bell, to think that contented workers were productive workers was to approach human behavior in terms of "cow sociology"; that is, the idea that contented cows give more milk. Counselors such as those at the Hawthorne plant were to be the new instruments of controlling humans. When employees disclosed their innermost doubts and fears, they were more susceptible to managerial manipulation. The socially-skilled supervisor could move from using authority to coercing desired behavior to psychological manipulation as a means of exercising dominance. Another aspect of Bell's criticism was that the human-relations style of supervision was intended to replace efforts to improve workplace conditions. The social person, relieved of what Mayo called "pessimistic reveries" by the catharsis of counseling, would feel better and forget about all other problems.[49] Bell's contribution was valuable, but he did not address the position of unions vis-à-vis management's commanding power over labor in the prevailing system of industrial relations.

While authority is the exercise of power "requiring a more or less voluntary obedience," as Mills wrote in his critique, manipulation entails power exercised "unbeknown to the manipulated."[50] He signaled a "curious omission" in the literature on human relations—the almost complete absence of a discussion of labor unions—the same criticism that Mary B. Gilson had leveled at Mayo and Roethlisberger (and their researchers) in her 1940 review of Roethlisberger and Dickson's *Management and the Worker*, as we saw earlier:

> Unions do not seem to be viewed as part of the industrial scene; even "collective bargaining" may be referred to without mention of unions. Managers confront individuals as individuals

and in informal groups, but no descriptive consideration is given of the informal and formal groups which unions have formed in the heart of American industry.... Although these students are quite concerned with how effective loyalties are secured, they never study unions as centers for workers' loyalties, nor shop stewards as human relational agents, filling, in one way or another, the very social voids these students see problematically in the vast secondary worlds of work.[51]

It should be recalled that Mills wrote this article and his book, *New Men of Power* (1948), before the postwar industrial-relations regime had been established, during a brief pre–Cold War moment when organized labor still had the will and the power to wage strike battles in a state of "conflict with the powers of property." The structure of power in America was Mills's overarching intellectual preoccupation. He was constantly searching for agents who might disrupt, even overturn, existing sociopolitical arrangements. As Stanley Aronowitz reminds us,

> That he at first turned to the labor leaders and to the movements they had helped foster reflected Mills's growing conviction that elites, perhaps more than masses, made history or, at least negatively, were responsible for thwarting the possibility that movements from below could take power. But his attraction to the labor movement was also a reflection on the 1930s and 1940s, when perhaps for the first (and only) time in American history, those at the heart of the rationalized labor process of industrial capitalist development—the previously powerless unskilled and semiskilled workers—appeared to have taken center stage in the economic and political drama of American life.[52]

However, shortly after *The New Men of Power* appeared, Mills became radically disillusioned with organized labor. By the time he published *White Collar* in 1951, he no longer believed in trade-union leaders as a labor-based "strategic elite" constantly in "conflict with the powers of property," and the union as the "only organization capable of stopping the main drift towards war and slump." Now, unions were at best a liberal "pressure-group" that at the same time acted as an agent of repression.[53]

In defending their human relations approach against critics (in effect ignoring Mills's more radical critique), behavioral scientists argued that consensual forms of persuasion were preferable to the drive system and to the "spiritless ideas"—such as Taylorism—that underpinned it. Proponents of human relations contended that their methods would force managers to treat employees as "flesh and blood men and women, with sentiments, ambitions, and needs of their own ranging beyond the confines of the organization."[54] And they thought unions were necessary only where managers ignored the individual or espoused the Taylorist principle that workers were only interested in money.

Sanford Jacoby suggests that with hindsight each side in the debate over human relations clearly "exaggerated its claims." Contemporary critics underemphasized the positive contributions of human relations to personnel management: respect for the individual, sensitivity to emotions and personality, and a concern with fairness in the workplace. Human relations advocates, on the other hand, consistently downplayed the ways in which their methods overlooked power relations at work and thus helped management to forestall or undermine independent unions. "To say that unions were necessary only to combat the effects of Taylorism was doubly wrong: it misconstrued the purposes of unionism and exaggerated the virtuousness of post–Taylorist management."[55] Yet the aforementioned critics of human relations were less one-sided than suggested. They may have paid only little attention to psychological dimensions and downplayed the possible merits of human relations for personnel management in particular cases, but their focus on the neglect of power issues was much to the point. They correctly criticized the human relationists of following an approach that remained confined to the narrow interpretative framework of a "plant sociology/social psychology" concentrated on the microsociety of the workplace. It did not include the broader context of industrial relations, nor did it relate a factory's group-life to the wider social involvements and experiences of the different categories of personnel, let alone the surrounding community and wider industrial setting, including possible societal conflicts.[56] There can be little doubt that "human relations in industry" was neither less profit-based nor more humane than scientific management: "It was simply another way of getting things done, this time using groups, discussion, and other devices of democracy."[57] And, in retrospect, we may conclude that C. Wright Mills's critique was highly appropriate, and applies just as well to the Lewinian approach to industrial psychology that emerged in the 1940s.

Lewinian Social Psychology and "Democratic Social Engineering"

During the late 1930s and 1940s, the psychologist Kurt Lewin and his associates carried out a series of field experiments in a Southern textile firm, the so-called Harwood studies, that showed the superiority of managerial democratic leadership over autocratic forms. Democratic leadership styles and employee participation in group-decision making resulted in higher productivity than did traditional, authoritarian styles of management. Because participation caused both morale and productivity to rise, the Lewinians arrived at the same conclusion as Elton Mayo and his followers; namely, that conflict in the workplace could be eradicated by a more enlightened, integrative approach to workplace management. "This was essentially the same notion that had infused welfare capitalism since the early 1900s," notes Jacoby, "although this time around it was footnoted with empirical corroboration."[58] (This does not hold true for the paternalist and autocratic welfare work in company towns, though.)

Although the Harwood studies are usually not considered part of the "classical" human relations tradition, there are striking parallels with the concepts used by the Harvard group of Elton Mayo and his associates. The Lewinians believed leaders (managers) could manipulate participation (informal organization) through communications (social skill) to produce a good group climate (morale), thus enhancing satisfaction (integration) with the group life (social system) and improving performance (output).[59]

Lewin had also encouraged his disciple John French, who was in charge of the later field experiments at the Harwood Manufacturing Corporation, to set up a new program of leadership training in which all levels of supervisory management would participate. The emphasis was on practical methods such as role playing, socio-drama, group problem solving, and other so-called action research techniques. The general purpose of this training experiment was to equip the supervisors with more effective methods of "winning cooperation," "building trust," "improving morale" and "handling the disciplinary problems of their subordinates." In training these supervisors, various practices involving self-examination, feedback, openness, confidence building, and group problem-solving were used. Starting in 1946, these practices would later become integral parts of the sensitivity training programs developed by Lewin's disciples for workshops such as those at Bethel, Maine, which in turn, would become institutionalized as the National Training Laboratories.[60]

From the late 1940s onward, many Lewinians also participated in the social movement of "planned social change"—characterized by an ambiguous mixture of social control and democracy—that was driven by humanistic-progressive liberal ideas about supporting democratic forces aimed at "building a better world." These thoughts were shared by a broad cross-section of American social scientists at the time.[61]

In more recent years, Lewinian applied psychology has been criticized for its strong manipulative tendency in settings such as the production-oriented workplace.[62] However, in the 1950s the Lewin group largely escaped reproach, while Mayo's human relations approach met fierce criticism. An obvious ideological reason was that Lewin espoused Deweyan principles of democratic participation—albeit in a tightly circumscribed version of democracy—in contrast to Mayo's elitist conception of leadership. As Sanford Jacoby has pointed out,

Laborist liberals of the 1950s could find implicit support for trade unions in Lewin's theories, whereas Mayo's work, like that of earlier corporatists, denigrated unions. And whereas Mayo's laborist critics contended that "high employee morale" was merely a euphemism to describe workers who were "happy, contented, but typically docile," it was difficult to pin a charge of docility on Lewin's autonomous, participative work groups.[63]

Another reason for the different reception of these two approaches had to do with timing. While leadership training, attitude surveys, and other practices inspired by Mayo's human relations perspective were widespread in the 1950s—especially in large nonunionized firms—participative groups did not take hold until after the debate on human relations had died down. The instances of small-group participation that one finds before the 1960s comprised groups that usually did not allow workers to be directly involved in making decisions. Examples are Thompson (later called TRW)'s "new system" plants and Sears' rotating committees, which both provided a modicum of employee representation but in a form that inhibited wage bargaining and made it difficult for national unions to mount a takeover.[64]

Finally, the Mayoites, despite their prestigious affiliations, did not have the disciplinary credentials of the Lewin group. Lewin and his followers, nearly all of them university-trained social psychologists, published their research in mainstream psychological journals and otherwise maintained their academic ties. The Mayoites, on the other hand, had no disciplinary anchoring points and presented most of their findings in popular books and magazines. This made them vulnerable to accusations that their work was sloppy and suffered from unscientific, pro-management biases, and that they were committed to aims that contrasted with those of their professional but non-industrial colleagues. However, although those affiliated with Lewin's research center and the Institute for Social Research were scientific professionals, they also were "pragmatic realists" (or opportunists, if one wishes to put it that way) who pursued lines of research that government and industry were willing to fund. As relationships between industry and academia intensified, academic behavioral scientists ran increasingly the risk of suffering from their own "bias of the auspices."[65]

Historian William Graebner sees Lewinian applied psychology as part of a broader American tradition of psychosocial intervention practices that he has labeled "democratic social engineering." He defines this approach as "a method of social control utilizing the small group, discussion, leadership, and participation of the objects of control."[66] Democratic social engineering emerged in the 19th century, in response to the new mass society and the growing social problems associated with industrialization and urbanization. Its intellectual roots lie in the turn-of-the-century social sciences (primarily psychology and sociology), pragmatic philosophy, and Progressive education.[67] This ambivalent approach cannot be clearly defined as either coercive or uncoercive. It was actually understood both as a form of social control *and* as a variant of democracy. It would thus appeal to the political right and to the left, to conservatives as well as progressives—certainly in a nation such as the United States, so fundamentally ambivalent about authority. It was simultaneously an expression of American ideas of freedom and of societal order.[68]

Democratic social engineering was first consistently practiced in Sunday schools and youth groups (YMCA) as well as in the settlement houses and schools—all part of the struggle of the Progressive movement to contain class conflict, the new immigrants, and the excesses of industrial capitalism. It was especially influential between 1917 and 1947. Graebner describes three case studies illustrating his analysis of the practices in question: the Foremen's Clubs movement, launched in Dayton, Ohio, in 1917; clubs for the aged, called Golden Age Clubs, founded in Cleveland in 1940; and the early work on the family and the raising of children by pediatrician Benjamin Spock. From our perspective the first case study is highly relevant as it concerns a psychosocial intervention practice aimed at modifying attitudes and convincing foremen—at the time increasingly tempted to unionize—that their "natural allegiance" was to capital rather than to labor.[69]

Paradoxically, democratic social engineering consists of group decision-making with a *predetermined* influence objective. It comprises a system of authority that is ideally effective and yet "democratic." Its protagonists were attracted to social psychology, and in particular its Lewinian variant, because as a body of knowledge it confirmed the validity of group process ("intelligently controlled" by group leaders) as the ideal form of social reform *and* social control in a democratic culture. Graebner's judgment appears to be sound. The industrial psychology studies of Kurt Lewin and his associates, especially the Harwood studies, emphasized "democratic" group participation processes within management-defined production parameters. A closer examination of the successive experiments has shown that in each case a predetermined goal set by management was at stake with which the researchers and group leaders seem to have agreed.[70]

"Alienated" Employees in Big Corporations in Mid–20th Century America

By the middle of the 20th century, the problem of work in big corporations had come to be defined as the problem of alienation. For most people in those settings the work was boring and often employees did not have the satisfaction of seeing the final fruits of their labor. Industrial organizations also transferred their employees with impunity, uprooting and disconnecting them from their families and community life. It goes without saying, however, that in the prevailing management literature, the concept of alienation was used without its Marxist connotations associated with labor exploitation and industrial and social relations in capitalist society.

Many prominent business theorists at the time believed that corporations could solve the problem of alienation. "Human relations" advocate Elton Mayo thought that corporations could mend the torn fabric of society. In his seminal book, *The Concept of the Corporation*, published in 1946, Peter Drucker argued that the corporation was the representative institution of the society par excellence, because it was best suited to fulfill the aspirations and beliefs of the American people—what was "good for General Motors" really was good for the country. While Drucker admitted that the majority of Americans were not employed in corporations, he stated that work in corporations set the tone for work in other areas of society. Corporations should therefore give status and function to the individual worker and create good industrial citizens.

Drawing from the Hawthorne studies, Drucker came to conclusions about alienation. First, "it is not monotony and routine which produce dissatisfaction but the absence of recognition, of meaning, or relations of one's own work to society."[71] Drucker and kindred spirits among business theorists had been impressed by the energy and pride displayed by industrial workers during World War II. After the war, management thinkers began to wonder how to channel the motivation and commitment of the war effort into peacetime production. Drucker's second conclusion was that the problem of alienation in an industrial system could not be solved by giving more benefits, security, or wages. It could be alleviated only by giving people the responsibility and dignity of an adult. Meaningful work was primarily about the social and moral qualities of a job, not the particular work that one did. Needless to say, this meant downplaying the relevance of the intrinsic quality of work and the labor skills of workers.

Drucker also made the case for socially responsible corporations. He stated that the means used to strengthen the corporation and make it more efficient should also promote the realization of the core values and beliefs of American society.[72] Joanne Ciulla rightly criticizes Drucker for having been too optimistic about giving profit-oriented and self-interested corporations the heavy responsibility of fulfilling human aspirations and developing industrial citizens. She points to several obstacles to corporations delivering on their promise to live up to society's values and aspirations.[73] As Roosevelt's New

Deal advisors Adolf Berle and Gardiner Means argued in their classic, *The Modern Corporation and Private Property* (1932), corporations face serious challenges in behaving responsibly when the people who own the firm (stockholders) do not run it and the people who run the firm (managers) are not its owners.[74] On the one hand, corporations demand loyalty and are the source of jobs, wealth, and technological creativity. On the other hand, they can be disruptive social forces that corrupt the political process, pollute the environment, promote addictive products, and ruin people's lives.

Using organization theories and management techniques developed during World War II, the managements of large white-collar organizations in the following years began to mold their employees into their images of a good corporate citizen. Each company had its own image, and the good company man (they were mostly men at the time) was not necessarily the good family and community man. The quest for the crucial motivating factor(s) had come a long way from Taylor's simple equation of pay for performance. Management researchers began to dig ever deeper into the human psyche in their search for the elusive spirit that inspired enthusiastic human action and commitment, allegedly without concern for external rewards and without asking for more. Corporate managers also felt obliged to find a cause, a mission, or a set of ideals that would give work a social meaning and create the kind of commitment they had seen in the war effort. Work was no longer supposed to be simply an economic transaction; it was now a personal and social transaction. Work was a place where corporations molded employees into corporate citizens. The corporate ethos advocated by these management thinkers implied that corporations fought alienation between work and private life and sometimes won by making work a larger part of one's life.[75]

The New Salaried Middle Class

In the 1950s, the latter tendency drew criticism of social thinkers such as C. Wright Mills. In *White Collar*, his 1951 book on the new salaried middle class, Mills expressed his concern about the influence large corporations had over their employees. He gave a depressing depiction of white-collar work in large bureaucratic organizations. Despite its substantial numbers, the new salaried middle class, in its six decades of growth since the turn of the 20th century, had failed to become an independent political force, let alone achieve economic independence. Mills believed that the meaning of work for industrial and white-collar workers had diminished to the point where work no longer gave them inner direction and connection to society.

For Mills, the golden age of work was the 1850s, an era of family farms and small independent shopkeepers; for him, the "old" middle class included craftsmen and independent professionals like physicians, lawyers, and engineers. A key practice of the old middle class was "spontaneity in work" and perhaps more to the point, the almost vanished integrated life where work and private life are viewed by subjects as part of the same totality. He wrote that back then, work was well integrated into life, giving people deep roots in their community and society. This may have been the case for craftsmen and shopkeepers who lived and worked at home, but it probably was not for most other people. In Mills's hankering for the way of life of the old middle class (as he envisioned this), and particularly his adulation of the craftsman, one can see a clear streak of romanticism. That is why his description in the first section of *White Collar* about the demise of the old middle class of farmers reads like a lament rather than a dispassionate assessment.[76]

Mills did not celebrate the middle class as such, however; he had little sympathy for mom-and-pop store owners or other small-scale merchants. Their position as the exemplary embodiments of American ideology—individualism, competition, free enterprise, and so forth—far outweighed their economic importance. While large corporations had come to dominate key aspects of life, a considerable number of people still held on to the American Dream, defined as the chance to own a small business.[77]

Mills's description of the "modern office" points to the replacement of manual labor by machines and the increasingly factory-like character of the work: "As office machinery is introduced, the number of routine jobs is increased, and consequently the proportion of 'positions requiring initiative' is decreased. Mechanization is resulting in a much clearer distinction between the managing staff and the operating staff."[78] White-collar employees, Mills argued, were deprived of "work as purposive human activity" and therefore seek other satisfactions to compensate for the decline of work at the heart of meaning of life.[79]

Stanley Aronowitz points out that Mills's discourse on work bears a striking resemblance to Karl Marx's well-known view on alienated labor in the *Economic and Philosophical Manuscripts* (1844). For Marx, labor is first of all equated with purposive human activity that mediates man's relationship to nature, rather than with work as an instrumental activity, organized to produce specific products or yield income for other purposes. Labor transforms both nature and human nature, and just as labor changes nature, so nature changes human beings. Capitalism modifies that relationship in that it separates humans from nature, or, rather, nature becomes purely an instrumental object and people lose awareness that they are part of natural history. Those who own the means of material production appropriate the labor of others, extracting from the worker the maximum amount of surplus value in the course of business competition among industrialists. Alienation is the result of the concentration of ownership in few hands, the division of labor between mental and manual work, and rationalization of work in which routine replaces the worker's initiative.[80] Workers lose the ability to determine their life and destiny, when deprived of the right to conceive of themselves as the director of their actions. They are no longer capable to determine the character of those actions, define their relationship with other people, and own the things and use the value of the goods and services produced with their labor.

For Mills, white-collar work was in some ways worse than unskilled (industrial) labor. About the latter he wrote that "proles" suffer physically, but at least they are free when they go home, whereas white-collar workers not only sell their time and energy, they sell their personalities.[81] He called the white-collar worker the "new little man" who is politically apathetic, has shallow roots and no loyalties, and is always in a hurry but has no clue where he is going. In Mills's view, "Whatever history [the white collar people] have had is a history without events, whatever common interests they have do not lead to unity; whatever future they have will not be of their own making"[82] Willy Loman, the main protagonist of Arthur Miller's 1949 play, *Death of a Salesman*, personified Mills's "little man." Mills stipulates that Loman is "a man who by the very virtue of his moderate success in business turns out to be total failure in life."[83]

Ursula Huws has brought attention to Mills's gender-blindness. While he was writing his book, women were entering office work in unprecedented numbers, so that by the time of the 1960 Census they represented about two-thirds of all clerical workers in the U.S.—a proportion that had risen to three-quarters by the 1970 Census; yet Mills paid little attention to the female white-collar workers.[84] He only devoted six pages of his 378-page book to a discussion of the "white-collar girl" whom he characterized mainly in terms of her love life.[85] Gender played no part in Mills's depressing conclusion that white-collar workers would never develop distinctive forms of political agency and that even if they did, "their advance to increased stature in American society could not result in increased freedom and rationality. For white-collar people carry less rationality than illusion and less desire for freedom than the misery of modern anxieties."[86]

The counterparts of the new little men were what Mills called the "new men of power" in corporate America. Because these new men of power lived in a liberal democratic society whose self-proclaimed core values were freedom, equality, and self-determination, they felt obliged to keep employees happy in order to remain free of unions and hostile government regulations. Mills's concern was that the human relations industry offered corporate leaders the promise of finding new symbols that would publicly legitimate the enormous inequity of power that existed, and cultivate loyal and enthusiastic workers.

According to Mills, corporations focused on employee morale because the Protestant work ethic of individual self-improvement through hard work was not viable in large complex organization, where so much of the work was fragmented and meaningless, and there was little room for mobility and improvement. Personnel departments took the place of the Protestant work ethic, and morale had replaced morality as the motivation to work.[87] Since employers could not rely on a moral commitment to work among their employees, Mills contended that the goal of the personnel department was to develop cheerful and cooperative subordinates. By controlling employees' sentiments inside the workplace, employers could maintain and justify their power without alienating workers.

Mills claimed that the white-collar man was psychologically whipped into shape by the organization to fit its purposes, and then doomed to lead a shallow and petty life outside of work because he had sold his personality to that organization. In this case the integration of work and life that Mills appreciated so much in 19th-century America, was disastrous in its 20th-century incarnation. Work, as Mills described it, ruins rather than enhances life both at home and in the community. The real concern of critics like Mills was that too much emphasis on work destroys a person's life, not only because of the time it takes, but because of the strong influence of the organization on the individual. The reverse side of this argument was of course the employer's concern that the way people live their lives outside work might detract from their lives at work; hence organizations' attempts to mold employees into their own image.[88]

The Organization Man *and the Psychological Approach to Management*

In his 1956 book, *The Organization Man*, William H. Whyte, a friend and colleague of C. Wright Mills, shared some of the latter's concerns, only Whyte addressed people's need to belong.[89] Whyte's criticism was in line with that of other social critics in the 1950s who worried about people's conformity to institutions and burgeoning suburban life. Whyte built upon a social type that David Riesman had described in his book on American character, *The Lonely Crowd* (written with the assistance of Nathan Glazer and Reuel Denney), published in 1950.[90] Riesman recognized a social type, the "tradition-directed" people, who followed rules established a long time in the past and who rarely succeeded in modern society, with its dynamic changes. "Inner-directed" people operated on the basis of an internal "gyroscope." They relied on the potential within themselves to live and act on what they discovered, using their inner guidance system. Inculcated at an early age with the need to take an independent stance, such people kept their own balance wherever they were. And, in line with society's ideal of independence, they were driven to act guided by their own insights and hunches, undeterred by the views of others.

The increasing ability to consume goods and afford material abundance was accompanied by a shift away from both tradition- and inner-directedness. Now (at mid-century), when "the problems not only of mere subsistence but also of large-scale industrial organization and production have been for the most part surmounted," the other-directed type was "befitting a society of abundance." It proceeded by "radar" that constantly checked others' responses to one's actions to fit in with the group.[91] How to define one's self became a function of the way others lived.

Riesman and his associates found out that other-directed people were flexible and willing to accommodate others to gain approval. Those people needed assurance that they were emotionally in tune with others. The other-directed person wanted to be loved rather than esteemed, not necessarily to control others but to relate to them. Because large organizations preferred this type of personality, it became indispensable to business corporations and other institutions that thrived with the growth of industry in America.

Riesman argued that a society dominated by other-directed people values manipulative skills over craft skills and expense accounts over bank accounts. Business is fun and managers are supposed to be "glad handers" who joke with secretaries and charm their bosses and clients. According to Riesman, the other-directed person in corporate life tends to the needs of the company first, and is more loosely connected to the family, church, and community.[92] He contended that, although other-directed individuals are crucial for the smooth functioning of the modern organization, the value of autonomy is compromised. Society dominated by the other-directed faces serious deficiencies in leadership, individual self-knowledge, and human potential. However, the way to get out of this predicament was not to return to the old inner-directed model but to maximize the opportunities of another direction, to create social conditions under which sensitivities to others and to the inward life gave persons "autonomy" rather than leaving them merely "adjusted," or worse, unattached and "anomic."[93] In describing the psychological problems created by a "society increasingly dependent on the manipulation of people," Riesman's critique of the "false personalization" of the other-directed type unable to develop an individuated personality was similar to Mills's portrait of the alienated white-collar worker.[94]

Whyte focused his criticism of modern organizations, and big corporations in particular, on a "social ethic," that morally legitimates the pressure of society against the individual. This ethic rationalizes the organization's demand for commitment and loyalty and gives employees who offer themselves entirely—with heart, mind, and soul—a sense of dedication and fulfillment. Inherent is the belief that the group is a source of creativity and that a sense of belonging is the ultimate need of the individual. This ethic also assumes that psychologists and sociologists working in management disciplines can create ways to deliberately achieve such belongingness among employees.[95]

Whyte feared that psychologists and social engineers would thus divest people of their creativity and individual identity. He expressed concern about the inherent dishonesty of such a psychological approach to management and he criticized the social engineers' search for "the magic term which will combine manipulation with moral sanction."[96] More specifically he criticized the use of personality tests to weed out people who do not "fit in," and challenged what he saw as the unrealistic notion that organizations should be free from conflict. But perhaps Whyte's worst fear was that organizations would become "antiseptic hells," where the threat did not come from the likes of Big Brother's henchmen in George Orwell's novel *1984* but "a mild-looking group of therapists who, like the Grand Inquisitor, would be doing what they did to help you."[97]

The crux of Whyte's argument was that people became convinced that organizations and groups could make better decisions than individuals, and thus serving an organization became logically preferable to advancing one's individual creativity. He claimed this did not fit the facts, and he listed a number of examples of how individual work and creativity can produce better outcomes than collectivist processes. Whyte did not believe that people think or create well in groups: "The most misguided attempt at false collectivization is the attempt to see the group as a creative vehicle."[98] In his book Whyte describes an experiment on leaderless groups done at the National Training Laboratory. The idea of the exercise was that when the group "jelled," the leader would fade into the background and be consulted only for his expertise. These groups resulted in chaos but, as Whyte informs us, the trainers hoped that the resulting emotional exhaustion of the group would be a valuable catharsis and a prelude to consensus.[99] According to Whyte, the individual has to enter into the process somewhere, but he wondered whether we should openly bring individuals into the group process or "bootleg" them in an expression of group sentiment. Basically, Whyte saw the whole idea of leaderless groups as intellectual hypocrisy.

The power and authority of the group simply camouflaged the real power and authority that leaders had *de facto* over group members.[100]

The issues brought up by Mills and Whyte in their criticisms of work in modern corporations would resurface in the 1970s when there was a renewed emphasis on teamwork among white-collar employees by personnel departments in large corporations.

4

Taylorization During World War II and the Postwar Automation Movement

Driven by the innovations of Taylor, Ford, and Knudsen (at GM), the American system of mass production made significant progress during the first three decades of the 20th century, But it was at mid-century that the system entered its golden age and had an impact that reached far beyond the machine shop and the assembly line. During World War II the application of mass production methods to armament production and to the aircraft industry in particular, was instrumental in bringing about the massive output of Roosevelt's "arsenal of democracy." Taking their cue from Ford and GM, the U.S. defense industries organized their production around giant plants employing huge numbers of workers. In the aircraft industry this expansion created a two-million-strong workforce with very little previous experience of aircraft production. For example, of the 25,000 workers at the Curtiss-Wright's plant in Lockland, Ohio, only two percent of job applicants had any such experience.[1]

During the first years of the war, the aircraft industry underwent a rapid transformation from a small-batch, craft-based industry to a mass production, special machine-based industry. Special-purpose machinery, jigs and fixtures, essential for high-volume production, became commonplace, and so did larger, sturdier machines capable of handling the faster speeds and higher volume made possible with high-speed cutting tools. At the same time, the division of labor increased, with a greater emphasis on both special setup men organizing the machinery for long production runs and unskilled operators putting the machinery through its pre-set paces. This had already been routine in some industries—car manufacturing, for instance—but now the pattern of highly mechanized mass production became established throughout the metalworking areas of industry too. There were also some innovations, such as greater use of hydraulic controls and the potentials of electronic controls, as well as more precision casting that eliminated the need for a significant amount of machining.[2]

Management theorist Peter Drucker, who watched the wartime economy closely, wrote later about how U.S. industry recruited unskilled workers and, relying heavily on Taylor's methods, "converted them in sixty to ninety days into first-rate welders and ship builders."[3] Boeing attuned its production of the B-29 bomber—perhaps the most complex weapon system of the war—to the capabilities of this mostly unskilled workforce. Large sections of the B-29 fuselage "had the same measurement and fabrication characteristics," making it easier to build the plane. Subassemblies were then shipped to a final assembly line where "less experienced workers could literally bolt everything together more quickly and with fewer mistakes."[4]

During the 1940s and 1950s, the body of knowledge implicated in scientific management evolved into operations management, operations research, and management cybernetics. The development of the computer paved the way for a "command-and-control" technology along with management techniques such as operations research first created by the military during World War II. A crucial technology was programmable numerically-controlled machinery. As it progressed, largely under Navy contracts, it was engineers and other specialists who did the programming and operation of the computer, while the workers who operated the machines were excluded from that knowledge base.[5]

It was in 1946 when the Ford Motor Company installed new machinery on the company's assembly lines that their engineers coined the term *automation* to describe the changes this involved. However, they were not referring to the sophisticated electronic communications and servo systems[6] developed during the war, much less to the advances in computer control. Rather they meant that automating manufacturing processes entailed making automatic not only each production operation but also the transfer of product-in-process from one work station to another. This task was made easier if the product itself was in a liquid or gaseous form and could thus flow through pipes or membranes from one unit operation to another. Therefore integrated automatic control of an industrial process first appeared in the continuous-process industry, including products such as chemicals, oil, natural gas, fertilizers and so forth. It was here that careful and constant control over complex, high-speed operations became a necessity, and a high volume of product could offset the considerable capital investments for fixed automated facilities.[7]

In the metalworking industries, where most work was still done in labor-intensive batch operations on general-purpose machinery, the use of automatic industrial controls had barely begun to approach that of the continuous-process industries. Automatic controls were limited to fixed or "dedicated" single-purpose machinery such as heavy presses and combination machine tools used for machining engine blocks, and transfer lines. There was little flexibility or use of electronics and almost no feedback control or computer applications. Yet those parts of the industry which were involved in high-volume production became the center of experiments with so-called automation. These were found particularly in the auto and auto-supply industries; they most resembled continuous-process industries with their heavy capital investment in fixed, special-purpose equipment.

At a place like Ford, "automation" in the late 1940s simply meant an increase in the use of electromechanical, hydraulic, and pneumatic special-purpose production and parts-handling machinery which had been in existence for some time. Production machinery in metalworking had long been rendered "self-acting" by the use of mechanical stops, cams, hydraulic, and later electrical, actuators. Indeed, the 19th-century American System of Manufacturing (as it was called by a British commission in 1854) was based in part upon such self-acting, special-purpose machinery for achieving the repeatability vital to interchangeable-parts manufacture. By the end of the Civil War, screw machines, turret lathes, and other machines were designed to be mechanically paced through a pre-set sequence of operations. Transfer machines dating back to 1888, became widespread in the auto industry by the 1930s. The combination of self-acting equipment and automatic transfer machines made possible the integrated control of factory operations, pioneered in the metalworking industries as early as 1920 by A.O. Smith's Milwaukee automobile frame plant.[8]

In 1947, Ford's engineering executive Del Harder called for more of such automatic handling equipment, as well as sequence-control mechanisms for balancing the different operation lines in the automatic mass production of engine blocks. At that time, Ford's plants were already heavily mechanized, with sophisticated machines streamlining every job on the line. But factory hands still had to move parts and subassemblies from one machine to the next, which left workers in some control of the pace of production. The new equipment altered that. Machines took over the material-handling and conveyance functions, allowing the entire assembly process to proceed automatically. Although the change in workflow may not have seemed momentous at the time, this control over a complex industrial process actually had shifted from worker to machine.[9] Needless to say, the automated machines were set up by industrial engineers according to top management's preferences and policy choices.

Next to the pursuit of progress and productivity, there was another driving force of automation: managerial control of workers. The immediate postwar years were characterized by intense labor struggles. Managers and unions battled in most American manufacturing sectors, and the tensions were often strongest in industries essential to the federal government's Cold War buildup of military equipment and armaments. In many factories, union stewards held relatively much power over everyday operations; the workers called the shots regarding the speed and flow of work. Military and industrial planners saw automation as a means to shift the balance of power back to management.[10]

In addition to reducing the need for workers, particularly skilled ones, automated equipment provided business owners and managers with a technological means to control the speed and flow of production through the electronic programming of individual machines and entire assembly lines. When, at the Ford plants, control over the pace of the line shifted to the new automated equipment, the workers lost a great deal of the influence they had once had on the shop floor. By the mid–1950s, the role of labor unions in laying out plans for factory operations had become minimal.[11] This would prove to be an important principle in the march of automation in the years to come; in an automated system, power concentrates with those who control the programming.

The latter became apparent in the case of numerically controlled machines—the first were built in the 1940s and 1950s, based on existing tools that were modified with motors that moved the controls to follow points fed into the system on punched tape (or other storage medium).[12] These early servomechanisms were soon augmented with analog computers, and later with digital computers, creating the modern CNC machines that have revolutionized the production of machine tools and aircraft engines, along with some processes of car production. End-to-end component design and production were thereby highly automated through the merger of computer-aided design (CAD) and computer-aided manufacturing (CAM) programs in a single process.

Gradually, elementary robots also began to make some inroads in industry. In 1961 the first industrial robot, Unimate, was introduced at a General Motors plant in New Jersey. The machine transported die castings from an assembly line and welded these parts on auto bodies, a dangerous task for workers, who might be poisoned by toxic fumes or lose a limb if they were not careful. Following step-by-step commands stored on a magnetic drum, the 4,000-pound arm was versatile enough to perform a variety of tasks. Robots like Unimate also performed tasks such as loading and unloading machine tools.[13] By the early 1970s, robots were taking over production work that required flexibility and physical dexterity: cutting, welding, and assembling. During those years, the reliability of microprocessors (with new solid-state circuitry based on the transistor) improved to the point that Boeing, McDonnell Douglas, and the new Airbus industry consortium in Europe were all prepared to take advantage of digital technology in the design of new airplanes. By the end of the decade, automated systems were helping to build airplanes as well as taking over flight control.[14]

There was also a significant postwar change in the nature of the employment of scientific and technical professionals. The development of electronically mediated communications during and after the war brought a whole new cohort of these professionals to large corporations, such as IBM, Eastman Kodak, Sperry Gyroscope, and the aircraft companies. In this period, discovery and invention were rewarded and for the most part were not subject to the ups and downs of the economy. During World War II and the Cold War, funding for scientific and technical investigations was largely supplied by the government, which awarded contracts to private companies but owned the patents that derived from that research. After the war, however, many of these patents were sold or given to the companies in question, which used them for private industrial purposes. Meanwhile, universities that had performed much of the science upon which the new technologies were based entered into their own partnerships with these companies. In return for research grants to academic departments, universities agreed to share or hand over the patents.[15] By the 1970s, most computer scientists and engineers were no longer independent entrepreneurs, but had become employees.[16]

Automation and Deskilling

According to Braverman in his 1974 book on work degradation in the 20th century, the managerial control of blue-collar and white-collar work was aided considerably by mechanization/automation. For capitalists, the great advantage of machinery was that it not only increased the productivity of labor, but it also enabled the managers of capital to control workers impersonally and unobtrusively by mechanical means in addition to organizational means. More specifically, so long as it was well maintained, machinery had three major advantages over workers; it was invariably more persistent, consistent, and acquiescent. Thus, the machinery ensured that the same precise actions were performed repeatedly and without question. By comparison, a worker, however industrious and conscientious, would get tired, become distracted, perform variably, and protest, if necessary, about the conditions and rewards of work. In addition to these productivity advantages, capital also benefitted from savings by reducing the number of workers required, plus the training and time and pay of those retained. Therefore it came as no surprise that capitalists were eager to have machines designed and installed that incorporated the knowledge and skills of the worker, ideally to the point where the majority of industrial workers and service workers were reduced to monitoring the automatic production process.

In support of this part of his analysis, Braverman cites James R. Bright's 1958 study of automation in American industry. Bright studied thirteen manufacturing facilities, including automobile engine plants, a refinery, a bakery, an electrical-parts manufacturer, plating plants, and others. He observed varieties of automation in production and materials handling. (It should be noted, though, that deployment of computers in manufacturing was virtually nonexistent at the time of his study.) Bright concluded that throughout the thirteen plants he studied, workers were receptive and, in many cases, enthusiastic toward the new automated equipment. The major reason given was that automation took the heavy labor out of a job, making the job much easier.[17] Bright also clearly stated automation's effects on skills: "As the controls become more sensitive and responsive to the requirements of the operation, environment, and the task, the machine assumes responsibility, just as it has already assumed skill, knowledge, and judgment requirements."[18] He noted that this was one of labor's biggest concerns about automation, but he was convinced that new wage determination systems, coupled with sensitive implementation of the new technologies, could overcome any resistance brought about by skill dilution.

Braverman was less optimistic; for him, the transfer of skill into machinery represented a triumph of "dead labor over living labor," a necessity of capitalist logic. By substituting capital (in the form of machinery) for labor, Braverman believed that employers merely seized the opportunity to exert greater control over the labor process. As the work force encountered fewer opportunities for skill development, it would become progressively less capable and therefore less able to exert any serious opposition.[19]

Sociologist Robert Blauner before him had interpreted Bright's research findings quite differently. His seminal 1964 study on the effects of automation on "alienation" (defined in terms of powerlessness, meaninglessness, isolation and estrangement) contrasted workers' attitudes and experiences in four types of industrial organizations—craft-based (the printing industry), machine tending (the textile industry), mass production (the auto industry), and continuous process (the chemical industry). Because of its advanced degree of automation, the continuous-process form of production was considered to foreshadow the conditions of factory work and employment in a future dominated by automated technology.[20]

Regarding the social-psychological dynamics associated with the continuous-process form of production, Blauner reported a very different relationship between the labor process and the body of the worker than in other manufacturing processes. Skill and effort seemed to be uncoupled now. In the chemical industry, production depended upon capital investment in highly automated equipment. Workers were called upon to physically exert themselves only when the equipment broke down, which created an inverse relationship between manual effort and productivity. The technology had helped to shape a work environment that freed the worker's body from the kinds of disciplinary pressures that had been routine features of industrial life. For example, operators who were required to make the rounds of the equipment in the plant in order to read instruments and monitor plant functioning, could control the pace of their activities. The very act of making equipment rounds provided a physical variety and freedom of movement that contrasted sharply with the machine-paced work of the assembly line. This mobility typically placed the continuous-process operator out of sight of an immediate supervisor, escaping his scrutiny. As a result, the operators in Blauner's study stated that they felt considerable scope to do their jobs in their own way.

The question was whether the reduction of effort in continuous-process operations also meant a reduction of skill. In general, Blauner argued that the shift from a job-centered to a process-centered form of work organization meant that the individual contribution changed from one of providing skills to one of assuming responsibility. The operator was responsible for the trouble-free operation of the process, the quality of product being produced, and the preservation of expensive automated equipment.[21]

In presenting this part of his argument, Blauner cherry-picked from Bright's findings; that is, he selected only one of two dimensions of Bright's research which showed a mixture of an increase/decrease in skill with the most advanced mechanization, namely responsibility. In so doing, Blauner relegated to a footnote Bright's point that automation does not necessarily raise skill requirements; in some cases, it actually reduces skill requirements.[22] Braverman noted that all the other skill indicators used by Bright, such as dexterity, general skill, experience, decision-making, and so forth, showed that the skill requirements of advanced automation had either decreased or were nil. And he quoted Bright's conclusion that "there was more evidence that automation had reduced the skill requirements of the operating work force, and occasionally of the entire factory force, including the maintenance organization."[23]

Based on his comparative studies, Blauner formulated the now-classic, inverted U-shaped curve representing a trend in which alienation is at its lowest in the early industrial period when craft technology was dominant, increases steeply with the introduction of machine-tending technology, and reaches its peak in the assembly-line technology industries by the mid–20th century. But with the advent of continuous-process technology a counter-trend occurs and alienation declines from its previous high point "as employees in automated industries gain a new dignity from responsibility and a sense of individual freedom."[24] Blauner argued that rather than exacerbating industrial tensions, higher levels of automation actually begin to reverse some of the most prominent negative tendencies associated with the rationalization of manufacturing work. Continuous-process operators manifest a greater degree of identification with their managers and more loyalty towards their companies resulting in a heightened sense of mutuality and collaboration. However, in an important footnote, Blauner qualified this optimistic conclusion by suggesting that in the future, automation will not necessarily lead to "a continuation of the major trend toward less alienation" because of the diversity of automated technology and economic conditions.[25]

As a preferable alternative to Blauner's inverted U-shaped declining alienation curve, Braverman referred to Bright's inverted U-shaped curve of declining skill, and, in stark contrast to Blauner, argued that even in the most technologically advanced industries using continuous-process technology, such as the chemical industry, the automation of production places it "under the control of management engineers and destroys the need for knowledge or training [for the operators]."[26] As production jobs offered less opportunity for skill development than ever before, they came to have little relevance for the kinds of expertise needed at supervisory levels. Consequently, in this context, working one's way up from the ranks became a thing of the past (when the most skilled workers were often promoted to managerial ranks).[27]

Braverman's deskilling thesis became the subject of a plethora of critical comments (the most important were mentioned earlier in the introduction). It also spawned a large number of empirical studies in various sectors of both blue-collar and white-collar work that cannot be summarized here for the sake of brevity.[28] But, where necessary, pivotal changes in the quality of work and skill requirements will be indicated in what follows.

The Rise of Computer-Mediated Technologies in Professional Work

By the 1980s, the computer was no longer tied to the mainframe and was available as an independent center of control virtually anywhere. In office work this led to the rapid spread of the desktop personal computer and subsequently, the Local Area Network that transformed much white-collar work. Rather than creating the more skilled jobs envisioned by some, for the majority it brought more deskilling.[29] It also created more possibilities for more flexible forms of production in industry. But a more flexible system of production demands a more flexible workforce than under a Fordist regime, one that can be deployed, redeployed, replaced and reduced as needed.[30]

In the same years, scientifically-based technologies began to displace and recompose the skills of professionals, especially in engineering and medicine. For example, civil, electrical, and mechanical engineers were traditionally obliged to draw dozens of prints in the process of making relatively minor alterations in a switch, water system, road, or building. It was quite common for them to draft hundreds of drawings for a major design. The new technology of computer-aided design and drafting (CADD) electronically reproduced the broad outlines of drawings with a program that standardized many of their dimensions and also provided a menu of standard mathematical calculations that the operator might choose from. CADD increased drafting productivity enormously for routine design jobs and freed engineers to spend most of their efforts on purely design functions.

Initially, these engineers saw CADD as an historical opportunity to return to what they were trained to do, relieved of the burden of seemingly endless drawing. But at the same time CADD virtually eliminated the drafter's occupation, at least for the routine design functions. Now that most of the drawing (and the time traditionally needed for it) could be transferred to the machine, far fewer engineers and drafters were required even as the rate of growth of construction, industrial production, and technological systems escalated. Just as numerical controls drastically altered the production process when they were first introduced on a wide scale on machine tools in the 1970s, CADD transformed many subfields of engineering, especially those that involve routine designs.

The work of physicians underwent significant changes too, due to the introduction of computer-mediated technologies. Physicians who still performed direct patient care came to rely heavily on electronically produced test results. By the 1990s, in many hospitals and group medical practices, computer programs such as the CAT scan[31] had already taken over a significant portion of the physician's diagnostic and prescriptive functions. Whether this led to increased accuracy was not always clear. Physicians still had room for interpretation of what appeared on the monitor; results did not eliminate their options. But the computerization and mechanization of diagnosis and prescription, like CADD, tended to transfer intellectual functions to the machine. From the doctor's perspective, the patient had progressively been reduced to a series of abstracted pictures of particular parts of the body; in hospitals, patient care had now become almost exclusively the work of practical nurses and nurses' aides. The exceptions were patients with specific problems such as kidney and liver failures, obscure diseases, as well as those who could afford the services of the attending physician.[32] Workers in other professions increasingly met similar challenges posed by new digital technologies geared to the particular job contents in question.

5

The "New Nonunion Model" and the Great Risk Shift

Modern welfare capitalism remained restricted to a minority of large nonunion companies until the 1960s, and their practices spread only slowly to other firms. Organized companies such as General Motors were dominated by unions that either resisted the introduction of modern welfare capitalism or aimed to control it and take credit for it. Managements of smaller nonunion companies were skeptical of this form of personnel management or else lacked the necessary resources to pursue it, and thus held on to traditional approaches. But during the 1960s and especially after 1970, modern welfare capitalism began to spread rapidly because of changes in the business environment. Markets became more competitive and less predictable. Educational levels rose steadily and the work force qualities shifted away from manual work. These changes put pressure on the union sector; managers and unions had problems in changing their emphasis from obedience to responsibility or to satisfy the aspirations of younger and more educated workers, including many women—members of the postwar baby boom generation.

Instead of meeting the expectations of those workers, unionized companies treated their white-collar employees much like their unionized blue-collar workers, the dominant group of the company's workforce. Although this led to great salary and benefit gains for white-collar employees, it also came along with a managerial mindset that was rigidly bureaucratic and economistic. Union-sector companies increasingly were unable to attract the best of the younger and college-educated entrants to the labor market, while nonunion firms came to be seen as more desirable and interesting places to work. The values of educated workers tended to be more in line with nonunionized firms' emphasis on individual pay determination and merit. Workers with at least some college education were more likely than their less educated co-workers to view fairness in terms of "recognition of individual abilities" instead of "equal treatment for all." This orientation did not fit well with the unions' emphasis on standard wage rates, common rules, and seniority. Young, educated employees were more inclined to reject the labor movements' egalitarian orientation, thus eroding social solidarity among workers, leaving only the narrower loyalties of corporation and career.[1] According to Sanford Jacoby, the union sector's resistance to behavioral science in the 1950s and 1960s added to the problems, because behavioral science—premised on individualism and affective relationships with its personal and "participative" orientation—corresponded better to the expectations of these workers.[2] However, the latter assessment overlooks the possible problems associated with "democratic social engineering" in the form of leader-controlled decision making in participative groups with predetermined goals.

Here one should also remember that in the 1960s, the leadership model of the "sensitive" manager became popular at welfare capitalist companies. In 1960, MIT management professor Douglas McGregor articulated two contrasting views of work and management. Theory X management was authoritarian, resting on the same assumptions that Taylor had about workers: people are basically lazy, lack discipline, respond only to material rewards and punishments, and want security but not responsibility in their jobs. Theory Y was participatory. It assumed that people like to work (or at least do not dislike it), are self-motivated, have self-control, and want to have responsibility for their work. Around the same time that McGregor's book, *The Human Side of Enterprise*, appeared the National Training Lab had developed T-groups, or training groups, which would eventually evolve in a variety of other forms such as "sensitivity training," "encounter groups," and "integrity groups." During those years the emphasis of group research shifted from the study of how people worked together in groups to how groups could change individuals. A number of large companies used these training groups presumably to transform bossy managers into participative ones. But after much moving around on the floor together, exchanging gut level feelings, and trying to connect better with other participants, few managers actually were transformed. While participatory management and initiatives to make managers more sensitive might look good on paper (at least to these "enlightened" employers), they could also make work for employees more complicated. "Friendly," "caring" managers did not necessarily nullify the lines of power and authority in an organization, rather they masked them.[3]

In the 1970s, the fast decline of industrial unionism encouraged employers in the union sector to resort to the anti-union strategies developed by welfare capitalist companies after World War II, which were revitalized as part of a massive national assault on organized labor (see below). Thus, modern welfare capitalism spread beyond its borders to a new group of rapidly growing companies; many were in the technology and service sectors. It was also in those years that the union sector began to pay attention to the "quality of working life" from the perspective of the behavioral sciences, about which more later.[4] Jacoby emphasizes that more generally "modern welfare capitalism's emphasis on commitment proved well suited to managing college-educated workers ... [it] meshed neatly with the participative principles that were supplanting traditional Taylorist approaches to work organization."[5] Needless to say, this form of "participation" in terms of teamwork within technological-organizational structures and corporate cultures (deeply embedded in modern capitalism) was far removed from the ideal of participatory democracy in terms of "workers' control" envisioned by labor activists of the New Left.[6]

It should likewise be noted that the expansion of modern welfare capitalism coincided with the rise of neoliberalism, in which yet another round of corporate ideological warfare played a crucial role (after the wave that lasted from the late 1940s through the early 1960s). The National Chamber of Commerce expanded its base from around 60,000 firms in 1972 to over 250,000 ten years later. Together with the National Association of Manufacturers it amassed an enormous campaign fund to lobby Congress and engage in research. The Business Roundtable, founded in 1973, became the centerpiece of pro-business action. It united over one hundred of the nation's biggest corporations—from U.S. Steel and GM to AT&T and Bank of America—in an alliance to sway the government and public opinion alike. Unlike older business lobbying groups, the Business Roundtable was more than a (major) player in the political arena; it sought in effect to define the playing field, proving ultimately to be highly successful. Think tanks, such as the Heritage Foundation, the Hoover Institute, the Center for the Study of American Business and the American Enterprise Institute, were formed with corporate backing to polemicize and, when necessary, as in the case of the National Bureau of Economic Research (NBER), to construct technical and empirical studies and political-philosophical arguments broadly in support of neoliberal policies.[7]

The management offensive at the macro level was paralleled by corporate attacks on labor in the workplace as firms hired anti-union consultants in unprecedented numbers. Union busting became a sophisticated big business, with mass market seminars and crash courses, industrial psychologists seeking to contain the hearts and minds of the rank and file, consulting firms that instructed employers step-by-step how to defeat an organizing drive, and trade associations that customized each step for a particular industry.[8]

Along with this well-orchestrated campaign to defeat organized labor, numerous books and articles lauded the emergence of a "new nonunion model" to sell to the general public. These publications suggested an ideal model comprised of eight basic features that were shared by the large companies concerned:

Strong organizational culture: inspired by top management, based on treating employees fairly and securing their identification with the firm.

Single-status systems: companywide policies governing pay, benefits, and other programs, including profit sharing, which abolish occupational distinctions, and encourage flexibility in job and task location.

Employment stability: marked by internal hiring and promotion, training, and development, and layoffs as a last resort.

Generous compensation: managers seek to pay above-average salaries and benefits.

Indulgency pattern: minimizing rules of the workplace while taking an individualized, flexible approach to correct performance problems, including careful training of supervisors.

Behavioral science: extensive reliance on attitude surveys, employee involvement, team-based organization, and planned corporate cultures and value systems.

Influential human resource departments: with direct access to senior management.

Use of labor-relations consultants to thwart union organizing drives: new-model firms range from those whose motivation has little to do with union avoidance to fervent anti-unionists.[9]

What is most striking about this list is how much it resembles the practices that characterized modern welfare capitalism since its inception. Rather than being new, the "new nonunion model" of the 1970s and 1980s hardly differed from what companies like Sears, Eastman Kodak, and Thompson had been following since the 1930s. Their view of a capitalist work organization corresponded to a "unitary" management ideology in that it acknowledged only one source of authority and loyalty—the company—and considered unions to be unnecessary.[10] The only significant difference was the sixth item: behavioral science in relation to the use of team organization and sociotechnical principles to modify the traditional division of labor. The team approach was a marked change in that it transformed managerial thinking about the relationship between efficiency and specialization. Because of its cooperative premise, the team approach had little traction among unionized firms, but it flourished in nonunion companies because it was well geared to the basic character of modern welfare capitalism and especially the Lewinian strain of human relations.[11]

Understandably, the single-status system (mentioned in the second item) became more widespread as well.

The employer drives to establish single-status employment systems in manufacturing firms, which (re-)emerged in the 1980s, constituted a deliberate strategy to counter the problem that the prerogatives of skilled workers made it more difficult for production managers to meet targets. This also means that it is incorrect to assume that employers always welcome friction between occupational and skill groups, as a simplistic control perspective on labor may do.[12]

The most important reason why it could seem plausible to contemporary observers that this nonunion model was something completely new—a true "plant revolution"—had to do with the proliferation of new nonunion companies in the 1970s, the number far exceeding those of the previous three decades. Some of these plants were offshoots of partially unionized companies like General Mills, Mobil Oil, and Cummins Engines, whose managements now found it technically and organizationally feasible to move into economic-geographical areas where there was little risk that unions would follow. Others belonged to a new kind of entirely nonunion companies such as Intel, Digital Equipment, Texas Instruments, and Federal Express; many were part of booming high-technology and service sector industries.

On the other hand, a few older welfare capitalists resurfaced in the 1970s as exemplars, including IBM, Procter & Gamble, S.C. Johnson, and Thompson (by then renamed TRW—Thompson-Ramo-Wooldridge). They were all highly profitable and growing fast, notwithstanding their age. Several of these companies were experimenting with team-based production methods, which meant that their newest plants had fewer job classifications and wage grades than their older ones did. However, the remaining policies in the 1970s—sensitivity training, quality circles, attitude surveys, employee meetings—harkened back to the single-status communitarianism that had emerged with the rise of modern welfare capitalism, the emphasis on "human relations," and to the conservative business notion that employee representation was only desirable as long as it did not involve unionism.[13]

A Brief Interlude: The Quality of Working Life Movement

Oddly enough, the attacks on unionized labor during the 1970s into the 1980s overlapped with the emergence of what came to be called the Quality of Working Life movement. In 1973, the Department of Health, Education, and Welfare (HEW) published the report, *Work in America*, that marked the end of a decade of rising discontent about alienation on the job. This report was published a year after a wildcat strike at General Motor's Lordstown assembly line in Ohio drew a great deal of public attention to the nature of the worker grievances against the inhumanity of the work place. The Lordstown line was then the fastest in the world. Its labor force and its local UAW leaders were very young (an average age of 24 or 25). The strikers exhibited attitudes previously associated with the middle-class students and other young adults who had put their stamp on the alternative lifestyles of the 1960s. For the most part, theirs was not a grievance over hours and wages. It was a protest against the quality of the work, and it was at odds with their parent union's contract with GM, which promised high productivity and labor peace in return for high wages so characteristic of the postwar compact with corporate America.[14]

The report concluded that "a significant number of Americans are dissatisfied with the quality of their working lives. Dull, repetitive, seemingly meaningless tasks, offering little challenge or autonomy, are causing discontent among workers at all occupational levels." The "alienation and disenchantment of blue-collar workers" was matched by the "disgruntlement of white-collar workers" and the "growing discontent of managers," while the physical and mental health costs of all this chronic alienation on the job became the taxpayers' burden. The report also decried the "anachronistic authoritarianism of the workplace," which resulted in a lack of employee participation in decision-making. It recommended the "redesign of work" in ways that went far beyond personal job enrichment. Thus it underscored the belief that "having an interesting job is now as important as having a job that pays well."[15]

After the publication of this report, the Quality of Working Life (QWL) movement for a brief historical moment had some impact.[16] It must be recognized that the report was well received by many but not the Nixon administration. The findings contradicted Nixon's repeated assertion that Americans had abandoned the work ethic. Consequently, the Nixon administration did not do much with the report. Yet the study led to a Senate inquiry and fostered important research and experimentation in job redesign, worker participation, and "workplace democracy."[17] Several North American companies began experimenting with QWL. New plants were designed, organizational structures were flattened, teams were formed, rules were eliminated, and the purpose of management became defined as "to enable people to do work."[18] In these organizational change projects, workers formed cooperative work teams, assigned tasks and responsibilities, controlling their own time and scheduling. QWL allegedly involved a process of joint decision making, collaboration and building mutual respect between management and employees. This process was expected to cause a change in people—in how they felt about themselves, their work and each other. QWL advocates claimed that the altered work environment increased job satisfaction and facilitated better solutions to management and production problems. They pointed to the results of many of the experiments, which were described as "phenomenal," with productivity gains of 30 to 40 percent, higher quality products, and lower absenteeism rates.[19]

Although joint union-management QWL efforts were much celebrated at the time, many of the more advanced work reform experiments in the U.S. took place in new nonunion plants, such as the General Foods pet food factory in Topeka, Kansas. This was partly due to the fact that it was easier to introduce work reform in a greenfield setting, where neither workers nor first-line supervisors were locked into traditional attitudes and entrenched ways of doing things. Another part of the explanation was that even though some unions such as the United Auto Workers (UAW)[20] were champions of QWL, many other unions—and some vocal factions within the UAW itself—were deeply suspicious of work reform, seeing it as a management tool to undermine the union. Yet another explanatory factor was that, as noted earlier, companies in the 1970s had significantly increased their union-avoidance activities, so that the number of new nonunion plants increased steadily over the decade.[21]

Consequently, many of the new organizational forms met severe resistance, both inside and outside the companies involved. The resistance could also be partly explained by confusion about the QWL concept, which lacked a proper definition. On the other hand, much of the confusion may have been deliberate. The use of the vaguely defined, all-encompassing term Quality of Working Life allowed participants to avoid dealing with the political dimension of the work situation.[22] "The programs that most of those companies were promoting did not involve democratizing the workplace at all," opinioned the president of the Canadian Auto Workers union (CAW). Aimed at increasing productivity, he continued: "They are about cutting out any time at all that the workers have for themselves and convincing workers that what is good for the enterprise is good for them."[23] One article specifically about the QWL projects in American corporations that was published in the *Academy of Management Journal*, appears to hit the nail on the head, suggesting that managerial attitudes were at the core of the problem:

> It appears that the majority of business executives ... do not take the view that employees should have the right to participate, through the democratic process, in making organizational decisions. They do not even favor allowing employees direct input to the decision making process ... except when the nature of the problem is such that the traditional managerial prerogatives will in no way be affected.[24]

In many of the companies where innovations did occur, the participating managers were condemned and ostracized by their more traditional colleagues;

the innovations either faded away within a few years or were sidetracked, remaining restricted to marginal areas of the company. Many companies that started with QWL programs eventually modified or replaced them with other participation efforts deemed more suitable to their businesses. These replacements included suggestion programs, joint management/employee task forces, work redesign, and various communication schemes, all of which were characterized by employee participation that could be more easily handled and controlled by management.[25]

Changing Relationship Between Owners and Managers

During those years there was also a crucial change in the relationship between owners and managers of corporations. As noted earlier, managerial capitalism had emerged in the late 19th and early 20th centuries, and challenged the traditional regime of personal entrepreneurial capitalism built on competitive interaction among small firms within industries. The heyday of managerial capitalism, dominated by large public corporations, was the post–World War II period until the early 1980s, when owners left control and coordination to salaried professional managers.[26] To be sure, the rise of this "managerial class" had not altered the main objective of the firm, which was profit making for owners. But differences in opinion remained about exactly how best to reap those profits, such as whether to focus on capital investments for sound financial prospects of the firm in the long run or not. And, historically, there also tended to be different views regarding employment between the personnel department and the production division. While the personnel manager put emphasis on stabilizing labor relations, which required trading off short-term efficiency in the interest of achieving high employee morale, production managers might be skeptical about the claim that good employee relations contributed to high productivity.[27]

With the increased importance of shareholders focused on the maximization of stock value in the 1980s, owners of public corporations came to see management itself as problematic and an increasing target for rationalization. During the Reagan Administration, financial markets became the primary beacon guiding corporate decision making. Three policy changes around 1982 were of particular significance for spawning the shareholder value movement. First, the Department of Justice released a set of merger guidelines that substantially eased limitations on within-industry mergers. Second, the Supreme Court's *Edgar v. MITE* decision struck down a set of state laws limiting hostile takeovers of domestic corporations under the interstate commerce clause.

Third, based on an IRS ruling in 1981, corporations began to offer 401(k) plans to their employees as a supplement and, eventually, a replacement for traditional defined benefit pension plans. The first two of these changes helped unleash a wave of hostile takeovers aimed largely at the conglomerates built up during the 1960s and 1970s. After a decade of mergers, the largest firms actually ended up smaller than they were at the start, reducing aggregate corporate concentration in the economy. The third change reinforced the power of financial markets relative to corporations. It helped create a broad new constituency as an increasingly larger proportion of the population became invested in the stock market. It also helped channel the vast new pools of capital created through employee savings into mutual funds. Broad popular participation in the stock market, along with a relatively concentrated set of institutional investors, thus created a strong countervailing power to "imperial" corporate managers.[28]

At corporate ground level, one could witness a repositioning between ownership and control as a new mode of corporate governance based primarily on financial criteria and short-term prospects was imposed. The proclaimed objective was to protect external investors by limiting the obstacles that affected their control. Transparency, responsibility and accountability of management, contestability of corporate control, and top management compensation associated with the maximization of stock value were all advocated. Needless to say, the latter was not always associated with good firm performance in terms of industry building and growth in the long run; on the contrary, firm performance and top management compensation often proved to be inversely related—not even taking into account the lucrative severance packages ("golden parachutes") given to those who were asked to step down because of underperformance.

Owners of capital now became involved more forcefully in capital accumulation to arrest a crisis in profitability, and in so doing, clashed with managers, pushing many out of the corporation and a few into the ranks of real capitalists (through providing them with large stock options and huge bonuses). Stockholders made direct interventions in corporate management by forced mergers, acquisitions and leveraged buyouts, coupled with the rationalization of layers of management and intermediate technical labor, and delayering of command hierarchies. All this was supposed to be in the interest of simplifying and reducing the costs of managing the firm.[29] As a result, stable bureaucratic centers of the corporation—which provided a status hierarchy for the middle layers of employment within the firm—experienced levels of employment insecurity previously reserved for manual wage labor only.

From Braverman's perspective of management control over labor, the creation of these employment middle layers acted as a buffer and potential career ladder between capitalists and workers within the firm. But corporations now subjected these middle layers to continuous rationalization and cost-benefit analysis, and rearranged responsibilities downward to lower levels of the corporate hierarchy, while at the same time centralizing budgetary controls at the higher echelons. Increasing availability of information technology acted as the mechanism and new accounting techniques as the instrument for tighter controls by corporate staff over operational management.[30]

Shareholder primacy was the unquestioned bedrock for managers of the new public corporations. Managers of the more than 3,000 corporations that went public in the 1990s—in industries such as biotechnology, computers, energy, and business services—had no illusions about the purposes of their firms. These existed to create shareholder value, not to cater to various alleged "stakeholders." The chosen management policies were fully in accordance with this adage from the very outset.[31]

Welfare Capitalism in Distress

What happened in the United States during the 1980s and 1990s was a shift in norms regarding corporate governance that helped to legitimate hostile takeovers, downsizing by profitable companies, and a much greater emphasis on shareholder rights. The latter included a reallocation of resources from employees and other stakeholders to shareholders (including executives who owned options) and a shift of risk to employees, whose wages and employment became more sensitive to business conditions leading to a greater volatility of income, while most of them did not share in the corporate earnings associated with greater risk. There were a few notable exceptions to this trend during that period, such as Hewlett-Packard, Johnson & Johnson, and Toro, whose CEOs practiced stakeholder capitalism, balancing the needs of various corporate stakeholders—that is employees, customers, and suppliers as well as shareholders and management.[32]

At the heart of this great risk shift was the concept of "moral hazard," the term economists tend to use regarding the idea that by protecting people against risk, their behavior changes for the worse. Those who hold this view contend, for instance, that people with access to unemployment insurance will stay out of work longer because they receive income when not working, and people with health insurance will abuse the system because they do not have to pay (most of) the costs of medical care, while people with guaranteed pensions will save less for retirement because they do not need to feel responsible for their own old-age welfare. To combat the embedded notions of shared risk, conservatives emphasized the concepts of self-reliance, individualism, personal gain, and efficiency. The concept of moral hazard provided the intellectual legitimation for this broad-based attack.[33] In this reformulation of the prevailing discourse, public figures, consultants, journalists and academics operated as what Sunstein calls "norm entrepreneurs," helping to legitimize both the necessity and inevitability of the change.[34]

This sea change in corporate management meant that the "new nonunion model," and particularly its employment stability feature, came under heavy stress. Nonunion companies that had never before had a major layoff, fired thousands of employees. This was especially a shock to those employees who thought they had absolute job security. To their consternation, middle-level managers discovered that the elimination of their jobs furnished the chief cost savings to be realized from "restructuring," a euphemism for the compression of the multi-divisional form of the corporation's bureaucratic hierarchy which had become well-entrenched in American industry during the 1950s.[35] The enormous publicity these layoffs drew, contrasts sharply with the far less attention that was paid to the massive job losses of blue-collar workers some ten to fifteen years earlier. It was only when professionals and managers were at risk that the politically more influential middle class began to feel threatened and the mainstream media took notice, reporting the demise of career jobs.

Some welfare capitalist firms adopted dualist policies in order to preserve career jobs: flex workers carried out the tasks of what these firms saw as their least essential parts (usually jobs requiring less formal education) while maintaining a core of stable jobs with good benefits. In the 1990s Hewlett Packard, for example, started a Flex Force comprised of temporary employees, especially in clerical and service jobs, who received no benefits or employment security. Flex Force employees lost their jobs when markets slowed, thus cushioning Hewlett-Packard's core work force. Needless to say, this arrangement merely redistributed unemployment from regular workers to disposable contingent workers. It was unclear, however, to what extent the "career jobs" in question would really offer job security when push came to shove.

Other welfare capitalist companies such as 3M, for instance, chose a different course in the early 1990s, and at first aimed to maintain full employment by retraining and reassigning workers to other corporate divisions, an employment stabilization technique dating back to the 1920s. IBM did the same in the 1980s for more than ten thousand workers, but still took recourse to large-scale layoffs, thereby offering relatively generous early-retirement schemes to thousands more workers. Digital Equipment and Eastman Kodak followed suit, first bending over backwards to avoid laying off employees. But ultimately these companies' managements also resorted to massive layoffs, thus putting an end to their implicit no-layoff policies.[36] By the turn of the century, the arrangements of bureaucratized employment at welfare capitalist firms were increasingly eroding.

6

Renewal of "Flexible Mass Production" Through a Japanese Filter

For the most part, workplace "reform" in the 1980s was driven by very businesslike responses to industrial competition, especially from Japanese management, whose emphasis on teamwork and collective self-discipline was hailed as the panacea for the American/Western problem of deficient motivation.[1] A succession of management innovations followed: "quality circles," "problem-solving teams," "customer-centered goals," "worker empowerment," "employee involvement," "job enrichment," "autonomous work groups," and "company culture." Each of these was guided by theories and associated strategies of reorganization. A crucial component of this renewal wave was the revival and technological update of "flexible specialization" (sometimes called "flexible manufacturing" or "flexible accumulation").

In their influential book, *The Second Industrial Divide* (1984), Michael Piore and Charles Sabel argued that as a production system, Fordism is intrinsically inflexible in that it is unable to respond to variable demand, especially once mass markets have been saturated and consumers' tastes have changed in the direction of more individualized and higher-quality products, as happened in the 1960s. By the late 1960s, technologies were becoming available that could cater to the consumers' desires for ever greater variety. Subsequently, new computer technologies allowed companies, even small ones, to respond quickly to changes in fashion, thereby overcoming the crisis of declining consumer interest in standardized products. Piore and Sabel played an important role in upholding the Italian industrial districts in what was often called the "Third Italy"—that is, the Central and Northeastern regions of the country—as a mode of production and organization very different from the American Fordist model.

They claimed that the new regime of "flexible specialization" differed in important respects from the old system of mass production that was now obsolete. In their view, the new technologies were complex and difficult to operate and so could no longer be handled by workers trained in the simple routines of scientific management. The new flexibility was the keynote to a new age, one that heralded an end to stultifying labor and a return to craft-like methods of production in U.S. manufacturing. Piore and Sabel even dreamed of a revival of "yeoman democracy" in small cooperative enterprises that could respond quickly to shifting market opportunities.[2] In hindsight, they were wrong in their attempt to portray the Japanese auto production systems as a new form of "craft control," since the Japanese auto producers represented a production system and industrial structure quite different from the industrial districts of the "Third Italy." They also overlooked the fact that "Sloanism," the system of "flexible mass production" developed at General Motors in the 1920s, had already proven that the mass production model could effectively be accommodated to changing consumer demands.

The success of the Japanese auto companies prior to the 1980s was attributed to lower wages, greater government support, and/or automation. But continued success into the 1980s attracted international interest in their production methods and led to a reversal of the pattern earlier in the century when foreign auto makers visited American plants. Ford and GM executives went on fact-finding missions to Japan in 1981 and 1983 respectively, and found the key to Japanese success: lean production.[3] The diffusion of Japanese lean production (JLP) methods was further enhanced during the 1980s by the establishment of Japanese transplant production facilities (typically nonunionized) and joint ventures (typically unionized) in North America and Europe. The arrival of Japanese transplants in the auto industry in the U.S. played a pivotal role in the national debate about the relationship between technology and work in factories and offices. So many of the concepts—multiskilling, flexible specialization, worker empowerment, worker autonomy—that were used to define the role employees played in what was called the "new economy," had their origins in the methods of Japanese companies like Toyota and Nissan.[4]

Books by American and British management experts praising the superiority and transferability of Japanese lean production,[5] academic studies of the development of Japanese auto production,[6] and an account of the evolution of the Toyota production system by its creator[7] also played a part in disseminating information about the ins and outs of lean production and how to implement it. One book in particular, *The Machine That Changed the World* (1990), containing a mixture of academic research and management-style prescriptions, was influential in spreading the gospel of JLP. It was based on an intensive study of the automobile industry carried out by the International Motor Vehicle Program of the Massachusetts Institute of Technology (MIT). Its authors, James Womack, Daniel Jones, and Daniel Rose, suggested that the way Japanese companies organized production combined "the advantages of craft and mass production, while avoiding the high cost of the former and the rigidity of the latter," which was necessitated by the existence of a small market for a great variety of cars.[8] They also claimed that JLP involved upskilling rather than deskilling, and was fulfilling rather than alienating. The authors concluded that "by the end of the century we expect that lean-assembly plants will be populated almost entirely by highly skilled problem solvers whose task will be to think continually of ways to make the system run more smoothly and productively."[9]

Their claim was part of what appears to have been a generalized rebuttal of Braverman's contention that capitalist-driven technological advance and industrial rationalization results in the progressive deskilling of labor. A host of thinkers on both sides of the Atlantic now proclaimed flexible specialization as the coming of an age that might upskill employees. As in Britain, these proponents represented a wide swath in the U.S., from radical critics such as Fred Block, who envisioned "postindustrial possibilities" bringing "higher skill levels" to Shoshana Zuboff of the Harvard Business School who saw the prospect of "a profound reskilling."[10] Block foresaw a differentiated development regarding two basic components of skill:

> Skill depth refers to the time it takes to learn a particular task, such as machining a complex job. Skill breadth refers to the range of different types of knowledge that employees must have to carry out their jobs. Flexible technologies tend to reduce skill depth precisely because the relationship of worker to materials is now mediated by machinery. This kind of hands-on knowledge that production workers often accumulated over a long period of time can become obsolete.[11]

In the writings of these authors, information is seen to play a pivotal role in flexible specialization in several ways. One is that information and communication technologies (ICTs) are the major facilitator and manifestation of flexibility in production work. The new technologies are "intelligent"; their distinctive feature is that they incorporate considerable quantities and complexities of information. As such the programs that guide them are their fundamental components rather than any specific function they may perform. It is these information inputs that determine their degrees of flexibility, enabling cost-effective small batch production runs, customization of products and rapid changes in manufacturing procedures. Furthermore, it is this information constellation that provides flexibility in the labor process itself, since to perform well the operatives must be multi-skilled and adaptable, hence more "flexible" (which in itself advances the role of information). Where previously employees learned a set of tasks for life, so to speak, in the age of information technology they must be ready to update their skills as quickly as new technologies are introduced (or reprogrammed). This means employees have to be trained and retrained as a matter of routine, a preeminently informational task.[12]

Another way in which information is crucial, it is argued, stems from an increased reliance on programmable technologies. The very fact that the machinery of production is so sophisticated requires that workers possess information/knowledge of the system as a whole in order to cope with the inevitable irregularities, errors, or malfunctions that come with its operation. Not only does information technology stimulate regular retraining, it also demands that the employees become knowledgeable about its inner workings. In this way production workers become, in effect, information employees. In the terminology of Larry Hirschhorn, information technologies on the shop floor are a "postindustrial technology," which takes away many of the physical demands and tedium of assembly line work, but also requires "a growing mobilization and watchfulness that arises from the imperfections, the discontinuities of cybernetic technology." Therefore "learning must be instituted in order to prepare workers for intervening in moments of unexpected system failure," something which requires comprehension of the overall system and a constant state of "preparation and learning." In this way we may foresee "the worker moving from being the controlled element in the production process to operating the controls to controlling the controls."[13]

In addition, Hirschhorn states that flexible specialization encourages employee participation in the design of work. That is, the computerization of production provides a feedback loop to the operatives, which enables them to act by reprogramming the system in appropriate ways.[14] Here the worker is depicted as informationally sensitive, made aware by advanced technologies of what is happening throughout the production process, and able to respond intelligently to improve that overall system.[15] This is what Shoshana Zuboff refers to as the "reflexivity" that comes from working with ICTs, and the "informating" process that she thinks generates "intellective skill"[16] (about which more later).

Unsurprisingly, these theories of flexible specialization have garnered a great deal of criticism. First, some of the advocates display—often in spite of explicit denials—a strong trace of technological determinism. Some like Hirschhorn, for example, emphasize the cybernetic capabilities of computers, placing themselves too easily within a tradition which assumes that advanced technologies automatically lead to advanced skill requirements. From this perspective, "industrial technology" is "transcultural" in that it unavoidably "shapes social life in the same mould everywhere," only to be disrupted and liberated by "postindustrial technology" which brings flexibility.[17]

Second, flexible specialization is presented as the opposite of mass production and in some way contrary to the continuing dominance of corporate businesses. It is actually doubtful whether this is the case. As noted earlier, this position underestimates the flexibilities of big corporations that are well able to adopt new modes of working involving new technologies that enhance adaptability, and modular products that allow for significant product differentiation while continuing mass production practices.

Third, in spite of true instances of flexible specialization that may be found, mass production remains dominant throughout the advanced economies. Any suggestion of a market change is demonstrably incorrect. Still another objection that has been raised is that there is little new about flexibility as it has been a feature of capitalist enterprise since its inception. Nineteenth-century history is replete with examples of specialist enterprises catering to market segments (e.g., the rag trade or toy makers), but none of these has ever been presented as illustrative of flexible specialization. Of course, one would have to allow for their lack of computerized information technology, which is central to today's flexible specialization.

Fourth, while its proponents present flexible specialization only in positive terms, it can also be interpreted as the re-emergence of what others have termed "segmented labor." While there may indeed be a core of skilled, resourceful and versatile employees, there are also groups of much more vulnerable, "peripheral" people working part time, casually or on short-term contracts.[18]

Writing in 1991, David Harvey claimed that flexible specialization had potential for increased worker control, but that so far it had been introduced into the workplace almost completely in the capitalist terms of "flexible accumulation." In this form, competition had not increased innovation, but flexible manufacturing had cut costs by replacing workers with automated computer technologies. The control over workers had been privileged over skill-based autonomy and worker control. This new "postmodernist" flexible regime consisted of a power move in which small-batch, just-in-time productions runs did not empower skilled workers. Harvey also insisted that "flexibility has little or nothing to do with decentralizing either economic or political power and everything to do with maintaining highly centralized control through *decentralizing tactics*." He observed that the past few decades had seen an increase in the concentration of multinational capital. The difference was that this power was "now increasingly organized through networks of seemingly autonomous firms and activities."[19]

In the following pages the claims about upskilling associated with flexible specialization are subjected to closer scrutiny as part of an in-depth analysis of

Japanese lean production (JLP). This will be done primarily with reference to auto manufacturing since this was the source and the main focus of research of JLP.

Background of Japanese Lean Production

Japan's creation of more flexible and more productive forms of the assembly line harkens back to before World War II, although most of the new practices stem from the 1950s and beyond. At Toyota what came to be known as "lean production" emerged from situational pressures and borrowings from other nations. "Japanese" lean production was partly based on the rediscovery of earlier American practices, such as eliciting suggestions from employees. Another older practice that was rediscovered was tighter inventory control. (Between 1913 and 1930, Ford managers were intensively focused on reducing the amount of money that was tied up in parts inventories. Their successors paid less attention, however, and eventually there was considerable redundant duplication. On a larger scale, in the case of General Motors, separate divisions acted often more like rivals who duplicated one another rather than cooperating entities who shared costs and learned from each other.[20]) Selective appropriation of American methods brought to Japan by American consultants after World War II played an important role as well.

In the 1930s, American auto companies, particularly Ford, dominated the small Japanese auto market, and Ford cars sold in Japan were assembled from parts shipped in from the United States. Ford's plan to build a factory that would produce parts in Japan was torpedoed in 1936 by the Japanese government who imposed a protectionist policy, putting a halt to American production there. As a result, domestic companies grew to meet the local demand. Notably Nissan sought to replicate American mass production methods, although some innovations emerged within Japanese corporations. The tight orchestration of supply chains, that later would be called just-in-time production, was already being tried out in the 1930s. Japanese companies also appropriated some German manufacturing practices. During World War II, some Japanese aircraft companies adopted the German *takt* system—the practice of organizing work stations in sequence, and allocating a precise time for each station to complete its assembly tasks. Workers moving their section of the manufactured product together according to *takt* time would later be incorporated into the lean system.[21]

When the Japanese auto industry began to expand under heavy state protection after the war, the production system of the American auto industry was the primary reference point. However, both the product and labor market conditions in Japan were very different from those in the U.S. There was much less room for mass production in Japan; production volumes were significantly lower. The Japanese companies also had a wide product range; they had begun as manufacturers of light trucks. Moreover, the economic resources of the companies and the purchasing power of the home market were very limited. It was therefore necessary for the car manufacturers to adapt American methods to fit the efficient manufacture of lower volumes and, despite limited resources, to be able to expand. First and foremost it was the crushing defeat of independent Japanese labor unions (with only management-controlled company unions remaining on the shop floor after a number of dramatic conflicts in the early 1950s) that gave the auto companies the opportunity to develop just such forms of low-cost rationalization. This gave the companies a free hand in matters of shop-floor organization and the supervision and utilization of the work force. In addition, the defeat of the independent trade union movement in the Japanese private sector contributed to a critical lack of social momentum that could bring about a general social welfare policy as happened in Western Europe, or national contracts as in the unionized sectors of American industry. Consequently, employees' security, income development, and social benefits came to be fully dependent on the company they worked for. Lastly, small companies were devoid of union organization altogether. This helped strengthen the industrial dualism in Japan—the extremely large differences in wages and working conditions between big and small companies—that were already in place before the war.[22]

Japan had long been receptive to American ideas and techniques. This is nicely exemplified by NEC, which was founded in 1899 as a joint venture with the American firm Western Electric. After NEC's factories were destroyed by an earthquake in the early 1930s, NEC built a near-replica of Western Electric's Hawthorne plant in Tokyo. NEC also learned about the experiments conducted by sociologists at the Hawthorne plant, which suggested the importance of involving the crew members more in their work. After World War II, NEC and other Japanese corporations resumed learning from American models; a small group of engineers and scientists read the literature on statistical process control which had been used in U.S. defense industries. And during 1948 and 1949, visiting experts from the Bell Telephone Laboratories held seminars for the Japanese Union of Science and Engineering (JUSE), presenting practical examples to demonstrate the utility of statistical process control methods. In 1950, 1951 and 1952, at the invitation of JUSE, American consultant W. Edwards Deming explained to its members how statistical process control had improved U.S. war production by enabling managers to identify problems as either systemic (that is, requiring changes in the system) or personal (that is, poor work habits or lack of expertise among particular workers). By making a well-considered distinction between system problems and personal ones, a company could reduce the incidence of defective products from 15 to 20 percent to less than 5 percent. Deming concluded that statistical process control led to large savings and greater worker satisfaction. He also showed that reliable suppliers were invaluable, even if their prices were higher than cheaper but undependable suppliers. If the materials supplied were uneven in quality, some of the parts made from them would be flawed, leading to replacement costs larger than any savings achieved by purchasing cheaper materials. Deming mapped the whole system of production and consumption, and emphasized that the consumer was the most important part of it. While most American companies lost interest in statistical process control methods, the Japanese made good use of them.

Between 1950 and 1970, JUSE organized intensive courses for more than 14,000 engineers and the use of statistical methods became common in major Japanese companies, leading to impressive practical results that demonstrated the value of those courses. Japanese companies eager to learn more from the U.S. experience, benefited from the fact that between 1955 and 1965, the Japan Productivity Council sent 6,600 people to the United States on "productivity missions."[23] These were similar to the study visits of the so-called productivity teams of Western European countries within the framework of the Technical Assistance Program that was an integral part of the Marshall Aid to those countries.[24] After their return to Japan, members of the productivity missions gave lectures on their findings and, like their European counterparts, wrote reports that eventually led to 40,000 pages spread over more than 165 volumes.

Some practices later identified as Japanese actually were based on Japanese observations of things American. Take, for example, the idea of getting continuous input from workers attributed to two Toyota executives (Toyota's chairman, Eiji Toyoda, and an executive named Shoichi Saito); they saw how an employee suggestion system operated at Ford's River Rouge plant in 1950 during a three-month industrial tour of the United States. Toyota reworked the practice, made it integral to their system of work teams, and three decades later exported it back to American shores. Other Japanese businessmen observed that Hotpoint made several different models of refrigerators on a single line, and decided to try a similar practice with different models in the auto industry. A generation later this practice too was re-exported to the United States.[25] These and similar creative appropriations of things American and their re-exportation to the United States can be seen as examples of what has been called "Americanization in reverse" in another context.[26]

The Japanese business community continued to learn from other American experts after W. Edwards Deming's early visits. Particularly influential was Joseph Juran, who first visited Japan in 1954 to teach courses to engineers, serving as a consultant to several companies. His approach was less statistical and more pragmatic than Deming's. He insisted that quality control should become part of every employee's conscientious work habits. His approach fit well with Japanese developments that shifted the focus from managers to workers on the factory floor. In his depiction of this "reform" of the workplace, David Nye speaks of "process innovations" that "often came about through an extended dialogue with workers," who "became deeply involved in the synthesis that eventually came to be called 'Total Quality Control.'"[27] However, he fails to mention the power play that was involved in this "extended dialogue" between managers and workers, which would soon favor rather lopsided arrangements with management holding the most important cards.

With the benefit of hindsight, one can see that important aspects of a broader change pattern that would ultimately lead to "lean production" at Toyota, began during World War II at a truck factory where Taiichi Ohno was a manager. His experiences in his previous job in the spinning industry had taught him the value of focusing a factory's layout on the product (rather than mirroring administrative divisions), emphasizing small-lot production, and trying to do each job right the first time so as to minimize rework. After 1945, Ohno focused on how to improve the use of Toyota's existing equipment and factory space. Through trial and error, he learned that incremental changes in layout, inventory and materials handling, improved efficiency quite significantly. In 1948–49, overproduction created a vast inventory of unsold trucks that almost bankrupted the company. This was the impetus for Toyota to develop just-in-time production, minimizing its inventories and building vehicles in response to the "pull" exerted by actual orders. These changes also led to a thorough reconsideration of how to organize an assembly-line factory. In contrast to American companies' emphasis on speed of throughput, Toyota began to emphasize minimizing error. Ohno introduced the *kanban* system, in which cards of various colors were used to indicate assembly sequences and to keep track of inventory.[28]

At the same time, Toyota adopted some practices from Ford that two of its executives had observed during their 1950 visit to the River Rouge plant mentioned earlier. Impressed by the handling of parts and materials at the plant when they returned to Japan, they introduced many more conveyor belts at the Toyota factory and brought in electric fork-lift trucks to move pallets around. During the 1950s, Toyota continued to innovate by selectively appropriating ideas from Detroit and integrating them with its own creative contributions. Thus, over the course of time Toyota's production organization adopted various components of the Ford system by design and hybridized them with its indigenous system and original ideas. The continuity between the two systems became clear for everyone to see.²⁹

Compared with the management structure of Fordism, Toyota's managerial organization is marked by a complex combination of continuity and innovation. When the Ford system was developed at Highland Park in the 1910s, it created the conditions for a considerably more extended system of management control than had characterized earlier forms of industrial organization. This system was required as well, because of its high vulnerability to disruption. The Toyota system is even more dependent on comprehensive control and has a broader management structure as a result. The position of foremen on the shop floor is extremely important. Foremen distribute tasks, choose work methods, determine operation times, assess employees' attitudes and efforts, and determine wages and advancement opportunities on the basis of a carefully worked-out system for individual evaluations. If present at all, the union has no influence over either performance standards or individual wages. Further, in Japan (with its system of company unions), the foreman is also usually the union representative. Finally, the workers are organized in groups led by subforemen, which further strengthens the role of first-line management.

On the one hand, Toyota has not followed Taylor's ideal of having a highly specialized managerial apparatus with "functional foremen." On the other hand, however, production and shop floor management is even more densely staffed. In the early 1980s, for example, there was one subforeman for every five workers, one foreman for every fourteen workers, and one senior foreman for every forty-three workers. This dense managerial structure played a critical role both in avoiding disturbances and in mobilizing workers in rationalization activities.³⁰

Surprisingly, it took somewhat longer for the automobile producers than much of the rest of Japanese industry to adopt a formal emphasis on quality control. After Nissan first embraced it, winning the Deming Prize in 1960, Toyota did not want to be left behind, vulnerable to criticism for lack of quality. So Toyota followed suit, adopting and enforcing quality control measures, which also helped to achieve goals it had already set forth: to cut down rework, reduce waste, create customer satisfaction, and minimize the high expense of recalls. Toyota won the Deming Prize in 1965 and began transferring its system to suppliers in the late 1960s. By the early 1970s the Toyota system was fully developed (though refinements continued). In short, production of a limited range of products in large volumes was replaced by production of a large range of products in generally small volumes.³¹ In the rhetoric of these Japanese managers that meant "a shift in emphasis from maximizing equipment capacity and utilization rates to maximizing flexibility in responding nimbly to trends in demand."[32]

Systematic Analysis of Japanese Lean Production

It is worthwhile to consider the basic features of JLP more systematically from a sociology of work perspective. The essence of JLP is well expressed in the concept *kaizen*, meaning the continuous improvement (CI) of every phase of production in order to "increase production efficiency by consistently and thoroughly eliminating waste"—the uneconomic use of labor, machinery, parts, raw materials, space, and so on.[33] Waste is an unnecessary expense, understandably fueling the never-ending quest to identify and abolish it, while increasing the quantity and quality of the products. Managers implement workers' suggestions about the ways machines may be better arranged, unnecessary movements eliminated, bottlenecks avoided and defects discovered. As David Nye puts it, "At a *kaizen*-based factory it is assumed that everyone occasionally has ideas for improvements, and suggestions are solicited from workers in regularly scheduled meetings. No suggestion is considered too small, as lean production emerges from myriad small improvements that collectively become quite significant."[34] To motivate workers to embrace CI, Japanese companies promised job security in the form of lifetime employment.

Several interdependent practices were developed to achieve the reductions in waste and improvements in the volume and quality of the output; the three most important were just-in-time production (JIT), total quality control (TQC), and teamwork (TW). JIT refers to the supply of materials, parts, and sub-assemblies for the final assembly exactly when they are needed, rather than in advance, "just-in-case" they are needed, as happened under Fordism.[35] The inspiration for JIT was the American supermarket in the 1950s, which was organized so that "a customer can get what is needed, at the time needed, and in the amount needed."[36] This way of organizing production reduces the size of buffer stocks to a bare minimum and requires the use of *kaban* (or tag) to ensure that each part is available when and where it is needed in order to facilitate the continuous flow of production. It epitomizes a lean approach in that it saves materials, space, labor, and stock inventories. However, for JIT production to be effective, it is essential that components are produced and delivered defect-free by workers trained to check upon this and with the authority to stop the production line if necessary.[37] Thus, the smooth operation of JIT necessitates the involvement of workers in the process of quality control, which in turn reduces the numbers of inspectors and the accumulation of defective parts.

Moreover, to produce a variety of models economically, requires that setup times for machines be reduced to a minimum; otherwise the assembly line and those who work on it will be idle during the changeover of models. Toyota led the way in modifying the way in which the setup of machines for the manufacture of various parts and components of "flexible production" are done—a process that takes place in the machine shop, before the components are transported to the line for final assembly. Shigeo Shingo's book, *A Revolution in Manufacturing: The SMED System* (1985), is very important in understanding the Toyota system in this regard. SMED stands for Single Minute Exchange of Die. Whereas the changing of a die on a press or stamping machine previously had taken hours to perform, it now could be done in minutes. The importance of the SMED system lies in its contribution to the "hard" flexibility of industrial production. "Soft flexibility" involves changes to the appearance or styling of a product, such as occurred at the auto assembly line at Toyota, with its variety of dashboards, seats, radios, and carpets. "Hard flexibility" refers to something much more substantial; the ability to vary not merely the outward appearance but the basic engineering structure of a product, so that a single machine shop or assembly line can turn out, within a single day, more than one model of automobile, computer, or video (now DVD) recorder.

SMED literally refers to a single kind of procedure involving a single kind of machine, but Shingo's book covers a huge variety of setup operations involving every conceivable kind of machine. Evidently, the hard variant of flexibility was widely practiced in the Japanese engineering and electronics industries, and wherever it was put in place, engineers could adjust the output of machine shops and assembly lines to allow for sudden and unexpected fluctuations in demand. Shingo's attitude toward craft workers and their skills was much like that of Taylor toward the skilled machinists at the Midvale Company in the 1880s. Shingo thought that the "intuition" that was so much a part of their skills (and of which the craft workers were proud) gave rise to error and inefficiency. A better alternative, he believed, was to look at ways of simplifying and standardizing the work so that it could be performed by virtually anyone, which meant implementing strategies that lowered the skill level required for the setup itself.[38] This was at odds with a general belief at the time, namely that the most effective policies for dealing with setups should be to address the problems in terms of skill. Indeed, as late as 1990, the authors of *The Machine That Changed the World* claimed that SMED needed an "extremely skilled" workforce.[39]

Shingo also thought that the chief responsibility for designing these new, simplified routines rested with managers and engineers, not frontline workers. Like Taylor, Shingo tended to be critical of these workers, whom he regarded as the creators and defenders of inefficiency on the shop floor. As with all systems of scientific management, managers had to conduct "a detailed analysis of each elemental operation" so that the fastest and most efficient way of doing the job could then be worked out; from thereon, this "one best way" should be followed by frontline workers. Once the system was up and running, "quality ... improves, since operating conditions are fully regulated in advance."[40]

In addition to checking, maintaining, and correcting machines, as well as taking responsibility for die changes when production switched to a different model, "multi-skilling" was extended to the assembly line itself. This occurred through the development of "U-shaped" or "parallel-configured lines" which enabled a worker to perform tasks on both sides of the line.[41] Ohno noted that the reconfiguration of the assembly line made it possible for workers to operate as many as three or four machines if necessary.

In completing its development, JIT was applied beyond the production process itself, backward to the suppliers of parts and forward to the distributors of cars. From now on, parts were supplied when needed on a daily basis directly to the factory, while production was tailored to demand; both minimized stockpiling and saved on storage space.[42]

It is obvious that a successful JIT system is heavily dependent on total quality control (TQC), that was in this case applied to all aspects of auto production, from pre-production testing to eliminate design faults, to "a given level of quality determined by what consumers desire and are willing to pay for."[43] For example, keeping the factory clean and tidy is a TQC priority and the responsibility of every employee since it is conducive to the safety of labor and machinery; problems with either disrupt production. Workers also check their machines before they start to operate them and undertake preventive maintenance. Consequently, TQC is a company-wide exercise to improve quality at every stage of production; if a defect is detected, it is dealt with at source rather than at the end of the process by randomly selected inspections. Like JIT, TQC saves on time (fewer rework hours), on labor (fewer inspectors), and on materials (fewer defective parts). The emphasis on quality and the transfer of responsibility for it from management to the shop floor alters the role of production workers and therefore the necessary training of these workers.

In order to achieve *kaizen*, training in quality issues is followed up with time set aside for workers to study production methods and make suggestions about how to enhance the production process as members of quality control circles (QCC). According to Michael Cusumano in his 1985 study of the Japanese auto industry, formally structured QCCs were developed as work groups because it was thought that workers would then feel more comfortable since working in groups was common in Japanese schools. He also noted that Toyota and Nissan executives regarded QCCs as primarily concerned with increasing worker participation and morale. The main purpose of QCCs may be their human relations function, but they can also save money, as became apparent at Nissan, for example. Between 1974 and 1984 quality circles saved this company some $160 million, which amounted to about $5,000 per circle.[44] As a result of this integrative approach to quality assurance, in the late 1970s the recall rate of Japanese cars sold in the U.S. was one-third that of American companies.

The third component of the JLP system is teamwork (TW), which is vital to the efficacy of both JIT and TQC. The team concept is also used as a metaphor for friendly cooperation as in a sports team, a perspective that favors the propagation of a unitary company culture, manifested among other things, by single status uniforms and dining rooms. Both meanings of TW evoke social egalitarianism and feature prominently in the rhetoric of managerial discourses that encourage all employees to identify with the company, thus blurring distinctions within the workforce. The main focus here will be on TW production because it is considered central to the success of JLP; it is the dynamic work team that constitutes the heart of the lean factory.

Womack, Jones, and Roos discern three stages in the process of developing efficient TW. Workers are trained in a variety of skills to facilitate job rotation; they are taught additional skills, such as simple machine repairs to ensure continuous production; and they are encouraged to think creatively to resolve problems before they fester into major ones. Team leaders coordinate the work of teams as well as undertake assembly tasks, while responsibility is effectively transferred from management to work teams, not to individual workers. It is claimed that, as a result of teamwork JLP increases productivity, job satisfaction, and that—like JIT and TQC—TW can be transplanted successfully to other countries. For Womack et al. there is a sharp contrast between Fordism and JLP. Instead of the monotony of task fragmentation and extreme alienation, there is rotation of multi-skilled tasks and empowerment as part of creative work teams that produce a great variety of high quality products at lower costs. In their eyes, JLP is therefore the "new best way" and they assert that once fully implemented, companies will be able "to automate most of the remaining repetitive tasks" and "by the end of the century we expect that lean-assembly plants will be populated almost entirely by highly skilled problem solvers."[45]

But in contrast to what this and other celebratory accounts of JLP suggest, it certainly did not live up to these rosy expectations. According to Christian Berggren, writing in 1993, the prescription of Womack et al. that the West should adopt the Japanese production system lock, stock, and barrel was out of step with the debate in Japan at the time, and represented a regression in terms of working conditions as well as individual freedom, when compared to Western "best practice," epitomized by the Swedish concept of teamwork and production (which will be discussed later). By the end of the 1980s, the Japanese labor market had become increasingly tight and criticisms about industrial conditions, long working hours, and exacting physical environment were widespread. Manufacturing firms were encountering increasing recruitment problems and there was a high turnover rate among new hires. Moreover, Japan's Auto Workers' Union had become active in this field and now forcefully demanded a "new industrial policy." Berggren suggested that "The real challenge for the 1990s and the new century is to amalgamate the contributions of lean production and of European human-centered manufacturing to create new syntheses."[46] So far, such new syntheses have failed to emerge, however.

JLP Compared with Fordism

In order to fine tune the picture of JLP, this system will be assessed with reference to the key features of Fordism. These can be summarized as follows: (1) fragmentation and simplification of work via Taylorized tasks; (2) managerial control over the pace of work via the moving assembly line; (3) standardization of parts and a high volume of low-quality products.[47]

First, although the Taylorized fragmentation of tasks has been altered in JLP to the extent that workers are trained to perform a variety of direct and indirect tasks (assembly line work and preventive maintenance work, respectively), the essence of Taylorism is retained and even applied more thoroughly. Cusumano noted that at Toyota, Ohno introduced time and motion studies to revise "standard operation sheets to make it easier for unskilled workers to perform more efficiently" and sought "to redistribute worker motions and cycle times to eliminate idle time for a series of workers, and then remove one or more of them or have the last person on the line take over the tasks of its neighbor, and so on down the line."[48] While both techniques for improving productivity originally hailed from the United States, Ohno applied them much more rigorously, determined as he was to eliminate all unnecessary movements and idle time for machines or workers.

A study of a GM-Suzuki joint venture in Canada has shown that the rhetoric of continuous improvement (CI), job enrichment, and job rotation was severely at odds with the way in which CI was narrowly operationalized in practice. The emphasis was on cost reduction, not safety or skills, and the rotated jobs were learned easily and quickly, were highly standardized, and repetitive, involving very little discretion. For these reasons the term "multi-tasking" was considered to be a more accurate description of work under JLP than "multi-skilling."⁴⁹ Taylorism was also dominant in Nissan's factory in Britain, where the standardization of work was company policy, job rotation was rare (except to fill in for absentees) and job enlargement tended to be downward rather than upward, such as cleaning up the work space.⁵⁰

In its 1993 study, *Manufacturing Productivity*, the McKinsey Global Institute gave an account of Japanese flexible specialization, geared to the needs of McKinsey's U.S. corporate clients struggling to match the superior productivity of their Japanese counterparts. The general assumption in the chapters on the automobile assembly and the automobile parts and components industries, was that Japanese manufacturers set the standards of high productivity with methods that their U.S. competitors needed to emulate. McKinsey also singled out Toyota and its production system as the model for emulation by companies in other industries that it had surveyed, including steel, machine tools, and consumer electronics.⁵¹ According to Simon Head, the production system that McKinsey describes and recommends "is an advanced system of scientific management, firmly based on Taylor's original theories and practices, as refined by Shigeo Shingo and Taiichi Ohno." And he hastens to add that "Neither McKinsey, nor indeed Shingo, offer any support for the claims of Sabel and Piore, and of the MIT and Magaziner Commissions⁵²—that flexibility of production requires a workforce with 'very high skills,' including craft skills."⁵³

This becomes clear indeed from the skills required for most workers involved in flexible manufacturing in the automobile industry. In its analysis of skill, McKinsey drew a distinction between basic skills that are the "pre-hiring skills" of prospective employees, and their "post-training" skills that the employer must develop. McKinsey's unambiguous finding was that for auto manufacture, high productivity could be achieve with a workforce that only needed to have the most basic skills—the reason why post-training worker skills were undemanding as well. This was in accord with what Simon Head was told at the Nissan and Honda companies he visited in Europe.⁵⁴ According to McKinsey, Japanese companies screened applicants to find those with "attitudinal factors that make [them] more flexible, less likely to call in sick, and committed to remaining on the job for a long period of time."⁵⁵ Although McKinsey did not explicitly say what these pre-hiring skills were, one may assume that these were the skills of basic literacy and numeracy that, according to the Magaziner Commission, enabled an employee to "read a production schedule or follow an instruction card."⁵⁶ McKinsey did not count "craft-based individual excellence" as one of these skills. Tellingly, it considered the craft tradition of German industry as an obstacle to the achievement of high productivity, stating that "in Germany the focus on specialization has led to excessively high complexity in the production process."[57]

In retrospect, the Japanese companies concerned have revived a long-established American system of production that had been showing signs of aging, thus giving it a new lease on life. This has enabled U.S. manufacturers to improve their performance while maintaining a workplace regime that had existed for most of the 20th century. Admittedly, these Japanese methods have improved the output per worker, or labor productivity, of both Japanese and American manufacturing companies. But the new Taylorism developed by the Japanese came at a severe cost for labor. Like the old Taylorism, it undervalues employee skill and experience, subjects employees to a pervasive regime of monitoring and control, and enables an all-powerful management to treat its workforce as a commodity. It is clear that these enduring characteristics of scientific management have a most negative impact on the quality of working life. Historically, it was the role of labor unions to shield the industrial workforce from the more noxious aspects of the Taylorized system, notably its unending drive towards speed-up. But the resuscitation of scientific management by the Japanese came at a time when organized labor in the U.S. was in severe decline. In 2001, 14.6 percent of the U.S. manufacturing workforce in the United States belonged to labor unions, compared with 27.8 percent in 1983. And the "big three" Japanese automakers—Toyota, Nissan, and Honda—have all been successful in keeping the UAW out of their U.S. plants.[58]

Criticism has also been leveled at the idea that JLP is an improvement over Taylorism in that it reunites mental and manual labor. JLP involves a refinement of Taylorism, not a rejection of it. Workers have always used both their brains and their muscles, typically to make their work easier. What distinguishes JLP is the method used to collect workers' knowledge: workers share their knowledge with team members and the team's supervisor or manager in quality circles.[59] The introduction of a participative form of Taylorism is more effective because it reduces costs by cutting down on specialists and lessens antagonism by encouraging workers to be actively complicit in their subordination to the JLP goal of continuous improvement.[60] David Nye seems to suggest that the communication between workers and managers takes place on an egalitarian basis. The Japanese corporations in question "had abandoned hierarchical communication down a chain of command in favor of dialogue.... They assiduously encouraged workers to make suggestions, and workers' suggestions then became the basis for innovation. Institutionalizing dialogue between workers, managers, engineers, designers, and marketers improved quality, efficiency, and safety."[61] But the term "dialogue" is misleading here, as it hides the exploitative nature of the relationship between managers and workers in extracting practical knowledge from workers.

The second key feature of Fordist production concerns the assembly line. Proponents of JLP admit that this involves a tougher pace of work, but still consider it more fulfilling for workers. The alleged benefits of JLP assembly-line work are thought to derive from workers' ability to stop the line, the opportunity to perform multiple "skilled" operations in teams, and the sense of pride in producing high quality goods. But even advocates of JLP have found that workers in U.S. plants were put under pressure by management not to stop the assembly line.[62] A study of a nonunion Japanese automobile transplant located near Lafayette, Indiana, found that there was the tendency to limit the authority to stop the line to team leaders or higher ranking company officials only. And when the line speed was increased, it led to more hand and wrist injuries to workers who were expected to continue working with splints on their wrists. Furthermore, if the production quota were not met, worker overtime was made compulsory and announced at short notice.[63]

The intensification of work on a JLP assembly line has been confirmed by many studies, including that of the GM plant in California which became a Toyota-GM joint venture in 1984 (and closed in 2010). The old GM practice entailed 45 seconds of actual work performed during each minute. By contrast, the Toyota standard for work performed within a minute was 57 seconds; that is, only three seconds of "rest," or non-performance were allowed.[64] The extremely brief time reserved for this respite from physical effort only added to the stress already inherent to most types of work. The main sources of intensification in a JLP plant, according to the Nissan, United Kingdom study previously mentioned, were the requirement to help and/or cover for other team members and the extra responsibilities assigned to teams such as quality checks.[65] These accounts of the demanding nature of work in JLP plants are indicative of what labor experts Mike Parker and Jane Slaughter have called a "management by stress" system.[66]

Working on an assembly line in teams is portrayed by proponents as a distinctive and positive dimension of JLP. But there is also a clear downside to this teamwork—namely pressure. This has been publicly recognized by some JLP advocates, notably John MacDuffie.[67] Peer pressure is integral to a JLP system in which multiple responsibilities are assigned to teams. This setup forces co-workers in the team to cover for an absent, injured or slower team member. It turns the work group into the supervisor and disciplinarian of the underperforming worker, a feature reminiscent of the notorious group piecework systems of the 1920s. Thus, even if workers are less convinced of the unitary team concept, teams operate as a powerful horizontal supplement to hierarchical supervision that can "boost attendance, job performance, and kaizen activities."[68] Moreover, pressure to work hard can result from the internalization of corporate goals, even though there is often a discrepancy between the management TW rhetoric and the reality of infrequent and poorly attended team meetings at which only the team leader speaks. For workers, peer pressure is yet another form of social control.

A basic precondition for this system is an intense personnel selection system. Japanese companies tend to adopt a lengthy and highly selective recruitment process to weed out those who do not show the required attitudinal and behavioral attributes.[69] Applicants who have worked in the American auto industry are not given special consideration; quite the contrary, this is thought to be a disadvantage for learning the required new work habits. Further, applicants' formal educational background is not considered important. The screening process, as it was presented by a Toyota personnel director in 1990, is very rigorous. Applicants first undergo intelligence tests. The lower fifty percent are automatically eliminated. The remaining applicants have to do a dexterity test, and again the less gifted are taken out of the running. This is followed by tests designed to reveal the applicants' ambitions, initiative, and creativity. Group orientation and social skills are further bases for selection. According to Toyota's personnel department, the result of this process is a prototypical worker who is aggressively oriented to performance, who is bent on being the best, and who wants to succeed in a career.[70] Those hired are often put on temporary contracts on a trial basis with the promise of a permanent contract if they live up to company expectations.[71] It goes without saying that temporary nonunion workers are also more vulnerable, easy to lay off when necessary. JLP plants favor a compliant workforce that lacks independent trade union representation and is therefore more likely to cooperate with management over a range of production rationalizations. For their transplants in America (and more generally the West), Japanese companies have shown a clear preference for high-unemployment, somewhat rural, nonunion regions where the workers have few job opportunities, because this increases the likelihood of recruiting a loyal and dedicated workforce.[72]

For a better understanding of the Japanese model of teamwork, it is worthwhile to compare it to its Swedish counterpart, developed during the 1970s and 1980s at two of Volvo's car plants in Sweden: in Kalmar (existing from 1974 to 1994) and Uddevalla (from 1989 to 1993).[73] According to Christian Berggren, the Swedish model differed significantly from those of the Japanese automobile-assembly and automobile-related steel and rubber industries in Europe and North America. (These transplants were either fully Japanese-owned or had significant Japanese participation in joint ventures.) First, in the

Swedish case the organizational changes were strongly linked to changes in the production setup, which was aimed at creating conditions in which functional groups would have some technical autonomy. The work teams at the Japanese transplants, by contrast, were organized directly on the assembly line. Second, the Swedish version of teamwork was characterized by an endeavor to increase the workers' organizational autonomy and scope for independent decision making. The teams often selected their own leaders or group representatives and performed tasks that previously had been done by foremen and industrial engineers. Third, the role of first-line management was changed from having direct control over workers to coordinating, planning, and supporting the labor process. At the Japanese transplants, by contrast, teamwork usually went hand in hand with strengthening the managerial structure. In many cases—Nissan in Britain and Toyota in the state of Kentucky in the U.S., for instance—the team was tightly organized around the foreman. These forms of teamwork entailed a reduction of worker autonomy and an increase in managerial control. Fourth, in Sweden, the Metal Workers' Union strongly committed itself, both centrally and locally, to the development of the new organizational form. The union was especially interested in bolstering the teams' decision-making prerogatives, as well as the prospects for developing collective competence.

The Swedish model represented a social compromise between different interests: between management's aim to delegate tasks and responsibility without ceding control, and the union's aspiration to achieve a genuine shift in the balance of power. This meant, among other things, that the boundaries of the work teams' autonomy and decision-making power could not be deduced from some guiding concept. Rather, these boundaries were more like temporary settlements in a still-contested terrain. The labor market conditions, the role of labor unions, government policies and national institutions of the time must all be taken into account here. In the Swedish case, high employment levels and strong labor unions were decisive factors in the development of work patterns involving a qualitative enhancement of autonomy and self-management. The Japanese firms, by contrast, generally dealt with acquiescent unions and highly dependent workers who submitted to their relentless demands. With the exception of a brief period prior to the first oil crisis (1973), when "humanization of work" was an issue in Japan as well, these companies never felt obliged to confront and change the character of the work itself, such as its fragmentation, intensity, and inexorable mechanical control. Japanese workers resented the work but generally complied with the demands of their employers.

A comprehensive decentralization of decision-making prerogatives flowing from management to the work teams—as in the Swedish model—has considerable productive potential, but also involves the risk from the managerial perspective that workers will use their increased resources to defend themselves against the demands of the economic system by restricting both their own work efforts and management's insights into the production process. This is one of the reasons why work developments on the shop floor in the Swedish auto companies have often been hesitant and inconsistent. The Japanese model of team work escapes this ambiguity. Delegation of responsibility, for quality, for example, takes place within the framework of a tight regime, complete with precise visual control systems, intensive personnel selection, and a wide range of disciplinary measures. Thus the possibility of collective worker action and of various forms of opposition and restrictions of output is eliminated.[74]

Mike Parker and Jane Slaughter contend that this team concept is insidious in that it undermines unionism through a dubious form of participation in management decisions. The erosion of negotiated work rules in the auto industry leads to a deterioration in the rights-based quality of the workplace. Workers are well aware that failure to cooperate with management often leads to economic and organizational penalties in the form of layoffs, work transfers, and plant closures. Parker and Slaughter claim that the JLP system undercuts worker autonomy, retaking many of the most negative elements of the early 20th-century drive system of punitive supervision. Despite the rhetoric of worker participation, the team concept and other participatory schemes in this context are basically strategies to enhance management control. Far from offering a humane alternative to Taylorism, workers mainly "participate" in the intensification of their own exploitation, mobilizing their detailed firsthand knowledge of the labor process to help management speed up production and eliminate wasteful work practices.[75] It is probably best characterized by the oxymoron "flexible Taylorism."[76]

The third key feature of Fordism, the standardization of parts and low quality products, was overcome in JLP by making every effort "to put together a specialized, yet versatile production process through the use of machines and jigs that can handle minimal quantities of materials" to produce a variety of products without "undermining the benefits of mass production."[77] So, contrary to the claim that JLP is beyond mass production,[78] lean production is still mass production (as Taiichi Ohno has acknowledged and many others have confirmed). As the expert on Toyota's production methods, Shigeo Shingo, pointed out in relation to the voluminous production of Toyota's Corolla, Toyota's CEO made having small inventories a priority, choosing therefore to concentrate on small-batch manufacturing. The object, nevertheless, was to produce the *highest possible cumulative volume* of each product. Long *total* runs were (and are) decisive for carefully preparing the fabrication of each part, standardizing tools, methods, and operations, and streamlining suppliers in developing the JIT flow.⁷⁹ It would therefore be more accurate to describe JLP as a manufacturing system designed for a large number of small batches and Fordism as a system for the production of a small number of large batches.

The continued importance of economies of large-scale production to JLP is evidenced by the tendency of such companies to reduce model variations in order to cut costs. For example, in 2003, customers were offered a choice of 54 options for the Toyota Corolla and 130 for the Honda Accord, while there were over ten million options for the Ford Focus, and twelve million for the Vauxhall (General Motors UK) Astra produced in Britain.⁸⁰ Product variation was pioneered by GM during the rise of Fordism in the 1920s, and by the early 2000s, Western auto manufacturers were still ahead of the founders of JLP in terms of consumer choice. This flies in the face of Womack et al.'s assertion that it was only under JLP that a "true renaissance of consumer choice" was achieved.⁸¹

Finally, the JLP advocates' claim that the quality dimension of this "new best way of manufacturing" cars is a major improvement on Fordism has been confirmed by consumer surveys. But, as Stephen Edgell has pointed out, the JLP reputation for high quality products was dealt a severe blow in 2009–10 when Toyota had to recall over 8.5 million cars for safety checks following numerous complaints and accidents, some of which were fatal, linked to problems with braking, accelerator pedals, and slipping floor mats. After this global recall, the view that JLP, pioneered by Toyota, resulted in high quality products, was no longer indisputable.⁸² By 2008, lean principles had taken hold at each of the Detroit three (GM, Ford, and Chrysler) and they were producing high quality products according to expert reviews.⁸³ But recent recalls such as the one in 2014 by General Motors regarding faulty ignition switches of its small cars, throw some serious doubts on these claims as well.

In conclusion, the lean production system that has been implemented in manufacturing is a reformed version of Fordism, or *neo–Fordism*, with the following key features: (1) qualified Taylorized work tasks and limited job enlargement and rotation; (2) intensified work on a modified assembly line organized into teams with limited autonomy; (3) partial destandardization of parts and an increasingly limited range of higher-quality products.⁸⁴ This is in contrast to a *post–Fordist* interpretation of industrial JLP which recognizes the following key features: (1) re-unification of mental and physical labor, job rotation and multi-skilling; (2) flexible assembly line operated by teams of empowered workers; (3) nonstandardized parts and great variety of high quality products. This interpretation, which can be found in writings such as Womack et al.'s *The Machine That Changed the World* (1990), and Kenney and Florida's *Beyond Mass Production* (1993), proved to be wrong given the available evidence. It has been criticized for its management bias, relative neglect of JLP's negative impact on workers, and for exaggerating the discontinuities with Fordism.[85] In the end, lean production can best be called neo–Taylorism, for it still rests on both Taylorist and Fordist labor management premises.[86]

Generally, lean production also brought new ways to organize and extend work time. Nonstandard or contingent forms of work such as part-time, temporary, and "self-employed" contract work expanded enormously (with the increase of most of the part-time work being "involuntary" part-time employment). This meant larger proportions of flexi- and temporary workers who experienced job insecurity, and were deprived of important job benefits and social provisions. The majority of women in most forms of nonstandard jobs were women; their jobs paid less per hour than full-time work, and their hours were determined by the employer, not the worker in most cases.

Two other important developments in working time associated with lean production were longer hours, often due to increased overtime, and alternative work schedules. Like nonstandard work, overtime from existing workers allowed employers to meet the ebbs and flows of demand; it provided them with a buffer at layoff time which precluded the hiring of more permanent full-time workers. Overtime also played a key role in the alternative work schedules. Such a schedule does away with the standard eight-hour day, Monday to Friday week. Instead of day and night shifts (and the traditional three-shift system for 24 hours), the workforce is divided into three crews. Each crew works a ten- or twelve-hour day, sometimes three days on and three days off, while two of the "weeks" are stretched over the weekend. In most cases, the workers rotate crews. Both the longer day and the constant rotation have severe ramifications for health. Not only is the longer day more exhausting, rotation has a devastating effect on sleep—it interrupts the body's natural circadian rhythms. The longer day also increases the risks of accidents and injuries due to fatigue and exposure to various chemicals and materials.[87]

By the early 2000s, "lean" thinking had also been widely applied in nonmanufacturing sectors.[88] As will be shown later, lean principles have come to dominate call center services (supposedly to improve live agent call handling), and have been adapted to industries as diverse as insurance and health care. "Lean" has even been implemented in software application development and maintenance, as well as other areas of information technology, particularly in the case of Indian IT companies doing work outsourced by U.S. corporations.[89]

7

Industrial Rationalization of Retail and Service Work Intensified

The flexible manufacturing techniques of lean production are more marketing-led and customer-oriented than traditional mass production, and are characterized by a tighter integration of the stages from design and production to distribution or circulation. Just-in-time production enables the manufacturer to operate with minimal quantities of inventory—with components arriving as close as possible to the moment when they are required. It also allows production to be undertaken and completed, as far as possible, only on the basis of orders from customers (e.g., retailers), which tend to be based on information about actual sales. In this system logistics play a key role, allowing for the geographic dispersion of production. Flexible specialization relies on decentralizing production to small subcontractors who are capable of providing the diversity of output and the flexibility demanded by the market, as registered by, and filtered through, the main producer. With the advent of accelerated economic globalization, outsourcing has become ever more central to lean production, but far less place-bound than was the case with lean production in its original Japanese form. This practice, in turn, allows for pushing down labor costs, increasingly crossing borders in search of the cheapest workers.[1]

In the auto industry, which still tended to be the trend-setter in work and product reorganization, another significant change took place in the late 1990s with the introduction of "modular production." This system, in which first-line supplier firms provide assembled modules—like the entire interior of a cockpit rather than dozens of pieces—brought about a basic reorganization; first-line suppliers were brought in under tight control of the big assembly corporations, as happened at GM among others. Further down the chain, smaller firms produced for the now larger first-line companies. The reorganization of an industry involving long-distance, just-in-time, and international production by a few top corporations became possible because of the command-and-control technology that had become available (notably Total Quality Control, to be analyzed in the next chapter). The geographic decentralization of production through outsourcing, was actually enabled by a growth in centralized power. As Bennett Harrison put it, "*Production* must be decentralized into a wider and more geographically far-flung number of work sites, but *power*, *finance*, and *control* remain concentrated in the hands of the managers of the largest companies in the global economy."[2]

The system of extended lean production demanded an intensified and partly other means of control of the logistics that held it together. New technologies came into use to track and control workers on the move. In addition to the technologies used for domination of traditional workplaces, industrial capital likewise had to find a way to keep track of, and speed up the work, of truck drivers, field repair and maintenance people, and others who work beyond the immediate reach of supervisors. Like early operations research and numerical control, it was again the military that developed the necessary new technology—namely the Global Positioning System (GPS)—which tracks moving objects or persons via satellites thousands of miles above earth.

The renewed significance of logistics in both trade and lean production led to other technological changes in transportation. For example, at railroads (which had again become important due in part to containerization in sea transports) new efforts to reduce and control labor developed, such as Remote Control Operation (RCO) of trains in the rail yard and single-person operation over long distances. Automatic trackside detectors and Centralized Traffic Control have been eliminating brakemen, rear flagmen, and on-board maintenance crews. Taken together, these and other technologies reduced the responsibilities—as well as the job satisfaction and workplace control—of the service crew.[3]

Tracking employees in road transportation and delivery is becoming ever more intense and extensive. A worst case scenario from the perspective of workers' control is the constant upgrading of the systems employed by UPS. At the time of this writing, its trucks are full of sensors that report all kinds of events: when the driver opens the bulkhead door, when he backs up, when his foot is on the brake, when he is idling, when he buckles his safety belt and so forth. Thus, a high-resolution stream of data, including all that information and the truck's GPS coordinates, flow back to the UPS offices. This system, called "telematics," means additional pressure to that of the classic UPS protocols that a driver already had to follow. These entail strict guidelines derived from time-and-motion studies that tell the driver the most efficient way to do everything: how to handle the ignition key, which shirt pocket to use for his pen (right-handed people should use the left pocket, and vice versa), how to choose a "walk path" from the truck, and how to spend time while riding in an elevator. Now drivers are called to account for a variety of small transgressions. They have to justify bathroom breaks and any other deviations—"stealing time" in corporate speak—that could chip away at their SPORH count (Stops Per On-Road Hour). This also includes, for example, turning on the truck before putting on one's seat belt, which wastes gas.

All of the current and former drivers that investigative journalist Jessica Bruder interviewed in 2015, said that they felt like they were working in what can best be described as a panopticon, in effect, being monitored by management all the time.[4] (The panopticon is a type of institutional building originally designed by the English philosopher Jeremy Bentham. The design's concept concerned a prison built in such a way that all the inmates could be observed by a single watchman. The inmates themselves could not tell at any given time whether or not they were being watched. Today's digital variant that allows for constant, all-pervasive surveillance will be discussed in a later chapter.)

Other instances of intensified employee tracking can be found at companies such as FedEx and Amazon. At some of FedEx's warehouses, workers have been forced to wear a computerized package scanner, strapped to their right forearm. This enables management to meticulously gather data about the individual worker's manual operations and track their speed. At Amazon warehouses, management has introduced scanners that bring "management by stress" to an even higher level. Every time a worker scans a piece of merchandise, a countdown begins on his screen, indicating how many seconds he has to reach the next items. The worker's progress toward hourly goals is also tracked. When the worker deviates from the prescribed protocol and/or route, a supervisor will soon intervene.[5]

Just-in-Time Techniques in Retail

Over the past few decades, just-in-time techniques have also come to dominate the big box retail stores, with Walmart leading the way, optimally taking advantage of manufacturing and logistics brought by lean production. The system consists of a tightly controlled chain of suppliers, just-in-time movements of goods and the logistical and telecommunications technology that pulls it all together coming from Toyota and GM. The Taylorized work patterns, the extreme uniformity ("one best way") of everything, and the use of the term "associates" instead of employees or workers are also familiar components of lean production. Walmart has become the dominant retailer by strategically combining many of the methods and technologies discussed earlier: just-in-time delivery techniques and corresponding advanced logistics, an advanced IT inventory system, control over its suppliers, and globalization, meaning, above all, outsourcing to Chinese producers and suppliers. To this strategy, as Nelson Lichtenstein has pointed out, it has added a level of central control and managerial authoritarianism (rooted in the company's very beginnings in Arkansas) that goes far beyond what most corporations achieve.[6] Thus Walmart has created a "brave new world of business" as the poignant subtitle of Lichtenstein's book on Walmart signals.[7]

In recent years, Walmart has added control technologies that rely on factory discipline to extract higher output from its already overstretched shopfloor workforce. Foremost among these technologies is "Task Manager," a targeting and monitoring system, which Walmart introduced in its stores from 2010 onward. The system tells employees what to do, how much time this should maximally take, and whether they have met their target times. Employees sign on to the system by swiping their identity cards on a terminal, and the system then delivers its instructions. Employees who fail to meet the target times mandated by Task Managers are then punished, whereby management uses an elaborate system of penalties.[8]

Amazon equals Walmart in the use of monitoring techniques to track the minute-by-minute movements and performance of employees and in settings that go beyond the assembly line to include their movement between loading and unloading docks, between packing and unpacking stations, and to and from the miles of shelves at what Amazon calls its "fulfillment centers"—gigantic warehouses where goods ordered by Amazon's online customers are sent by manufacturers and wholesalers, to be shelved, packaged, and shipped to Amazon customers.

Amazon's management of shop-floor processes constitutes an extreme variant of Taylorism. Management experts take the basic workplace tasks at Amazon, such as the movement, shelving, and packaging of goods, and break these tasks down into subtasks, usually measured in seconds. Then they rely on time and motion studies to find the fastest way to perform such subtasks, and subsequently reassemble the subtasks to make this "one best way" the process that employees must follow. On the packing lines there are modern-day versions of "functional foremen," supervisors and line managers (in Amazonspeak, "co-workers" and "leads"), whose collective task is to fight "time theft" by workers and keep the line moving, but also to try to find ways of making it move faster. The paramount purpose is to continue pushing up employee productivity, while keeping hourly wages at or near poverty level.[9]

Walmart also pays very low wages and fails to provide affordable health insurance (with good coverage and low insurance deductibles) for a majority of its domestic retail workers. Many of these workers belong to the working poor and have to rely on public "safety net" programs, such as the Supplemental Nutritional Assistance Program or SNAP (commonly known as food stamps), the federal-state Children's Health Insurance Program (CHIP), Medicaid, Medicare, and subsidized housing—next to Earned Income Tax Credits—to make ends meet.[10]

The abovementioned "lean" techniques have been so powerful in their retail application, and so successful in cutting costs and then prices, that it forced Walmart's competitors to follow suit, just as Toyota and GM have forced other car makers to emulate their "lean and mean" strategies. For the same reasons Walmart managed to grow without taking recourse to mergers or acquisitions as corporate America typically tends to do. The exception was abroad where Walmart bought up stores and chains, such as Asda in Britain. At home Walmart grew through the simple expansion of capital, the wringing of tax concessions from state and local governments, and so forth. But its competitive edge and lead in the retail sector was based first and foremost on its ability to keep prices low by keeping its direct labor costs low (which was of course also the major reason for Walmart's virulent anti-unionism), by the stranglehold it exercised over its suppliers by virtue of its sheer size, and by extensive purchasing from China in particular.[11]

Industrial Rationalization in Interactive Service Work

In the early 1970s, Braverman assessed the state of affairs within retail in terms of worker skills and management control. He argued that recent technological advances—notably computer- and checkout systems that involve bar code scanning—eroded the skill requirements of the checkout worker further still, while simultaneously increasing centralized management control, whereby the checkout counter "adopts as its own the assembly line or factory pace in its most complete form."[12] The introduction of scanning technology was a form of work intensification in that it enabled the checkout operator to process at least twice as many customers than previously, when items were recorded using a manual keyboard. Further differences with retail sales work as it existed prior to Taylorist rationalization included reduced training, pay, and job prospects. And just like the early years of Fordism, labor turnover increased markedly and an anti-union attitude by employers became widespread. Retail automation became associated with reduced staffing levels, especially of full-time workers, as well as deskilled workers, typically women and young people, who are employed when needed on a part-time basis, such as at lunchtime and weekends.[13]

Robin Leidner has introduced the helpful designations "interactive service workers" and "specialist service workers." The first category includes employees who engage with service recipients (e.g., customers, clients, etc.) either face-to-face or voice-to-voice; an emotional component is at its core. Specialist service workers on the other hand perform tasks that pivot around knowledge.[14] The distinction between emotion workers and knowledge workers does not mean that knowledge is unimportant in the first case or that emotion is irrelevant in the second case; it is a matter of centrality rather than exclusivity, as Leidner makes clear. Here the focus is on face-to-face interactive service work; at the end of Chapter 9, call center work (the major form of voice-to-voice interactive service work today) will be scrutinized. Specialist service work will be examined at various places in subsequent chapters.

The similarities of industrial and interactive service work highlighted by Braverman, were also observed, albeit in a less critical way, by Theodore Levitt, who argued that the efficiency and quality of service provision could be improved by adopting the methods of mass production along the lines of the McDonald's chain of fast-food restaurants. Levitt credited the success of McDonald's mainly to the application of industrial mass production to a people-intensive service production system, whose Fordist aim was to produce a high volume of low-priced standard goods speedily and cheaply. As with the mass production of cars, the mass production of burgers is characterized by fragmented and simplified work tasks, single-purpose machines organized in the form of an assembly line, and the use of standardized parts and products. For example, the raw materials, such as the meat, are pre-measured, pre-packed, and cooked with the aid of lights and buzzers which signal when to turn the burgers, thus eliminating any discretion on the part of the workers.[15]

Levitt's analysis of McDonald's as an exemplar of a Fordist approach to interactive service work was corroborated by John F. Love's historical account of McDonald's.[16] In 1948, after several years of experimentation, the McDonald brothers closed their small but successful drive-in restaurant and changed their business model in an attempt to take their enterprise to a higher level. The kitchen was redesigned to facilitate speedier and higher volume production, china was replaced by disposable bags and cups, the menu selection was reduced to either a hamburger or a cheeseburger (with a given set of condiments), and customers placed their order at a service window, together streamlining the service production process. The price was cut from a competitive 30 cents to an unheard-of 15 cents per burger. Their new type of fast-food restaurants was based on speed, volume, and lower prices, along with a strict adherence to detailed, standardized work procedures. In the 1950s, McDonald's was transformed into a national corporation in the United States, and then became an international in the 1970s under the directorship of Ray Kroc, who saw to it that every McDonald's restaurant followed the same technological and organizational specifications. The McDonald's operations manual described in detail the correct way for workers to perform every task and the correct way for managers to run a fast-food restaurant like an assembly line.[17]

Levitt's Fordist characterization of McDonald's was also confirmed and extended by George Ritzer, who argued that the principles of the fast-food restaurant pioneered by McDonald's—notably bureaucracy, scientific management, and the assembly line—were spreading to the whole of American society, and further across the world. Ritzer analyzed McDonaldization from a neo–Weberian perspective (with its focus on the rationalization of work and society) in terms of four basic dimensions: efficiency, calculability, predictability and control. He concluded that McDonaldization has many things in common with the Fordist industrialization of work: Taylorized work tasks, single-purpose machines and conveyor belt assembly, standardized parts and the speedy delivery of a high volume of inexpensive low-quality products. Moreover, in addition to being monitored by managers, subject to extensive operating rules, and controlled by machines, fast-food workers are also put under pressure by the presence of customers who expect to be served quickly and politely.[18] On the other hand, for their part, customers are incorporated into the assembly-line process too, in that they are expected to collect and dispose of the products they purchase.

Ritzer also paid attention to the interactive dimensions of the service work involved in McDonaldization. Drawing heavily on research by Leidner,[19] he extended the earlier analyses by noting that in fast-food restaurants, it is not only the tasks that are standardized, but also what workers say and how they appear to customers, which are standardized via scripts and appearance codes: "The scripting of interaction leads to new depths in the deskilling of workers."[20]

The requirement to follow scripts, subscripts, wear uniforms, and show appropriate expressive behavior (smiling), not only point to standardization and deskilling, but also to the emotional labor intrinsic to interactive service work. The concept of "emotional labor" originates in Arlie Russell Hochschild's seminal book, *The Managed Heart: Commercialization of Human Feeling* (1983), which builds upon the pioneering analysis of the commodification of feelings and appearances by C. Wright Mills.[21] Hochschild defined emotional labor as "the management of feeling to create a publicly observable facial and bodily display."[22] Based on her analysis of flight attendants, she showed that while they are performing manual tasks such as pushing a meal trolley and thinking how best to distribute refreshments, they are also expected to be friendly and reassuring. Hochschild presented the flight attendants as her paradigmatic emotional laborer, though the practice she identified involves many types of middle- and lower-income service workers: shop, hotel, and restaurant workers, secretaries and receptionists, nurses and home-care workers, as well as the workforce of customer relations as a whole. Such emotional labor relies heavily on these workers' reserves of enthusiasm and empathy, sources of self that they see as deep and integral to their individuality. Hochschild was concerned that the employer demands corrode and distort our inner self and blur the distinction between the self that is inherent to our individuality and the self we have to present to the outside world in order to fulfill our obligations as emotional laborers.

The strategies that employees deploy to deal with the rigors of emotional labor originate in private life, but in the course of their transfer from the private to the commercial sphere, these strategies must undergo a radical transformation. In the private sphere, our reliance on them is shaped by us and by the rhythms and daily occurrences of our lives. But once transposed to the commercial sphere, the strategies become components of production and the white-collar assembly line. Hochschild concluded that interactive service workers who are required by their employing organizations to express certain emotions, such as friendliness, while disguising their true feelings, experience alienation from both the service product and the labor process. For this, she drew directly on Marx's theory of alienation.

Hochschild's argument that all interactive service workers who perform emotional labor are alienated has not gone unchallenged. Marek Korczynski has pointed out that not all worker-customer relations are marketized, unequal and fleeting. He contrasted the low alienation of service workers in public or voluntary organizations with the high alienation in worker-customer relations experienced by market-driven, instrumental interactive service workers in profit-driven organizations.[23] On the other hand, however, Jackie Krasas Rogers found in her in-depth study of a small number of temporary clerical workers that one of the main social costs of this type of flexible work is alienation from work, from other workers, and from oneself.[24] Yet another U.S. study showed that the more staff in a highly bureaucratic fire department were consulted by their superiors, the less alienated they were in terms of powerlessness, meaninglessness and estrangement. Conversely, and generally speaking, the more authoritarian the leadership style, the more alienated the personnel.[25] One can find support for this in an exploratory study of quick service restaurant staff. Here alienation proved to be unevenly distributed, indicating that it was not caused by the type of technology used, but by the style of management in different restaurants.[26] Overall, these studies suggest that contemporary work situations retain several possible sources of alienation, "sufficient to temper any overly optimistic generalization about the historical decline of alienation."[27]

As becomes clear from Hochschild' account of flight attendants' appearance codes (that covered everything from hairstyles to shoe styles), interactive service work also involves an aesthetic dimension, called "aesthetic labor," which concerns "embodied capacities and attributes," including both visual and aural appearances.[28] What is distinctive about interactive service work therefore is the presence of the recipients of services, which complicates the contest over control in this type of work. In theory, the complex alignment of each interest group is unstable, but in practice, as in the case of McDonald's, "the interests of managers and customers converged, diminishing workers' control and allowing customers to augment management's control strategies."[29] This was because customers not only shared the managerial concern for a quick and courteous service outcome, but they supplemented the managerial supervision of service workers via "the power to direct, evaluate, and reward or punish workers."[30] The servility of interactive service workers to customers as well as management is reinforced by the increasing usage of consumer service reports, the results of which are used to evaluate and discipline workers.[31]

McDonald's system of mass production of food has been emulated by many other food and non-food service organizations, such as Pizza Hut and Disney World. This has contributed to the mass consumption of a wide range of services, resulting in the growth of low-skilled, low-paid, repetitive, dead-end jobs that are widely referred to as "McJobs."[32] Unsurprisingly, there is a strong similarity between McDonald's emphasis on uniformity and teamwork and Japanese work practices.[33] The team concept, for instance, is central to McDonald's methods of managing and working, indicated most clearly by the term "crew." Operating as a team is imperative due to the tendency to minimize staffing and idle time, much the same as in the Japanese lean production-type of car factory. Some monitored variation from otherwise highly standardized scripts is also allowed "to avoid sounding like robots."[34] Crew members can attend monthly meetings at which the company conveys information to its employees. They can offer suggestions (which are hardly ever used) and complain in "real approach to problems" (RAP) sessions that are held at the end of a shift two or three times a year (which are not popular with restaurant managers). Workers can also be part of "quality action teams" that deal with specific issues such as health and safety. Tony Royle has argued that these forms of "McParticipation" focus mainly on communication and in reality are more concerned with preserving managerial prerogatives than empowering workers.[35] They constitute the McDonald's equivalent of teamwork and quality circles that are additions to a long-standing commitment to continuous improvement of how things are done on the shop floor.

In the late 1990s, when its market share in the U.S. fast-food market was declining, McDonald's introduced its version of just-in-time production called "Made for You" that involved new technology to further reduce labor costs and increase the speed at which food was served. As investigative journalist Eric Schlosser wrote, "Advanced computer software essentially runs the kitchen, assigning tasks to various workers for maximum efficiency, predicting future orders on the basis of customer flow."[36] Since restaurant crews do not start assembling an order before it is placed, it means that every order can be customized, whereas previously special orders were discouraged because they disrupted the assembly line process. Thus the achievement of individual choice (within the constraints of the given variety of products) at low mass production prices, called "mass customization," was made possible by the combination of two Japanese systems: the adaptable marketing system and the flexible manufacturing process or lean production.[37] These innovations enabled fast-food restaurants to adapt their Fordist procedures so that they could offer individualized products and respond quickly to the demand for a greater, though still limited, variety of products. For example, customers at McDonald's can request a burger with or without pickles and can select from an expanded menu that includes eggs, fish, and chicken—albeit in a standardized form. This suggests that the Fordist fast-food system has been modified in a way comparable to neo–Fordist Japanese lean production in order to meet new market conditions—namely, increased competition and changing consumer preferences.[38]

McDonald's and other similar service sector corporations have thus far been able to resist attempts to unionize fast-food workers in the U.S. Excluding trade unions, obviously enables employers such as McDonald's to maintain managerial prerogatives, pay low wages, provide poor working conditions and hardly any benefits. Resigning is one of the few ways to express job dissatisfaction. Fast-food corporations historically have been under very little pressure from their workers to improve the intrinsic or extrinsic rewards of their workforce.

This is rapidly changing, however. Beginning in November 2012, fast-food workers in various American cities—as well as nation-wide—have organized strikes and demonstrations for higher wages, better working conditions and the right to form a union without retaliation from their managers. Since December 2013, these collective actions have focused specifically on raising the minimum wage nationwide to $15 per hour; unions such as SEIU (Service Employees International Union) helped to organize at community level. Labor activists and fast-food workers were joined by home care assistants, child care aides, employees at discount and convenience stores, airport workers and others who work low-wage jobs. By 2015, this movement mushroomed in size and influence (now including Walmart workers too), and in response, fourteen cities, counties, and states around the country approved a $15 minimum wage through local laws, executive orders and other means. Dozens more ballots or legislative proposals were introduced around the country as well. With the exception of a few jurisdictions which had already enacted the raise in 2015, the new minimum wage was to be introduced in subsequent years in remaining locales according to phased-in schedules.[39] New York and California were the first states to adopt the $15 minimum pay with a phased-in schedule in April 2016.

However, at the time of this writing the federal minimum hourly wage remains as low as $7.25 (which has been in effect since 2009). This while in certain places around the country with high costs of living, $15 per hour is still below a living wage level.[40]

8

Enhanced Top-Down Management Systems in Manufacturing and Office Work

There is a crucial difference between the original Japanese model of lean production and that selectively adopted by companies in the U.S.; the latter did not promise job security to their core labor force. The cost-cutting measures of Japanese lean production were adopted without the related employment policies, which model has rightly been called "lean and mean."[1] By contrast, the original "Toyotist" model—that offered employment security to a core labor force in exchange for cooperation, but at the same time created a large buffer of less privileged workers without the same rights and benefits—might be called "lean and dual."[2] This guarantee of life-time security to core workers was either modified or abandoned altogether as Japan's economy ran aground in the 1990s.

Initially, Japanese lean production was characterized by the right of workers to stop the assembly line. Rather than relieving pressure on those workers, this was intended to reveal flaws or problems in the system, but faded out in practice as work measurement became more sophisticated or more universally applied. In the original lean production concept, teams were the major way of implementing constant improvement in the practice of "quality circles." In addition to increasing productivity and the ideological effort to foster a "common sense" among workers about their shared interest, the team concept was a means to bring the workers' knowledge of the production system into management's domain, where it could be incorporated into their programmable control system.[3]

Total Quality Management

Employee participation increasingly gave way to more blatantly top-down systems of measurement and management, notably with the rise of Total Quality Management (TQM) programs in the 1990s. In many cases teams were eventually eliminated and/or their previous functions deemed redundant. The emphasis came to rest on top management setting the course; "strong leadership" came into vogue again rather than the softer quasi-consensus style of the 1980s.[4] Nowhere was this better illustrated during those years than in the prevailing corporate culture concept.

TQM's guiding principle, "Do it right the first time," meant that quality control should be done along the way, not only at the end of the process. TQM was likewise based on the old business adage, "The customer is always right." But TQM was basically a synthesis of virtually *all* the useful management insights garnered since scientific management, combining Japanese management quality circles, group dynamics, teamwork, leadership, corporate culture, and statistical process control into an all-encompassing work practice. Managers enthusiastically embraced TQM because so much of it was familiar. Contrary to what management writers at the time suggested, there was nothing new under the sun here. Already in the 1930s, W. Edwards Deming had argued that (contrary to popular belief) if one increased the quality of one's product, this would lead to increased productivity. Instead of doing quality control on the finished product, one should do it continuously throughout the production process. Deming taught this practice to the Japanese and so did management consultant Joseph Juran in the 1950s and 1960s. Juran himself offered a simple definition of quality; it basically revolves around a product's "fitness for use," the product or service should offer what the customer wants or needs, and has a right to expect from it.

The U.S. military adopted the ideas of Deming, Juran, and other quality theorists like Armand V. Feigenbaum and began to examine its practices through their filter. It was a navy psychologist, Nancy Warren, who actually coined the term Total Quality Management. In 1988 the Federal Quality Institute was established to introduce government officials to TQM and provide training, consulting, and information to their agencies; the U.S. government from then on embraced and promoted TQM. In 1987, for example, the Department of Commerce created the Malcolm Baldrige National Quality Award to reward corporate performance and stimulate competitiveness. The core values and basic features of TQM as publicized by promoters are customer-driven quality, leadership, continuous improvement, employee participation and development, fast response, design quality, long-range outlook, management by fact (which usually means hard data), partnership development, corporate responsibility, and citizenship. It is clear from this list that TQM was more than a system of production; it also had profound implications for employer-employee relations.[5]

In his edited volume on TQM and leadership (published before the revived tendency toward strong leadership became effective in the 1990s), Richard J. Pierce states that front-line supervisors should act like leaders, which in his view means that they must become "more participatory and less authoritarian." This entails listening to employees' ideas and, when appropriate, implementing them. But in Pierce's view employees, too, have to change. They must realize that "improved quality performance on their part, while vital, may bring no added compensation ... but in the long run, productivity and quality improvement are necessary for survival."[6] While Pierce refers here to survival of the company, implicit in his statement is the survival of the employee at that company—the stick (veiled threat) replacing the carrot (job security) offered previously.

The rhetoric of TQM advocates holds the noble idea of reinstating a craft ethic that includes pride in workmanship and the intrinsic value of a job well done. This is in itself a positive and rewarding model of work, as Joanne Ciulla points out. But she hastens to add that it should always be considered in relation to the kind of work in question as well as the context in which a job is done. In this setting, the employer wants employees to act and feel (as craftsmen tend to do) that they are not engaged exclusively in an economic transaction, while at the same time reminding them that management is engaged in a purely economic transaction—a truly paradoxical situation for workers.[7] It is fair to say, however, that Pierce harkened back to Deming, who back in the 1930s had argued that business should abolish the practice of paying for performance. Since workers rarely control the resources that affect output, he believed they should not be rewarded or penalized on the basis of productivity.[8] In theory at least, workers in a "participatory" workplace have more control over the labor processes and therefore are responsible for the success or failure of their work. But Deming's idea can be taken out of context and misinterpreted as a legitimation for blaming employees and not sharing more of the company's profits with them, which has often been the case in reality.

By the late 1980s and into the 1990s, business management books were teeming with the words *trust, commitment,* and *loyalty,* which became an integral part of the TQM vocabulary. Part of the appeal of "quality" was that it allegedly was not only an effective way to manage, but was also good in some moral sense of the word (and associated with the term "corporate responsibility," one of the criteria for the Malcolm Baldrige award). Richard Pierce asserts that quality is a matter of ethics and that it requires ethical leaders all along the line and at the top of the company, giving customers what they want.[9] While this is a strong statement of ethical commitment to customers, the relationship between company and employees (and other stakeholders) does not receive this degree of moral consideration. Most TQM theorists imply that employees are treated ethically because they are allowed to participate in decisions, management listening to their ideas. But this entails a meager definition of an ethical arrangement. The mere fact that employees participate does not mean that their relationship to management is ethically sound. People can participate in fraudulent business practices or they may even "participate" because they are afraid of losing their job or are afraid of their boss.

A study of fear in the workplace found that people are usually afraid of retaliation, reprisals, and retribution. Other sources of fear relate to matters that people in the organization are afraid to deal with, such as the boss's management style, which ranked as the number one taboo topic of conversation, followed by co-workers' performance, then compensation and benefits.[10] Needless to say, if workers are most fearful talking about a boss's management style, then it will be virtually impossible to assess what they really think about TQM and reengineering, or any other management initiative for that matter. Increased productivity may very well be the result of factors such as fear that bear no relationship to "teamwork and coaching."[11]

The Rise of Business Process Reengineering

The 1980s was a decade when a number of organizational and technical alternatives to rationalized, bureaucratic office work practices existed. But these alternatives became casualties of managements' unrelenting quest to reduce labor costs by using office technology and associated organizational changes to further control labor processes. In 1985, the U.S. Congress Office of Technology Assessment carried out a series of case studies of different industries to understand how changes in office technology affected employment patterns, job training, organizational structures, job content, and skill. In their report, *Automation of America's Offices*, the researchers concluded that it was not the technology itself that was shaping the changes in skill requirements and job content, but rather the choices made by management.[12] According to Joan Greenbaum, writing in 2004, their predictions, based on careful analysis, suggested changes in work that have since occurred. In general, the researchers believed that the workplace developments of the early 1980s would become more pronounced in the following decade. They pointed especially to an increasing tendency among management to reduce labor costs by cutting back-office jobs, limiting the growth of middle-management costs, and hiring more part-time and temporary workers. The ongoing standardization of work meant that management was able to move work around to wherever wages were less. It was epitomized by the proliferation of call centers, from bank balances to software technical support. Translating complex, in-person services into the more routine procedural steps of telephone scripts meant that this kind of work could be moved anywhere and done at any time. It also meant that corporate headquarters, which had migrated from the city centers to the suburbs in the 1970s, were able to move out of the city and even out of the country altogether, out of reach of inner-city and minority workers.[13]

During the recession of 1990–91, there were structural job shifts that led to huge cuts in the number of payroll or full-time jobs, a compression of job titles into the remaining ones, and a surge in the "contingent" or "work for hire" workforce. Along with these three types of changes came the increasingly common phenomenon of people working from home either as "telecommuters" (on the payroll) or as self-employed freelancers. There was also the increasing tendency to recruit merely formally self-employed workers, that is, to manage employees as if they were self-employed, and to insist on "mind-set flexibility." Practices such as management by results and performance-related pay, coupled with contracts in which working hours were unspecified, unremitting work pressures and fear of redundancy, all combined to produce a situation in which the coercive power of the manager was internalized. As Ursula Huws points out, this method of management is closer to the work rates of the putting-out systems rather than the time-based pay (albeit with machine-based work) of the factory. And it muddies the relationship between worker and employer; problems are exacerbated when there is a geographic separation between them, with employees working from their own homes, using computers with a telecommunications link to deliver work assignments.[14]

All of these changes were driven in large part by the management practice of Business Process Reengineering (BPR), an up-front means of reducing the workforce, often by eliminating steps in the production or service-providing process through the application of new technology. Reengineering was an important addition to a toolbox of techniques that gave top management more control over which jobs could be standardized, which could be integrated through computer technology, and which could simply be built into preprogrammed computer applications.[15]

BPR was combined with TQM to flatten organizational hierarchies, reorganize work processes, redefine required skills, and introduce new technologies. Increasingly, allegedly "objective" measurement (never as scientific as suggested) was employed and standards such as "benchmark metrics" and "cycle time analysis" were hailed as preferred tools to obtain higher levels of worker performance. The existing corporate way of organizing work, with its job ladders and relatively secure jobs, was being transformed to resemble the entrepreneurial ideal—one where workers had to fend for themselves.[16]

Business Process Reengineering was the brainchild of Michael Hammer and James Champy, who introduced the concept to a wider audience in their 1993 book, *Reengineering the Corporation: A Manifesto for Business Revolution*. More than all the other management innovations of the 1980s and 1990s, reengineering held the promise of making the work that an individual does more interesting. Information technology made it possible for one person to have access to the information of many workers. In this context, the term *kanban* became popular in indicating a method for managing knowledge work with an emphasis on just-in-time delivery which does not overload the team members. (In this approach, the process, from defining a task to its delivery to the customer, is displayed for all participants to see. Team members pull work from a queue on the computer screen.) In addition, Hammer and Champy insisted that "People who once did as they were instructed now make choices and decisions on their own instead.... Managers stop acting like supervisors and behave more like coaches. Workers focus more on the customer's needs and less on their bosses."[17]

Hammer and Champy presented their reengineering approach explicitly in terms of its appeal to, and connections, with "American-ness." The solution was for the U.S. to become more American—to rediscover its roots. Business Process Reengineering was to capitalize on "the same characteristics that made Americans such great business innovators: individualism, self-reliance, a willingness to accept risk and a propensity for change."[18] American inefficiencies were not due to fundamental weaknesses, but to the country's recent complacency and inertia. The recommended panacea was salvation through a rediscovered national authenticity, which meant a clean slate, a fresh start, couched in evangelical-sounding conversion terms by reengineering's leading advocate: "This isn't tinkering; it is all or nothing. A total reversal of history is required; and total conversion—'Don't automate, obliterate.'"[19] Part of the persuasive effect of the rhetoric deployed by Hammer and his ilk regarding corporate culture change lay, as Keith Grint put it, "in the resonance that it 'reveals' between American past glories and future conquests.... American industry is weak now *because*, rather than despite the fact that, it was so strong before; and American industry will be strong again *because* of, rather than despite, American culture."[20] Thus, this harking back to America's "past glories" (from a corporate business perspective) offered a usable past for contemporary managerial purposes.

In his 1996 book, *Beyond Reengineering,* Hammer tried to explain why the modern American football team is "an almost perfect model" for the reengineered organization. The head coach sits on the sidelines and motivates and supports players, while the position coach nurtures and develops players so that they can execute the coordinator's plans.[21] But no explanation is given as to where one gets these coaches who are willing to give up the power they have held in the past to stand on the sidelines. Do they take something like sensitivity training? Or do companies hire new managers with these traits? In business schools, people do not tend to learn and develop skills or personality traits associated with nurturing, coaching, and the ability to refrain from using positional power. Most MBA students, at least in U.S. business schools, take only one or two management courses that contain bits and pieces borrowed from sociology and social psychology of work (corporate culture, leadership styles, decision-making in small groups, etc.), while the rest of their curriculum focuses on other aspects of business, such as finance and advertising.[22] Obviously, the managerial concepts of teamworking and leadership at issue here are highly ambiguous. The next section considers the discrepancy between the managerial rhetoric and the reality of the management practices in question.

Managerial Attempts to Control and Inspire "Creative" Workers

Until around 1980 employers used to demonstrate a rather benign attitude toward engineers, designers, and other "creative" workers with regard to financial compensation and discretion as to task fulfillment. This was possible because more than most other U.S. employees these workers could be expected to display loyalty to the firm. When necessary, they could also be induced to demonstrate "heroic self-exploitation." The most important reason to treat these creative workers well, however, was economic. Except for some engineering-intensive industries, design and administrative work constituted a relatively minor cost of production. Labor-intensive industries producing for protected markets—a description that fits most U.S. economic sectors between 1918 and 1977—generally could afford to absorb the costs of "intellectual slack time."[23]

With the rise of accelerated economic globalization in the 1980s, employers were faced with a radically different marketplace, however. Efficient and rapid product development, intricate coordination, reliable communications systems, and promptly dealing with "exceptions," were the basis for getting competitive products to global markets as quickly as possible. Managers also faced a dilemma: if design, coordination, and dealing with "exceptions" (unanticipated disruptions in the process) are the most important value-adding work in the global production system, how can managers then make predictable the work of those employees who handle non-routine problems?

Taylorist command-and-control systems alone have never been adequate to manage these types of workers. Taylorism in fact can only be applied to some aspects of design and administrative work. When employers try to extend Taylorist control techniques to design and managerial workers, the results are ambiguous at best. This poses a fundamental problem: managers seeking to extract the greatest value from "creative" workers need to manipulate not only behavior but imagination; they must inspire along with control.[24] The techniques most favored by American employers to inspire imagination—cheerleading and appeals to professionalism—have also been the least reliable, however. These methods take time and if deployed too often may generate resistance.

Management's earlier attempts to get a grip on "creative" workers' imagination were thoroughly Taylorist in spirit, if not in the literal application of the "one right way." Managers tried to attach work deconstruction techniques to operations research methods (OR) and management by objectives (MBO) systems, but neither combination was particularly successful. OR is a modeling system for laying out and scheduling the individual tasks broken down by workflow designers; it is basically an extension of the rationalist assumptions of Taylorist fragmentation, "scientifically" recombining the tasks of individual workers (whose work had been broken up in separate parts earlier by "scientific" work rationalization). It offers little in the way of facilitating work design itself. MBO attempted to rationalize the decision-making process for managers and other administrative workers by encouraging them to start with the desired long-term and intermediate outcomes rather than a standard set of administrative procedures and control techniques. Organizationally, MBO was the first widely used management system to lay out procedures and guidelines for making choices in ambiguous situations. Analytically, it was thus the opposite of the one-size-fits-all practices mandated by Taylor's "one right way."[25]

OR and MBO were among the first attempts to systematize indirect command-and-control systems aimed at "creative" workers. This in contradistinction to the older human relations efforts to systematize the psychological reward systems U.S. managers have used to affect worker behavior and attitudes. MBO in particular showed managers they did not have to choose between either "hard" control systems designed by industrial engineers or the uncertain effects of "responsible autonomy" and inspirational meetings. Engineering-based behavior measurement could be combined with carefully constructed "soft" systems of the kind James March and Herbert Simon call "bounded rationality." The challenge would be to find the right balance.[26]

The 1980s and 1990s produced command-and-control systems such as Continuous Improvement (CI), Total Quality Control (TQM) and Business Process Reengineering (BPR) that according to its proponents struck just that right balance. In the spirit of MBO, the goal of these "quality" and "process" movements was to provide managers with reliable ways to predict and control "outcomes" rather than measure and monitor behavior. Their common formal purpose was to reduce value-adding time, product and process defects, and costs. In this respect, they all owed large and obvious debts to Taylorism. TQM and BPR were enthusiastically adopted by U.S. managers in part precisely because they legitimated and rejuvenated the traditional Taylorist preoccupation with unnecessary motions and unnecessary people.

Like Taylorism, the process-centered, command-and-control systems assumed that all workplaces are systems that can be rationally designed, modified, and made routine, predictable, and efficient. Taylor's "eliminate unnecessary motions" was transformed into "continuous improvement." "Soldiering" was rooted out through *kanban* and lean production or some other form of "management by stress."[27] Like Taylorism, all were concerned chiefly with getting fewer workers to produce more in less time and ultimately at lower costs. All relied heavily on techniques that operationalized workflows in order to measure outcomes ranging from time-to-market cycles to deviations from specification to customer satisfaction. They relied on a variety of sophisticated computer-based "real time," that is, continuous, measurement systems. For U.S. workers—whether engaged in "creative" or "routine" work—the consequences of the new work redesign systems were usually the same as those produced by Taylorism: intensified labor, more job competition and insecurity, and downward pressure on wages.

The new command-and-control systems differed from each other in some important ways. Continuous Improvement (CI) and TQM were the more incremental approaches. They sought steady decreases in product and process variations and the constant evolution of "robust" design and product processes. BPR, at the other extreme, demanded more fundamental results: a massive restructuring of process and workflows. BPR's goal was to reduce not just defects and variations, but to do so through radical simplification and downsizing. Whereas TQM and CI kept silent on speedup and job loss, BPR openly advocated stripping organizations down to their "core competencies" and "core processes" while aggressively outsourcing the rest.[28]

CI, TQM, and BPR and similar systems were not simply modern variations of work measurement and direct control, however. They went far beyond simple measurement, task disassembly, and speedup. Like Taylorism, they sought to maximize output and product quality at the lowest possible unit costs. Unlike traditional Taylorism, though, TQM and other process-centered strategies sought to eliminate defects in the organization of the production process as a whole. In what Philip Kraft has called a "radical departure" from Taylorism, these process-centered systems rejected rigid distinctions between design and production and consequently rigid distinctions between design and production workers. He referred to the fact that CI, TQM, and BPR valued, even "coveted" the ideas and tacit knowledge of all workers, including traditional direct workers:

> If Taylorism is about separating mental and manual work and then constructing a rigid hierarchy to administer and police that separation, process-centered management systems are about systematically appropriating ideas and knowledge from all workers through a system Harvey (1989) calls "flexible accumulation." It may just as accurately be called flexible appropriation and flexible control.[29]

The system in question might indeed be "flexible" as indicated, but it was still managers who, with the assistance of their reengineers, appropriated ideas, tacit knowledge and expertise from the workers involved. And this meant that now any worker, not only direct workers, could thus be divested of part of his/her labor power. And, ultimately, managers were the ones who decided which components (if any) of this "knowledge base" be incorporated into the technical-organizational control systems, and in what ways.

In contrast to traditional Taylorist rationalization, which is linear, serial, and segmented, TQM and BPR emphasized both the design of the product and the design of the process required to make it. This meant, as Philip Kraft readily admits, that managers and designers had to have a tighter and more immediate control over process as well as product variation. Process-centered, command-and-control techniques offered them a way to do this. "Over-the-wall" design, production, inspection, testing and service—whereby each fragmented part of the total process was carried out with little regard to what comes before or after it—were replaced by "design for manufacturability" and "concurrent engineering." It was the difference between inspecting finished products for defects (= traditional quality control) rather than reducing variation and defects in the process itself.[30] However, contrary to what Kraft suggests, this is not a radical departure from Taylorism. Coupled with the adoption of Just-in-Time inventory, Statistical Process Control techniques, and the striving for ISO 9000 certification (a quality assessment by third-party bodies based on external audits), TQM in many cases appeared to represent an updated form of scientific management. TQM resulted in a more pronounced division between conception and execution, concentrating conception more clearly at the top management level with the consequent loss of discretion at middle-management and technical levels.[31]

In Kraft's interpretation, which reflects the new management thinking at that time, traditional Taylorism focuses on the labor process of the individual worker rather than the production process as a whole (even though Taylor was well aware of the significance of the work group strategy, and Fordism, with its crucial Taylorist components, did consider the whole production process). It is assumed that a finished product is the sum of individual tasks and individual "value-adding" transformations. An individual's work is deconstructed, recombined, and then reinserted in a linear process populated by workers whose behavior is similarly fragmented and closely coordinated by supervisors.

As Kraft reminds us, critics of Taylorism have always pointed out that in practice, U.S. managers routinely ignore the assumptions of radical individualism and hyperrationality. Taylorism often backfires, particularly when crucial parts of the labor process rely on tacit knowledge and non-prescribed coordination. Moreover, the focus on the individual labor process becomes even more of a problem when global competition increases the demand for "flexibility," "quality," and speed. Global production requires the coordination and administration of diffuse, constantly changing, and even "virtual" organizations. This compels managers to conceive of production as an integrated system of design, development, production and distribution rather than a collection of individual tasks, which is made possible by the new computer-based technologies. Controlling the workers in this setup requires managers to reject the traditional divisions between design and production and between production and process. It also compels them, however reluctantly, to reject rigid distinctions between conceptual and manual labor.[32]

In this managerial reconceptualization of work as a collective activity, computer-based, process-centered control systems permit managers to concentrate on concurrent (direct and indirect) control systems, process integration, and task reassembly rather than merely on task deconstruction. But in so doing, as noticed earlier, managers are obliged to rely on normative control mechanisms such as peer pressure through management-defined and -controlled teams, and identification with the firm by means of motivational seminars and tent revival-like inspirational meetings.[33]

Managers must also look for new ways of determining the value added by previously invisible but crucial "indirect" workers, such as system designers and technical support staff. Product development and data processing are redefined from overhead activities to products with "internal customers," that is, other transformational workers in the overall workflow for the "value chain." Work that was once considered merely overhead, such as communications and warehousing, or peripheral, such as process design and consumer service, is now reconceptualized as integral to the larger production process and the overall "value chain." This also means that managers need new ways to measure, monitor, and maximize "value." In the end, this is allegedly accomplished by transforming all workers—direct workers and "guard labor" (workers who do not add value, but only bookkeep or monitor goods-in-process) as well as "creative workers"—into "design workers." It is assumed that managers can control value-adding workers by making everyone standardize, speed up, measure, monitor, and control their own work. In other words, CI, TQM, and BPR are thought to be attempts to dissolve the distinctions between production, design, process flow, and control. Process-centered production control claims to collapse the distinction between conception and execution and between productive and unproductive labor, which, if true, would be the reverse of Taylorism.[34]

Controlling and inspiring the workers in this collective activity process means reinventing an old management tool: the team. Management-defined and -controlled teams are nothing new, as we have seen. Since at least the days of human relations and welfare capitalism at Sears in the 1940s, they have been part of the management repertoire. Conventional teams were specialized and tended to have the same flaws of serial, over-the-wall functional divisions of labor as traditional Taylorism did. In contrast, CI, TQM and BPR, with their obsession for facts and data and controlling variables, use "multifunctional teams" to shift some decision making from managers to "the people who actually do the work." In other words, these systems readily permit some workers some flexibility in fragmenting and combining their work processes under some circumstances. TQM and BPR encourage employees to "surface" tacit knowledge in order to systematically incorporate it into "rational" processes. Oddly enough, managers called this transformation of worker knowledge into "fact-based management," *empowerment* (supposedly of employees).

This practice of "empowerment" depends in turn on two major "soft" components, which are both rejections of traditional systems of fragmentation. The first is an emphasis on flexible organizational structures. The goal is to shorten communication times and reduce communications "distortions," that is, to reduce the production of "bad data" or inaccurate information. This is done through the creation of teams equipped with an array of appropriate computer-based technologies. In practice, teams are the means to push traditional supervising, coordination, and reporting functions down the production and process chains of command. The decision-making authority offered to these "self-directed teams" is a preeminent example of what March and Simon meant by "bounded rationality."[35] It is the right to choose among a limited range of options that have been designed into the system at a higher level of design or coordination. Information and communication technologies, which can be used to monitor in "real time," provide built-in surveillance and control to higher management.

The second component is a systematic emphasis on ideology or "culture" as a control mechanism. BPR, TQM and their variants involve comprehensive management "philosophies" of workplace relations. There is of course nothing new about managers trying to influence the way workers think and feel about their condition and their relationship to their employers. But the normative offensive that accompanies TQM and BPR is of a different kind than previously on offer. It is focused on changing attitudes mostly about the relations of power and control. Now normative control mechanisms are intended to alter the beliefs and behavior (the "corporate culture") chiefly with regard to the definition of the "customer" and the functions of middle management. Power and control are usually given labels like "flexibility" and "cooperation." The notion of customer is broadened to include all transformational workers in the value chain. Middle managers are allegedly transformed from police and supervisors to (what are confusingly called) "coaches," "leaders," "facilitators," and "resources" who are supposed to inspire rather than prod workers. At the other end of the transformational chain, direct workers are informed ("indoctrinated" is perhaps a better word) that they are engaged in a "win-win" quest with their employers. Cooperation and "jointness"[36] are supposed to replace us versus them adversarial relations, except, perhaps, when joining forces against a common enemy such as foreign competitors. Obviously, employers could turn such arguments easily into a case against unions.

Finally, invoking the belief system associated with this team work allows managers to "surface" tacit knowledge as well as hidden agendas. The unrelenting pressure of "satisfying the customer"—that is, to work faster and produce more—combined with the social pressures of team membership can induce team members to reveal their attitudes and opinions, more particularly to "confess their individual sins and seek forgiveness from the group"[37] In other words, teams make it easier for managers to apply group pressure to underperforming workers.

As seen from a helicopter perspective, sociotechnical practices—the design of technology and social relations within the workplace to facilitate productivity and commitment—are thus used as a form of control. It goes without saying that workplaces have always been sites of enculturation. But under the new conditions of capitalism, worker empowerment, participation in corporate culture, and the inculcation of corporate values became a business strategy involving "a new soft-touch hegemony."[38]

The ideology of "empowerment" reflected the new management point of view that delayered or flattened organizations—meaning organizations in which teams monitor and intensify their own behavior—can extract value more efficiently and more quickly than traditional systems of managerial control. The real power distribution of BPR and TQM and similar process-centered systems was most evident when they were combined in a multi-tiered control strategy. Together, they continually refined engineering-based control systems for routine processes, radically reorganized whole production systems and workflows, and reviewed the "core competencies" of the firm on an ongoing basis. Kraft summarizes the typical combination of tiers as follows:

1. *Continuous Improvement for routine processes characterized by simple, repeatable tasks.* Repeatable events range from conventional mass production processes in manufacturing and data entry work to customer service, sales, or other activities relying on scripts of similar limited "decision trees," to combining "off-the shelf" modules to write computer software. The goal is to eliminate both variations in the product and "slack," mostly inefficient labor. This is the area of traditional Taylorism, where increasingly IT-based fragmentation and disassembly of tasks are being used.
2. *Total Quality Management for "problem surfacing" and dealing with less routine and more "creative" work.* This is where "responsible autonomy" is combined with *kanban* to produce "self-directed, autonomous, high-performance work groups." It is also where "hard" (engineering) and "soft" (human resource) managers struggle over the exact balance of measurement and inspiration. The focus is first and foremost on "systems"—and embedded control structures—rather than on tasks. The goal is to devise ways to eliminate defects in the production system itself. Here "defects" means employing more people than necessary, not just deviations from product specifications. Successful TQM makes "exceptional" work routine. It can then be pushed down the command-and-control chain and managed by continuous improvement techniques.
3. *Business Process Reengineering for effecting radical change and solving complex or crisis-level problems.* BPR is done under the direction of senior managers and consultants who are allowed to downsize or otherwise sharply reduce costs and cycle times in a fast tempo. Once an enterprise is radically reengineered, its systems can be handled by TQM and CI teams and processes.[39]

In this organizational setup, BPR deals with fundamental questions about the very purpose of the enterprise and overall structural change. TQM and

Continuous Improvement focus on the middle and bottom of the process hierarchy. The goal of each separately and in combination, is to minimize exceptions—variations, defects, waste, anything that does not "add value"—and to codify and normalize as many "erratic" processes as quickly as possible.

Ultimately, the whole constellation very much remains a top-down system with managerial power concentrated at the top. The work teams are inhibited in their capacity as "self-directed, autonomous work groups" by the constraints imposed by higher management. Studies in the late 1980s and 1990s of "self-managed" teams found a relatively limited delegation of authority. And studies about the amount of decision-making autonomy in working on these teams proved that the empowerment rhetoric was often empty and the managerial prerogative largely intact; only a small minority of teams elected their team leader. With respect to TQM, there is clear evidence that while workers responded positively to attempts to draw on their expertise and the reduction of close supervision, existing hierarchies nevertheless narrowly limited attempts to delegate power and expand involvement for employees and even (mid-level) managers.[40]

Reengineering and the Enhanced Industrialization of Office Work

The revival of the mass production model by the Japanese and their Western followers took place on the very eve of the IT explosion in the U.S., so that, timewise, the new Taylorism was very well positioned to influence how information technology could be used in the U.S. service industries as well. But the Japanese approach to scientific management was also operationally in line with the qualities that computers and their associated software could bring to the control of business processes in these industries.

With the surge of IT investments in the 1990s, reengineers could now try to apply the rigorous discipline of scientific management to the more elusive processes of the service industries. There was a major difference with manufacturing, however: while in manufacturing the frontline worker on the shop floor had been the prime target of the new Taylorism, in service industries, reengineers have extended the reach of the labor practices in question upward to middle management and even beyond.[41]

Earlier we saw how William Henry Leffingwell spearheaded the movement aimed at applying the principles of scientific management to the service industries. However, many forms of white-collar work were not easily subject to measurement, standardization, and control, as Leffingwell's successors found out. It proved difficult to assign standard times to tasks that varied according to both their content and the skills of those who performed them.

Another major challenge for scientific managers was that the technologies of the office did not provide managers with immediate, up-to-date feedback about the performance of employees. The clerical labor practices lacked one of the essential characteristics of the classical assembly line, which was that the moving line itself provided the primary source of real-time information about employee performance. It was clear to supervisors when production was behind schedule, and who was responsible, just by observing the line, and so forth. It is true that typewriters could record a typist's strokes per minute, but that information then had to be collected and analyzed. Similarly, supervisors could record their employees' telephone conversations, but calculating the average length of calls was onerous and time-consuming.

The rather disappointing track record of white-collar Taylorism helps explain why the reengineering movement of the 1990s, which focused on the application of scientific management in the contemporary service economy, took its cue less from Leffingwell's American heirs and more from the Japanese automakers, with their successful renewal of scientific management's industrial model. With the coming of the networked computer and its workflow software, Leffingwell's vision of a white-collar assembly line subject to the rigorous control of the labor process—similar to that of the assembly line in manufacturing—was within reach.[42]

In Leffingwell's preoccupation with the mail-order world, the primary focus was on order fulfillment; the sequence of tasks that had to be performed for a written order to become goods sent off to the customer. Order fulfillment also figured prominently in the promotional texts and handbooks of leading reengineers of the 1990s such as Thomas H. Davenport, Michael Hammer and James Champy. As Simon Head notes, the description of order fulfillment by Hammer and Champy in their bestseller, *Reengineering the Corporation* (1993), shows a striking resemblance to Leffingwell's 1917 description of the process. At the very outset, both emphasize the importance of mapping in detail the process that a business is actually following; that is (in this case), how a business really operates in fulfilling its customer orders. This is followed by the critical task of finding out which steps can be shortened, joined together, speeded up, or eliminated altogether. In addition, the reengineers underline the necessity of looking at the amount of time wasted by moving paperwork between different departments of a business or between employees working within a business department.

Both Leffingwell, and Hammer and Champy, recommend the formation of "cross-function teams"—groups of workers made up of different specialists—

as a way of reducing this time. These proponents also seek to reengineer mechanical devices to speed up processes, with the scientific manager focusing on conveyor belts, elevators, telephones, buzzers, horns, and the reengineer on computers and their software. But there is a crucial difference. The contemporary reengineer has come much closer to reproducing the rigor and disciplines of scientific management in an office setting than Leffingwell and his successors ever did. This is due to IT's phenomenal powers regarding measurement, monitoring, and control, which neither Leffingwell nor all other office managers of the pre-digital age had at their disposal.[43]

In the Leffingwellian office, "real time" monitoring remained mostly confined to the supervisor's patrolling the line and looking over the shoulders of the clerks at work. With modern-day reengineering the balance between "real-time" and "after the fact" monitoring changes dramatically and real-time monitoring takes an unprecedented scope. Managers are able to peer into workers' computers with their own computer and software, meticulously time an employee's work, record and time workers' telephone calls, and monitor to the nearest second their every movement: to the bathroom, the water fountain, coffee machine or the lunch room. By means of automatically generated graphs, statistical tables, pie charts, etc., they can analyze from every conceivable perspective the performance of an employee or group of employees over a specified period of time (hourly, daily, weekly, annually or over more years) with up-to-the minute analysis.

The use of information technology as a reengineering tool has three major implications. The first is the impact of information technology on the substantive tasks that constitute the process to be reengineered. The second concerns the impact of information technology on the structure of work; how tasks are divided between employees and the degree to which tasks can be measured and timed. The third aspect is the impact of information technology on the control and monitoring of employees by management.

Firstly, does IT require higher "new workplace" skills from those performing the tasks involved, or does the technology partially (or wholly) perform skilled tasks itself and leave employees only a residue of lesser skills? The main tendency seems overwhelmingly to have gone in the latter direction; clear indications for this can be found in the published work of leading reengineers.[44] An eminent example is the credit loan sector. With a few exceptions (which are still handled by experts), regarding credit loans to clients, the functions once divided among various departments now became the responsibility of a single employee, called the "deal structurer," who now handles the entire credit-granting process. The same applies to the "case manager" for an insurance company, whose reengineered job is comparable to the job of the deal structurer.

Case managers and deal structurers now perform whole sequences of tasks that used to be performed by entire departments or specialists; today they are supported by PC-based workstations that run an expert system and connect to a range of automated systems on a mainframe. In difficult cases that might be beyond the capabilities of the expert system, the case manager calls for assistance from a senior underwriter or even a medical doctor—one of many uses of Leffingwell's "exception principle."[45]

Pioneered in the 1970s in early efforts to diagnose diseases and discover mineral deposits through artificial intelligence technology in the 1980s, developing expert systems turned into a discipline called "knowledge engineering." The idea was that one could package the expertise of a scientist, an engineer, or a manager and apply it to the data of an enterprise; the computer would effectively become an oracle. In principle that technology could be used to augment a human's capabilities, but as a productivity tool its purpose was more often than not to displace workers; software companies in the 1980s would sell it to corporations based on the promise of cost savings.[46]

Generally speaking, reengineering entails overriding an individual's professional judgment in decision making by "intelligent" systems which substitute a series of standard rules; for example, in determining eligibility for a bank loan (as mentioned above) or mortgage, prioritization for hospital treatment, or the offer of a university place for an applicant. As soon as the labor involved in processing such decisions has been standardized, it becomes possible to quantify its outputs, turning the function into a separate profit center or cost center, externalizing it, or subjecting it to competitive bidding.[47]

In *Reengineering the Corporation,* Hammer and Champy acknowledge that the purpose of expert systems is to enable the less skilled to perform work that until now has been carried out by the skilled employees. They write: "The real value of expert systems technology lies in its allowing relatively unskilled people to operate at nearly the level of highly trained experts."[48] Thomas Davenport gives the example of American Express, which managed to significantly improve the cost, time, and quality of credit authorization by streamlining the process through an expert system called "Authorizer's Assistant," derived from the knowledge of its best authorizers.[49] Simon Head concludes that—contrary to Hammer and Champy's suggestion that they do "richer and more demanding work" than their specialist predecessors—the deal structurer and case manager are "essentially computer operators who feed the right information into the machine, follow the machine's recommendations, and make sure that difficult cases that the machine might not be able to handle are forwarded to a team of human experts."[50]

Secondly, there is the role of information as a reengineering tool that changes the structure of work. It is claimed that the classic division of labor, advocated by Adam Smith and practiced by Taylor, Ford, and Leffingwell, are superseded. The tasks that make up a labor process are no longer broken down into a sequence of separate steps to be divided among workers, with each worker assigned a particular task. Instead, with information technology, the tasks of a process can be brought together and performed in their entirety by a single worker. This "compression of tasks" is touted as a "radical departure" from the way work had been organized since the Industrial Revolution.[51]

But these claims are highly problematic, since the tasks performed by the reengineered deal structurers are not comparable to the tasks performed by their specialist predecessors and therefore, the two activities cannot be lumped together under the same heading. Lacking most elements of research, calculation, and judgment, the activities of the deal structurer/computer operator should preferably be described as "operations," comparable to the activities of the machine tool operators working at computer-controlled machines. Once the deal structurer's operations have been separated from the specialist's tasks, it becomes clear that the former's job is definitely located within the traditions and practices of scientific management. While by 1900, Taylor's machining "software," the Taylor-Barth slide rule, could be used to automate the substantive machining judgments involved in each machining operation, with reengineering, expert systems are in place to automate the calculations and judgments performed by specialists.[52]

The third aspect concerns the impact that information technology as a reengineering tool has on the relations between managers and employees. Very misleading is the rhetoric of the "new workplace" that reengineering experts tend to draw upon to describe this relationship. They suggest that with reengineering, managers would "stop acting like supervisors and become more like coaches,"[53] as mentioned earlier, and that the new setting would be characterized by a "culture of facilitative management," in which "trust is extended whether or not direct management control is now exercised."[54] Notably absent is the crucial fact that tasks of monitoring and control have been subject to partial automation, so that fewer managers are needed around the office, evidenced by the waves of layoffs of the early and mid-1990s which hit middle managers especially hard. This downsizing was not so much the result of management's withering away, as the reengineers claimed, but foremost of these managerial workers becoming redundant.[55]

Highly relevant at this point becomes the distinction between the power of information technology to "automate" and its power to "informate" that Shoshana Zuboff makes in her book, *The Age of the Smart Machine*. Automation "replaces the human body with a technology that enables the smart processes to be performed with more continuity and control" as in, among other things, Henry Ford's machine shops. But contemporary technology "simultaneously generates information about the underlying productive and administrative processes.... It provides a deeper level of transparency to activities that had been either partially or completely opaque."[56] Zuboff coined the term "informate" to describe this "unique capacity" of information technology to provide information about the tasks in which IT itself is engaged. Thus, workflow software can not only prescribe that tasks or operations be performed in a certain sequence, but also record whether the prescribed sequence is in fact followed. If a task involves the use of the telephone as well as the computer, software can monitor the call according to the importance of the customer or the value of his/her order. Software can coordinate the monitoring of what the employee is saying on the telephone and the monitoring what he/she is doing on the computer screen. Software can also record the times when employees are away from the telephone or computer.

Informating, in Zuboff's view, would mean using computer systems to increase skill levels in clerical positions, thus giving responsibility and knowledge back to those doing the work through new forms of work organization and newer office technologies:

> Activities that had once been extracted from the professional domain and rationalized in lower level jobs could now be reintegrated with those higher level positions. For example, bank workers could interact directly with the database, perform analyses, and develop ideas. The remaining clerical positions would take on a quasi-professional status, requiring information management and business knowledge.[57]

The scenario Zuboff sketches came to be called "professionalization of clerical work," the reverse of professionals getting to do "clericalized" work. Writing in the late 1980s, Zuboff left open the question of how this power of technology to "informate" would actually be used: whether it would be used by management to strengthen its supervision and control, or whether, as the reengineers have argued, this power would be made available to employees, so that they could analyze and improve their own performance.

A problem with informating, however, is that it will most likely be implemented only when managers (or the consultants they hire) are able to demonstrate that overall labor costs are decreasing and that the remaining employees are more productive. Another problem with this skill-enhancement scenario is the fact that the invisible dimensions of a clerical worker's skill—the more tacit and harder to quantify aspects of the job—rarely are included in job descriptions or evaluations. Thus, in the event that clerical work is going to be made more professional, workers may be expected to perform with more skills, but will not necessarily be compensated for the new knowledge and skills they bring to the job. This proved to be particularly true of computer skills.[58]

With the benefit of hindsight, we now know that the faith in upskilling of clerical work did filter up to front office and professional jobs, but most work that had already been rationally divided remained automated and in the 1980s was "either relegated to isolated parts of the office building or hidden behind cubicle partitions."[59] Joan Greenbaum attributed this later to the fact that, in the 1980s, the movement to lower labor costs took on a new momentum, as work was further divided or recombined so that it could be done with fewer workers:

> The new policies were coated in the rich language of "enhancing human resources," making it seem that much was being done to improve skills and jobs. But ... employment figures and salaries in the 1990s illustrate that management continued the rationalization of tasks and jobs that had already been standardized and simplified, while at the same time identifying new tasks and functions (like paraprofessional and technical jobs) that could be molded into standardized jobs. By the end of the 1980s more reliable software was being developed to reintegrate previously rationalized tasks and standardized services. And a new angle was pursued to combine work organization with software. This was to create standard products and services. In this newer round of cost-cutting, the emphasis was not only on making workers and software more predictable, but carving up services so that they too would be standardized and predictable.[60]

Standardizing services and software to speed up the pace of work was always an intended goal. This strategy also made inroads into professional work that until then had not been timed or monitored because it was assumed that thinking was required, and the common sense view was that this could not be measured. This too was to change in the 1980s, when complaints about increased time pressure became as common among professional and managerial staff as it had been among clerical workers. This was partly due to the proliferation of fax machines, voice mail, and software applications like databases and spreadsheets that were expected to produce almost instant results. But another contributing factor was the changing definition of professional work, bringing it more in line with measured results and standardized services. Many professional workers found that in order to get their work done, they had to work longer and harder—an intensification of work that would be taken to a further extreme in the 1990s. This also entailed the clericalization of professional work that continues today, as most professionals and managers are expected to do their own word processing and handle their phones, faxes, and e-mail.

In clerical jobs, what seemed at first to be small incremental changes led to enormous increases in the pace of work. These small changes included no longer having to get up to put a piece of paper in the typewriter, file a document, mail a letter, or look up information in a manual or other material publication. In addition, having keystrokes counted sped up the pace for many back-office clerical workers. By the second half of the 1990s, employees complained about repetitive strain injuries (RSI), particularly tenosynovitis and carpal tunnel syndrome, resulting from prolonged rapid use of the keyboard (along with incorrect hand posture and finger handling of the mouse). Eye strain and severe headaches—due to staring at a computer screen all day long—also became troublesome.[61]

There is overwhelming evidence today that in almost all cases, in various industries, management has shown its determination to claim the "informating power" of technology for itself rather than sharing it with its middle- and lower-level workers. According to Simon Head writing in 2003, this flew in the face of then-prevailing wisdom that the "old economy" businesses that deploy IT are increasingly resembling the "new economy" businesses that create and supply that technology, so that the skill, proficiency, and flexibility of the Silicon Valley workforce is manifesting itself all over the economy and at all skill levels.[62]

In 1989 the MIT Commission on Industrial Productivity signaled "new patterns of workplace organization" in U.S. manufacturing that required the "creation of a highly skilled workforce," one that was incompatible with "the ways of thinking and operating that grew out of the mass production model."[63] As mentioned earlier, in 1990 another influential commission on U.S. manufacturing, named after its chairman, Ira Magaziner, described in detail and along similar lines, what would be required of workers in the new, "Japanese" workplace.[64] Likewise, influential human resource experts in the 1990s claimed that IT use went hand in hand with a new workplace organization that included broader job responsibilities for front-line workers, decentralized decision making, and more self-managing teams. However, this is not what happened, as Simon Head signaled later:

> Neither the plant and office-level evidence, nor the evidence of the trade literature, supports this vision of a newly skilled workforce empowered by information technology going about its business within autonomous, self-directed teams. At the upper echelons of "old economy" companies, new and advanced skills may be required of those who oversee the implementation of reengineering and ERP projects. But the sponsors of these systems habitually use them to simplify the work of middle- and lower-level workers, surrounding their tasks with elaborate regimes of business rules, and setting up all-seeing systems of digital monitoring to make sure that the rules are being obeyed. Perhaps the chief error of those proclaiming the coming of the autonomous, self-managed workplace has been their failure to allow for the sheer intrusiveness of the digital workplace and its technologies.[65]

There is a final aspect of reengineering that makes the practice a modern-day version of scientific management. This concerns the reengineers' methods, how they actually go about altering and speeding up labor processes. It involves an iron grip of central control over those processes by management. Similar to Taylor's original stance in this regard, Hammer and Champy write: "The push for engineering must come from the top of the organization ... because people near the front lines lack the broad perspective that reengineering demands ... it is axiomatic that reengineering never, ever happens from the bottom up."[66] Much like Taylor viewed the skilled machinists at Midvale in the 1880s, today's reengineers are also intolerant of workers' criticism and resistance to their approach. Like all scientific managers, reengineers believe that their "one best way" is based on objective, scientific truth, not opinion or speculation. They therefore perceive those who oppose the scientific manager's "one best way" as reprobates who refuse to acknowledge this truth, often deliberately so, and this helps explain why managers from Taylor up to today's reengineers have often demonstrated so much intolerance towards their opponents.[67]

Furthermore, in contrast to the often-heard claim by management experts that reengineering is not the same as downsizing or eliminating jobs, in reality reorganizing and reengineering in the 1990s resulted in fewer jobs and in more jobs being done with the same number of people. This process would rapidly spread as well to government agencies, educational institutions, and to smaller and newer firms. A major way in which reengineering resulted in downsizing was through collapsing job ladders and/or simply canceling job titles, so that workers had to take on more functions, becoming more "flexible." This type of corporate delayering affected everyone and was to remain top management's policy of choice in many organizations in succeeding decades. It also had a significant impact on the internal labor markets in question, because it resulted in fewer entry-level positions for newcomers to office jobs and fewer opportunities of promotion.[68]

The impact was different depending on gender and race. For most of the period that job ladders and internal labor markets dominated the organizational landscape—particularly from the 1940s through the 1970s—whiteness and a college degree appeared to be necessary for movement beyond the lower organizational rungs. Job ladders worked well for white, college-educated men in organizations where the ladder progressed up through middle management. The career patterns were less effective for white college-educated women who—depending on luck (of department or supervisor)—might make it to the professional ranks but then faced a "glass ceiling" somewhere around middle management. There were even less career opportunities for white women who came in through the clerical route, where job ladders tended to end with the title of office manager. For people of color, particularly those entering through the mailroom or back-office clerical department, career ladders were almost nonexistent. Moreover, job segregation by race/ethnicity and gender was also reflected in the number of declining occupations. The effects of the restructuring of work could clearly be seen throughout the administrative sector, where a number of jobs simply disappeared. For example, keypunch operators, overwhelmingly black and other minority women, was phased out by the end of the 1980s. In the 1990s, there was a sustained decline of key administrative support (clerical) job categories. In addition, as companies relied ever more on voice mail and electronic mail, the job of receptionist also began to disappear. In its stead, because of increased security concerns, male security guards have become more likely to be the ones to greet visitors in the entrance hall, as offices have increasingly been transformed into locked corridors and closed-off areas. Telephone operators, with a job that once provided a bridge to better work for many women, began a significant decline in the early 1990s, leaving only 176,000 operators in 1995.[69]

As part of the first wave of the reengineering process, job ladders were replaced by different sorts of broadbanding; that is, bundling jobs together in bands that involved a wide range of presumably interchangeable skills and operational responsibilities. Broadbanding went something like this: people within a band or category—for example, administrative support—were expected to assume responsibilities for a greater number of tasks. This often involved working in teams, so that any worker could fill in for any other worker. It was generally also assumed that this flexibility increased productivity, and anecdotal evidence seemed to confirm this; most office workers felt they were producing more, as did the companies they worked for.

A double standard was evident in this creation of teams and broad bands in the process of reengineering of jobs. On the one hand, managers were told to invest in people, as business magazines emphasized human potential and building what was called "human capital"—arguing that people can be expected to increase their "worth" for the company by acquiring and improving skills through training. On the other hand, however, managers were told to cut back as many people as possible. Job bands might, in theory, unleash creativity by giving people license to do more and different tasks (if this was indeed a form of "liberation" for those workers), but the bottom line was to eliminate positions to reduce costs.[70]

The Fading of Commitment, Loyalty and Trust

A great irony of the 1990s was that business practices emphasized downsizing, while at the same time business books and business rhetoric focused on "commitment," loyalty," and "trust." Employers wanted these qualities from their workforce, but many employees were aware that their employers were no longer willing or able to reciprocate. "Commitment" had become a highly-valued asset, particularly in companies that had cut the workforce and significantly increased employees' workloads. It is ironic that the less stability and loyalty companies had to offer employees, the more commitment they demanded from them. Obviously, when employees sense or know that the company will instantly drop them if deemed necessary to stay competitive, loyalty seems absurd to them. The affection and loyalty that employees hold for their company will be genuine if it remains loyal to them even under the most dire circumstances. This is because the company (that is, its top management) has kept its word and stuck to its moral obligations. This company loyalty may have produced a workforce that is resistant to change, but usually this does not mean that they are totally inflexible.

Further, if you trust a person, you can do business with a handshake, but if not, you will try to get all transactions and agreements written down on paper. When there is no trust in an organization, people fill this vacuum with formal rules, contracts, and laws, which requires enforcers and lawyers. Cooperation can be obtained with legal contracts, but running an organization without trust is not only unwieldy and devoid of goodwill, but potentially dysfunctional. Trust is a moral and emotional relationship between people, which is hard both to get and give. It requires honesty, mutual respect, and a rather consistent track record of moral behavior. In his insightful book *Trust*, Francis Fukyama characterizes trust as the backdrop of a culture; it leads to what he calls "spontaneous sociability."[71] This emerges when cooperative groups of people—like garden, amateur sporting, or book reading clubs—pop up naturally in a culture. In the workplace, spontaneous sociability might be what top managers, focusing on business culture change, have been trying to orchestrate and engineer since the beginning of the 20th century. Spontaneous sociability occurs when people work as a team, not because management merely declares that they are a team, but because they truly trust each other and agree to work together toward a common goal. Paradoxically, a number of companies attempted to implement Total Quality Management, while simultaneously downsizing the workforce. Through arrogance, stupidity or naiveté, the managers in charge had the illusion that they could build team spirit while employees were worried about losing their jobs and felt that they were competing with their "teammates" for jobs.

When *commitment* effectively boils down to time at work, *loyalty* to something one pays for, and *trust* to a legal contract, these terms are emptied of moral meaning, with negative ramifications for everyday workplace culture.

No matter how carefully companies acted and how many services they provided, those who survived massive job cuts still suffered. Downsizing changed the social compact that had been forged among corporations, government, and organized labor during the Cold War period. The adage then was that as long as you did your job well and the business made some profits, over time you would reap the benefits of the American Dream: a house, a car, and a raise every year.[72] However, it should not be forgotten, that the firm-centered, collective bargaining system that underpinned this compact remained confined to the unionized, and primarily white male workers in industrial companies. This system was patriarchal and racially inflected; the segmented labor market kept the majority of working women and people of color in nonunionized jobs outside the industrial core.[73]

While TQM and reengineering offered many organizations more efficient ways of organizing work, the question remains to what extent teams and the other features of these managerial programs really motivated employees. The extraordinary gains in productivity and quality and the ability of firms to "do more with less" (in quality control terms: reduce "waste" of all kind, including "redundant" workers) might just as well be attributed to the work ethic of fear than to any shrewd management intervention. Explicit fear, such as knowing that you will be fired, has limited benefits and induces negative responses; it can depress, paralyze, debilitate or infuriate you. This is a major reason why employees seldom receive much advance notice about layoffs. Yet, subtle fear based on uncertainty about the future compels many people to work very hard. Worries about falling behind in some undefined competition, drives many people to put in long hours. Managers fear losing business and worry about taking vacations, because they do not want to miss out on anything. Employees may eventually burn out or self-destruct, but they will put in more hours, at least for a while. During the past few decades company men and women worked longer hours and tolerated greater pressure than William H. Whyte's prototypical organization man of the 1950s. Unlike the ideal type of Protestant work ethic described by Max Weber, the work ethic of fear does not hold out hope of salvation, but only offers the opportunity to work more and at a frantic pace.[74]

Contrary to the late 1950s, the sustained management efforts to build "teams" and emphasize the value of groups in the workplace has not given rise to much concern of social critics, let alone broader public outcry, about the loss of creativity and submission of individual identity to group identity. In fact, managers tend to care more about the problem of individuals who are not team players. Like so many of their predecessors, the majority of management theorists and practitioners today still think that groups and teams by definition are the basis of all that is worthwhile and productive for the company.⁷⁵ There is a counterstrain among social psychologists and management theorists, however, who emphasize that cohesive groups and teams are not always the best way to work or make decisions in organizations. Researchers such as Irving Janis have demonstrated the disadvantage of "groupthink," a condition in which members of a group make faulty decisions because group pressures lead to a deterioration of "mental efficiency, reality testing, and moral judgment."⁷⁶

Moreover, organizations still use psychological tests to select new employees and identify existing employees' individual personality traits at critical moments in their careers. These are no longer the psychological tests that Whyte discussed in his book, but others such as the Myers-Briggs test, used to describe a person's personality traits. For example, some people are extraverted intuitive thinking judges, or ENTJs. The test is supposed to tell employers that these individuals are natural born leaders. Some organizations still use tests to select conformist workers; that is, to see how well they work in groups. Today companies sometimes use tests such as the Gordon Personal Profile to predict management success. These tests aim to detect leadership qualities and the ability to make decisions without a group. Whereas for Whyte personality tests were an affront to a person's dignity, autonomy, and privacy, many employees today see (or at least are believed to see) them as a tool for self-knowledge and development. However, the problem is that when one takes these tests in the work setting, self-knowledge comes at the price of self-exposure and possibly unfair labeling. While much has changed since Whyte's time, writes Joanne Ciulla, his general critique of the corporation probably still holds true, even though most employees seem to care little or simply accept these tests as part of their job.⁷⁷

9

Enterprise Resource Planning: Business Process Reengineering Taken to the Next Level

Networks became as central to the business world of the early 1990s as stand-alone personal computers were in the 1980s. By 1994, 87 percent of large firms and 32 percent of smaller companies had installed some form of local area network (LAN). An increasing number of organizations also adopted wired area networks (WANs), which linked computers in different departments, buildings, and cities. It was at this time that the Internet, previously an academic and scientific network (originating from a U.S. Defense advanced research project), was beginning to be opened for commercial purposes. By the mid–1990s, agreements between hardware and software companies, along with industry-wide standards, resolved most of the preexisting hardware and software compatibility problems. The standards gave these companies room to carve out their market niches, as the further evolvement of the Internet would clearly show.

Setting such network standards dovetailed nicely with plans to remove middle managers by incorporating the information and reports they had up until then generated, directly into databases that could be retrieved and shown on different computer screens, whenever and wherever necessary. Network standards also matched reengineering plans that called for abolishing lower-level tasks like data entry and repackaging them (at least for the time being) into integrated jobs. Moreover, networks enabled managements to divide their labor force geographically and obtain more output from the same number of workers—or, where possible, fewer workers. This was yet another aspect of Business Process Reengineering; shuffling employees, offices, and functions around in attempts to lower real estate expenditures as well as labor costs.[1]

As noted earlier, much of this reengineering activity took place under the label of "empowerment," which led to a lot of confusion and cynicism. An implicit assumption of the popular management literature at the time was that empowerment strategies should enable employees to contribute more effectively to task goals and organizational effectiveness. Despite this rhetorical twist, in reality empowerment was nothing more than another management tool.[2] In adopting a "power-sharing" perspective on empowerment in which employees were given "bigger jobs," many senior managers expected their newly "empowered" employees to feel good about the changes. Many employees, however, complained about being expected to do both their own and their (former) boss's jobs without being properly compensated. They resented being told they were empowered when in fact they had no real say in the work they carried out, the direction of the company or its normative orientation. They also disliked the fact that they had little time or energy for themselves, their families or friends. Some employees even suggested that "empowerment" had become a nice-sounding word for virtual slavery in the 1990s.

This state of affairs can be seen in terms of a shift in strategy from the more obvious direct control to the more subtle "responsible autonomy" form of managerial control. As Andrew Friedman has suggested, such a shift is consistent with the reduction in the number of white-collar workers available to perform monitoring and control functions.[3] In order to be successful, however, responsible autonomy demands an elaborate ideological apparatus to ensure worker co-optation. But the ideology of empowerment as it has been implemented in many organizations has been ineffective as evidenced by the extent of employee cynicism towards it. Instead, fundamental tensions that exist within organizations have come to light. This suggests that the very term "organizational empowerment" associated with the managerial strategies in question may be a contradiction in terms: "Given that it is a very critical organizational function to control employee behavior and to subvert employee needs for the requirements of the organization ... how can an organizationally-based empowerment strategy result in anything more than power-sharing in its most limited form?"[4]

In retrospect, it is noteworthy that the changes in office work practices in the first half of the 1990s were mostly made without the infrastructure of the Internet. In 1990, the pieces were coming together of what would become the World Wide Web through programs that could share both textual and graphic information. The second milestone, in 1995, was the beginning of the widespread use of the web browser called Netscape Navigator, an interface program that enabled users to visually link text and graphics (which would lose most of its usage share to Internet Explorer during what is called the "first browser war" of the late 1990s and early 2000s). The second half of the decade was marked by speeding up of outsourcing through corporate efforts to raise stock prices by lowering labor costs and through the use of distribution technologies—connected mainly through Internet expansion.[5]

Hyper-Reengineering

By the late 1990s, reengineering had evolved into Enterprise Resource Planning (ERP), a form of hyper-reengineering that brought together single business processes and aimed to weld them into giant mega-processes. Spearheaded by the German software maker SAP, the reengineers of ERP were driven by a vision that business processes great and small—from the ordering of office furniture to the designing of strategic plans—could all be made to operate together with the smooth predictability of the mass production plant.

Early versions of SAP software pertained to three major components: logistics, financials, and human resources. The first included the main manufacturing processes: materials management, production planning, quality assurance, and plant maintenance. The second component combined procedures, such as financial and asset accounting. The third was termed "human resources," and included such things as personnel administration, planning, and development. It has become the software industry's convention that ERP refers to the integration of these three activities. Processes whose integration with the central core materialized later—such as customer relations management (CRM) and supply chain management (SCM)—are usually described as add-ons to the original ERP.[6]

The problem with ERP is that it is essentially the old engineering of the early 1990s writ large, according to Simon Head, writing in 2003. First-generation reengineering took single business processes such as "order fulfillment" and subjected them to an assembly line discipline. Basic ERP takes these single-stand-alone processes, and joins them together. But the methods used by reengineers to overhaul a business process are virtually identical to those used by Frederick W. Taylor more than a century ago. First, the software team observes in minute detail exactly how these employees carry out their work. Customarily, the team seeks out the ablest workers and interviews them at length to find out why some workers are more productive than others. Like Taylor's scientific managers, the software team then leaves the workplace and draws up a plan describing how the process ought to be reengineered, focusing on the "best practices" of the best workers. After having obtained the final green light from senior management, the team will then incorporate its insights into workflow software, which will thereafter govern the routines of all those engaged in the process.[7]

This is followed by advanced ERP which extends the "digital welding" of basic ERP to the structure of entire businesses. However, reengineers have turned toward this advanced variant of their practice without having first solved the problem that has plagued reengineering from the very outset, that a practice based on the discipline and control of the assembly line is not attuned to contexts in which human agents discuss, argue, negotiate, and strike deals, as they are prone to do in service industries.[8]

In both customer relations management (CRM) and supply chain management (SCM), scientific management is firmly established as the controlling management perspective. This means that the closer integration of these two processes with the existing processes of ERP simply reinforces the already dominant role of scientific management in the ERP machinery. As Head claims, nevertheless CRM offers an opportunity to bring software and employees together in ways that can enhance the skills, judgment, and earning power of employees. Workers could be properly trained to make use of all the information that CRM software can bring into play when an agent deals with the customer. This entails the possibility of "to informate" as Zuboff puts it. But this opportunity is consistently disregarded by representatives of scientific management with its digital scripts, monitoring and control techniques, and micromanagement of employees' working life.[9]

Supply chain management builds on what is already a strong supply chain element in basic ERP, which automatically links the sales, production scheduling, and credit checking of a business. The supply chain of extended ERP lengthens the chain to include a company's customers and suppliers, and also uses the Internet as a possible means of communication between the three parties. The most remarkable achievement of supply chain history is Henry Ford's set up of a chain that linked raw material and finished product at his Highland Park and River Rouge plants. The product manuals of contemporary companies that are leaders in supply chain technology contain more heavy technical jargon than those of Ford, yet the unchanging nature of supply change management often shines through.

Among the skills required of a contemporary supply chain manager is the ability, with the help of user-friendly graphs and charts, to make sense of the information the system sends to his/her workstation. The manager has to recognize when the system is indicating that something is faulty, and then has to evaluate the system's recommendations about what corrective action should be taken. However, in one critical respect the contemporary supply chain manager is much more an object of scientific management than his/her counterpart in Ford's supply chain system. The manager's working life becomes visible to the gaze of his/her superiors in much the same way that the work of the call center agent (to be discussed later) is visible to his/her all-seeing supervisor, who, at any time, can activate the system to find out whether the supply chain manager is meeting predetermined goals. It is the third phase of ERP that is built around systems that gather and analyze information about all aspects of company activities at virtually every level. By subjecting managers to the discipline of process, the old distinction between the manager and the managed is being eroded. But in this newly "transparent" enterprise, some managers are more subject to the real time surveillance that is at stake here. Managers who cannot hide possible poor performance are the kind of managers who deal with supply chains. There is only one group that escapes this real-time surveillance—the CEO and his senior colleagues.[10] They are not the objects of the electronic gaze, because they *are* the electronic eye, monitoring all the others, and have thus "panoptic power," to use Foucault's term.

In his book, *Discipline and Punish: The Birth of the Prison* (1975), Michel Foucault develops the concept of "panoptic power" and its embodiment in an institution: the panopticon. Its archetype is the prison with the architectural plan originally conceived by the English philosopher and social theorist Jeremy Bentham in the late 18th century. No true panopticon prisons of Bentham's designs have ever been built; it is the underlying concept that is relevant here.[11] The panoptic prison was to be a twelve-sided polygon formed in iron and sheathed in glass in order to create the effect of what Bentham called "universal transparency." A central tower, with wide windows, opened onto the inner wall of the surrounding polygonal structure, which itself was divided into narrow cells extending across the width of the building. Each cell had a window on both the inner and outer walls, allowing light to cross the cell, thus illuminating all the inhabitants to an observer in the central tower, while that observer could not be seen from any one of the cells. Mirrors were also placed around the tower to direct extra light into these apartments.[12] (Needless to say, the modern, high-security prison becomes a high-tech panopticon once closed-circuit television cameras are installed on or near the ceiling of its cells and hallways.) "The major effect of the panopticon," Foucault writes, is "to induce on the inmate a state of conscious and permanent visibility that assures the automatic functioning of power."[13] For power to be exercised in this way, the inmate does not have to believe that he is under constant observation, but only that the possibility of being observed is constantly present.

In her book, *In the Age of the Smart Machine*, Shoshana Zuboff elaborates on how Foucault's terminology and analysis can easily be applied to the non-punitive setting of the business corporation. Scientific managers have sought to attain panoptic power ever since Taylor envisioned his shop floor planning departments, with their large numbers of "functional foremen." But it is only with the arrival of the modern computer, and the computer's empowerment through the attachment of monitoring software, that panoptic power has become a real and pervasive presence in offices and factories. Once the computer is up and running, the possibility of managerial monitoring and control is omnipresent, though at any given moment the employee can never really be sure whether or not this power is actually being exercised.

The concept of panoptic power has become applicable to the whole business, not just those parts of it that are inhabited by frontline workers; much of the managerial workforce is also the object of panoptic power. By the end of the century, companies like SAP were marketing monitoring and control systems that occupy all four office walls within the executive suite, giving the CEO and his fellow executives a panoptic view of the entire enterprise, including the detailed activities of all levels of management, except for the highest.[14] In 2001, the American Management Association reported that 77.7 percent of companies acknowledged that they electronically monitored their workers on a routine basis.[15] The actual percentage was most likely higher, naturally, since we may assume that not all companies involved were willing to publicly admit the surveillance of their own workers. As Andrew Ross put it: "It turned out that supervision of workers' time and actions was even more systematic in the computerized workplace than it had been under the factory foreman."[16]

Call Centers as "Digital Assembly Lines," with Some Exceptions

There are white-collar workplaces where further information rationalization diminishes the opportunities for middle- and lower-income workers to do skilled work. As part of the corporate bureaucracy that intersects with customers in areas such as marketing, sales, and customer service, the work of the front office requires a minimum of human interaction that cannot easily be subjected to today's advanced automation of the corporate back office. The prototypical front office worker is the call center agent enclosed in his/her cubicle, communicating with customers via telephone, e-mail and the Internet. As research on call-center work has shown, it involves an endless stream of short job cycle routine tasks characterized by software-driven scripted conversations and the fulfillment of quantitative (e.g., number of calls answered) and qualitative (e.g., rapport) performance targets to deliver a standard service to as large a number of customers as fast as possible. This all takes place in the presence of customers that requires call-center workers to perform standardized emotional labor, while they are subject to constant surveillance and monitoring by supervisors armed with specialist software. Meeting target times is a particular problem since managers—especially in the absence of unions—may increase the speed of the process by reprogramming software in an instant, reminiscent of classic Fordism and neo–Fordist lean production. This adds to the stress of the work, especially in light of lean (read under-) staffing policy.[17]

As Simon Head highlights in his thorough analysis of call center work, three strands of technology are combined within the call center.[18] First, "knowledge management" and "data warehousing" software can clarify each encounter between agent and customer with a virtually unlimited volume and variety of information. Data warehousing can include the entire history of the customer's relations with the business, the customer's own financial history regarding purchases in the past, and any information about the company's products that may be of interest to the customer. Knowledge management software presents this information in whatever form management deems desirable. Second, a technology known as computer telephony integration (CTI) permits, yet constrains, exchanges between agent and customer to take place using a combination of telephone, fax, e-mail, and Internet. Third, information technology has the power to integrate the call center, the corporate front office, with the corporate back office; that is, the departments responsible for specific tasks as scheduling, purchasing, manufacturing, accounting, and repairing.

Head rightly emphasizes that these information-gathering technologies have the potential to enhance the skills of the call center agent. As nexus to all these information flows, the agent could be allowed to decide how best to persuade the customer to place an order or renew a contract. With the full history of a customer's past dealings with the company literally at their finger tips on the computer screen, agents need to know how to assess that history and decide very quickly how best to go about persuading the customer to use the company's products and services. With the complex products of banking, insurance, or health care, agents must be able to completely understand their product lines and match them to customer needs or desires. Moreover, in every costumer transaction the agent must also work toward cementing the customer's loyalty to the company.[19]

The impact of information technology on the life within a call center is threefold. First, there is the impact of information technology on the substantive tasks that the processes of the industry encompass. Second, there is the impact of technology on the structure of this work; in effect, the sequencing of tasks, their division among employees, and their susceptibility to timing. And third, there is the impact of technology on the relations between managers and employees, which raises the question about whether a technology is used to strengthen or weaken management's powers of surveillance and control.

With two of the call center industry's processes, sales and marketing, the structure of work and its substantive tasks cannot easily be separated. This is because the shaping of a key element of the sales and marketing process—the telephone or Internet conversation between agent and customer—can itself be a substantive task for the agent. While, for instance, case management or deal-structuring processes are repetitive and predictable, this is not true of a sales encounter between a call center agent and a customer. In principle, the call can go wherever the customer and the agent want it to go. An essential task of the agent is to ensure that the call moves in the direction desired by the company.

However, most software companies concerned do not offer the agent much room to maneuver, as they have created an elaborate system of technology designed to manage the sales encounters from beginning to end, with the "verbal interaction" between agent and client taking place according to pre-arranged formulas. The agent loses the power to manage the call and instead has to follow instructions provided by CRM (Customer Relations Management) software, which represents the detailed preferences of management.[20]

Next to sales and marketing as two of the call centers' leading processes, there is a third, customer service, that entails handling customers' questions by phone or over the Internet concerning products or services. The reengineering of this third CRM process hits upon problems of knowledge management and control that are, in some ways, more demanding than those encountered in the reengineering of sales and marketing. At the center of a well-constructed online service is an expert system that incorporates the input of experts in the production, use, functionality and replacement of the products being supported. This acknowledgment of the merits of expert input goes hand in glove with the scientific manager's typical lack of respect for frontline workers' knowledge and expertise. As representatives of reengineering will argue, in a typical pre-knowledge management technical service call center, each team member brings a set of skills and real-world experience to the job that may or may not match up with the customer's needs. Some of the individual approaches of these agents will certainly be more appropriate to particular inquiries than others. Reengineering attempts to replace this untidy and unreliable knowledge base with a well-organized, complete expert system—"just as Taylor's work-sheets once displaced the rule-of-thumb notions of the Midvale machinists."[21]

But Simon Head claims that the technologies of Customer Relations Management have the potential of accommodating a different regime of workplace skills that leaves experts still in charge. From his own very different experiences with a Microsoft call center based in the Canadian Maritimes and a Toshiba call center (whose location is not disclosed) when trying to find a diagnosis and remedy for his failing laptop computer, Head learned that call centers too can be centers of skills and that it is within the power of the central management of such businesses to effectuate this. "The critical difference between the Microsoft and Toshiba CRM regimes," Head argues, "was that the online database available to the Toshiba agent was not a passive backup for the agent's own expertise, which he might call upon as he needed. Rather, it was a *substitute* for his expertise, an automated and authoritative expert system embodying rules drawn up by expert scientific managers that governed every aspect of the CRM transaction."[22] Most businesses likewise deliberately choose *not* to adopt a human skills-centered system, shaped by the drive to keep labor costs low and to fill the ensuing skills gap with the data bases, digital scripts, and expert systems embedded within the prevailing command-and-control systems.[23]

In sales, marketing, and customer service, the converging of reengineering and information technology has led to unprecedented managerial power to control how employees do their work. Knowledge management prescribes what information is made available to workers and when. Scripting spells out the exact wording the employee must use in conveying the information to customers. Rules engines and their "prescribed action responses" (led by algorithmic programming) determine the exact sequence in which tasks must be performed. But next to these digital control techniques that can be used to micro-manage an agent's activities, the control of employees and their work has a whole other dimension: all-pervasive monitoring. The special task of a host of software products is to constantly keep a watchful eye on employees so that managers can be sure that their business rules are being followed. Monitoring software detects and records any violation of the rules in real time as it occurs. This software can also detect immediately if an agent is not working fast enough and risks failing to meet production quotas.

There are at least five distinct types of monitoring software, according to Head. First, there are the "classic" forms of monitoring software that embody the Taylorist preoccupation with timing and measurement. Second, there are quality monitoring products that ease the manager's task of measuring the agent's "soft skills"—his/her personal warmth and politeness, and whether his/her friendly demeanor has strengthened ties of intimacy and loyalty between the company and its customers. Then, third, there is the software with even more intrusive effects. These are "total monitoring" products that simultaneously monitor what is happening on the agent's screen and what s/he is saying on the phone. This allows management to see whether the agent is following the prescribed script and accurately conveying the information and recommendations laid out by product databases. Fourth, there is software that monitors Internet and e-mail conversations between agent and customer; this can, if necessary, add another layer of monitoring to the monitoring of telephone conversations. And finally, there are the digital technologies that are embodied in many of these monitoring products, which make possible the scope and intensity of the multidimensional monitoring in question.[24]

Thus, reengineers have developed technologies for the front office that subordinate the skills of the call center agent to an industrial-like assembly line discipline. Virtually every aspect of the agent's labor process is pre-arranged. Decision-support software pre-decides which products the agent should promote, and how. Detailed script technologies display on the computer screen the exact conversation, word for word, that the agent must follow in dealing with customers. And monitoring technologies track every facet of the agent's work, whether via telephone, e-mail, or the Internet. The data allow supervisors to see from moment to moment, in minute detail, whether or not their employees are doing their job exactly as prescribed by workflow software, and are meeting their production targets.[25]

In short, these standard systems design practices are intended to bear down further on workers through computer software applications that are built to dictate rather than involve the workers who actually know what the systems do. With this type of all-encompassing managerial control, it is no longer possible for experienced office employees working with computer applications or in IT departments to "override the system." The denied opportunity to override (or bypass) the system is a common experience in today's front office jobs. It happens frequently at times when a customer calls with a problem that is not listed on the computer screen. When call center agents cannot answer a customer's question, this is considered a loss of productivity, because the computer system itself is designed to record only the transactions listed on the menu. This means a lot to workers, since performance evaluations and possible pay raises are based on numbers of transactions. In this way, systems that cannot be worked around are not only an additional method of monitoring workers but also an extra burden to them.[26]

The call center industry meets all the standards that Leffingwell envisioned regarding a white collar workplace governed by scientific management. Head puts it poignantly: "The lined-up cubicles of the call center are digital assembly lines in which standardization, measurement, and control in combination create a workplace of relentless discipline and pressure."[27] But he hastens to add that although technology has been the indispensable agent of such a regime, this use of IT is not inherent to technology itself but always reflects management's preferences and choices:

Agents do not have to be "simple conduits," their work governed by the digital script. Nor does their talking, walking, eating, and resting have to be measured and controlled by the nearest second. The electronic eye can always be dimmed to allow agents some freedom to deal with customers as they judge best. But for that to happen, managers have to give up some of the enormous power that IT has handed them. So far, they have rarely been willing to do this.[28]

In manufacturing, scientific management works by speeding up the pace of work in tiny increments. Computers and their software entail powers of measurement and control that make them formidable instruments of speed-up by management. For many years, labor unions have been the worker's best defense against excessive speed and they still are to some extent. But with the demise of organized labor over the past few decades and relentless union busting by many business corporations, its countervailing power has waned. And worse, unions have hardly gotten a foothold in the call center industry, which in the U.S. is located mostly in right-to-work states. The Communications Workers of America (CWA) and the International Brotherhood of Electrical Workers (IBEW) have been successful in some of their attempts at organizing call center workers in other states. But U.S. corporations that only a few years ago received millions of taxpayer dollars in the form of subsidies to establish local call centers have increasingly off-shored these jobs to India, the Philippines, Egypt, Mexico, Honduras and other developing countries.[29] At the time of this writing, legislation is pending in both the U.S. House and Senate that aims to address the multiple threats posed by increased offshoring. The United States Call Center Worker and Consumer Protection Act of 2016 (H.R. 4604/S. 2593) is designed to keep jobs in the U.S. and improve protections and service for consumers.[30]

However, even though managers at call centers have overwhelming power over their workers, as Head rightly claims, it should also be recognized that there are limitations to managerial control of this type of work, which is never "total." These limitations stem from the contradictory logic involved; the need to be simultaneously customer-friendly (a major source of job satisfaction) and cost-efficient (a major source of job dissatisfaction). From the standpoint of capital, management is just as concerned with the quality of service (particularly in association with repeat business related to customer satisfaction) as with efficiency costs, since both are rooted in the need to maximize profits and avoid failure in the competitive market. Together, they contribute to the relentless emotional intensity of the work which stresses workers out, increases absence due to sickness, fuels labor turnover, lowers performance, and reduces the call center workers' capability to engage positively with customers.[31] In attempts to alleviate these problems managements at a number of call centers have taken recourse to a range of employee involvement techniques such as teamwork, job rotation, suggestion schemes and quality circles. This points to a trend towards integrated systems of technical, bureaucratic and normative controls, intended to create an "assembly line in the head."[32] As with other management projects of participative management, there is often a discrepancy between the unitary managerial rhetoric and the actual practices of employee participation. For example, teams are often supervisor-led and associated with peer pressure; team meetings are often brief or skipped altogether, and quality circles lack authority and autonomy.[33]

In call centers that deal with more complex problems, such as technical support that requires the employment of knowledge workers, tasks are less routinized, specialists work together to answer questions, and enjoy more discretion within a less-bureaucratic network organization. Call centers in which nonstandard problems are the norm, operate in a knowledge-intensive environment characterized by learning, problem solving and sharing of contextually-specific, tacit knowledge designed to provide a high-quality customized service. Usually the knowledge workers involved aim to creatively and optimally use a sophisticated expert system. Yet even in such empowered, high-trust work situations, knowledge workers tend to experience peer pressure to complete tasks and projects within certain time and budget limits as imposed by the targets set by managers, who are monitored too, albeit to a lesser extent than non-specialist workers.[34]

Clearly, not all call centers are alike. The organization of the work can vary within and between call centers; much depends on the complexity of the work, the segment of the market served and where it is located, since market and employment conditions vary between localities (or countries), or a combination of some of these factors. But several studies have shown that the majority of call centers veer toward the Fordist technologically-driven, low-cost, lean production model.[35] Finally, there has also been an increasing tendency of further automating jobs in call centers by introducing voice-response systems, which allows customers to interact with a company's host system via a telephone key pad or by speech recognition.[36] The ability to identify customers allows services to be tailored according to the customer profile. The caller can be given the option to wait in line, choose an automated service, or request a callback. As yet, call centers mostly use these systems to identify and segment callers.[37]

10

Twists and Turns of High-Tech Jobs and the Reengineering of Skilled White-Collar Work

The shareholder-type system of capitalism that became prominent in the 1980s is associated with weak ties, low trust, and short time horizons, and tends to impinge negatively on career jobs and workers' job security. Not all employees regretted the change in corporate governance, however. In the 1990s, a significant segment of the younger generation of workers in private business—that is, educated people in high technology, global finances and associated new services, such as those found in Silicon Valley, New York's Silicon Alley, and on Wall Street—were in favor of, and even celebrated, labor mobility.[1] This was a time when the economist Robert Reich in his influential 1991 book, *The Work of Nations*, argued that, given the loss of high-volume manufacturing jobs, the key to national competitiveness in the global economy now lay in what value American workers would add to products and services.

As Bill Clinton's first Secretary of Labor, Reich glorified the status of "symbolic analysts," whose skills in problem solving, strategic counseling, and knowledge management would be paramount. The idea was that these analysts held an occupation involving the nonstandardized manipulation of symbolic information (data, words, oral and visual representations), and continuously accumulated mobile, transferable and hence, highly valuable skills that were independent of fixed organizational or national location. Reich calculated that up to 20 percent of U.S. jobs were occupied by symbolic analysts involved in the creative manipulation of symbols, images, and ideas. These included a wide variety of professionals: engineers, consultants, coordinators, designers, managers, brokers, advertisers, artists, marketers, academics, stylists, and so forth.[2]

For U.S. managers, the increased economic significance of these categories of "creative" workers exacerbated an old problem; it accelerated the need to rapidly as well as efficiently appropriate the labor of "value-adding" workers. The major challenge to managers was how to make "creative" workers think faster, which (as described earlier) they tried to do through rejuvenating an older management practice of control and inspiration.

It turned out, however, that this was not the fastest growing occupational group in the new economy. The largest growth would come in the low-wage sector, which Reich described as in-person services: security guards, cashiers, waiters, janitors, hospital and sales attendants, and nursing home aides. However, the status and caliber of Reich's symbolic analysts made their jobs a goal toward which all workers were encouraged to aspire and a role model to adopt for their children's education. This segment of the workforce—much more influential than their numbers would suggest—harbored what Andrew Ross has called the "no-collar" people. Their technologies were "revered like the sacred fire that Prometheus stole from the gods," and high tech was one of the few sectors of the economy where the United States was still leading the way.[3]

On the other hand, it was also acknowledged that with the increased use of the Internet certain kinds of jobs were destined to become obsolete. Routine Web use promised a reduction in the time and energy that people spent looking for goods and services: information, news, entertainment, food, shelter, and the abundance of consumer items. If almost everything could be researched, or ordered, or even consumed online, then most of the middlemen—brokers, retailers, salespeople, travel agents, editors, publishers—who ran the current systems of distribution would lose their jobs as a result of "disintermediation," then a widely popular management term. This trend was not expected to result in mass unemployment, however. For the time being, at least until the information technology industry resorted to its own downsizing, the proliferation of jobs in the new economy sector was supposed to be able to compensate for layoffs elsewhere.[4]

Thus, America's response to the challenge from China in the 1990s was to shift toward high tech, which became the rallying cry for both business and political leaders alike. According to the prevailing conventional wisdom, "the U.S. economy had become 'postindustrial'—well on the way to realizing the prognostication that it is a service economy, and it is better to let others such as the Chinese and the Koreans produce material goods because industrial production causes pollution and is inconsistent with our collective aspiration to become a nation of ... 'symbolic analysts.'"[5] Several leading economists claimed that traditional U.S. manufacturing was doomed because China and the rest of Asia were becoming the workshops of the global economy with their millions of low-cost, moderately skilled workers. America's new high ground would be the knowledge economy—the Internet, IT, scientific research, product development, corporate services, finance—areas where American universities would generate high-end skills and where start-ups would smartly lead the United States to a long-term innovative advantage. The older generation stimulated the so-called Generation X to stake its future on becoming engineers, computer programmers, and systems architects—an army of "knowledge workers" whose knowledge economy expertise would protect them from low-cost Asian competitors. The dawning of the digital age, its advocates asserted, was changing the global balance of economic power back in America's favor.[6] Stanley Aronowitz and William DiFazio adroitly summarize this viewpoint and the associated policy changes regarding education for the labor force:

> The communications/information boom would create a world of almost unlimited opportunities for young people, provided they put their collective noses to the grindstone and learned math, science, and the elements of computer programming. In [the 1990s], the dot.com boom appeared to refute our claim [regarding the demise of what the authors call "real jobs"]: opportunities for the computer literate sprang up, chiefly on the two coasts [especially New York's Silicon Alley and California's Silicon Valley], but also in select cities like Atlanta and Austin and in many university towns. Quickly, new financial and economic moguls such as Microsoft, Apple, Sun Systems, Intel, and computer makers such as Hewlett-Packard and Dell seemed to challenge the old oligarchic companies like General Motors, General Electric, Ford, and U.S. Steel for dominance. Schools at all levels gave wide berth to computer-mediated occupational programs and enrollments sharply rose as young people, finding that factory jobs were disappearing, entered higher education in the confident belief that schooling was the key to their collective futures ... many institutions of higher education save the elite universities succumbed to forge "partnerships" with cutting-edge technology corporations that were eager to assist university and college administrations to tailor their curriculum to the new economic reality.[7]

Certainly, the number of IT jobs in the U.S. showed a marked increase in the late 1990s. According to the Bureau of Labor Statistics, the number of computer programmers grew from 553,000 in 1995 to 669,000 in 2000, while the number of systems analysts jumped from 933,000 to 1,787,000 in the same period.[8] Next to the growth of these more traditional and higher salaried computer occupations, IT support jobs such as database administrator, help desk technician, webmaster, and IT specialists were growing even faster, although the Bureau of Labor Statistics was not capable of keeping track of them. There was also the important fact that, as the Internet and computer applications became omnipresent, IT jobs were no longer confined to IT industries but had spread throughout all organizations—including health care, schools, art institutions, and sports. The U.S. Commerce Department reported that, at their high point in 2000, IT occupations totaled 5.4 million, although this seems to include computer manufacturing jobs, which were the first to be outsourced abroad.[9]

An important factor in the case of IT work was that in the last decade of the 20th century, the division between the work of project managers and systems analysts weakened. While computer programming in the 1960s was largely a craft, procedural programming languages like COBOL were introduced to speed up code production. By the late 1970s data-processing management experts had developed so-called structured programming, intended to reorganize programming work so that managers could better control it.[10] Instead of the assembly-line rigid labor divisions tried by managers in the 1970s and the structured programming of the 1980s, the 1990s restructuring of such work led to more being done with fewer people. This could be accomplished, partly, because programming was then based on structured programming languages and standardized system development tools that had been developed over the previous periods. From a management perspective, what could not be done by dividing and standardizing the work could instead be accomplished by using more standardized tools, techniques, and software.[11]

Easier-to-use programming languages with routine coding procedures resulted in a devaluation of programming skill, so that by the early 1990s programmers' salaries were no longer rising as they had been before. By now computer programs were designed as packaged products to be sold on the market, thus enabling businesses and consumers to buy off-the-shelf software. Additionally, object-oriented programming languages like JAVA and C++ were becoming popular. These languages were designed to integrate databases with software routines. This meant that each "object" of information from a database, such as a name, Social Security number, and address, could be used in any number of different programs without programmers having to recode it.[12] On the other hand, programming skills, in terms of number and range of programming languages, application tools, and Web design principles continued to expand in the late 1990s and into the new century. Companies were also raising the educational bar, requiring at least a bachelor's degree, and in some areas, graduate degrees in Computer Science or an MBA in Information Technology for employment.[13]

There was a remarkable convergence of technologies, and the monopolistic dominance of global markets by a few standard suppliers, notably Microsoft, which led to the increasingly generic nature of many business functions and processes. The design of off-the-shelf software increasingly dictated the nature of business procedures, forcing many small firms, for instance, to use standard procedures for project management, accounting, or database management, because they lacked the intellectual, technical, and financial resources to create their own custom-made solutions in an increasingly complex technological environment. (This tendency would be partly counter-balanced in later years by the emergence of an array of standardized software packages—including desktop or Web-based applications—that are geared toward as many different types of small businesses.) As organizations developed their business processes in these near-interchangeable ways, it became increasingly easier for these same processes to be seen as separable functions, which could be outsourced, "in-sourced," or sold on as profit-making services to other organizations.[14]

Office workers expected to be treated professionally and therefore did not think they needed union protection. In the past, American white-collar workers were not open to unionization or collective action at the workplace. The white-collar middle class seemed more interested in individual advancement—as promised by the various technology and information revolutions—than in fighting collectively for workplace rights. As corporate employees, they bargained individually with their managers for higher salaries and annual increases. But there was also a strong reluctance on the part of the large entrenched, white-male industrial unions to organize office workers, who were, for the most part, better educated and alien to them. By conceding the "qualified," credentialed intellectual workers to management, leading industrial unions severely diminished their capacity for industrial action. It was only at the end of the 20th century that union organizing of professional and technical workers heated up as a growing army of workers became subjected to the deskilling format of industrial work and unions started to take more notice of these segments of the labor force. This became evident in a surge of unionization among engineers and computer experts in some of the largest corporations.[15] The Communications Workers of America (CWA) made inroads among Technical, Office and Professional (TOP) workers, particularly in the high-tech Seattle area. (Yet an attempt to organize Microsoft's Seattle professionals had little success, even though the company had just instituted a two-tier salary structure. The first tier enjoyed more or less secure employment and benefits but lower salaries than the second tier, which had no benefits or job security at all.) And the Professional Employees Department of the AFL-CIO, representing four million technical, professional, and skilled white-collar workers, held a nationwide campaign to organize technical and professional workers.

Likewise, legal actions such as the one by IBM employees over the loss of their secure pension benefits resulted in an employee association affiliated with the Communications Workers of America. Furthermore, in 1998, temporary workers at Microsoft—who called themselves "permatemps," because many worked more than two years—formed the Washington Alliance of Technology Workers and affiliated with the CWA. Six years earlier, permatemps at

Microsoft had filed a class-action lawsuit against Microsoft for the way the company hired and treated its contingent workers, improperly denying them benefits such as stock options, pensions, and health coverage. They asserted that the company maintained a fiction that they were temp workers by hiring them through temp agencies to avoid paying them those benefits. They maintained that they were actually permanent employees, and therefore deserved the same benefits as regular workers. In December 2000, Microsoft settled the case for $97 million. The settlement covered temp employees who worked at Microsoft from January 1987 to June 2000; 8,000 to 12,000 former temporary workers were estimated to qualify for an award under the settlement.[16]

The Ups and Downs of No-Collar Workers

The most celebrated work in the second half of the 1990s was that of the no-collar, new media workers—programmers, commercial artists, and young businesspeople—who developed websites and multimedia projects. These emerging (and merged) occupations grew out of older job categories, and developed with such breakneck speed that by the turn of the century, jobs, companies, and indeed the whole IT industry, had become heavily involved in what would soon be known as the dot-com bubble.

In the late 1990s, when many small Internet and new media firms were growing and being bought out by larger firms, the IT industry was a major driving force of the booming stock market. Financial analysts and others representing financial firms put together proposals for initial public offerings (IPOs) to create and sell shares in the new firms in what the analysts promised would be the new economy. Workers in these new hybrid companies—artists and designers from advertising and entertainment, MBAs and marketing experts in business consulting, information technology specialists—were often offered the chance to buy the stock offerings. For most workers, the stock options became (what seemed to them) far more wealth than their salaries or even bonuses could ever have delivered.

Hyped by fabulous stories in the popular press and other media, the new employer-owner millionaire came to symbolize the possibilities of the new postindustrial economy in much the same way that stories of Horatio Alger (the fictional rags-to-riches character) did in the industrial period of the late 19th century. For young people entering these firms, the lure of individual wealth, represented by shares in stock, held out the promise of more interesting job prospects and a better work life than the corporate career ladder paths of those (mostly men) among their parents' generation.[17]

Indeed, the Internet-intensive firms were supposed to be different in their work practices and working conditions. In theory, workers who were owners (at least of stock certificates) were to have more decision-making power over what they did and the chance to acquire new skills and use them in more creative ways. Unlike older, more bureaucratic or hierarchical management models, the new economy was to be characterized by flattened channels of communication between workers and their managers. Working hours, dress codes, and office walls as well as office furniture were to reflect a more flexible working culture. To be sure, these characteristics were in place for hundreds of thousands of workers who did manage to get a job at Internet-intensive companies, but for many others these characteristics were elusive.[18]

In *The Corrosion of Character* (1998), the sociologist Richard Sennett discussed the sociopsychological implications of the new developments in American capitalism in the 1990s for middle-class workers at the epicenter of the global boom in high-tech industries, in financial services, and in the media. He argued that flexi-time, the flexible scheduling of both full- and part-time work, operated in "about 70 percent of American corporations," and tended to be used as a form of social control since it was a matter of reward from above rather than a right achieved from below. Sennett also stipulated that an individual's identity was less dependent upon work than in the past.[19] He further contended that the surge in corporate downsizing was the preeminent occurrence of the postmodern age, with consequences that went far beyond the labor market. As career durations contracted, so too did people's time horizons and personal relationships. The new man/woman saw a way here to get rich by thinking short term, developing his or her potential by job-hopping in places like Silicon Valley with weak personal ties and short time horizons, which eroded people's moral strength by loosening the bonds of trust and commitment, and divorcing will from behavior. Both transiency and inequality were the price paid for the increased liberty.[20]

In a later publication Sennett qualified his account of the growth of flexibility by noting that the institutional changes he described referred only to the cutting edge of the economy: high technology, global finance, and new service firms with three thousand or more employees (yet he estimated that different forms of nonstandard work added up to about a fifth of the American labor force). But these firms had a cultural influence that went far beyond their numbers; they pointed to new conceptions of personal skills and abilities. The qualities of the ideal self in these workplaces were a source of anxiety because the new conceptions were experienced as disempowering by the mass of workers. Sennett argued that in the new flexible organization of work, capital was liberated but workers were devastated. The identity they once obtained via work was undermined by diminished loyalty, trust, and knowledge; that is, erosion of the value of accumulated experience, thus hollowing out ability. Ironically, this impaired organizational efficiency, especially during an economic downturn.[21]

The changed status of craftsmanship was a pivotal issue here, according to Sennett. Whereas craftsmanship requires mastering and owning a particular domain of knowledge, the new version of talent was not content-specific or content-determined.[22] Dynamic firms and flexible organizations that were leading the way in the "new capitalism" emphasized the ability to rapidly process and interpret changing stocks of information and practice.[23] Work at the cutting edge of the "new capitalism" in North America and Western Europe entailed an emphasis on *potential ability* in relation to the practices of flexible institutions. The latter was also the basis of the associated meritocratic scheme in evaluating talent, whereby the discovery of a certain kind of potential ability was equated with justice, as Sennett suggested.[24]

As his findings confirmed, strong institutional ties or company commitments were not ranked very high on the list of no-collar workers' priorities, especially in the job-hopping sector. But it should be recognized that, by the mid–1990s, change, risk, individual mobility, and discrete job experiences had entered the workplace almost everywhere, eroding the prospects of stability, solidarity, or a long-term career. Job security was less of an expectation in all sectors of the economy. A layoff was no longer the opposite of employment. Andrew Ross even suggests that it had become "a routine aspect of work in America and was almost understood to be part of a job description."[25]

The downside of what Sennett called the "new capitalism"—but which with the benefit of hindsight can better be seen as speeded-up capitalism-as-usual—became all too clear when the dot-com bubble burst in the stock market in the spring of 2000. The information technology industry, which was at the center of the 1990s boom, was caught in the maelstrom of the 2001 recession and the ensuing "jobless recovery." Between March 2001 and March 2004, the IT industry plunged and many people were laid off by companies in Northern California (Silicon Valley), New York City (Silicon Alley), and other Internet-intensive areas. As a whole, the IT industry lost about 403,000 jobs, more than half of which were eliminated during the economic recovery as U.S. corporations continued to pursue restructuring tactics aimed at achieving immediate reductions in labor costs. The employment declines were partly due to cyclical factors, but flexible staffing arrangements and offshore outsourcing played a crucial role in more long-term structural changes of the IT industry.[26] According to a rough estimate, more than a million other employees in a wide range of older industries like finance, insurance, and legal sectors, were then laid off in the U.S. too.[27]

While the overall economic patterns of the 1990s appeared as an accelerated version of capitalism-as-usual, a new set of work relations had emerged out of the economic turmoil of the late 1990s and early 2000s. But the new work relations did not appear to reflect the rosy picture that was given of them in the mid–1990s: worker-owners with many jobs to choose from and flexible working conditions. Instead, one could witness a major shift in employment relations for people entering the labor market as well as for experienced workers. The shifts were apparent in the way workers—all workers from factory floor to freelance professionals—were expected to be more flexible in terms of their job expectations, salary, contractual arrangement, time spent doing work, and skills.[28]

There was an important factor at work here that should not be overlooked. The number of tasks involving standard generic computer-related skills had been growing rapidly, as measured in terms of the numbers of people whose jobs involved these skills exclusively or in terms of the proportion of the time spent on these tasks by workers whose jobs also required other skills (or both). This created a double-edged sword. The fact that the skills were now generic had made it easier to hop laterally from job to job, company to company, and industry to industry. But by the same token each worker had also become more easily dispensable and replaceable. The combination of this new occupation mobility with the huge expansion of the potential labor pool also made it much more difficult to build stable group identities based on shared skills (which might be helpful to neo craft-based, exclusionary unionization). Attempts to construct barriers around skill groups were thwarted by the speed of change. Any investment of time and effort in learning a new software package might be wiped out in a matter of months by the launch of a new replacement. As existing hierarchies were challenged through direct communication between senior and junior members of staff and cutting out middle layers of managers, new divisions may have been created that opened up an unbridgeable gap between these same head office staff members and their fellow employees at a remote call center or data-processing site.[29]

The Corporate Office Will Be Everywhere

More generally, the much-heralded new economy of the 1990s, with its supposedly recession-proof character built on productivity generated by technology, did not materialize in the 21st century. In 2002, the Bureau of Labor Statistics reported that 32.1 million jobs in the U.S. had been lost, many of them in occupations requiring skill and higher education.[30] The Bureau also reported that 37.1 million jobs had been created, but, as is well-known, this figure is misleading since these newer jobs included part-time and low-wage sales jobs like those at Walmart. By now it was becoming clear that the combination of incorporating routine parts of jobs into complete software and databases, coupled with the decreasing costs of information infrastructure, enabled corporations in the U.S. (and elsewhere in the global North) to offshore many of those jobs to developing countries in the global South and ex–Soviet bloc countries in Europe.

The other parts of the narrative about the changing nature of work had been seen on a smaller scale throughout the 1990s: the increasing part-time and contingent nature of the jobs that stayed in the country; the extended reliance on defining work in terms of projects of products instead of specific hours worked; enhanced expectations that consumers would do their own work in buying products and services, on the Internet or on the phone; and the enormous reductions in the costs of computer hardware, software, and networks. All of this came together to create what looked like the perfect storm, pulling jobs out of the country and making the remaining ones more stressful and more risk-laden. For many of the remaining workers, these risks included uncertainty about where the next job or project would come from, as well as the very down-to-earth risk of getting sick and not having medical insurance or paid sick leave.

Corporate globalization's first wave had started two decades earlier with the exodus of jobs making shoes, cheap electronics, and toys to developing countries. After that, simple service work, like processing credit-card receipts, and digital toil, like writing software code, began fleeing high-cost countries. Now corporations that had previously outsourced jobs in the areas of product design, technical support, and employee benefits to subcontractors in their home countries, were shifting those jobs to overseas subcontracting firms. It became ever more evident that all kinds of knowledge work could be done almost anywhere.[31]

All these changes are part of the by now familiar economic pattern of shifting financial risk from large organizations to smaller ones, and from higher management to the individual worker. In the 1980s, there was much managerial talk about needing "just-in-time" products to compete in the global market. By the late 1990s, in addition to flexible product inventories, employees too had become a just-in-time variable. Originally "just-in-time" meant that parts and products would be produced, as they were needed, thus reducing the expense of keeping inventories. In the world of office work, just-in-time workers were those drawn from the contingent workforce, where companies hired them only during peak periods. This had many advantages for the firm, but hardly any for the workers involved, with the notable exception of self-employed consultants in professional areas, many of whom said that they preferred this arrangement.[32]

By the early 21st century, a "just-in-time" production process had spread further and been introduced throughout the white-collar sector, not only in the U.S. and Japan, but around the world. Typically, parent companies, including large companies in India, squeezed competitive prices out of subcontracting firms, who in turn squeezed lower-priced contracts out of the large reserve labor pool of individual freelancers and self-employed workers, many of whom were willing to take whatever work became available to make a living.[33]

The Corporatization of Higher Education

One of the most visible settings to see how the nature of work and the places it is carried out have changed is the university, where increasingly corporate business models have been introduced. Along with the broader tendency of neoliberalization and the dismantling of the public sphere (including university education as a public good),[34] just-in-time production and service delivery has expanded enormously through the large increase of full-time and part-time contingent instructors. According to the American Association of University Professors (AAUP), from 1993 to 2011 the percentage of faculty members without tenure surged nationally from 57 percent to 70 percent.[35] In 2014, more than 75 percent of faculty members were adjuncts and more than half of these lived below the poverty line.[36] Traditionally, the majority of adjuncts had been graduate students, for whom teaching part-time was a kind of apprenticeship for working their way through their doctoral studies. Increasingly, however, universities have taken recourse to hiring more part-timers and non-tenured faculty to cut labor costs and increase the number of sections and courses taught, and thus raise revenue for the university. Linked to the need for income by unemployed and part-time professionals, this managerial policy has resulted in a growing army of freelance academics, who are often facing scattered and very time-intensive work.

Of course, the quality of tenured or more permanent university jobs has also changed. Especially at universities outside the Ivy League, professors experienced increasing workloads, ranging from more students per semester to more papers to grade, to more time spent on a computer, answering e-mails and doing administrative work. E-mail and course websites along with computer applications like Blackboard (to put together supplemental materials to students) became a common extension of the educational environment.

For-credit online courses were increasingly part of the curriculum as well. Taken together, this easily led to overwork with its human costs. Many faculty, like other professional workers, were also faced with the extension of their workday due to the blurred boundaries between home and work, and work-related Internet usage and digital communications with students after work hours.[37]

Furthermore, university professors, like medical doctors (see later in this chapter), increasingly found their decision-making constrained by bureaucratic levels of managers and administrators. Ironically, at the same time that managers of large business corporations and influential consultants were claiming that the older hierarchical corporate structure was inefficient, this model was being held up as the way to go forward to formerly independent professionals in higher education and health care. But there is nothing new in this pattern, for increased levels of management have been added to control workers thought to be too independent—from craftsmen in the early industrial period to book-keepers and accountants in the white-collar world of the early post–World War II period. From this historical perspective, one would expect that once managerial control over the workers and the work process was achieved, top management would release some hierarchical reins (and delayer the organizational hierarchy), as professionals then internalized the demands and no longer needed to be reminded routinely of the rules.[38]

The overall trend at universities appears not to have gone in this direction, however. On the contrary, the more intensive top-down management practices that are part of business reengineering have also entered the world of academia. In particular, the approach called Balanced Scorecard (BSC), which was originally developed for business organizations, has increasingly become influential at universities as well over the past twenty or so years. This occurred not only in the U.S. (where in 1993 the University of California at San Diego was the first to adopt the BSC), but also in several other countries across the globe by way of U.S. consulting firms and business schools. (BSC was taken to an extreme in the United Kingdom with the introduction of the Research Assessment Exercise (RAE) in 2006–2007 as part of the production regime mandated by all British governments since Margaret Thatcher's time, requiring academics to turn out a designated number of books, monographs, or articles in scholarly journals over a four- or five-year period.[39])

BSC is the brainchild of Robert Kaplan, an academic accountant at the Harvard Business School, and Boston consultant David Norton.[40] In line with Kaplan's accountancy background, the methodologies of the BSC concentrate on the setting up, targeting, and measurement of statistical key performance indicators. These are classified under four headings: financial performance, internal business processes, innovation and learning, and customer service. The multiplication of key performance indicators also offers many more opportunities for top-down monitoring and control. This is reflected in Kaplan and Norton's usage of the language of aviation and autopilot to describe the BSC at work. The Balanced Scorecard is compared to the dials and indicators in an airplane cockpit, with the CEO, his or her senior executives, and their system designers in control.

The BSC control regime relies on a proliferation of performance indicators whose targets must be met. In the case of research, this leads to the measurement and targeting of a scholar's output and measurement of the time taken by the scholar to do the research, the money the research brings in, the indexes of impact and esteem surrounding the research, and the grades awarded for research submitted in the assessment exercise. Other performance indicators (such as the number of graduates and postdoctoral students enrolled, degrees and diplomas awarded etc.) are used with regard to education, down to the level of individual faculty members.

Management consultants presented the Balanced Scorecard as a prominent tool that could be used to "strategize" and monitor organizational performance, continuously "benchmarking" this with key elements of the strategic plan that top management should have designed. After the BSC approach was introduced in an academic setting, the workplaces of faculty came to be dominated by (at least in this context) unfamiliar managerial language. Now there were "departmental line managers" who carried out monitoring, diagnostic, prescriptive, and sanctioning tasks with regard to the department's members on behalf of higher management. In order to survive in the much more competitive climate, faculty felt obliged to pursue highly calculative strategies in publishing and otherwise making their research public. They tried to find out, for example, whether an academic conference they were going to attend would count as an "indicator of esteem." Above all, they thought through as best as they could how to come up with at least the minimum, but preferably more than the designated number of books and journal articles of a certain quality through strategic publishing.[41]

In implementing the BSC in higher education institutions, tools such as Strategy Map have come into use "to enhance clarity." This is thought to be especially useful to guide middle management and operational staff, as well as other non-technical stakeholders. Using a strategy map, they are all able to visualize how their activities contribute to the institution's strategic goals and final outcomes. A strategy map is purportedly a handy tool to give a graphical snapshot of the strategy of the institution so as to clarify the linkages among the strategic objectives, the initiatives, and specific actions to be accomplished.[42]

It aims to offer a visual framework that illustrates patterns of the cause and effect chain connecting the desired outcomes to the key drivers that are essential to achieve them. It thus may provide a visual insight into how individual actions of employees contribute to strategic objectives and subsequently to the overall performance of the organization. It supposedly enables workers to collaborate and coordinate their actions in order to achieve maximum efficiency and effectiveness while executing the institution's "mission." Unsurprisingly, such a map is structured in a top to bottom fashion, mapping out a destination/goal and thereby illuminating the route to be taken to achieve it. Once implemented, the monitoring by the institution's board and top management is expected to be easier. A strategy map consists of five basic components: Financial Perspective, Learning and Growth Perspective, Internal Process Perspective, Stakeholders Perspective, in addition to the "Vision, Mission and Strategic Thrusts." As such it provides a more practical, some would say rather trivial, way of implementing the BSC framework in higher education.

According to this framework, a key element of higher education institutions is achieving results in terms of products and services that cater to the customers and other stakeholders; this is the reason why the stakeholders perspective (however problematic the precise meaning of "customers" may be) has been given high priority.[43] However, based on an extensive survey of higher education institutions around the world, some proponents have suggested that it would be more appropriate for non-profit universities to use the BSC with the financial perspective instead of the customers/stakeholders perspective at the top of the scorecard.[44] This involves the questionable belief that once an institution's financial strategy is clearly defined and purposely implemented to focus on the educational outcome, this will translate into overall success of the academic institution.[45] Needless to say, this is emblematic of the financial pressure that especially public universities are often under. And it leaves intact a highly centralized command and control structure (much more coercive than normative in its setup), which is adverse to an alternative organizational structure and culture that befits the classic humanistic mission of the university.[46]

There is also a trend of increased automation of the teaching part of professorial labor. This is evident in a recent push to use computers to grade papers, which has triggered a public protest, in the form of a well-researched online petition, posted in March 2013, by a small group of academics, primarily consisting of English professors and writing instructors.[47] Within a couple of months, the petition had been signed by over four thousand professional educators, as well as public intellectuals, including Noam Chomsky.

Using computers to grade tests is not new, of course. For years, computers have been used to handle the trivial task of grading multiple-choice tests.

Machine essay grading draws on advanced artificial intelligence techniques; the basic strategy closely resembles the methodology behind Google's online language translation, and is also deployed for plagiarism detection. Machine learning algorithms are first trained using a large number of writing samples already graded by human instructors. The algorithms are then applied to new student essays and can do so almost instantaneously. Techniques such as these very often match or even outperform the best efforts of human experts, according to its supporters. Indeed, a 2012 analysis by researchers at the University of Akron's College of Education compared machine grading with the scores awarded by human instructors and found that the two systems "achieve virtually identical levels of accuracy, with the software in some cases proving to be more reliable." The study involved nine companies that offered machine grading solutions and over 16,000 pre-graded student essays from public schools in six U.S. states.[48]

But other studies of machine scoring of essays reached negative conclusions on various dimensions, including the inability to recognize important qualities of good writing, such as truthfulness, tone, complex organization, logical thinking, or ideas new and relevant to the topic. Moreover, some of the algorithms used are so reductive as to be absurd; for example, sophistication of vocabulary is reduced to the average length or relative infrequency of words, or development of ideas is reduced to average sentences per paragraph.[49] According to Nicholas Carr, "Automated essay-grading algorithms encourage in students a rote mastery of the mechanics of writing. The programs are deaf to tone, uninterested in knowledge's nuances, and actively resistant to creative expression."[50]

Martin Ford, author of *Rise of the Robots* (2015), thinks that despite the controversy surrounding it, algorithmic grading is likely to become more prevalent as school managements continue to seek ways to economize. In situations where a large number of essays need to be graded, the approach is thought to have obvious advantages. Next to speed and lower cost, an algorithmic approach offers objectivity and consistency in cases where multiple human graders would otherwise be required. The technology also gives students instant feedback and is deemed well suited to assignments that might not otherwise receive detailed scrutiny from an instructor. Most likely this kind of grading will, at least for the foreseeable future, be consigned to introductory courses teaching basic communication skills. For the time being, English professors need not fear that the algorithms are on the verge of invading upper-level creative writing seminars. But their deployment in introductory courses might eventually displace the graduate teaching assistants who now perform these grading tasks.[51]

At the time of this writing, machine scoring of essays is often associated with massive open online courses—enrolling thousands of students. One type consists of writing courses (especially first-year composition) that some universities have introduced by way of experiment. The ability of experienced instructors to offer close and continuous individualized feedback to student writers, which may improve their writing skills, is by definition prohibited by the basic structure of these courses.[52] One of the most disruptive impacts is expected to come from online courses offered by elite institutions, however. In many cases, these courses attract huge enrollments, and they will therefore be an important driver of automatic teaching and grading. Since early 2013, edX, created by MIT and Harvard University in May 2012 and then expanded to become an international consortium of elite universities, offers online courses (including some that are free of charge) in a variety of disciplines; it has made its essay-grading software freely available to any educational institution that wants to use it. In short, according to Ford, "algorithmic grading systems have become yet another example of an Internet-based software building block that will help accelerate the *inevitable* drive toward the increased automation of skilled human labor."[53] However, his judgment leaves out the possibility of different choices being made regarding the development of artificial intelligence, including the option of keeping humans "in the loop."

Reengineering in a Service Industry with Highly Skilled Employees: The Medical Sector

With the arrival of "managed care," medicine has become the latest service industry targeted by industrial reengineering. The lead employee in health care, the physician, is a high-wage, highly skilled worker, and the attempts of the managed care industry to subject the physician to the disciplines of "process" represent perhaps the most dramatic example of reengineering's upward mobility in the "new economy" of the late 20th century.

It was the decline of the old fee-for-service system of health insurance that induced the rise of managed care in the late 1980s. Medical insurance benefits were part of the company-provided welfare safety net that employees at business corporations enjoyed from the 1940s into the 1970s. After the defeat in 1949 of congressional legislation that would have established a National Health Service, and the stagnation of the Social Security (pension) system, unions in basic industries such as steel, auto, electrical, communications, oil, and transportation had negotiated a "private" welfare state. Thus they deflated efforts to enact a publicly financed universal health-care program and extend the welfare state.[54]

A major weakness of the old system was its failure to control health care costs. Between 1965 and 1983, per-capita health care expenditures in the U.S. increased at a rate of 12.5 percentage on average per year, nearly 5 percent more than the underlying rate of inflation. The problem of rising health care costs became acute in the late 1980s when yearly increases in health insurance premiums of 15 to 20 percent became normal.[55] Since then a large share of the cost burden has been shifted from companies to their employees. In 1980, for example, 70 percent of Americans who worked at companies with one hundred or more employees received health insurance coverage fully paid for by their employers. But from then on employers began demanding their employees pay an increasing portion of this coverage. Many small businesses made employees pay for most, if not all, of the health insurance costs.[56]

The way in which the relationship between insurers, employers, and physicians developed led to inflation of health care costs. The monthly premiums that insurers charged to businesses on behalf of their employees were calculated on a cost-plus basis, which reflected the existing costs of health care and a markup for profits. As long as the insurer could pass on the higher costs of health care in the form of higher monthly premiums to be paid by the employer, physicians could be overcautious, mitigating their own risk by ordering multiple tests, drugs, or surgical procedures for their patients. The acceleration of health care costs inflation in the late 1980s prompted employers to look around for ways to control their health care expenditures. Managed care seemed to offer a means of breaking these links between higher medical costs and rising insurance premiums.

Large employers such as General Motors would contract with selected managed care organizations (MCOs) such as Aetna or Humana for the insurance of all or part of their workforce. The MCO offered the corporation comprehensive coverage of its workforce for a fixed payment per insured employee. A major drawback for employees of companies that enrolled with MCOs was that their choice of physicians was restricted. The most restrictive of the MCOs, the health maintenance organization (HMO), limited the employee's choice of physicians to a panel approved by the HMO. The preferred provider organization, or PPO, came at a higher fee to employees and allowed them to select a physician "out of network." The promise of MCOs, whether of the HMO or PPO variety, was to keep insurance premiums rising in line with the economy's overall rate of inflation.

Unlike the old fee-for-service industry, MCOs took on the power to control medical costs. This control was greatest for those MCOs that owned their own network of hospitals and directly employed their own medical workforce of doctors, nurses, and administrators. But even when MCOs had to negotiate with independent hospitals, physicians, or groups of physicians, MCOs could use their control of covered patients to knock down the prices they would pay for surgical procedures, doctor's consulting fees, and hospital stays. An important fact regarding the industrialization of service work, is that MCOs also relied on bureaucracies of case managers, *often medically untrained*, to contain medical costs. Working on the telephone, and with the MCO's rule book at hand, case managers subjected the decisions of physicians to "utilization review," telling them which drugs, procedures, tests and treatments they could and could not prescribe for their patients.[57]

In the early and mid-1990s, the managed care model was successful—at least in terms of falling rates of health care inflation and the rising percentage of the employed population insured through MCOs. Measured by the rise in the average premium paid by employers with a workforce of two hundred or more, the inflation of medical premiums fell from 11.5 percent in 1991 to 8 percent in 1993, and to 2.1 percent in 1995. Employers responded with a spectacular increase in the percentage of employed private sector workers enrolled with managed care companies, from 25 percent in 1988 to 80 percent in 1997.[58]

Yet the number of employers who required their workers to pay a higher proportion of health care premiums continued to rise. Other employers canceled company-financed health plans entirely, stating they could not afford them. So pervasive was this risk/burden shift that by the mid-2000s, only 18 percent of workers were receiving full health care coverage paid by their employers, while another 37 percent received partial help but had to pay a large chunk of the medical insurance themselves. The remaining 45 percent received no employer support whatsoever.[59]

The employees who were enrolled in MCOs through their employers have never shared the employers' enthusiasm for the managed care system. A September 2000 poll in *Business Week* showed MCOs to be just as unpopular as the tobacco industry among the American public. Seventy-one percent of those interviewed judged MCOs "poor" or "fair" in the service they provided their customers, while only 18 percent judged their service to be "good" or "excellent." And in the summer of 2002, a Harris poll found that only 17 percent of the public believed that a health care system dominated by managed care "works pretty well and only minor changes are necessary."[60] The growing unpopularity of managed care meant that the U.S. patient population became ever less willing to accept the denials of care handed down by MCO case managers. They regarded those decisions as often arbitrary and unfair, dictated by the MCO's own drive for revenues and profits.[61]

One should be aware that the ideas that drive the managed care industry are rooted as much in management theory as in medicine; management consultants have written many of the chief texts of managed care,[62] while most of them lack any medical qualifications. They set out to transform the practice of medicine, but none has been to medical school, none has practiced medicine, and none has ever examined or diagnosed a single patient. Only one kind of specialized knowledge is required for tasks such as "organizational design," and that is knowledge of reengineering. Medical reengineers simplify existing processes and speed them up; for instance, patients spend fewer days in the hospital, are allowed fewer visits to the doctor, and those visits that do occur are rigorously timed and shortened. Medical reengineering also creates new processes that did not exist before, for example, patients with routine symptoms may be diagnosed over the telephone (or smartphone more recently). Like in a regular call center, automated expert systems pose scripted questions that are then relayed, via a "call taker," to the patient. Treatment of the chronically ill can be reengineered as well, as patients with cancer or heart disease can become objects of "disease management." The processes mentioned so far belong to the operational side of a business, the mostly routine activities that are performed by semi- or unskilled workers. There are many such operational processes in managed care, the ordering of medical supplies, the billing of patients, the procedures of an MCO's own call center.[63]

The reengineering at the lower level of process in managed care is well exemplified by a project called the Idealized Design of Clinical Office Practices, or ID-COP, which was developed in the late 1990s by Donald Berwick and Chuck Kilo, both of the Institute for Health Care Improvement, and both well-known experts in health care efficiency. For them, the ideal clinical office best resembled a Japanese automobile plant: "Tenets of lean production that emanated from Toyota are central to the ID-COP design.... We need to create some health care Toyotas, and we need to understand the path to get there." Berwick praised Taiichi Ohno, cofounder of the Toyota system, as a "ferocious foe of wasted human effort" and, as with the engines and chassis on the Toyota line, patients visiting an ID-COP facility had to be processed in and out of the doctor's office at the maximum possible speed.[64]

A revealing example of managed care's reengineering of a lower-level process is the use of "telephone triage" systems to deal with the supposedly routine complaints of patients. In this respect, managed care has borrowed heavily from the processes of the call center industry. Similar to a call center devoted to sales or marketing, the "call taker" need have no expertise in the subject discussed with the caller. The expectation is that the software guides the call taker in the right direction through a "sophisticated tree analysis" by means of a list of questions and responses based on the information that the caller supplied.[65] Furthermore, technologies exist that supplement the skills of the physician in the same way that design software supplements the skills of the engineer. These include diagnostic systems that facilitate the identification of illness, scanners that provide visual images of disease, and Internet search engines such as Medline that can give the physician immediate access to a wealth of specialized literature. But the managed care industry is also deeply engaged in reengineering what are "higher" processes, and these are the core professional activities of the physician: his or her screening, diagnosis, and treatment of patients.[66]

Managed care's most ambitious claim is that it has developed methods of medical decision-making that are superior to the methods habitually used by physicians. Medical reengineers have developed technologies that circumscribe the physician's expertise and subject him or her to industrial discipline. The physician does not control these technologies—they are the tools of medical directors and case managers employed by managed care organizations. These involve databases incorporating decision-making algorithms that "decide" on the proper length of a patient's hospital stay, set out the appropriate length of time a physician gets to spend with his/her patients, and rule on the treatments that patients should or should not receive. Other software systems that exist set targets for each physician's "clinical productivity," and then monitor whether physicians are meeting their goals.[67]

On the face of it, MCOs are not well placed to impose such medical standardization on the work of practicing physicians. As noted earlier, most medical reengineers have absolutely no medical qualifications, nor can they make up for this deficiency by pointing to the presence within MCOs of highly qualified physicians who might provide medical judgments superior to those of front-line physicians. With few exceptions, MCO "medical directors" are no longer practicing physicians who actually take care of patients. Fewer still are doing advanced medical research. Rather, they have become medical administrators who pass judgment on the medical decisions of others, though they themselves often lack the relevant specialized knowledge. It is here that information technology comes into play as the primary hub of decision making in managed care. In the literature of managed care there is the pervasive belief that the greater the size of the medical databases at the hands of MCOs, the more likely it is that they will hit upon the "best ways" of treating patients.[68] This means, basically, that the lead role in working out how patients with specific clinical features should be treated is not played by physicians but by information systems.

In "planned medicine," the most important decisions physicians have to make concern the broad classification of their patients, and what counts in this classification is not the patient's "individualized" or "idiosyncratic" profile and symptoms, but those characteristics and symptoms that the patient may share in common with a "clinically significant subgroup." This will determine which subgroup the patient will be assigned to. Once the physician has placed the patient into a particular subgroup, he or she has already made his/her most important decision, as the patient's further treatment has instantaneously been decided by the machine. Algorithms have already "analyzed the patient base" to which the patient now belongs, and also determined "which patients need specific services."[69]

The practice of this managerial medical system has profound implications for the relations between physicians and their co-workers. As MCOs try to shrink the responsibilities that have always set physicians apart from nurses or social workers, administration can have their way, integrating the physician within medical processes that are standardized, repetitive, and subject to rigorous timing and monitoring in the manner of the Toyota-style clinic mentioned earlier. The new team structure removes doctors as the essential link in the chain of every patient's care. Thus, the health care system as a whole has been shifting away from the encounter-based care between doctors and patients.[70]

In considering the effects of recent automation in medicine, it should be taken into account that, by the mid–2000s, the U.S. government began to aggressively promote health information technology. Early in 2004, George W. Bush issued a presidential order establishing the Health Information Technology Adoption Initiative, with the goal of digitizing most U.S. medical records within ten years. In the summer of the next year, researchers at the RAND Corporation in California published a report with a rousing prediction about the future of American medicine. They claimed that the U.S. health care system could save more than a whopping $81 billion annually and improve the quality of care if hospitals and physicians changed over to automated record keeping.[71] In June 2005, the Department of Health and Human Services established a task force of government officials and industry executives, the American Health Information Community, to help stimulate the adoption of electronic medical records. The conclusions of the RAND research encouraged the federal government to hand over billions of dollars in financial incentives to hospitals and doctors to have the systems installed. Shortly after his inauguration in 2009, President Barack Obama announced a program to release an additional 30 billion in taxpayer dollars to subsidize purchases of electronic medical record (ERM) systems. A new wave of investment followed, as some three thousand doctors and four thousand hospitals used the opportunity to profit from this program.

However, when Obama started his second term in 2013, RAND published a new report that sketched a very different scenario of information technology in health care. The annual aggregate expenditures on health care in the U.S. had grown from circa $2 trillion in 2005 to roughly $2.8 trillion. Yet, despite the increased use of health IT, quality and efficiency of patient care were only marginally better than before. It was also worrisome that the ERM systems that had been installed with government funds, showed problems with "interoperability" as critical patient data remained locked up in individual hospitals and doctor's offices. The reason was that the EMR applications employed proprietary formats and conventions that imposed brand loyalty to a particular IT system.[72] The latest RAND conclusions about the unfulfilled promises of health IT are confirmed by studies in other countries, such as Great Britain and Australia, where EMR systems have been up and running for some years.[73]

As more data about individual patients are collected and stored in the form of electronic records, digitized images and test results, pharmacy transactions (and in the near future, readings from personal biological sensors and health-monitoring apps), computers will become more adept at finding correlations and calculating probabilities in ever finer detail. Given the current stress on achieving greater efficiency in health care, a Taylorist approach of optimization and standardization is likely to take hold throughout the medical field. The already strong trend toward replacing personal clinical judgment with the statistical outputs of so-called evidence-based medicine will gain further momentum. Doctors will be increasingly subject to pressure—if not outright managerial fiat—to give up more control over diagnoses and treatment decisions to software.[74]

In response to all of this, doctors and registered nurses working in managed care have become much more interested in workplace control. They complain that administration has subverted their autonomy, that decisions concerning patients' health are no longer the exclusive domain of the health professional. Treatment regimes are now handed down to them, often dictated from above. Management exercises control over issues of diagnosis, treatment—including choice of medication—and the organization of the professional's time. Moreover, the practice of medicine is itself subject to machines: computers, electronic scans, MRIs and so forth. But it is also subject to the pressures of science as commercial enterprise, in the drugs promoted to the hospital and the doctors by big pharmaceutical companies. And now that health care is managed by large corporations—some of them for profit—the once independent physician works under constant surveillance.

These developments have become topics for some union intervention. In those places where doctors have become unionized—by 2014, about 15,000 in several organizations, most of them affiliated with the Service Employees International Union (SEIU)—questions of autonomy are a lightning rod of organizing drives. Yet once a drive is over with, health care unions tend to revert to making traditional trade union demands regarding salaries and benefits.[75]

The Side Effects of Automation in Medicine

The introduction of automation into medicine, as with its introduction into other professions, has effects that go beyond efficiency and cost. As physicians come to rely on computers to aid them in more facets of their everyday work, the technology is influencing the way they learn, the way they make decisions, and even their bedside manner.[76] A study of primary-care physicians who adopted electronic records, conducted in 2007 and 2008 by Timothy Hoff, a professor at SUNY University at Albany School of Public Health, shows evidence of "deskilling outcomes," including "decreased clinical knowledge" and "increased stereotyping of patients." The seventy-eight physicians who were interviewed were from primary-care practices of various sizes in upstate New York. Three-fourths of the doctors were routinely using EMR systems, and most of them said they were afraid computerization was leading to less thorough, less personalized care. They told Hoff that in using the computers they would regularly "cut-and-paste" boilerplate text into the reports on patient visits, while when they dictated notes or wrote them by hand they "gave greater consideration to the quality and uniqueness of the information being read into the record." According to those doctors, the very process of writing and dictation had alerted them to be careful and forced them to slow down and "consider what they wanted to say." The physicians complained that the homogenized text of electronic records can diminish the richness of their understanding of patients, undermining their "ability to make informed decisions around diagnosis and treatment."[77]

Doctors' growing reliance on the recycling or "cloning" of text clears away nuance. The cost of diminished specificity and precision is compounded as cloned records circulate among doctors. The reading of dictated or handwritten notes from specialists has long provided a significant educational benefit for primary-care doctors, deepening their understanding not only of individual patients but of everything from disease treatments and their efficacy to new ways of diagnostic testing.[78]

Moreover, the more rigid way that computers present information tends to foreclose the long view of a patient's medical history. Although flipping through the pages of a traditional medical chart today may seem outdated and inefficient, it can provide a doctor with a quick yet meaningful sense of a patient's health history, spanning many years. Faced with the computer's relatively inflexible interface, doctors often end up scanning a patient's records for only the last two or three visits, all information before that is consigned to the electronic dustbin.[79]

The automation of note taking leads to another negative side effect. It introduces a "third party" into the exam room; that, is, the computer itself "competes with the patient for clinicians' attention, affects clinicians capacity to be fully present, and alters the nature of the communication, relationships, and physicians' sense of professional role."[80] In a study conducted at a Veterans Administration clinic, patients who were examined by doctors taking electronic notes reported that "the computer adversely affected the amount of time the physicians spent talking to, looking at, and examining them" and also tended to make the visit "feel less personal."[81]

The intrusiveness of the computer creates yet another problem that has been widely reported. EMR and related systems are set up to provide on-screen warnings to doctors, which can help avoid dangerous oversights or mistakes. If, for instance, a physician prescribes a combination of drugs that could trigger an adverse reaction in a patient, the software will highlight the risk. But most of the alerts turn out to be unnecessary. They are irrelevant, redundant, or just simply wrong. Studies show that primary-care physicians routinely dismiss about nine out of ten of the alerts they receive. This nurtures a condition known as "alert fatigue." Doctors then dismiss the alerts so quickly when they pop up that they end up ignoring even the occasional valid warning.[82]

To fully understand a complicated medical problem or complaint, a clinician has to listen carefully to a patient's story, while at the same time guiding and filtering that story through established diagnostic frameworks. The key is to strike the right balance between grasping the specifics of the patient's situation and inferring general patterns and probabilities derived from reading and experience. Computer automation can streamline patient visits and bring useful information to bear, but by requiring a doctor to follow templates and prompts too slavishly, it can also "narrow the scope of inquiry prematurely" and even lead to misdiagnoses by provoking an automation bias that gives precedence to the screen over the patient. Doctors can begin to display "screen-driven" information-gathering behaviors, scrolling and asking questions as they appear on the computer rather than following the patient's narrative thread.[83]

Experiences in Other Skilled Professions

Unsurprisingly, there are drawbacks to the deployment of computer software by other professionals as well. Compare, for example, the use of decision-support software in corporate audits by accountants. The applications speed up the work, but there are signs that as the software's capacities improve, the accountants become less capable. One study, conducted by a group of Australian researchers, examined the effects of the expert systems used by three international accounting firms.[84] Two of the companies employed advanced software that, based on an accountant's answers to basic questions about a client, recommended a set of relevant business risks to include in the client's audit file. The third firm used simpler software that provided a list of potential risks but required the accountant to take a closer look at them and manually select the salient ones for the file. The researchers gave accountants from each firm a test measuring their knowledge of risks in industries in which they had performed audits. Those from the firm with the less advanced software manifested a significantly better understanding of different forms of risk than did the accountants from the other two firms. The decline in learning associated with advanced software affected even veteran auditors—those with more than five years of experience at their current firm.[85]

Other studies of expert systems led to similar findings. The research generally indicates that while decision-support software can help novice analysts make better judgments in the short run, it can also make them mentally indolent. By diminishing the intensity of their thinking, the software in question retards their ability to encode information in memory, which decreases the likelihood that they develop the rich tacit knowledge essential for true expertise.[86] Computers do a superior job of sorting through lots of data quickly, but human experts remain subtler and wiser thinkers than their digital partners.[87]

The shortcomings of automated decision aids can be subtle, but they have real consequences, particularly in fields where analytical errors have far-reaching repercussions. For example, it has been suggested that miscalculation of risk, exacerbated by high-speed computerized financial trading programs, played a significant role in the near meltdown of the world's financial system in 2008 as these "robotic methods" of decision making led to a widespread "judgment deficit" among bankers and other Wall Street professionals.[88] But other processing mechanisms contributed to this too. Computer Business Systems and their constituent information technologies (about which more later) were at the core of Wall Street's insidious operations before and during the crash. Wall Street professionals relied on these technologies "to create a virtual assembly line on which something as simple as a single subprime mortgage at the start of the line could become by the time it reached the end a molecule within a financial derivate so complex that it was beyond the powers of the IT system themselves to manage or keep track of."[89] But one should also not forget that the ramifications of financial deregulation, along with fraudulent and unethical behavior among those financial wheelers and dealers, have played an important, if not decisive role as well.[90]

11

Technology-First Automation and the Double-Edged Sword of Decision-Support Systems

This is a good place to pause for a moment to examine more closely the problems that may arise in using computer software to replace human skills or, as in the case of expert systems, to purportedly augment those skills. It is important to recognize that, rather than being an automatic result of "inevitable" technological progress, the trajectories of automation that set the parameters of employees' job contents and working conditions are ultimately the result of choices and strategic plans made by top managements (with the help of computer technology consultants and software engineers).

When people tackle a task with the aid of computers, as Nicholas Carr points out, they often become liable to a pair of cognitive impediments: *automation complacency* and *automation bias*. Both reveal the traps we may fall into when we take the route of performing important operations without thinking about them. Automation complacency comes into play when a computer induces a false sense of security in us. We then become so confident that the machine will work flawlessly, adequately handling any challenge that may arise, that we allow our attention to drift. We disengage from our work, or at least from the part of it that the software is handling, and as a result may miss signals that something is wrong. A simple example is that when the spell checker is on as we use e-mail or word-processing software, we become less vigilant proofreaders. Errors that get overlooked can lead to annoyance and at worst, to embarrassment. But automation complacency can also have devastating consequences. In the worst cases, people become so trusting of the technology that their awareness of what is happening around them fades completely, and they tune out. If suddenly a problem emerges, they may be perplexed and waste precious moments trying to reorient themselves.[1]

Automation complacency has been documented in many high-risk situations, from battlefields to industrial control rooms to the bridges of ships and submarines, as well as the flight decks of airplanes. Office workers can fall victim to complacency too, as for example, has happened in the case of architects' declining attention to detail with the introduction of design software in the building trades. With software-generated plans, at least initially, they tended to be less careful about verifying measurements.[2]

Automation bias is closely related to automation complacency.[3] It emerges when people give undue weight to the information arriving on their monitors. Even when the information is wrong or misleading, they believe it. Their trust in the software becomes so strong that they ignore or discount other sources of information, including their own senses. Automation bias occurs, for example, when people are trying to find their way in an unknown environment, slavishly follow flawed or outdated directions from a GPS device or other digital mapping tools, and get lost or go around in circles.

Automation bias is a particular risk for people who use decision-support software to guide them through analyses or diagnoses. For example, since the late 1990s, radiologists have been using computer-aided systems that highlight suspicious areas on mammograms and other x-rays. This has altered the way radiologists read images. In some cases, the highlights aid in the discovery of disease, helping radiologists identify potential cancers they might otherwise have overlooked. But the highlights can also have the opposite effect. Biased by the software's suggestions, doctors may end up paying merely superficial attention to the areas of an image that have not been highlighted, which sometimes leads to overlooking an early-stage tumor or other abnormality. The prompts can also increase the likelihood of false positives, when radiologists have patients return for unnecessary biopsies.

A study in England showed that automation bias has had a greater effect on radiologists and other professional image readers than was previously thought. The researchers found that computer-aided detection tends to improve the reliability only of "less discriminating readers" in assessing "comparatively easy cases."[4] But it can actually diminish the quality of expert readers' performance in evaluating tricky cases. As they rely ever more on the software, the experts are more likely to overlook certain cancers.

There is also evidence that the subtle biases instigated by computerized decision aids may be an inherent part of the human cognitive apparatus for responding to cues and alarms.[5] By directing the focus of people's eyes—and instantaneously triggering their inbuilt responses to such changes in their perceptual field—the aids distort their vision.[6] Martin Ford, a seasoned expert in computer design and software development, by contrast, argues that computers are rapidly getting better at analyzing images; he can quite easily imagine that in the not-too-distant future, radiology will be almost exclusively practiced by machines that hardly ever fail to do the job correctly.[7] Whether his optimism is realistic at this juncture remains to be seen.

The Underrepresentation of Human-Centered Automation

In the prevailing technology-first approach, expert systems are designed to replace, rather than supplement human judgments. And with each upgrade in an application's data-crunching speed and predictive capability, the programmer shifts more decision-making responsibility from the professional to the software. In the emerging field that is variously known as Machine Morality, Machine Ethics, or Friendly AI, there have even been experiments to develop computer models for moral decision making.[8] Researchers in the Netherlands, for example, have come up with the prototype of an "ethical machine" that could possibly be used in medical practice (and criminal justice). They claim that their "moral reasoner" can produce the verdicts of medical ethicists and health judges in real-life cases and can handle the emotional differences between logical identical problems. This ethical machine, allegedly gifted with "twofold autonomy and a touch of personality," also deals with character traits such as honesty and humility that play a role in actual human moral behavior.[9]

In particular cases the technology-first approach may also bring extreme risks with it. The oft-quoted example is the overuse of flight automation in aviation, which can put a plane and its passengers in mortal danger. Evidence collected by the Federal Aviation Administration (FAA) from crash investigations, incident reports, and cockpit studies, indicated automation-induced errors on the part of flight crews. A heavy reliance on computer automation (using a digital "fly-by-wire" system) entails too much time spent flying on autopilot and only little time on manually controlling the plane. This can erode pilots' expertise (psychomotor and cognitive flying skills), dull their reflexes, and diminish their attentiveness, leading to a deskilling of the crew.[10]

Yet there are other ways to deal with the interaction between humans and automation technology, as Nicholas Carr points out. Human-factors experts have long urged designers to move away from the technology-first approach and instead turn toward human-centered automation.[11] Rather than beginning with an assessment of the capabilities of the machine, human-centered designs take off with a careful evaluation of the strengths and limitations of the people who will be interacting with the machine. This connects technological development again with the humanistic principles that motivated the original practitioners of ergonomics, a field that began to emerge—together with its more theoretical cousin, cybernetics—as a formal discipline during World War II. Inspired at first by the war effort and then by the drive to incorporate computers into commerce, government, and science, a large group of psychologists, physiologists, neurobiologists, engineers, sociologists, and designers began to deploy their varied skills to studying the interaction of people and machines. Their aspiration was to bring people and technology together in a productive, resilient, and safe symbiosis, a harmonious human-machine partnership that would get the best from both sides.[12]

The principal aim of human-centered automation is to divide roles and responsibilities in a way that not only capitalizes on the computer's speed and precision but also keeps workers engaged, active, and alert—in the loop rather than out of it. Striking this kind of balance can be achieved in a number of ways. A system can be programmed to shift control over critical functions from the computer back to the operator at frequent but irregular intervals. Cognizant that they may need to take command at any given moment keeps people attentive and engaged, fostering situational awareness and learning. A design engineer can put limits on the scope of automation, making sure that people working with computers perform challenging tasks rather than being assigned passive, observational roles. Giving people more to do, helps to sustain a phenomenon called the *generation effect*.[13] This has everything to do with the advantage of learning by doing, the well-known phenomenon that active involvement during the learning process is more beneficial than passive perception.

At this point one should recognize the possible negative consequences of the increasing reliance on external storage of information in the digital era. As Carr explains concisely:

> For millennia, people have supplemented their biological memory with storage technologies, from scrolls and books to microfiche and magnetic tape. Tools for recording and distributing information underpins civilization. But external storage and biological memory are not the same thing. Knowledge involves more than looking stuff up; it requires the encoding of facts and experiences in personal memory. To truly know something, you have to weave it into your neural circuitry, and then you have to repeatedly retrieve it from memory and put it to fresh use. With search engines and other online resources, we've automated information storage and retrieval to a degree far beyond anything seen before. The brain's seemingly innate tendency to offload, or externalize, the work of remembering makes us more efficient thinkers in some ways. We can quickly call up facts that have slipped out of mind. But that same tendency can become pathological when the automation of mental labor makes it too easy to avoid the work of remembering and understanding.[14]

As the computer programs of Google and other software companies become adept at doing our thinking for us, we come to rely more on the software and less on our own cognitive skills and memorized knowledge. We will be less inclined to be actively preoccupied with knowledge generation. We then end up learning less and knowing less, and also become less capable. As computer scientist Mihai Nadin has observed with regard to modern software, "The more the interface replaces human effort, the lower the adaptivity of the user to new situations."[15] In place of the generation effect, technology-centered automation leads to the reverse: a degeneration effect.

Explicit knowledge (also known as declarative knowledge) about how to carry out a task has its limits, especially when the task has a psychomotor component as well as a cognitive one, like learning to drive a car, which provides a model for the way humans gain complicated skills. To achieve mastery, you need to develop tacit (or procedural) knowledge, which is only possible through real experience—by rehearsing a skill over and over again. The more you practice, the less you have to think about what you are doing. Responsibility for the work moves from your conscious mind, which tends to be slow and faltering, to your unconscious mind, which is speedy and fluid. As you thus free your conscious mind to concentrate on the more subtle aspects of the skill, and when those aspects, too, become automatic, you proceed to the next level. If you keep going, pushing yourself, assuming that you have some natural aptitude for the task, you will ultimately possess the full expertise. This skill-building process, through which capability comes to be exercised without conscious thought, is called *automatization*. It involves widespread, deep adaptations in the brain: "Certain brain cells, or neurons, become fine-tuned for the task at hand and they work in concert through the electrochemical connections provided by the synapses."[16] And through these neural modifications, the brain develops *automaticity*, a capacity for rapid, unconscious perception, interpretation, and action that enables mind and body to recognize patterns and respond instantly to changing circumstances.

Automaticity (sometimes called *proceduralization*) can be seen as a kind of internalized automation—the way the body makes difficult but repetitive work routine. Physical movements and procedures get wired into the brain, laid down in muscle memory, and interpretations and judgments are made through the instant recognition of environmental patterns registered by the senses. The conscious mind's capacity for absorbing and processing information is surprisingly limited. Without automaticity, our consciousness would be permanently overloaded. Even very simple acts, such as reading a sentence in a book or cutting a piece of wood, would strain our capabilities. It is automaticity that gives people more mental leeway.[17]

The transference of performance of tasks from the conscious realm to the subconscious that goes with automation often creates problems. Carr gets to the crux of the matter: in relieving us of repetitive mental exercise, automation relieves us of deep learning. In effect our minds are not being challenged. Our brains, he writes, are "not fully engaged in the kind of real-world practice that generates knowledge, enriches memory, and builds skill."[18] The problem is worsened by the way the dominant setup of computer systems distances its users from direct and immediate feedback about their actions.

To counter these effects, a system design can be engineered so as to give the operator direct sensory feedback on the system's performance by means of audio and tactile alerts, as well as visual displays, even for those activities that the computer is carrying out. Regular feedback, too, heightens engagement and helps operators stay vigilant. A kind of application that deserves special attention here is adaptive automation, in which the computer is programmed to pay close attention to the person operating it. The division of labor between the computer software and the human operator is adjusted continually, depending on what goes on at any given moment. When the computer registers that the operator has to perform a tricky maneuver, for example, it might take over all the other tasks. This enables the operator to concentrate fully on the critical challenge in question. Under routine conditions, the computer might hand more tasks over to the operator, increasing their workload to ensure that they maintain their situational awareness and practice their skills. By thus putting the analytical capabilities of the computer to humanistic use, adaptive automation aims to keep the operator at the peak of the so-called Yerkes-Dodson curve, preventing both cognitive overload and underload. (The Yerkes-Dodson law refers to the phenomenon that as a task becomes harder, the optimum amount of mental stimulation decreases. Both an unusually weak stimulus and an unusually strong stimulus impedes learning—a moderate stimulus inspires the best performance. The law is usually depicted as a bell curve that plots the relation of a person's performance at a difficult task to the level of mental stimulation, or arousal, the person is experiencing. In other words, humans tend to learn and perform best when they are at the peak of the Yerkes-Dodson curve, where they are challenged but not overwhelmed, and enter the state of flow.[19])

In line with these findings, Raja Parasuraman, a well-known expert on the personal consequences of automation, argues that decision-support applications (embedded in expert systems) work best when they deliver relevant information to professionals at the moment they need it, without recommending specific courses of action.[20] The smartest, most fruitful ideas emerge when people are offered room to think. As John Lee (who agrees) puts it, "A less automated approach, which places the automation in the role of critiquing the operator, has met with much more success." According to Lee, the best expert systems present people with "alternative interpretations, hypotheses, or choices."[21] The added and often unexpected information helps counteract the natural cognitive biases that sometimes distort human judgment. It stimulates analysts and decision makers to look at problems from a different perspective and consider broader sets of options. Lee emphasizes that the systems should preferably leave the final verdict to people themselves. Set up in this way, an expert system will truly "informate" its users along the lines that Shoshana Zuboff suggested in the late 1980s.

As AI technologies, including vision, speech, and reasoning, progress, it is increasingly possible to design for humans to be either in or out of "the loop," that is, into or out of the computerized systems that are being created in virtually all sectors of the economy. There is clearly a choice here for system designers: focus either on creating intelligent machines that replace humans, or on how human capabilities can be augmented by the same machines. To be sure, this is a philosophical and ethical choice, rather than simply a technical one.[22] But this is not just a question of the personal preferences of engineers and designers; it involves politics at the societal level, and decisions by government regulators. A precondition for the introduction of human-centered engineering on a larger scale would be a transformation of the prevailing economic system. This is because the ongoing progression toward ever more automation is fundamentally driven by capitalism. Technology-centered mechanization/automation has been going on for many years; the only difference today is that accelerating progress is supposedly pushing it towards its ultimate limits. Up until now this was assumed to involve exponential progress according to Moore's Law—a well-established rule of thumb that says computing power roughly doubles every eighteen to twenty-four months. Moore's Law is a misnomer, however—it is rather a conjecture that semiconductor producers subsequently adopted as an industry standard. Experts now say this "law" is dead, as the rate of progress in question is actually slowing down.[23]

For any "rational" business operating under the given political-economic circumstances, the adoption of labor-saving technology will tend to be irresistible in many cases.[24] Martin Ford explains the capitalist logic and the mindset of business executives that is at issue here. In order for a more human-centered system to be economically competitive to a technology-centered one, it has either to be significantly less expensive (to offset the higher labor costs) or it has to produce results that deliver substantially greater value to customers (and ultimately generate enough additional revenue) to make those extra costs a rational investment. It seems highly unlikely that either scenario would be viable in the vast majority of circumstances. In the case of white-collar automation, for example, both systems would be composed primarily of software, so one would not expect a major cost differential. In a few areas central to a business's primary focus, the human-centered system might have a meaningful advantage (and the ability to increase revenue over the long run), but for the majority of more routine operational activities this again seems unlikely. Moreover, there are additional costs when the business hires workers; the more workers employed, the more managers and human resources staff are needed. Those workers also need offices, equipment, and parking spaces. They also introduce relatively more uncertainty: they get sick, perform poorly, take vacation, have car trouble, quit entirely and bring potentially many other issues with them.[25]

It becomes ever more apparent that changing this pattern of decision making would require modifying the basic incentives built into the market economy. This would mean direct government intervention into the private sector, which is highly unlikely to happen in the U.S. Still, it should be remembered that much of the basic research done in the IT sector was financed by the U.S. government, which included subsidies to private companies. The Defense Advanced Research Projects Agency (DARPA) created and funded the computer network that ultimately evolved into the Internet.[26] And the exponential progress of information technology was brought about partly by university-led research funded by the National Science Foundation. This means that today's computer technology is to some extent the result of the support that American taxpayers have funneled into federal coffers in the decades after World War II.[27] There has been some movement toward regulation of areas of high automation-related risks such as aviation, however. In a 2013 safety alert for flight operators, the Federal Aviation Administration suggested that airlines encourage pilots to assume manual control of their planes more frequently during flights, thereby taking a stand, albeit a tentative one, in favor of human-centered automation. In contrast to European-based Airbus which pursues a technology-centered approach, Boeing has opted for a more human-centered approach in designing its aircraft since the introduction of fly-by-wire systems some thirty years ago.[28]

The Increased Potential of Computer-Aided Decision-Support Systems

The expanding ability of decision-support systems to take control of certain aspects of professional decision-making reflects dramatic gains in computing. Great advances in processing speed, enormous decline in the costs of data storage and networking, and breakthroughs in artificial intelligence methods such as natural language processing and pattern recognition, have changed the situation. Computers have become much more adept at reviewing and interpreting vast amounts of text and other information. By detecting correlations in the data—traits or phenomena that tend to be found together or to occur simultaneously or sequentially—computers are often able to make accurate predictions. Through machine-learning techniques like decision trees and neural networks[29] that chart complex statistical relationships among phenomena, computers are also able to refine the way they make predictions as they process more data and receive feedback about the accuracy of earlier forecasts.[30]

The increased deployment of computers is now happening virtually everywhere in elite professional work. As we have seen, the thinking of corporate auditors is being shaped by expert systems that make predictions about risks and other variables. Other financial professionals, from loan officers to investment managers, also rely on computer models to guide their decisions. Wall Street is now largely dominated by correlation-searching and -calculating computers and the quantitative analysts who program them. The overriding tendency among brokerage and investment banking firms is to continue automating the system while diminishing the number of traders. This is not only the case with regard to the trading of simple stocks and bonds but also in the packaging and dealing of complex financial instruments, with all the risks this entails. Predictive algorithms are also increasingly being used in the domain of venture capitalism, where top investors have long prided themselves on their personal qualities in attaining entrepreneurial success. Venture-capital firms now use computers to search for patterns in records of entrepreneurial success, and then place their bets based on this information.[31]

Similar things are happening in the field of law. For years, attorneys have relied on computers to search legal databases and prepare documents. Recently, specialized software has taken on a more central role in law offices; the critical process of document discovery has been largely automated. Traditionally, junior lawyers and paralegals read through a great amount of correspondence, e-mail messages, and notes in research of evidence. In the early 2000s, new applications of artificial intelligence techniques emerged based on natural language understanding, such as "e-discovery," for the automated processing of the relevant legal documents required to disclose in litigation. It soon became possible to scan millions of documents electronically and recognize underlying concepts and even discover so-called smoking guns—that is, evidence of illegal or improper behavior. This happened at a time when litigation against corporations routinely involved the review of millions of documents for relevance. The machines detect not only relevant words and phrases but also chains of events, relationships among people, and even personal emotions and motivations. Thus, a single computer can take over the work of dozens of well-paid professionals. Comparative studies showed that the machines could operate as well or better than humans in analyzing and classifying documents.[32]

Legal software firms have gone further, and are developing statistical prediction algorithms that, by analyzing thousands of past cases, can recommend trial strategies, such as the choice of venue or the terms of a settlement offer, providing high probabilities of success. Software will soon be able to provide assessments that up until now required the experience and insights of a senior litigator. Lex Machina, a company started in 2010 by a group of Stanford law professors and computer scientists, may be leading the way here. With a database covering some 150,000 intellectual property cases, it runs computer analyses that predict the outcomes of patent lawsuits under various scenarios, taking into account the court, the presiding judge, participating attorneys, the litigants, the outcomes of related cases, and other factors.[33]

It is IBM's super computer system Watson, however, that has been lauded as a major breakthrough in the use of computer technology in highly-skilled professional work. Watson embodies an artificial intelligence technology capable of answering questions in natural language. The computer system was specifically developed to answer questions on the TV quiz show *Jeopardy!* In early 2011, it competed against two former winners and won the first place price of $1 million. Watson was not connected to the Internet and, essentially, searched a vast database of documents for potential answers, and then determined (by working simultaneously through a variety of prediction routines) which answer had the highest probability. But it performed this set of tasks so quickly that it was able to beat exceptionally smart people in a tricky test involving trivia, wordplay, and recall.[34]

A massive collection of reference information formed the basis for Watson's responses. This amounted to about 200 million pages of information, including dictionaries and reference books, works of literature, newspaper archives, web pages, and nearly the entire content of *Wikipedia*, along with historical data from the *Jeopardy!* quiz show. Watson's operation involved thousands of separate algorithms, each geared to a specific task. This included searching within text: comparing dates, times, and locations; analyzing the grammar in clues, and translating raw information into properly formatted candidate responses.

Repurposed as a diagnostic tool in the medical field, Watson's big data-analysis capability provides the opportunity to obtain precise answers from a huge amount of medical information that may include textbooks, scientific journals, clinical studies, and even physicians' and nurses' notes for individual patients. Watson has an impressive ability to dig into vast collections of data and discover relationships that might not be obvious, especially if it concerns information drawn from sources that cross boundaries between medical specialists. By 2013, customized versions of Watson were helping to diagnose problems and refine patient treatment plans (by looking for the best evidence-based treatment options) at major medical facilities, including the Cleveland Clinic and the University of Texas's MD Anderson Cancer Center. The organizations involved in this program are careful to stress that the AI technologies will be to augment physicians' clinical expertise and judgment, not replace them.[35] Still, it certainly seems plausible that one day Watson will substitute physicians' diagnostic work in particular cases.

Other obvious applications of the Watson system are in areas like customer service and technical support. In 2013, IBM announced that it had teamed up with Fluid, Inc., a major provider of online shopping services and consulting. The project aims to incorporate into online shopping sites the kind of personalized, natural language assistance that a knowledgeable sales clerk in a retail store would provide. It will not take long before this type of capability becomes available via smart phones, and shoppers will be able to access conversational, natural language assistance while in brick and mortar stores. IBM also sees a role for Watson in the financial industry, where the system may be instrumental in providing personalized financial advice by delving into a wealth of information about specific customers as well as general market and economic conditions. Within a year of Watson's victory on *Jeopardy!*, IBM was already working with Citigroup to explore applications for the system in the company's massive retail banking operation.[36] IBM also foresees further applications in such fields as law and education. Spy agencies like the CIA and NSA are also reportedly testing the system.[37] Shrouded in secrecy, they may already be using customized versions of Watson at the time of this writing.

In November 2013, IBM announced that its Watson system would move from the specialized computers that had previously hosted the system, to "the cloud." This means that Watson would now reside in massive collections of servers connected to the Internet. Developers would be able to link directly to the system and incorporate IBM's computing technology into custom software applications and mobile apps. This move of cutting-edge artificial intelligence capability to the cloud is very likely to be a powerful driver of further white-collar automation. The progress in software automation in question will be far less visible to the public than innovations in robots that produce tangible machines often easily associated with particular jobs. White-collar automation will very often involve information technology consultants descending on large organizations and building customized systems that have the potential to fundamentally change the way the business operates, while at the same time abolishing jobs for "potentially hundreds or even thousands of skilled workers."[38] Other observers of the various forms of artificial intelligence made possible by big data, do not expect such heavy job losses, however: "In some cases, human analysts are replaced, but often the computers speed up a process and make it more accurate alongside human workers."[39]

As part of their effort to turn Watson into a practical tool, IBM researchers allegedly confronted a primary tenet of the big data revolution—the idea that prediction based on correlation is sufficient, and that a deep understanding of causation is usually both unachievable and unnecessary. A new feature named "WatsonPaths" lets researchers see the specific sources Watson consulted, the logic it used in its evaluation, and the inferences it made during the process of generating an answer. According to Martin Ford, Watson's designers are "gradually progressing toward offering more insight into *why* something is true."[40] It is still highly questionable, however, whether this feature will really lead to deep insights into underlying causal relations. At best, it makes transparent the specific data bases that the computer uses in generating answers, the algorithms being applied, as well as the outcomes of their calculations of probability. As Nicholas Carr correctly comments,

> Predictive algorithms may be supernaturally skilled at discovering correlations, but they're indifferent to the underlying causes of traits and phenomena. Yet it's the deciphering of causation—the meticulous untangling of how and why things work the way they do—that extends the reach of human understanding and ultimately gives meaning to our search for knowledge.[41]

If people come to see automated calculations of probability as sufficient for their professional and social purposes, they risk losing, or at least weakening, their incentive to seek explanations.

One must remain cognizant that today's computer scientists who develop a system such as Watson, are taking a very different approach to artificial intelligence that is both less ambitious and more effective than the original AI strategy. Their goal is no longer to replicate the *process* of human thought but rather to replicate its *results*. These scientists take a particular product of the mind—a hiring decision, for instance, or an answer to a trivia question—and then program a computer to accomplish the same result in its own mindless way. In other words, the replication of the output of thinking is not thinking: "The workings of Watson's circuits bear little resemblance to the workings of the mind of a person playing *Jeopardy!*, but Watson can still post a higher score."[42] Journalist Stephen Baker spent a year with the Watson team in doing research for his book *Final Jeopardy!* He found that "The IBM team paid little attention to the human brain while programming Watson. Any parallels to the brain are superficial, and only the results of chance."[43] In short, current AI looks intelligent but it is an artificial resemblance. This could change in the future. Designers might begin to build digital tools that more closely mimic human minds, perhaps even drawing on the rapidly improving capabilities for scanning and mapping brains.[44] But for this to happen, it seems there is still a long way to go.

So far a truly creative or innovative machine has not appeared on the scene, as Erik Brynjolfsson and Andrew McAfee correctly point out. They mention software that can create lines of English text that rhyme, but none that can write a true poem. Likewise, programs exist that can write clean prose, but none that can figure out what to write about next.[45] Moreover, there are similar problems with the recent use of fully automated news reporting. Narrative Science, Inc., founded in 2010, has built a comprehensive artificial intelligence engine that it named "Quill." It is used by top media outlets, including *Forbes*, to produce automated articles in a variety of areas, including sports, business, and politics. The company's software generates a news story approximately every thirty seconds, and many of these are published on widely known websites without acknowledgment of the use of this service. These stories are all generated by algorithms without human involvement.[46] They may thus perhaps be able to fully substitute routine reporting by humans, but not quality reporting that also offers relevant contextual information, and certainly not investigative journalism. Brynjolfsson and McAfee also say they have never seen software that can create good new software—until now, such attempts have failed badly.

Such creative/innovative activities have one thing in common: *ideation*, the creative process of generating, developing, and communicating new ideas. (Importantly, an idea is understood here as a basic element of thought that can be either visual, concrete, or abstract. Ideation comprises all stages of a thought cycle, from innovation to development to actualization.) Computers can easily be programmed to generate new combinations of preexisting elements like words. This is *not* recombinant innovation[47] in any meaningful sense, however. Ideation in its many forms is an area where humans have comparative advantage over machines today. That entails "thinking outside the box," which is precisely what computers and robots remain miserably poor at doing, as they stay strictly confined within the frame of their programming.[48]

Martin Ford disagrees with this argument, which implies the association of the concept of creativity exclusively with the human brain, itself the product of evolution. He refers to recent attempts to build creative machines that incorporate genetic programming techniques. Genetic programming allows computer algorithms to design themselves through a process that mimics Darwinian natural selection. Research using genetic algorithms as "automated invention machines" by computer scientist John Koza produced designs that allegedly were competitive with the work of human engineers and scientists in a variety of fields, including electric circuit design, mechanical systems, optics, software repair, and civil engineering. This would suggest that "creativity may be something that is within reach of a computer's capabilities"[49]—a conclusion that appears to be inflated, however.

Consider the usage of Watson programmed for the field of medicine, where it has shown promising results that seem to indicate that this system may ultimately be able to trump real physicians in making good diagnoses. Yet, while computer reasoning based on predefined rules and inferences from existing examples can address a large share of cases, human diagnosticians will still be needed even after Watson "finishes its medical training" through "self-learning" because of the idiosyncrasies and special cases that will arise. "Just as it is much harder to create a 100-percent self-driving car than one that merely drives in normal conditions on a highway," Brynjolfsson and McAfee write, "creating a machine-based system for covering all possible medical cases is radically more difficult than building one for the most common situations. As with chess, a partnership between Dr. Watson and a human doctor will be far more creative and robust than either of them working alone."[50]

Watson's programming is just one of many new software applications aimed at leveraging the enormous amount of data now being collected and stored within businesses, organizations, and governments across the global economy. Nearly all of that data is now stored in digital format and is therefore accessible to direct manipulation by computers. The vast majority of this data is "unstructured," that is, it is captured in a variety of formats that are often difficult to match up or compare. This is very different from traditional relational database systems where information is arranged neatly in consistent rows and columns that make search and retrieval fast, reliable, and precise. The unstructured nature of big data has led to the development of new tools specifically geared toward making sense of information that is collected from a variety of sources.

Rapid improvement in this area is a major example of the way in which computers are, at least in a limited sense, beginning to encroach on capabilities that were once the exclusive domain of humans. The ability to continuously process a stream of unstructured information from sources throughout our environment is, after all, one of the things for which *homo sapiens* is uniquely adapted. The difference, of course, is that, in the realm of big data, computers are able to do this on a scale that would be impossible for a person to attain.

The insights derived from big data analyses typically arise entirely from correlation calculations which tell nothing about the causes of the phenomenon being studied. An algorithm may find that if A is true, B is likely also true. But this cannot tell whether A causes B or vice versa—or if perhaps both A and B are caused by some external factor. In many cases, however, and especially in the realm of business where the ultimate measure of success is profitability and efficiency rather than deep understanding, correlation alone can have extraordinary value. Big data can now offer management an unprecedented level of insight into a wide range of areas; everything from the operation of a single machine or the labor of a single human worker to the overall performance of a multinational corporation can potentially be analyzed at a level of detail that would have been impossible before.[51] This is where IT-powered industrial reengineering has come to fulfill a crucial role in the reorganization of work in business corporations and other organizations.

12

The Extensive and Intrusive Reach of Computer Business Systems

Today, the information technologies that emerged in the late 1990s under the name of Enterprise Resource Planning (ERP) have become even more powerful and far-reaching in their effects on American working life. As Simon Head makes clear in his recent book *Mindless*, the industrial rationalization brought about by what are now called Computer Business Systems (CBSs), has spread all across the economy.[1] It has extended from its old primary base in manufacturing to encompass much of the service economy—from wholesale and retail to financial services, secondary and higher education, health care, customer relations management and human resource management, public administration and corporate management at all levels (except the highest). It has also reached higher up in the occupational hierarchy to include the professional and administrative middle class: physicians as well as call-center agents; teachers, academics, and publishers as well as "associates" at Walmart and workers in Amazon's "fulfillment centers"; bank loan officers and middle managers as well as fast food workers.[2] Simon Head neatly summarizes the general trend as follows:

> With the coming of the networked computer with monitoring software attached, industrial regimes of quantification, targeting, and control now pervade the white-collar world: how many patients, litigants, customers with complaints, students with theses, and future home owners with mortgages have been processed or billed per day or week, and how many *should* be processed or billed, because the digital white-collar line is subject to speedup no less than its factory counterpart?[3]

CBSs enforce the rules that determine how work should be done and with a power and speed non-existent in the pre-digital age. Yet, the systems do not make the rules; they have no will of their own. The rules are set out by the work of a number of interested parties: the senior executives who know broadly and indicate what kinds of rules they want; the system providers who supply products whose designs are close to the executives' wishes; and the corporations' own in-house designers who can adjust the purchased IT products according to local needs.

These systems are fusions of different technologies that are brought together to perform highly complex tasks in the control and monitoring of businesses, including their employees. The technologies of the Internet are critical to CBSs because they provide the foundation for computer networks that can link the workstation of every employee or group of employees within an organization to that of every other, irrespective of location and status. Other essential components of the CBS control regime are entities known as "data warehouses" and "data marts" which store the big data that are the lifeblood of the system and prepare those properly for CBS core processing. Data warehouses contain the raw material of the system: gigantic quantities of information that encompass data on millions of transactions performed daily by tens of thousands of employees. Data marts "cleanse" and order this information so that it can be used to evaluate performance in real time and in line with parameters set by management. The fusion of data warehouses and data marts with the monitoring capabilities of CBSs provides the groundwork of a very powerful system of top-down workplace control by management.

Most CBSs also contain a third critical component: systems that mimic human intelligence in performing the cognitive tasks that are vital to the business processes to be managed by the system. Their presence within the system is essential if complex interactions between humans—in health care, higher education, customer service, and human resource management—are to be fully subject to the industrial disciplines of measurement, standardization, and speed. A prominent example of such industrialization via expert systems (discussed earlier) is their use by HMO case managers to make binding decisions on the treatments that patients should or should not receive from their physicians.[4]

CBSs are being promoted heavily by business academics, especially at the Massachusetts Institute of Technology (MIT), and management consultant agencies such as Accenture and Gartner. Unsurprisingly, these systems are also hawked by their producers: IT companies such as IBM, Oracle, and the German corporation SAP, as well as Scheer AG of Saarbrücken, Germany, a *Mittelstand* software company that has had a strong and enduring impact on SAP, the world leader in terms of market share for CBSs. As Simon Head notes, their product manuals are full of abstract, quasi-scientific jargon that puts off anyone outside the specialist communities from deciphering them. The texts speak of business events and occurrences, critical business situations, process instances and flows, process improvement metrics, and event-driven process chains (EPCs). This language of what Head calls "digital managerialism" conceals a significant transformation; the primary focus of management are no longer flesh-and-blood humans but their electronic representations. Employees have become the numbers, coded words, cones, squares, and triangles that represent them on digital screens. "The human-contact side of management—the tasks of explanation, persuasion, and justification—fades away as workplace rules and procedures become texts showing up on employees' computer screens, while the whole apparatus of monitoring and control is instantly recalibrated to accommodate the new metrics."[5]

At the beginning of the main product manual for its Websphere Business Monitor V6.1, IBM aims to market its software to a wide range of professional, white-collar workplaces. The manual describes how its control technologies empower "financial institutions to track and manage loan processes in real time," enable a "government agency to gain visibility into the operations of a social service agency," and equip managers in health care "to gain an overview of all operations within a hospital, including the management of insurance claims processing, scheduling of testing, equipment needs, and staff assignments."[6] SAP and Oracle stake out similar claims, and all three corporations have published a host of research documents and "executive briefs" indicating how their monitoring and control systems apply to all the major sectors of the manufacturing and service economies.

IBM gives a vivid sense of the sheer density of control within its systems. It lists eight mutually reinforcing "views" of the workplace that managers empowered with its systems can acquire. The key to understand these CBS control systems is the picture of the workplace embedded in the eighth "view," which displays "graphical cues about a user's process statistics."[7] It consists of graphical, electronic representations of processes as "an event-driven process chain" in which the (mostly) computer workstations constituting the process are represented as squares, triangles, or oblongs on the screen, linked to one another in a virtual chain, and thus displaying the life cycle of the process from beginning to end.

Contrary to what one might expect, the managerial need to monitor and control is much greater in the white-collar economy than in the blue-collar. In the case of the archetypical manufacturing process, the automobile assembly line, the discipline of the line is enforced by the repetitive simplicity of the work procedures performed on the line, all meticulously calibrated and timed in advance according to the principles of scientific management. This control regime applies whether the worker performs a single unvarying routine, as in the early Ford plants, or a routine that varies at the margin, as in Japanese systems of lean production now adopted everywhere in the U.S. auto industry. The moving line itself is also a powerful, all-seeing monitor, because the failure of a worker to perform his/her assigned task within the designated time immediately becomes manifest in the form of a defective, incomplete work piece moving on to the next worker on the line.

However, once the move is made from the blue- to the white-collar line, the strict disciplines of manufacturing fade away, and the human dimension, with all its potential for error and indiscipline, becomes more pronounced; from a management perspective, so does the need for a panoptic monitoring regime to correct these human errors and non-compliances without delay.[8] With the "process events" of customer relations management, human resource management, financial services, and public administration, there is still a place for human judgment—and so for human error—along with the human capacity to derail a process and prevent it from achieving management's target for its *Key Performance Indicators* (KPIs), such as the sales and profits for corporate divisions or the numbers and values of fee-paying students professors have attracted to their classes. With these white-collar processes, there is no physical, mechanical line to ensure that the process events are performed by the right people in the right order and in the right amount of time. When the workstations along the line are run by humans, the operator may send the information "work piece" to the wrong computer, or, if the work divides into subtasks performed on a single computer, the operator may not execute the tasks in the right order and within the designated time frame.

There may also be unauthorized process "loops" created by employees. For example, a "human resource" operative may hire an employee while omitting steps mandated by the system such as the requirements to "install [the employee] in a learning environment" or "install by special trainer." Or a physician may prescribe a treatment not authorized by an HMO's treatment rule book. Although the monitoring and control processes embedded in the systems are designed to deal with this undisciplined human behavior, the dominant image that emerges in the manual is one of human beings set alongside the inanimate components of process as abstracted entities fully subject to the manipulation and control of the corporate "process assemblers." These are the engineers who take senior management's preferences for what a process should look like and build these into the fully elaborated process model they then come up with. A process assembler can use the graphical tools on the computer screen to pull the services needed from a palette into the process map. The process assembler can also drag and drop relationships among data, people, systems and services, as well as identify and mark the measurement points.[9]

It is at this point that this corporate business system of IBM shows the features of an all-pervasive digital panopticon. Employees at all skill levels and ranks have all become disembodied objects of speed and efficiency tied to these electronic symbols on the screen, which process assemblers move around as they see fit and with the real, corporal people having to follow strict orders. IBM also claims that the system helps managers "perform corrective action based on real time information" when necessary. Corrective actions include "transferring work times" away from workers who may not be meeting their target and "suspending the process altogether" so that an investigation of employee error can be undertaken without delay."[10]

Scheer AG's monitoring software also is pitched for its power to "evaluate various behavior patterns" and to test whether "secondary paths on the event tree" taken less frequently by the human agents are "disruptive and should be eliminated." The company also focuses on new sources of disruption—e-mails, chat rooms, discussion forums, blackboards, instant messages, and Web conferences—insisting that the undisciplined use of all these tools has to be replaced by their "order creation in the value creation chain."[11] The product manual of IMB's Domino Administrator 8 gives a clear indication how this "ordered creation" of e-mail use can be achieved. The document contains separate sections on topics such as "Tools for Mail Monitoring," "Creating a Mail-Routing Event Generator," "Tracking a Mail Message," "Generating a Mail Usage Report," "Viewing Mail Usage Reports," and "Controlling the Mail Tracking Collector."[12]

The development of such elaborate systems of control shows how the power of CBS technologies extends to virtually every human activity performed in the workplace. It also indicates how irresistible the temptation is for executives to avail themselves of such powers even if the activities in question may be ill-suited to be objects of control. In trying to find ways of tracing employees who abuse their use of e-mail, businesses may do so by setting up a panoptic 24/7 system that monitors the entire workforce all the time, which in turn, fosters a culture of mistrust and discourages the use of e-mail as a creative outlet for employees otherwise subject to rigorous managerial control by means of their Key Performance Indicators.[13]

Measures to correct the unauthorized, the disruptive, and the dysfunctional are the end products of elaborate systems of monitoring and control that need some further exploration here. Again it is the event-driven process chain that is the essential entry point. A highly illuminating account of EPCs as control mechanism can be found in Scheer AG's volume *Corporate Performance Management*. IBM and SAP texts provide similar, though less detailed and less systematic accounts of EPCs.

Scheer's monitoring system revolves around the representation of an ideal

EPC embedded in the system's memory. This "ideal" is a process archetype that exemplifies exactly how management wants the process to be performed, whether it is the hiring of an employee, the treatment of a patient in a clinic, the packaging of a mortgage, or the assembly of a computer on the line. These archetypical EPCs set the pathways that the work item, whether physical or virtual, must follow as it goes its way between the process stations, the time assigned to each stage of the process, and the quantitative values for the KPIs that management may attach to the process.

The number of KPIs that management can attach to a process is unlimited. In the product manual for its Business Process Management system, IBM lists thirty-three possible KPIs for a product sales department, including profit margin per transaction, profit per customer, customer average days to pay, contribution to profit by product, and percentage of deliveries on time. The system also allows managers to attach KPIs to a process without the employees being informed about this. IBM's research Red Book for its Websphere Business Monitor V1 outlines how a "dashboard KPI" can be created for a manager's "personal use" and is not visible to others in the organization.

Central to this monitoring is an automated comparison between the values of the ideal process instance embedded in the system's memory, and the values of the actual performance of employees in the present or recent past. If the comparison is with past process instances, the system can create a composite event tree of these past instances, which will show the average of its KPIs and possibly also provide evidence that there may be a systemic flaw in how the processes have been executed. Managers can also take a look at their subordinates' screens without their knowing it and see how the process is being executed in real time.

Of course, the goal of this monitoring is to find cases where there are discrepancies between the KPI values attached to real-world process instances and those embedded in the ideal process. The discovery of such a discrepancy is the first stage of a three-stage procedure that has to be fully gone through if the malfunction is to be properly dealt with. The second stage is tracing the causes of error, and the third the prescription of a remedy. The search for causes involves a central feature of CBSs, that is, their capacity to "drill down" to find the causes of dysfunction. Here the manager scrutinizes the electronic images of process instances on his dashboard, each with their own electronic process chain, to find the wrongdoer(s).[14]

If the culprit is a single employee, the manager's search may end with an examination of the single process instance for which the employee has been responsible. If s/he has taken too long to perform a "business event" such as the processing of a mortgage application, this may be due to the fact that s/he has included unauthorized procedures, which the electronic image of the process instance will indicate. If the culprit is a work team or whole department, it may be necessary to create a composite process chain to detect where exactly the weak link in the process exists. In the CBS product manuals there is an unrelenting emphasis on the need for speed in the execution of processes and for speed in the detection and correction of process error.

Importantly, Corporate Panoptics as the monitoring and control of business process, and Business Process Reengineering as their restructuring, are no longer distinct activities; they are now fused as a continuous activity. The inefficiencies detected by constant monitoring become the raw material for the equally constant activity of reshaping the processes to make them run faster and more efficiently. The working lives of employees are deeply affected by this constant change, but they are no more involved in the decision-making about how it occurs than the hardware and software systems that stand between them and their superiors.[15]

The powers and skills of managers (except those at the highest level) too are diminished by the arrival of Corporate Panoptics. As the monitoring, analysis, and reshaping of business processes are increasingly automated, the role of middle and lower managers becomes one of gazing at control screens, not unlike shift workers in a highly automated steel mill, and waiting for something unusual to happen. Moreover, their own performance is as much subject to monitoring as their front-line subordinates, and equally visible to their management superiors.

The heavy automation of new-generation CBSs seems to suggest the workings of artificial intelligence (AI), but this is misleading. Each of the inventories of rules that govern the work regimes of CBSs is the result of decisions made by senior executives and then embedded in the system by the process assemblers, whether it is the structure of the event-process tree, the timings linking the workstations on the tree, the KPIs attached to the process, or the continuous interplay between Business Process Reengineering and Corporate Panoptics. It is these executives who choose the rules used to assess which process improvements should be authorized and which should not. The non-experts, whether lower managers or front-line workers, have little or no say in the constant shaping and reshaping of the processes that follow.[16]

In the contemporary service economy, dominated by CBSs, what matters are the judgments, human interactions, and even the speech of employees, and the agents of control are the networked computers empowered with workflow and monitoring software, with expert systems attached, and the whole ultimately governed by senior executives. Moreover, because employees in such fields as health care, financial services, customer relations, and human resource management are dealing with fellow human beings in all their complexities, the rules of the system necessarily proliferate and mutate as they try to cope with the numerous contingencies that can emerge in these encounters.

Thus, every aspect of work—the timing of tasks, the sequence in which they are performed, the operation of expert systems—becomes subject to rules that can be altered, elaborated, and enforced at the touch of a managerial keystroke. "What we are witnessing," Head claims, "is the emergence of a new white-collar working class, subject to all the regimentation and discipline of its factory predecessor, but lacking the latter's solidarity, its willingness to organize and to fight its cause in the workplace."[17]

Head points out that China is a hospitable environment for Computerized Business Systems and Corporate Panoptics because these are simply corporate variants of centralized control that mimic the Communist Party's own system. Outsourcing production to China is logical for Western corporations searching to reduce costs, because a Chinese workforce can, at least for the time being, be subjected to pressures that have no parallel in the U.S. Moreover, leading American consulting firms are earning lots of money as they superimpose Computer Business Systems and Corporate Panoptics on the management structures of Chinese state-owned enterprises either recently privatized or being prepared for privatization.[18]

Automated Systems in Human Resource Management

The control implications and intrusiveness of CBSs become very clear in the domain of human resource management. Engineers have come up with a "process recombinator" that allows the corporation to order and reorder the processes and subprocesses of human resource management. Leading agents in this reengineering are process designers who use the CBS software to embed corporate preferences in the detailed operations of the system. "People analytics" software is instrumental in automating decisions about hiring, pay, and promotion. This elaborate apparatus of control once again bears the strong imprint of Taylor's scientific management, as is the expertise of senior executives and system designers whose guidelines about how hiring an employee should be done become embedded in the system's enforceable rules.

Another powerful instrument of top-down control in human resource management is the automated personality tests such as the Myers-Briggs test and the Wagner Enneagram Personality Style Scales (WEPPS) used by corporations to evaluate the suitability of their prospective employees.[19] A company like Xerox now relies exclusively on computers to select applicants for its fifty-thousand call-center jobs. Candidates fill out a half-hour personality test at a computer, and the hiring software immediately assigns them a score indicating the likelihood that they will perform well, reliably show up for work, and stick with the job. On the basis of this, the company makes offers to those with high scores and sends low scorers away.[20]

In his book, Simon Head devotes a chapter to the management of "emotional Labor" in human resource management, basically a case study of how the philosophy of CBSs, with its emphasis on process and process engineering, shows up even in places where information technology itself is absent. The HRM experts concerned rely on a model of the human mind as itself a process machine whose inner workings can be modified in the interests of corporate efficiency. In the "emotion management" theories that dominate this field, "process" fulfills a leading role as an analytical tool. The usage of the language of "process" by emotional labor theorists allows them to make their work comfortable and familiar to corporate HRM operatives immersed in the mindset and control mechanisms of process. In frequently using the word "process" in descriptions of the mental and emotional phenomena that HRM operators have to deal with, they can consider their work to be a kind of process reengineering of the soul.

Behavioral psychologist James Gross of Stanford University seems to have been a kind of guru of emotion theory geared to HRM.[21] Gross defines the subject matter of emotion regulation theory as "the processes by which individuals influence which emotions they have, when they have them, and how they experience and express these emotions."[22] He proposes an input-output model, in which individuals receive stimulation from the situation and respond with emotions. Gross is the originator of the two analytical concepts that dominate HRM thinking about the regulation of emotional behavior: "antecedent-focused emotion regulation" and "response-focused emotion regulation."[23]

He distinguishes four strategies that individuals can follow in adjusting their emotions to an event that, viewed from an HRM perspective, is a breakdown of the input-out model: situation selection, situation modification, attention deployment, and cognitive change. In the case of employees subject to corporate display rules and the emotional labor attached to them, "situation change" "and situation modification" are effectively ruled out. The choice is between "response modification"—repressing felt emotions and faking false ones—and "antecedent-focused regulation," with its "attention (re)focus" and cognitive change. The HRM emotional labor theorists see as their leading task to sort out which of these variants of emotional labor might be best for employee productivity and the bottom line. Needless to say, Arlie Russell Hochschild's criticism (in *The Managed Heart*) of the alienation and exploitation involved in commodified emotional labor (discussed earlier) is at odds with comparisons of the relative utility to business of the two variants of cognitive regulation. Her concern is with the integrity of the managed heart itself, while most of the academic literature on "emotion regulation" is concerned with how the strategies of emotional labor can best contribute to efficiency and the bottom line. She questions businesses' right to manipulate and market the sources of self in question that are deep and central to our individuality. As Head poignantly describes the problem, "At its worst emotional labor seizes upon the feelings, perceptions, and judgments that constitute who we are, pushes them aside, and substitutes a body of imposed perceptions and feelings that originates not in ourselves but in the judgment of HRM specialists relying on research telling them which mental mix will best serve the interests of the business."[24]

Finally, an important caveat must be made here to the previous characterization of CBSs, which is based on Simon Head's reading of the product manuals in question. He suggests these manuals are gateways to enter as far as possible into the world of CBSs.[25] But he has been criticized for being too prone to take the claims of the engineering manuals at face value.[26] An obvious shortcoming of this approach is that it does not trace precisely how the instructions in the manuals are applied in every day work practices and how the employees concerned respond to them. Given the available evidence, however, it is undeniable that the predominant aim of top management's usage of such systems is to attain greater technical-organizational control over employees as well as lower-level managers. To what extent these attempts are successful in particular cases is another question, which can only be answered by detailed empirical research of CBSs in situ—research that is still mostly absent at the time of this writing.

A Reversal of Contemporary Business Practices?

An underlying theme in Head's account of Corporate Business Systems is that an emphasis on human-centered automation rather than the prevailing technology-first approach would make workers partners rather than competitors with machines, in a mode that restores the dignity of work. This is similar to Nicholas Carr's view (mentioned earlier) that too much automation can erode human skills—in some cases with disastrous consequences, as occurred with increased cockpit automation in aviation, for example. But while Simon Head also sees the prevailing engineering "design philosophy" as an obvious problem, he targets the underlying causes, calling for a reversal of contemporary business practices.

In doing so, he tends to underestimate the sea change necessary to retain good jobs for the majority. Head offers a powerful indictment of contemporary Anglo-American capitalism regarding its degradation of workers' skills and the reduction of their relative rewards. He argues that it is not technology as such but rather the "hard armor of corporate power" and its predominant work culture that bears the brunt of the blame. He cites examples of alternative, employee-friendly work cultures, such as codetermination and labor-management in Germany as it took shape at the Chemnitz machine-tool plant he visited in 1992; the Scandinavian employee participation practice in software design (especially strong in Norway and Denmark); the Mondragon cooperatives in the Basque region of Spain; the John Lewis Partnership, a high-quality retail chain in Britain; Lincoln Electric (with generous profit sharing for employees and a policy of "no layoffs" even during recessions) and the employee-friendly expert systems at Xerox in the U.S. In each case business practices augment, not degrade, workers' skills, pay and benefits. But within the context of global capitalism, such practices have become rare exceptions. Head himself acknowledges that these work cultures have usually taken root for reasons specific to a particular location or company and are not easily replicated elsewhere.[27] Another problem is that in his endeavor to recreate a worthwhile world of work, Head never acknowledges the possibility that automated machines may be destroying jobs permanently, a major topic of the next chapter.

"Politics," Simon Head insists, needs to create a "dominant coalition" from among "the majority of Americans who are losing out in today's economy" to overcome the "new authoritarianism of the digital age." In his view, this coalition would include "low-income minorities and whites of the Walmart and Amazon world" but also "middle managers and middle administrators whose real incomes have been steadily eroding, and even non-elite professions of the non-concierge economy suffering the same fate."[28] The political debate should be central here, and involve a progressive critique of the economy that includes the issues of white-collar industrialism being applied to ever-widening segments of the service economy.

Needless to say, the capitalist-industrial and political-institutional conditions at the current juncture pose enormous, if not insurmountable, challenges for such a broader coalition of countervailing forces to overcome. A viable coalition of this kind has not emerged yet and does not appear to be in the offing. Some might say this would involve a kind of revival of what happened during the New Deal era. But, as Jefferson Cowie convincingly argues in his recent book, this was "the great exception" to deeply ingrained patterns of American political practice, economic structure, and cultural outlook; it was the result of short-lived, historical circumstances generated by the trauma of the Depression and World War II, and therefore would be extremely difficult, if not impossible, to reproduce today. Ironically, the most successful economic era for the nation's working people coincided with the suspension of some of the most defining features of U.S. history. "The cultural homogeneity of the postwar era—while deeply flawed, problematic, and forced—made the United States just a bit closer to Northern European–style politics, providing, in Richard Hofstadter's terms, a 'social-democratic tinge' where it existed neither before nor after."[29] In the vigorous, sometimes violent political struggles in America, the values of collective economic security tended to be trumped rather consistently by other forces. But during the New Deal era, for once, Americans found sources of unity, however objectionable some elements were.

The New Deal order by and large remained confined to the white, male industrial working class, into which members of the second-generation "new immigrants" from Southern and Eastern Europe had by that time become integrated. Among the most obvious differences between then and now is the integration of people of color into the fabric of mainstream American society. To secure the cooperation of the Southern committee chairs in Congress, the FDR administration excluded much of the South's people and industry from the scope of New Deal social legislation. Neither the Wagner Act nor Social Security covered agricultural labor or domestic service, which together employed more than 60 percent of the African American labor force, and nearly 75 percent of those who were employed in the South. Thus the Roosevelt administration effectively abandoned those workers to the Jim Crow South. The civil rights movement eventually changed this structure; yet as Cowie points out, the reforms of the Fair Deal and the Great Society did not focus on New Deal–style collective action but on individual rights, thereby retaking a longstanding American political tradition. The most important democratic advances of U.S. history—for example, the Emancipation Proclamation and the Civil Rights and Voting Rights Acts—are landmarks in a continuing struggle to expand individual rights.[30]

Finding another source of unity, hopefully one not based on exclusion, is necessary if people are to challenge once again the problem of economic inequality.[31] This also demands a clear recognition that today's industrial rationalization—by means of digital information technology—is closely intertwined with a new organization of production and distribution of goods, often married to business forms other than the traditional U.S. public corporation (to be discussed in Chapter 14). This poses even greater challenges than before for forging a broad counter-movement as suggested.

13

Robots: Cooperating with or Replacing Human Workers?

Big data and the accompanying "smart algorithms" are having a direct impact on workplaces and careers as employers, particularly large corporations, increasingly track numerous metrics and statistics regarding the work and social interactions of their employees. While the initial purpose of all this data collection and analysis is typically more effective management and assessment of employee performance, it could eventually be used for the development of software to automate much of the work being performed.[1]

As noted earlier, employment for many skilled professionals is already being significantly eroded by advanced information technology. They are not the only ones under threat. As Martin Ford explains in his well-received book, *Rise of the Robots* (2015), most jobs are, on some level, fundamentally routine and predictable with relatively few people being paid primarily to engage in truly creative work or innovative thinking. As machines take on that routine, predictable work, workers will face unprecedented challenges as they attempt to adjust.[2]

In the past, automation technology tended to be relatively specialized and to disrupt one employment sector at a time, with workers then switching over to a new emerging industry. This is the trend John Maynard Keynes foresaw in his futuristic 1930 essay, "Economic Possibilities for Our Grandchildren," in which he coined the term "technological unemployment" to indicate the unemployment caused by machines replacing human behavior. Automation, he claimed, could put people out of work permanently, especially if more and more tasks kept getting automated. But Keynes was early to point out that technology was also a powerful generator of new categories of employment, and that technological unemployment was only a "temporary phase of maladjustment."[3]

The situation today is quite different, however; current developments point to a sea change. Information technology is a truly general-purpose technology, and its impact is likely to become less labor-intensive as new technology is assimilated into existing business practices. At the same time, the new industries that emerge will nearly always incorporate powerful labor-saving technology right from the start; think of Google and Facebook in Internet software; IBM and Oracle in the technologies of Computer Business Systems; and Apple in consumer electronics. Google and Facebook have become household names and achieved massive market valuations. They can refrain from manufacturing altogether, and hire only a small number of people relative to their size and influence. Apple retains an elite core of managers, designers, and technicians in the U.S., but outsources most of its manufacturing to China (more specifically to Taiwanese companies that have extensive operations there, such as Foxconn whose plants are being further automated) and Southeast Asia.[4]

Robots have become part of the work carried out in virtually every sector of manufacturing, from automobiles to semiconductors. However, those industrial robots are for the most part blind actors in a tightly organized performance, and rely primarily on precise timing and positioning. In the rare cases where robots have machine vision capability, they can typically see in just two dimensions and only in controlled lighting conditions. Until recently, progress has been slow in making machines that can replace human workers in areas like pattern recognition, complex communication, sensing, and mobility.[5]

The challenges to automate such routine manual jobs point to what has come to be known as Moravec's paradox. This is "the discovery by artificial intelligence and robotics researchers that, contrary to traditional assumptions, high-level reasoning requires very little computation, but low-level sensorimotor skills require enormous computational resources."[6] As Hans Moravec himself put it, "it is comparatively easy to make computers exhibit adult level performance on intelligence tests or playing checkers, and difficult or impossible to give them the skills of a one-year-old when it comes to perception and mobility."[7]

One possible explanation of the paradox is in terms of evolution. All human skills are implemented biologically, using "equipment" designed by the process of natural selection. In the course of human skills' evolution, natural selection has tended to preserve design improvements and optimizations. The older a skill is, the more time natural selection has had to improve the design. Abstract thought developed only very recently in evolutionary terms, and consequently, we should not expect its implementation to be perfectly efficient.

More specifically, evolution has encoded in the highly evolved sensory and motor areas of the human brain, millions of years of experience about the nature of the world and how to survive in it. Examples of skills that have thus been evolving include recognizing a face, moving around in space, judging people's motivations, catching a ball, recognizing a voice, paying attention to things that are interesting, anything to do with perception, attention, visualization, motor skills, social skills and so on. In contrast, the abstract reasoning that we associate with "higher thought" is a relatively recent acquisition, developed over a few thousand years. Some examples of skills that have appeared more recently are mathematics, engineering, human games, logic and much of what we now call science. It often requires simpler software and less computer power to mimic or even exceed human capabilities on these types of tasks.[8]

On the other hand, many things that humans find easy and natural to do in the physical world have been remarkably difficult for robots to master. Robotics experts have found it extremely difficult to build machines that match the skills of even the least-trained manual worker. Regarding physical work, humans have a huge flexibility advantage over machines. Automating a single activity like soldering a wire onto a circuit board or fastening two parts together with screws is rather easy, but this task must remain constant over time and take place in a "regular" environment. For example, the circuit board must show up in exactly the same position every time. Companies purchase specialized machines for such tasks, have their engineers program and test them, and then add them to their assembly lines. But each time the task changes—when, for example, the location of the screw holes moves—production must screech to a halt until the machinery is reprogrammed.

Many of today's factories may be highly automated, but they are not full of general-purpose robots. Their production technology consists mostly of dedicated, specialized machines that are expensive to buy, configure, and reconfigure. In those factories human workers are scarce, but they are not absent, although a lot of the work they do is repetitive and mindless.[9] It consists of tasks that have not been automated because appropriate specialized machines either do not exist yet or, if they do, the companies in question have chosen not to buy them because it is still cheaper to deploy human labor instead.

There are recent innovations in robotics that offer new opportunities to automate part of the remaining manual tasks. Boston-based Rethink Robotics was founded in 2008 to pursue nontraditional industrial automation; building robots that can handle the many imprecise tasks currently done by people in today's factories. Its poster child Baxter, released in 2012, is a humanoid manufacturing robot that can easily be instructed to perform a variety of repetitive tasks and only costs $25,000. Baxter is basically a scaled-down industrial robot designed to operate safely in close proximity to humans, contrary to the robots which, until recently, were large and needed to be caged off to ensure safety. In contrast to industrial robots which require complex programming, Baxter can be trained simply by moving its arms through the required motions, which can be done easily by nontechnical workers. To teach the robot a new repetitive task, a worker only has to guide the robot's arms through the requisite motions and Baxter will automatically memorize the routine. If multiple robots are used in a workplace, the knowledge of one trained Baxter can be transplanted to the others by plugging in a USB device that loads the machine with that digitalized information. The robot can carry out a variety of tasks, including light assembly work, transferring parts between conveyor belts, packing products into retail packaging, or tending machines used in metal fabrication. Baxter also has a two-dimensional machine vision capability, can pick up individual parts and even perform basic quality-control inspections.[10]

Other new types of robots are now entering the final frontier of machine automation, where they will compete for the few relatively routine, manual jobs that are still assigned to human workers. For example, Industrial Perception, Inc., a Silicon Valley start-up company, has designed and built a highly specialized machine focused specifically on moving boxes with maximum efficiency. The robot has a remarkable capacity located at the nexus of visual perception, spatial computation, and dexterity. This capacity is needed to resolve the complexity of problems such as moving a stack of boxes of varying shapes, sizes, and colors that have been piled up in a rather disorganized way—precisely the type of visual challenge that the human brain has evolved to overcome but engineers are facing in designing capable robots. The imaging technology that powers this robot's ability to see in three dimensions involves a webcam-like device, called Kinect, that uses what is, in essence, sonar at the speed of light. Seen as a one-to-one replacement for human workers, the Industrial Perception box handler is a significant move into what has been one of the last strongholds of unskilled human labor, that of warehouse workers, longshoremen, and lumpers (freight handlers).[11]

Large online retailers are increasingly taking the opportunity to automate jobs in their warehouses and distribution centers as well. In 2012, Amazon— a leader in advanced warehouse logistics—purchased a company called Kiva Systems that makes robotic sorting systems for warehouses, hoping to eventually automate the bastions of the badly paid, meticulously controlled warehouse jobs that are still open to humans. A year after the acquisition, Amazon had about 1,400 Kiva robots in operation and had only begun the process of integrating the machines into its massive warehouses. But by the spring of 2015,

Amazon already "employed" 15,000 Kiva robots.[12] The company's constant cost-benefit analyses had apparently led to decisions to significantly step up its replacement of human workers by robots.

In modern consumer goods logistics, there are two levels of distribution: storing and moving whole cases of goods, and retrieving individual products from those cases. The Kiva robots can only perform tasks at the first level. These mobile robots are intended to save human workers the time of walking through the warehouse to gather individual products to be shipped together in a composite order. Rather than having workers going through the aisles selecting items, a Kiva robot simply zips under an entire pallet or shelving unit, lifts it, and brings it directly to the worker packing an order. The robots navigate autonomously using a grid laid out by barcodes attached to the floor. Thus, while the humans work in one location, the Kiva robots maneuver bins of individual items at just the right time in the shipping process, and the humans pick out and assemble the products to be shipped. These robots are deployed to automate warehouse operations at a variety of major retailers in addition to Amazon, including Walgreens, Staples, Toys "R" Us and the Gap.[13]

The skills needed for these robots to distinguish the different shapes, sizes, and textures of the objects on the shelves are beyond the capability of current robot technology. Today's automation cannot yet fully replace human hands and eyes; especially the ability to quickly recognize objects among dozens of possibilities and pick them up from different positions remains a big challenge. But humanoid robots like Baxter or more impersonal systems like the ones Google's robotics division is developing, come closer to resolving this issue. While "techno-optimists" tend to believe that it may not take long before such robots are working in an Amazon warehouse alongside teams of mobile Kiva robots, others remain skeptical about this.[14]

Another important development involves the highly automated distribution centers that the Kroger Company, one of the largest grocery retailers in the U.S., has opened in recent years. Kroger's system has the capacity to receive pallets containing large supplies of a single product from vendors, and then disassembling them and creating new pallets containing a variety of products that are ready to ship to stores. It is also able to organize the way products are stacked on the mixed pallets so that stocking of shelves is optimized once they arrive at stores. The automated warehouses do not need human intervention, except for loading and unloading the pallets onto trucks. Like the Kiva robots, Kroger's automated system leaves some jobs for people. These are primarily in areas that require visual recognition and dexterity, such as packing a mixture of items for final shipment to customers. But, as noted earlier, these are precisely the areas in which innovations like Industrial Perception's box-moving robots are "rapidly advancing the technical frontier," as the techno-optimist Martin Ford suggests.[15]

Access to the cloud is an important driving force of the current robot revolution. Its impact may be most dramatic in areas like visual recognition that require access to vast databases as well as powerful computational capability. Much of the computation required by advanced robots can be offloaded to huge data centers, while also giving individual robots access to network-wide resources. This makes it possible to build less expensive robots, since less onboard computational power and memory are required, and also allows for instant software upgrades across multiple machines. If one robot employs centralized machine intelligence to learn and adapt to its environment, then that newly acquired knowledge can become instantly available to any other machines accessing the system—making it easy to scale machine learning across large numbers of robots.[16]

Still, computers remain as yet comparatively weak in activities that involve moving through and interacting in the physical world, even as they get so much better at cognitive tasks. Advances like the Baxter robot and Kinect devices that can map a room, show that much progress has been made in giving machines real-world capabilities, but there are still many "simple" manual tasks that robots have a hard time mastering, or cannot master at all, at least for now. Brynjolfsson and McAfee give the example of a towel-folding robot to illustrate how far we are from resolving Moravec's paradox. A team of Berkeley researchers equipped a humanoid robot with four stereo cameras, and algorithms that would allow it to view towels, both individually and in piles. The robot successfully grasped and folded the towels, even though it sometimes took more than one try to grab them correctly. But it took an average of more than twenty-four minutes per towel! The robot spent most of that time trying to find out where the towel was and how to grasp it. Findings like these suggest that cooks, gardeners, repairmen, carpenters, plumbers, dentists, janitors, home health aides, and others doing service work that is nearly impossible to automate, are not about to be replaced by machines any time soon. All of these jobs involve a lot of sensorimotoric work, and many of them also require the preeminently human skills of ideation, large-frame pattern recognition, and complex communication. Not all of them are well paying but at least they are not subject to close competition with the machine.[17]

According to the theory of skill-biased technological change, which was once popular among economists (especially in the 1990s), the new information technologies, by definition, favor people with more human capital. Technologies like factory automation, computer-controlled machines, automated inventory control, payroll processing software, and word processing have been deployed for routine work (involving routine jobs that are close substitutes to software-driven computers), replacing workers on the factory floor, in clerical tasks, and doing rote information processing. By contrast, technologies like big data analytics, high-speed communications, and prototyping[18] have augmented the contributions that involve more abstract and data-driven reasoning, and in turn have increased the value of workers with the right engineering, creative, or design skills. The net effect has been a declining demand for less skilled labor and an increasing demand for skilled labor.

Brynjolfsson and McAfee, who apparently accept this theory, claim that a broader reorganization in business culture may have been an even more important path for skill-biased change. Pivotal to companies' reengineering projects has been the usage of digital technologies to reorganize decision-making authority, incentive systems, information flows, hiring systems, and other aspects of their management and organizational processes. This combined usage of organization and technology not only increased productivity but also tended to require more educated workers and reduce demand for less-skilled ones. The reorganization often eliminated a lot of routine work, leaving behind a residual set of tasks that required relatively more judgment, skills, and training.[19] This is not exactly how things have panned out in reality, however.

In the new century, the numbers of the more educated workers needed after the technical-organizational reengineering projects have remained comparatively low. The millions of new jobs created in the 1990s during the tech bubble, especially in the IT sector, were good jobs that began to disappear after corporations automated or off-shored jobs, or began to outsource the IT departments to centralized "cloud" computing services. Throughout the economy, computers and machines were replacing more and more workers rather than increasing their value; wage increases lagged far behind growth in productivity. Both the share of national income going to labor and the labor force participation rate fell dramatically. The job market continued to polarize as middle-class jobs requiring a moderate level of skills were disappearing. One result of the loss of middle-skilled routine jobs was that these workers were forced to compete for low-skilled manual jobs, thus raising the supply relative to the demand for manual workers. This has led to a decline in wages for those with relatively low skills, including high school graduates, and high-school dropouts.

The hollowed-out middle of the job market is likely to expand as robots and self-service technologies take away more low-wage jobs, while artificial intelligence systems and their increasingly sophisticated algorithms, put a variety of high-skill occupations at risk.[20] The impact of the accelerating information technology is intertwined with globalization, however. The line between the two will blur further as higher-skill jobs become more susceptible to electronic offshoring.[21] The latter tendency is acutely evident in the increasing offshoring of a variety of research and development work since around 2000 to China and India, which continues to erode the U.S. high-tech base.[22]

14

Digital Information Technologies and the Nikefication of Production and Work Organization

For a better understanding, the current impact of digital information technologies on employment and the quality of the remaining work in America needs to be put into its proper context. Oddly enough, this concerns the decline of the U.S. public corporation as we once knew it. As Gerald F. Davis explains in his thought-provoking book, *The Vanishing American Corporation*, the retreat of the corporation is due partly to economic crises and industry consolidation. However, the overarching reason is the increasing obsolescence of the corporate form, which coincides with the steep rise of enterprises that are organized differently—both legally and financially; most are limited liability companies.[1]

The modern U.S. corporation (one that issues shares on the stock market) emerged in the first three decades of the 20th century and its defining features were analyzed in Berle and Means' classic work, *The Modern Corporation and Private Property*, first published in 1932.[2] The U.S. public corporation evolved around mass production and mass consumption, fueled by a continent-sized consumer market. Economies of scale meant that bigger was more efficient. This also meant that many firms required capital on a scale too large to be funded by private partnerships or banks; they had to raise capital by selling shares on the stock market. A distinguishing feature for most of the 20th century was massive size, and big firms were almost always listed on the stock market.

The public corporation came to dominate the U.S. economy at midcentury and continued to grow bigger in terms of assets and employment until around 1980. As Davis points out, today's corporations bear little resemblance to the companies analyzed by Berle and Means. Moreover, there are far fewer of them than there used to be; in 2012, the United States counted less than half as many publicly traded domestic corporations as it did in 1997. Their number had declined by over 21 percent just between 2008 and 2009.[3]

Most of the public corporations that remain are ill-equipped and their managements little motivated to provide bureaucratic employment, more specifically long-term employment opportunities for economic advancement, and benefits such as health insurance and retirement provisions.[4] Ironically, the retreat of the public corporation has much to do with the success of the shareholder value movement, which effectively reduced the corporation from a social institution with enduring features to a mere "nexus of contracts" among voluntary, individual participants. As noted previously, policy decisions early in the Reagan years simultaneously created the conditions for the hostile takeover wave that disintegrated the existing corporate order and propelled the shareholder value movement that replaced it. This movement was driven to a great extent by the growth of individual pensions and retail investments which resulted in the concentration of corporate ownership in the hands of financial institutions, particularly mutual funds and exchange-traded funds (ETFs). By 2010, 75 percent of the largest 1,000 corporations' shares were held by institutions, not individuals. Among those institutions were huge shareholders such as "asset manager" BlackRock which, as of 2011, was the single largest shareholder of one in every five corporations in the U.S., often including the largest competitors in the same industry. Likewise, the mutual fund Fidelity was the largest shareholder of one in ten U.S. corporations. Never before—not even at the height of "finance capitalism" in the early twentieth century—had the United States witnessed corporate ownership this concentrated within a small number of financial institutions.[5]

It must also be remembered that Berle and Means' premise that large corporations typically make or transport tangible products, or provide infrastructure,[6] is no longer tenable. In 1950, the biggest private employers were AT&T, General Motors, U.S. Steel, General Electric, Sears, Bethlehem Steel, Ford, Chrysler, Standard Oil (Exxon), and Westinghouse. These were predominantly large manufacturers and technology firms with a long-time horizon and concomitant employment practices, including well-developed career ladders. By 2010, the biggest private employers were Walmart, Target, UPS, Kroger, Sears, Holdings AT&T, Home Depot, Walgreens, Verizon, and Supervalu [without e]. Nine of the twelve largest employers were retailers, and none were manufacturers. Walmart alone employed as many Americans as the twenty largest manufacturers combined. In retail, wages and benefits are modest at best, turnover is high, and career mobility extremely limited.[7] Large retail also has characteristically different forms of work organization than large-scale manufacturing. Whereas Ford's River Rouge plant employed over 100,000 people at its peak, a typical Walmart Supercenter employs about 400 people in a highly modular format.[8]

Moreover, corporations are no longer as long-lived as before. The image of corporations as similar to feudal manors does not accord with a world of high corporate turnover. From the 1930s until the late 1980s, there was remarkable stability at the core of the corporate economy in comparison with the preceding era. Since then, the situation has seriously deteriorated; for instance, of the thirty firms included in the Dow Jones Industrial Index in 1930, sixteen of them still existed in 1987. But by 2009, all but three—Chevron, Exxon, and GE—were gone due to bankruptcies, mergers, hostile takeovers or radical reorganizations in which the original firms were no longer recognizable. Three other firms—GM, AIG, and Citigroup—also exited from the index as they temporarily became government-supported enterprises through massive taxpayer bailouts in the wake of the latest financial crisis.[9]

There is another tendency that may point to the diminishing life expectancy of the public corporation. Companies that have gone public since the dot-com collapse of 2000 often defy standards of corporate governance—for instance, by giving founders permanent control via super-voting shares. Their rationale for going public is to pay off employees and early investors, rather than to raise capital to invest in long-lived assets. This suggests that such firms may not be sustainable as public corporations in the long run, although demand for returns by investors may keep them going for some time.[10]

Nikefication

Behind the declines in assets and numbers of employees concentrated in individual corporations are substantial changes in the organization of production in the U.S., which Davis summarizes as "Nikefication." Nike is well-known for its modular model of producing shoes and athletic gear; while the company engages in the design and marketing of its goods, manufacturing is done almost entirely by overseas contractors, primarily in East Asia.[11] In other words, Nike's "core" involves developing intellectual property, not manufacturing physical goods. The underlying premise is that high value-added activities (the knowledge-based work of design and marketing), should be done by the company that owns the brand, while lower value-added activities, such as assembly and supply chain management, can be contracted out. Although the Nike model of "disaggregated production" has a long history in apparel, thanks to Wall Street pressures and the availability of an outsourcing sector the model spread widely throughout the electronics industry and is now standard practice in industries from consumer packaged goods to pharmaceuticals to pet food and many others. So-called "turnkey" manufacturers and distributors have taken over core economic activities from name-brand corporations. Dozens of companies like Apple, Ericsson, and Sony sold their factories to generic manufacturers so that they could focus on their "core competencies" of design and brand management. The existence of a large sector of generic manufacturers, often operating abroad, allows even the smallest company to produce on a large scale. A major result of this movement is that a company can be large in revenues and market capitalization while remaining quite small in employment numbers and assets.[12]

Thus, the public corporation in the U.S. has increasingly become unnecessary for production, and unsuitable as a platform for stable employment and the provision of social welfare. In nearly every industry, modular production systems have been adopted, allowing both large and small firms to contract out the manufacture and distribution of physical goods. In the scenario of ongoing offshoring regarding the production of a wide variety of such goods to China or elsewhere, U.S.–domiciled corporations are unnecessary for much of large-scale production. Many of the large firms that remain employ most of their workers outside of the United States; these include GE, IBM, GM, United Technologies, and Citigroup. Of the manufacturers that do continue to employ substantial numbers of Americans, several of the largest are military contractors who receive from 50 to 90 percent of their revenues from the U.S. government; Boeing, Lockheed Martin, General Dynamics, Northrop Grumman, and Raytheon are among the twenty largest manufacturing employers in the U.S.[13] Importantly, much celebrated high-tech companies, following the Nike model of production, create relatively few jobs in the U.S.[14]

The Limited Liability Company as the New Default

The growth of generic manufacturers and distributors, along with the widespread availability of cloud services—which has made the "virtualization" of an industry by separating design and brand management from production that much easier—have lifted the barriers to entry in many industries that previously were dominated by traditional corporations. As Davis suggests, with the help of a credit card and a Web connection, it is not hard to create an enterprise. Information and communication technologies help to do so smoothly, from creating a legal structure to hiring temporary employees to contracting out production and distribution. Coordinating activities used to be the corporation's strong asset. But now the corporation is increasingly outmaneuvered by alternative business forms that are more flexible and less costly.

The economies of scale that were a decisive factor in the creation of the modern corporation have disappeared in many sectors. Entrants can scale their business up or down rapidly by renting rather than buying capacity, and their low costs mean that in many domains their products or services are the preferred choice for consumers. For example, Vizio grew to be the best-selling brand of LCD televisions in the U.S. by 2010, beating Samsung and leaving Sony far behind; Vizio offered low-cost TVs assembled by a Taiwanese partner and sold through big-box retailers like Costco. Vizio chose to forgo investment in assets or employees; it had fewer than 200 when in late 2007 it had sold about as many televisions in the U.S. as Sony (with 150,000 employees). Today Vizio has expanded its business into sound equipment and laptop computers, but it still has only 400 employees.[15]

Such lightweight private firms with modest time horizons have little reason for bearing the costs (financial and otherwise) and disadvantages of going public, which can be substantial. Raising capital on public markets imposes a set of requirements for accountability and transparency. Public companies need to issue quarterly and annual reports explaining what the corporation does, who is running it, and how it is doing. A public corporation is required to share its balance sheet explaining its assets and liabilities. It also needs to issue an income statement documenting its revenues and expenses; a reputable outside accountant is necessary to verify these documents, and expensive.

Public corporations are also required to disclose a large number of other things, such as the board members, their qualifications and other commitments; how much executives are paid; what risks the company faces; the state of its labor relations; and more. These disclosures also make it easier for actual or potential competitors to see what the company is up to, which is another kind of cost. Corporations also are subject to regulations that other forms of business are not. Corporations that issue shares have to deal with a long list of federal regulations about their corporate governance and other aspects of how they do business; these inevitably create financial costs. Public corporations bear other costs that are implicit. The public expects safe products, fair wages, and decent employee benefits. When corporations fail to live up to these expectations, their required disclosures are a significant source of information for journalists and activists who want to hold them accountable. The same information is not available about a company like Koch Industries, which is privately owned and therefore not required to tell the public, for instance, what the Koch brothers earn. Social activists concerned about a number of issues—including the working conditions in the factories of contract manufacturers abroad, child labor practices, environmental pollution impacts on climate change, and so forth—inevitably find it much easier to target listed corporations than other kinds of businesses.

Finally, beyond the demands of regulators and the scrutiny of the media and social movements, public corporations today face unprecedented levels of activism by hedge funds demanding changes in personnel, finances, and strategy. There have always been costs associated with being a public corporation, but the threshold today is high enough that the costs may not be offset by the benefits.[16]

To be clear, Davis does not suggest that all public corporations are doomed. What he claims is that the public corporation will no longer be the default way of doing business. Low entry costs mean that various alternatives become plausible, and if they are cheaper, they will come to dominate. Of these alternatives the most popular is the LLC (limited liability company); it has become one of the most prevalent business forms in the United States. It combines the pass-through taxation of a partnership or sole proprietorship with the limited liability of a corporation. LLCs are simple and cheap to set up (in almost every state), highly flexible, and easy for tax purposes, as returns flow through directly to owners. Income from public corporations is taxed twice, once at the corporate entity level and again when distributed to shareholders, thus more tax savings often result if a business is set up as an LLC rather than a corporation.[17] Davis's assessment leaves out the important fact that many U.S. corporations use offshore tax havens and other accounting tricks to avoid paying federal income taxes. (A large loophole at the core of U.S. tax law enables corporations to avoid paying taxes on foreign profits until they are brought home; this is known as "deferral." Consequently, many corporations choose never to bring these profits home and never pay a single penny of U.S. taxes on them.[18])

For several years now new businesses have been far more likely to organize as an LLC than a corporation. Companies owned by private equity firms are often organized as LLCs. Legal forms with additional purposes beyond profit are the L3C (low-profit LLC) and the benefit corporation. Alternative ways to channel capital to business include private ownership (for example, family business), private equity, and new forms such as crowdfunding. These are compatible with alternative legal structures, but LLCs tend to be the default.

If creating an enterprise is inexpensive and requires little investment and few dedicated assets, then low-cost legal forms are attractive. And even on a larger scale, the benefits of the public corporation to entrepreneurs are diminishing, due to all the inherent costs mentioned earlier.[19] One thing should not be forgotten, however. The increasing use of business forms having the LLC format (in one way or another) does not necessarily mean that business leaders on the whole have less political clout than they used to have. On the contrary, there is empirical evidence regarding the enduring existence of a power elite with business leaders at the core (who are increasingly those at the helm of privately held companies).[20] The powerful influence of private business is obvious in politics at all levels of government. Recently, wealthy individuals—typically self-made men who made their fortunes mostly in finance and energy—have thrown their weight around in presidential politics.[21] They did so especially through contributions to what are popularly dubbed "Super PACs," a new form of Political Action Committee which emerged in response to the 2010 U.S. Supreme Court ruling in *Citizens United v. Federal Election Commission*.[22]

From Job Ladder to Job to Task

Already in the 1990s, observers signaled the "death of the career," as careers had devolved into jobs, with employees often moving from firm to firm, or working as independent contractors. At most corporations a career system is no longer in place today; they still provide jobs, but no job ladders that offer a trajectory for upward social mobility. In some sectors, one can witness another shift—traditional jobs are giving way to discrete, dispersed tasks. This means doing specific pieces of work for specified financial compensation—not as an employee, but as an independent contractor. Uber, the ride-hailing online platform—whereby drivers use their own cars to provide "taxi rides" to customers—is the most prominent example of this new form of work.[23]

Aided and abetted by the fact that much of the population carries a smartphone with GPS, Uber and similar digital platforms make it possible for consumers to contract for microwork (walking a dog, picking up groceries, wrapping gifts, watering plants) for a set fee. In some cases, potential contractors bid against each other to offer the lowest rate. For instance, at Mechanical Turk (MTurk), Amazon's online labor market platform for "human intelligence tasks," this has led to a deplorable situation in which many "Turkers" routinely earn less than the minimum wage.[24] Because they are not employees, but rather "freestanding micro-entrepreneurs," the minimum wage legislation does not apply. Gerald Davis expects this new form of what he calls "platform capitalism" (rather than the less accurate term "sharing economy," at least regarding the for-profit platforms[25]) to spread to any kind of task that can be easily specified, to the extent that the law allows (there is always the possibility of new employment legislation regulating this kind of work). Skill need not be a barrier to using this format either; platforms can require that their "micro-entrepreneurs" document their qualifications (e.g., a commercial driver's license or a shelf-stocking certificate). In principle, any task that has not been automated or outsourced, and that requires only minimal special training, can be subject to "Uberization."[26] Critics who see the for-profit platforms as creators of a growing "precariat"—a "class" on the precarious edge of economic security—are probably right in arguing that the "sharing" is not trust, but desperation. They signal the race to the bottom, with risk shifting from companies to individual "micro-entrepreneurs."[27]

Overall, automation and outsourcing, along with the rapid cycle time for products, imply that long-term corporate employment is becoming obsolete in the U.S. for the majority of the workforce. Even short-term employment may become rare and unpredictable. Consequently, the employment-based social welfare system in the U.S. is increasingly maladapted to the realities of employment in this country, and therefore withering away. Davis gives the vivid example of companies like Eastman Kodak which provided health insurance and retirement pensions partly to encourage employees to invest in firm-specific skills, and both parties tended to benefit from long-term attachments. He compares this with short-lived contemporary enterprises such as the company behind the (once very popular) Flip video camera, produced from 2006 until March 2011.[28] Given the expected brief lifespan of such companies, it makes little sense for them to build strong corporate cultures with generous benefits intended to ensure commitment, and it makes even less sense for an employee to risk learning firm-specific skills for a company that is likely to exist only for a few years.

It is true that a number of firms—often high-tech and heavily capitalized—continue to experiment with newer welfare provisions for their tenured employees, such as child care, medical benefits for same-sex partners, and generous vacation plans, while also offering attractive profit-sharing plans and stock options, as well as expanded educational opportunities. But much of what remains of corporate welfarism in America is in disarray, and may even be declared officially dead in the not-too-distant future.

A Possible Way Out?

Due to automation, offshoring, Nikefication and the decline of the public corporation as it existed during its heyday after World War II, job ladders and real jobs provided by U.S. corporations have been disappearing in many sectors of the economy; they may never come back again. Most of the new businesses do not offer that many jobs, let alone stable employment and good benefits, except for a limited number of core employees. Further, the paramount influence of Corporate Business Systems makes attempts at attaining (greater) "relative autonomy" regarding the remaining jobs in large organizations seem futile. This is not an issue on the agenda of most labor unions in the United States. Union density in the private sector is low anyway, if the employees in a workplace are unionized at all. (In 2015, the percentage of wage and salary workers belonging to a union was 11.1 percent. This masks the big difference in union density between the private and public sectors. While in the private sector only 6.7 percent of the workers were unionized, 36.3 percent in the public sector were.[29]) The few groups of employees involved in struggles for workers' rights that do include calls for workplace control (in the sense of having a real voice in decision making regarding technology and work organization) continue to meet resistance from their employers.

Alternative forms of work organization like those at online platforms or locally in the "sharing economy" do not make up for the job losses at corporations by any stretch of the imagination. The creation of jobs by massive work projects focused on repairing crumbling infrastructures and building new ones (including, among other things, renewable energy and energy saving ventures) across the country might bring some significant relief. (The U.S. government did such things on a relatively modest scale during President Barack Obama's first term, through the introduction of an economic stimulus package in response to the 2008 financial crisis.[30]) But there is as yet no broad movement on the scale needed with enough political clout to bring such efforts to fruition. The prospects for alternative systems that have been proposed to deal with the disappearance of jobs, and permanent unemployment—for example, those including a basic income guarantee or a full-fledged negative income tax (larger than the current Earned Income Tax Credit, and universal[31])—seem bleak too.

At the present time, the question of the IT-informed industrial rationalization of work and its ramifications for the quality of work and job requirements—at many levels, in virtually all sectors—is barely on the public agenda. As things currently stand, it seems unlikely it will emerge as a hot button issue in American politics any time soon.

Conclusion

Taylorism, as a set of managerial principles and techniques regarding the rationalization and standardization of the work process in terms of "the one best way," aimed at gaining economic efficiency through improved work organization and greater labor productivity. It grew out of the systematic management movement in America during the late 19th century, and developed first in the manufacturing industries. From there scientific management, in a broad sense, spread to other sectors of the economy and continued to have an impact on the quality of work and control structures of labor in a wide variety of work settings.

Scientific management evolved in an era when mechanization and automation were still in their infancy. The ideas and methods of scientific management extended the American system of manufacturing in the transformation from craft work (with humans as the only possible agents) to mechanization and automation. By deconstructing production processes into discrete, unambiguous units, scientific management laid the groundwork for automation, anticipating industrial process and numerical controls in the absence of any machines capable of carrying out the tasks. Taylor and his followers, however, did not foresee the extensive removal of humans from the production process. In their world, it was humans who would execute the optimized processes. Concerns over skill-eroding and labor-displacing technologies arose later on with increasing mechanization and automation.

The middle ground between the craft production of skilled workers and full automation is occupied by systems of extensive mechanization and partial automation operated by unskilled and semiskilled workers. Such systems depend on algorithmically controlled workflows and knowledge transfer, which require substantial engineering to succeed. Although Taylor's intention for scientific management was simply to optimize work methods, the process engineering that he and his associates pioneered also tends to build the skill into the equipment and processes, removing the need for skill in the workers accordingly. As demonstrated in the previous chapters, this type of approach has governed most industrial engineering since then.

Industrial rationalization was first and foremost embodied by the new automotive production technology that evolved in the Ford Highland Park plant in the early 20th century. Although Ford's technology was used to improve productivity in the automotive industry, its principles could be applied to any kind of manufacturing process, and even (to some extent) to the service sector. It would become the dominant industrial technology for most of the 20th century. Fordist "mass production" is typically based on a technical division of labor that is organized along Taylorist lines, subject (in its immediate production phase) to mechanical pacing by moving assembly-line techniques (including the usage of special-purpose machinery), and governed overall by the supply-driven principle that production must be unbroken and in long runs to secure economies of scale. The assembly line itself as well as the single-purpose machinery allied with it, employed unskilled and semiskilled workers, but other types of worker (craft workers, foremen, engineers, designers etc.) were employed elsewhere. Ford managers and engineers achieved forms of control through the strict supervision of workers, the design of machine tools, and the setup of line production.

Earlier on, one could also witness the spread of industrial rationalization's logic into the service sector, starting with retailing: self-service restaurants since the 1890s and self-service shops since the 1910s. Beginning in the aftermath of World War I, through the efforts of Taylor's disciple Leffingwell, the rationalization of office work evolved too by implementing Taylorized principles to work tasks that could be routinized, and by applying the "exception principle" to difficult cases that could not be properly handled by ordinary clerks. These exceptional cases were then handed over to experts for resolution. The clerk's decisions about which cases met this principle were based on criteria determined by management, and did not require much independent thinking. As we have seen, the exception principle still plays a significant role today in the setup of customer services, and more generally call center work, albeit in settings with very different office technology.

In their attempts to keep a check on labor, managements deployed control strategies other than scientific management. A distinctive feature of the U.S. scene was the exceptionally high degree of hostility that employers demonstrated toward both the regulatory state and organized labor. Welfare capitalism was their way of fending off labor militancy and political radicalism, as well as government regulation. Welfare capitalists went to great lengths to quash union organizing, strikes, and other collective labor actions, through combinations of stick and carrot methods, including violent repression, worker sanctions, and work incentives and benefits (in exchange for loyalty). However, the assaults on labor by major employers until the New Deal era, were made possible by the opportunities resulting from greater state repression than in many other industrialized countries at the time.

Welfare capitalism first emerged during the intense industrial developments from 1880 to 1900, and gained prominence in the 1920s. Welfare work, as it was also called, initially evolved in companies controlled by their founders, who were driven by an ethical impulse (a mixture of moral, paternalistic and *noblesse oblige* motives, often underpinned by religious beliefs), which was combined with a large dose of self-interest, however. Like scientific management, welfare capitalism aimed to prevent collective labor action and improve production, though its methods were more indirect, focusing on the workers' conditions outside the workplace. Promoted by business leaders during a period marked by widespread economic insecurity, social reform activism, and labor unrest, it was based on the idea that American workers should look not to the government or to labor unions but to the benefits provided by private-sector employers for protection against the fluctuations of the market economy. Employers pursued these types of welfare policies to encourage worker loyalty, productivity, and dedication to the job.

Welfare work was frequently manipulative and patronizing to workers, with the most paternalistic programs being directed at women and immigrants from Eastern and Southern Europe. Skilled workers—almost all men, native-born or from Northwestern Europe— tended to receive more clear-cut economic incentives for loyalty, including wage bonuses, retirement and profit-sharing plans. By strengthening skilled workers' ties to the firm, employers sought to weaken craft union traditions, speed the pace of work, and hasten the introduction of new technologies. For the latter purpose, piece-rates and other incentive wage systems were also used, especially in the metalworking industries, where Taylorist practices had taken a strong foothold. However, it sometimes had the opposite effect, making workers more reluctant to accept technical innovations or job transfers, both of which might lead to lower earnings. Therefore, career-based workplace policies—promotion ladders, seniority rules, and dismissal restraint—were introduced next to incentive wage systems. Gradually the "drive system" gave way to more enduring work relationships, coupled with the welfare services the employer provided outside the workplace. This effectively meant the bureaucratization of employment.

In the 1920s, the push for a "moral capitalism" led from above helped fuel the rise of the labor movement in the 1930s when capitalism was in crisis. The

Great Depression restricted the growth of welfare capitalism, but never fully bankrupted it. Welfare capitalism silently transformed itself in response to New Deal policies which made company unions unlawful and endorsed collective bargaining rights, while an emerging welfare state began to provide workers with elementary protections against the risks of industrial life. One must remember, however, that the New Deal order remained by and large confined to the white, male industrial working class. From the late 1930s on, welfare capitalism gradually was modernized by a group of corporate businesses, spearheaded by firms such as AT&T, DuPont, IBM, Procter & Gamble, Standard Oil, Eastman Kodak, and Sears which had not been unionized and had gone through the Depression with little or no harm to their core business. They still offered relatively generous welfare plans, but now the benefits took the form of supplements to Social Security and other government programs.

By mid-century, the human relations approach had become a mainstay within welfare capitalist firms. It focused on how the attitudes and feelings of workers affected their job performance. According to this approach, in contrast to scientific management, work was not just a physical and technical-organizational process, and motivation was about more than financial incentives. The human relations management techniques emphasized the importance of the relationship between supervisor and workers and the dynamics of the groups formed by the workers. Managers had to learn how to understand employees, and especially how to talk and listen to them, by attending special training programs. In this way, the human relations approach sought to foster work-group solidarity in conjunction with workers' commitment to the values of the formal organization.

It represents a form of normative control, and can be very manipulative as is well-exemplified by the extensive program developed at Sears, the corporate center of the human relations movement during the 1940s and early 1950s. A combination of employee attitude surveys and interviews provided management with much intelligence about their employees, who were steered toward having a cathartic experience designed to relieve "emotional stress" through counseling. The Sears program aimed to change an employee's behavior without his/her knowledge or consent. It was also deceptive about the survey's true objectives, and the program consistently adopted a managerial perspective on workplace relations, as in its definition of "morale" and its deliberate intention to stave off unions.

A similar critique applies to Kurt Lewin's approach to industrial psychology that emerged in the 1940s, which showed that democratic leadership styles and employee participation in group decision-making caused both morale and productivity to rise. There are parallels with the thinking of the human relationists. Likewise, the Lewinians believed leaders (managers) could manipulate participation (informal organization) through communications (social skill) to produce a good group climate (morale), thus enhancing satisfaction (integration) with the group life (social system) and improving performance (output). However, while leadership training, attitude surveys, and other practices inspired by Mayo's human relations perspective were widespread in the 1950s, Lewinian-style participative groups did not get real traction until the 1960s.

Lewinian applied psychology can be situated within the broader American tradition of "democratic social engineering," which emerged in the late 19th century. This type of social engineering first took off in Sunday schools and youth groups (YMCA) as well as in the settlement houses and schools that were part of the Progressive movement. Paradoxically, democratic social engineering consists of group decision-making with a *predetermined* influence objective. It comprises a system of authority that is ideally both effective and "democratic." Its proponents were attracted to social psychology, and in particular its Lewinian variant, because as a body of knowledge it confirmed the validity of group process ("intelligently controlled" by group leaders) as the ideal form of social reform *and* social control in a democratic culture.

In the 1950s, problems of "alienation" and "the need to belong" became leading topics in social critiques of white-collar work in large corporations. According to C. Wright Mills in *White Collar*, this type of work was in some ways worse than unskilled industrial labor; white-collar employees had to sell their personalities in addition to the time and energy they invested in their work, whereas industrial workers were at least free in their leisure time. The human relations industry offered corporate leaders the chance to develop new interpretative frameworks that would publicly legitimate the enormous power imbalance between the "new men of power" and ordinary citizens, and purportedly help to produce loyal and enthusiastic workers. The focus was on employee morale because the Protestant work ethic of individual self-improvement through hard work was not viable in large complex organizations, where so much of the work was fragmented and meaningless, and there was little room for mobility and improvement. Mills claimed that the white-collar man was psychologically shaped by the organization to fit its chief objectives and then destined to lead a shallow and petty life outside of work.

William Whyte in *The Organization Man*, targeted a "social ethic" that rationalized the organization's demand for commitment and loyalty and gave employees who committed themselves wholeheartedly to the organization, a sense of dedication and fulfillment. It implied the conviction that the group is a source of creativity and that belongingness is the ultimate need of the individual. This ethic also presumed that psychologists and sociologists working in personnel management could develop techniques to engineer a sense of belonging. Whyte was apprehensive that such an approach would deprive people of their creativity and individual identity. He went further, specifically criticizing the use of personality tests to weed out people who did not fit in, and challenged the notion that organizations should be conflict-free. Whyte's worst fear was that organizations would come to be dominated by a climate of all-pervasive conformity, where the threat for individuals lay not in an Orwellian type of coercion or repression but in psychological manipulation by an amicable group of "therapists."

The core of Whyte's argument was that people would become convinced that organizations and groups can make better decisions than individuals, and thus serving an organization should take priority over advancing one's individual creativity. He claimed this viewpoint was not in line with the available evidence, and went on to give several examples that showed that individual work and creativity can produce better outcomes than collectivist processes. Whyte did not believe that people think or create well in groups. He found disingenuous the whole idea of "leaderless" decision-making groups, whereby the leader, consulted only for his expertise, would fade into the background once the group members started to work well together. Whyte maintained that the power and authority of the group simply masked the real power and authority that leaders had over group members.

The issues that Mills and Whyte raised then would resurface again in the 1970s, when there was a broader public outcry about "alienation," culminating in the 1973 U.S. government report *Work in America*, which spawned the short-lived Quality of Working Life movement. Ultimately, it had little long-term traction, even though there were no indications of diminishing alienation in many jobs. In addition, a renewed emphasis on teamwork in large corporations emerged, which drew little social criticism along the lines of Whyte's argument, however.

From the mid–20th century on, there has been the tendency of what George Ritzer has called the "McDonaldization of society," whereby the principles of the fast-food restaurant pioneered by McDonald's were adopted by an ever growing array of retail, leisure and media services. McDonaldism has much in common with the Fordist industrialization of work: Taylorized work tasks, single-purpose machines, and conveyor belt assembly, standardized parts, and the quick delivery of a high volume of inexpensive, low-quality products. In addition to being monitored by managers, subjected to extensive operating rules, and controlled by machines, fast-food workers are also put under considerable pressure by the presence of customers who expect to be served quickly. Meanwhile, the requirement to show appropriate expressive behavior points to the emotional labor intrinsic to interactive service work.

The continued industrialization of white-collar work also brought with it the issue of speedup and its consequences. Office automation eliminated many menial tasks but also led to new physical complaints and psychological strains among employees. A major problem for management was that much of white-collar work resisted the rigorous standardization and measurement of scientific management, while the technologies of the office did not offer managers direct, up-to-date feedback about the performance of employees. Both challenges could be overcome with the arrival of networked computers and associated workflow software. But the reengineering movement of the 1990s, which sought to apply scientific management principles to the contemporary service industry, borrowed (for office management) less from Leffingwell's American successors and more from the Japanese automakers, with their renewed scientific management's industrial model, which became known as "lean production." Now rigorous control of the labor process similar to that of the assembly line in manufacturing became a real possibility. Moreover, the reach of the reengineered work practices was extended upward to middle management and beyond.

—⁂—

Prior to the 1960s, welfare capitalism remained limited to a minority of large nonunion corporations and their practices only slowly took hold in other firms. But during the 1960s and especially after 1970, welfare capitalism began to spread rapidly because of changes in the business environment. This included more competitive and volatile markets and a workforce shifting away from manual work, along with different aspirations of younger and more educated workers (including many women) in white-collar jobs. The values of those workers tended to be more in line with nonunionized firms' emphasis on individual pay determination and merit. These employees were more inclined to see fairness in terms of the recognition of individual abilities and rights instead of "equal treatment for all" with its emphasis on standard wage rates, common rules, and seniority rights upheld by workers in unionized firms. Thus, welfare capitalism spread beyond its borders to a new group of rapidly growing companies, many of which were in the technology and service sectors.

The "new nonunion model" of the corporate firm presented to the general public at that time was not as new as suggested. In fact, it was very much like what leading welfare capitalist firms had been following since the 1920s. The only difference was the behavioral-science-driven use of team organization and sociotechnical principles to alter the traditional division of labor. The team system spread rapidly, at first within nonunion firms, as it dovetailed nicely with the basic character of modern welfare capitalism and especially the Lewinian strain of human relations that by now had become influential. This went hand in hand with a more widespread adoption of the single-status employment system of the "unitary" concept of the firm, which did away with occupational distinctions and encouraged "flexibility" in job and task allocation. This system was extended to manufacturing in the 1980s when Japanese lean production was first introduced.

Supporters of "flexible specialization" and lean production were optimistic about the links between advanced manufacturing systems and the utilization of skilled labor. They posited a polarity between mass production and some form of flexibility that breaks with Taylorism and Fordism. Likewise it was assumed that the first wave of office automation largely confirmed Braverman's degradation of work thesis, but that the second wave emerging in the 1980s was ushering in a reintegrated labor process and multi-activity jobs.[1]

As we have seen in this book, the move towards flexible specialization was not as innovative as some influential management writers suggested. It was anticipated by "Sloanism," the flexible mass production already developed at General Motors in the 1920s, and did *not* entail a break with Taylorism. It is true that skill variety is necessary to exploit arrangements such as just-in-time and modular production that are part of lean production. But variations or new responsibilities such as self-maintenance may be small, and a more accurate description is that of an enlarged number of interchangeable tasks carried out by replaceable labor, or a broader scope of skills, not higher ones.

Much of the restructuring of work took place in jobs that had been designed to reintegrate or put tasks back together, shifting the pattern of the division of labor. Yet the newer division of labor, often combining mental and manual tasks, was built on the earlier basis of divided work. There was indeed much continuity with the past, in that lean production retained many Taylorist elements. For example, in manufacturing plants, the work of line operators still overwhelmingly involved following a prescribed procedure and offered little discretion. Learning was dominated by an obsession with standardized work procedures based on a more sophisticated application of Taylorist techniques.

Other management techniques such as Total Quality Management (TQM), which were buttressed by benchmarking systems, likewise required a concern for standardized procedures and uniform, dependable practices. Business Process Reengineering (BPR) gave top management even more control over the standardization of jobs by integration through computer technology and built-in programmed computer applications.

Advocates of TQM and teamworking have argued that organizations are moving away from models of managerial control to ones of "self-managed" teamworking driven by commitment. As noted in this book, this appears to be a much too optimistic conclusion. Usually, this kind of teamworking still entails relatively limited delegation of authority, while the empowerment rhetoric is often empty regarding the amount of decision-making autonomy that teams actually exercise; the managerial prerogative remains largely intact. In most cases, the extent to which control practices have been changed is negligible. Evidence shows that existing corporate hierarchies still constrain attempts to delegate power and expand employee involvement. While TQM and teamworking hand over some responsibilities to teams and operators, tasks are more closely monitored and strictly controlled. Added to the managerial armory of external surveillance is often extensive peer surveillance of behavioral norms and outcomes such as attendance and productivity. Thus, "self-management" becomes self-policing aided by digital panopticons—information and communication technologies that allow management to have an omnipresent eye on the shop or office floor.

One should also recognize that managerial projects to foster commitment among employees still constitute a form of control, namely normative control. Criticism has rightly been leveled at the "totalitarian" nature of management controls, such as corporate culture and Business Process Reengineering.[2] Such criticism may apply even more to newer versions of reengineering, Enterprise Resource Planning (ERP) and Corporate Business Systems (CBSs), with their all-pervasive digital control structures across the firm extending to the activities at all levels of management except the highest.[3] Only the CEO and his senior colleagues dodge the real-time surveillance at stake here.

Overall, managerial control over workers in corporate life has come to rely—to a much greater degree than ever before—on the technological and organizational constraints built into the command-and-control systems that were introduced in many firms during the past decades. This is exemplified most recently by the increased pace of work dictated by CBSs, with their intensive targeting and monitoring through "performance evaluation" systems, and subsequent deskilling of employees with expert systems. However, one must be wary of an overdeterministic view of technology and account for the possibility of management incompetence and worker resistance. Uneven and incompetent management implementation may indeed stymie the effectiveness of these control systems. But what about worker resilience that may also come into play? This is of course very much dependent on the countervailing power that labor has at its disposal. With the decline of organized labor and relentless union busting by many employers, worker power has waned. It must also be remembered that generally unions have not been inclined to address issues of workplace control. In those places where professionals have become unionized—as, for example, doctors in some health care organizations—questions of autonomy are a theme of organizing drives, but once a drive is over these unions tend to slip back to making the usual demands regarding salaries and benefits. Further, the uncertainty for workers of getting and keeping a regular job grew dramatically in the 1980s and 1990s, as employment contracts became more unsettled and the category of wage labor more problematic. Long-term unemployment grew, and the length of job tenure shortened, while temporary, part-time, and other forms of contingent work flourished. All of these conditions have contributed to a loss of confidence in labor as a source of opposition to the management-dominated control and monitoring systems.

—⁂—

With the rise of financial capitalism and the increased importance of shareholders focused on the maximization of stock value, owners of capital re-intervened in the management of the corporation during the 1980s and 1990s. Control by owners came to dominate corporate governance, which by then was primarily based on financial criteria and short-term prospects. The great risk shift at issue here involved a reallocation of resources from employees and other stakeholders to shareholders (including executives who owned options) and a shift of risk to employees, whose wages and employment became more sensitive to business conditions.

The implication for welfare capitalist firms was that its "new nonunion model" and particularly its employment stability feature, came under fire. Several of these companies laid off thousands of employees, which now included a growing number of middle-level managers who were shocked to discover that their jobs were no longer protected. Some welfare capitalist firms adopted dualist policies in order to preserve career jobs. They had flex workers carry out the tasks which were the least essential to the firm, while buttressing a core of stable jobs with good benefits. Other welfare capitalist companies took a different course in the early 1990s, and first aimed to maintain full employment by retraining and reassigning workers to other corporate divisions, an employment stabilization technique dating back to the 1920s. But ultimately, these companies also found it necessary to resort to layoffs, thus reneging on their job-security promise.

By the turn of the new century, company-provided welfare provisions were sharply reduced and a huge share of the cost burden was shifted from employers to their employees. Corporations significantly reduced their contributions to their employees' health care costs, and shifted from defined benefit pensions to employee-funded defined contribution plans. There are some notable exceptions to the ongoing deterioration of welfare capitalism. These include firms—usually high-tech—that continue to experiment with welfare provisions such as child care and longer vacation packets, and still offer profit-sharing plans and stock options. Yet much of corporate welfare capitalism is in dire straits and may even die out in the somewhat longer run.

—⁂—

The development of expert systems has been crucial in the use of information technology as a reengineering tool. "Informating" (Zuboff's term) would mean using computer systems to increase skill levels in clerical positions, thus giving responsibility and knowledge back to the employees involved. As has become apparent, this skill-enhancement scenario has not materialized. In various industries, the informating power of technology has mostly been used by management to strengthen its supervision and control over middle- and lower-level workers rather than enable them to directly analyze the information in the database, come up with ideas, and improve their own performance. This tendency has even become evident in call center work that deals with more complex problems and uses a more sophisticated expert system, but—with only few exceptions—still allows the employees little leeway for analyzing the database and developing creative answers to questions.

The attempts of the "managed care" industry since the late 1980s to subject the medical sector to industrial reengineering is a dramatic example of reengineering's upward reach into the higher echelons of professional work. Importantly, management consultants have written many of the books on managed care and direct the transformation of medical practice, but most of them lack any medical qualification whatsoever. Medical reengineers focus on simplifying existing processes and speeding them up. In addition to the routine processes of the operational side of the "medical business," reengineering is also deeply engaged in "higher" processes which involve the core activities of the physician: screening, diagnosis, and treatment of patients.

A Taylorist approach of optimization and standardization is likely to become more pronounced throughout the medical field. And so is the trend toward replacing the physician's clinical judgment with the statistical output of what is called evidence-based medicine, whereby doctors are increasingly pressured to relinquish more control over diagnoses and treatment decisions to software. As previously noted, using decision-support software also brings the risk of automation bias with it in making analyses or diagnoses. Furthermore, automation bias is related to automation complacency, which has been found in a variety of high-risk situations with technology-first automation including, among other things, industrial control rooms and the flight decks of airplanes. It has also occurred in office work as, for example, in the case of architects' and other designers' declining attention to detail with the introduction of design software.

The potential of computer-aided decision-support systems taking over certain aspects of professional decision making has greatly increased with the arrival of IBM's super computer system Watson a few years ago. This tendency has accelerated since then with the move to "the cloud." But it must be remembered that a system like Watson has been developed by the prevailing artificial intelligence approach that aims to replicate the results rather than the process of human thought. It upholds a primary tenet of the big data revolution; the idea that prediction based on correlation is sufficient for making good decisions, and that a deep understanding of causation is usually neither achievable nor necessary. Basically, the system is "mindless" and has only a cursory resemblance to intelligence.[4] The use of Watson programmed for the field of medicine, for example, has shown promising results regarding diagnosis. But while computer reasoning based on predefined rules and inferences from existing examples can address a large share of cases, human diagnosticians will still have a role to play even after Watson is done with its "medical training" through "self-learning," because anomalous cases will always emerge.

―∞―

The introduction of robots in manufacturing and big retail has led to displacement of workers and in some cases, to improvement of the quality of work for the remaining lesser-skilled workers. On the other hand, robots have created and sustained good jobs for the relatively small numbers of industrial and software engineers and other highly-skilled workers who are involved in designing, programming, and maintaining those robots. Yet artificial intelligence systems with increasingly sophisticated algorithms are eroding the employment of those workers too, and are expected to put a variety of high-skill occupations at risk. As we have seen, no skilled profession, not even medicine, is immune to the efforts of the "reengineers."

Overall, managerial control over workers in corporate life has come to rely (to a great extent) on the technological and organizational constraints built into the command-and-control systems that were introduced in many firms during the past few decades. It is also noteworthy that scientific management—in the guise of Business Process Reengineering—has led to the erosion of employment via both automation and offshoring. Both were made possible by the deskilling of jobs, aided by the knowledge transfer that scientific management achieved. Jobs that once would have required skilled work first were transformed into semiskilled work and then became unskilled. At that point the competition between workers (and worker populations) reached a culmination point. Jobs could be offshored (giving one human's tasks to others, which could be good for the new worker population abroad but not for the old) or they could be eliminated through automation (giving a human's tasks to machines). Either way, the net result in the "homeland" was that jobs started to pay less, and then disappear.

One can even see a modern variant of the putting-out system in various places today. Indeed, this system has been revitalized with the Internet, as distributive service work can create virtual factories composed of workers who only meet online, and employers who contract labor services without building a bureaucracy or firm as was common to many industries in the last century. These employers draw in labor from across borders and temporal zones, thus ensuring continuous production and extract higher productivity (by significantly lowering overhead operating costs) than in a fixed center like a factory or office.[5]

Moreover, facilitated by sophisticated digital information and communication systems, businesses have been offshoring high-skilled professional jobs as well, particularly jobs in IT-enabled knowledge services that include research and development, computer programming, engineering support, product design, equity analysis, radiological analysis, medical transcription, tax-return processing, title searching and more. For the time being, these jobs are primarily outsourced to India. There is also an increasing number of high-tech product companies, including some in Silicon Valley, that have started outsourcing innovation work to India and China. This kind of offshoring, with workers not physically relocating, yet still making their daily presence as contributors to the core business of American corporations felt, can be viewed as a form of *virtual* labor immigration.

These latest developments must be put into proper context, which concerns the decline of the traditional U.S. public corporation, coinciding with the rise of enterprises that are organized differently, both legally and financially. Due largely to the success of the shareholder value movement, the corporation has typically been reduced from a social institution with enduring features to a "nexus of contracts" among voluntary, individual participants. The remaining public corporations, along with newly listed ones, are not set up to offer bureaucratic employment; specifically, long-term opportunities for economic advancement, and benefits such as health insurance and retirement provisions. Changes in the organization of production and distribution of goods subsumed under the label "Nikefication" have significantly contributed to the dismantling of the familiar large-scale corporation. Automation and outsourcing, and the rapid cycle time for production, have made long-term corporate employment a thing of the past for the majority of the workforce. Even short-term employment may become hard to come by, as well as unpredictable. As a result, the employment-based welfare system in the U.S. is increasingly ill-suited to the realities of employment here, and therefore continues to degenerate. The recent shift from jobs to tasks—doing specific pieces of work for specified financial compensation, not as an employee but as a freestanding contractor—only makes things worse. Profit-oriented digital platforms, such as ride-hailing platform Uber and Amazon's online labor market, Mechanical Turk, do not alleviate, and may even exacerbate the precariousness of people who can find no other work. This trend is only weakly counterbalanced by the non-profit, shared economy platforms allied to worker-controlled cooperatives and other projects.

Looking at the wider terrain regarding the business practices that undergird the prevailing management strategies today, it is clear that a broad coalition of countervailing forces—if not a truly democratic political revolution with a focus on the quality of working life—would be necessary to upend these practices. It is also obvious that the current political-institutional and capitalist-industrial conditions pose enormous challenges to the success of such a coalition (should one emerge). Meanwhile, there appears little evidence of this happening in the foreseeable future.

Chapter Notes

Introduction

1. Managerial control strategies regarding earlier forms of labor such as indentured service, craft apprenticeship, the household economy, and the institution of slavery, are beyond the scope of the present work. For managerial control of slave labor in the 19th-century American South, see David Brion Davis, *Inhuman Bondage: The Rise and Fall of Slavery in the New World* (New York: Oxford University Press, 2006), 193–204; Robin Blackburn, *The American Crucible: Slavery, Emancipation and Human Rights* (London: Verso, 2011), 307–17; Kenneth M. Stampp, *The Peculiar Institution: Slavery in the Ante-Bellum South* (New York: Vintage Books, 1956); William K. Scarborough, *The Overseer: Plantation Management in the Old South* (Baton Rouge: Louisiana State University Press, 1966).
2. Mark Wardell, "Labor Processes: Moving Beyond Braverman and the Deskilling Debate," in *Rethinking the Labor Process*, ed. Mark Wardell, Thomas L. Steiger, and Peter Meiksins (Albany: State University of New York Press, 1999), 4.
3. Harry Braverman, *Labor and Monopoly Capital: The Degradation of Work in the Twentieth Century* (New York: Monthly Review Press, 1974), 24–25.
4. Michael Rose, *Industrial Behaviour: Research and Control*, 2nd ed. (London: Penguin, 1988), 315–17.
5. Against this, it has been argued that Braverman's historical referent tends to be an ideal-type craft worker based on a philosophical-anthropological view, where conception and execution are not separated by social and technical relations imposed by a central authority, rather than any specific historical form of a classical craft worker. "Classic" sociological studies often include such a critical dimension. In the United States, Albion Small, Robert and Helen Lynd, and C. Wright Mills are among the more notable in this tradition. From this perspective, Braverman's outline of the ideal craft worker represents a call for a more humane workplace, and is an important reminder that analyses of the workplace should include a critical human dimension. Wardell, "Labor Processes," 5–6.
6. Rose, *Industrial Behaviour*, 320.
7. Christopher Lasch, *The True and Only Heaven: Progress and Its Critics* (New York: W.W. Norton, 1991), 168–225.
8. Rose, *Industrial Behaviour*, 317–18.
9. Braverman, *Labor and Monopoly Capital*, 304.
10. Paul Attewell, "The Clerk Deskilled: A Study in False Nostalgia," *Journal of Historical Sociology* 2, no. 4 (1989): 369, 384.
11. Braverman, *Labor and Monopoly Capital*, 329.
12. *Ibid.*, 335.
13. *Ibid.*, 70.
14. *Ibid.*, 223, 244.
15. *Ibid.*, 339.
16. David Stark, "Class Struggle and the Transformation of the Labor Process: A Relational Approach," *Theory and Society* 9, no. 1 (1980): 92.
17. Rose, *Industrial Behaviour*, 315–20.
18. One other flaw that must be mentioned here is Braverman's gender-blindness, evidenced by his failure to examine the extent to which the meaning of skill is influenced by ideas about gender as well as technical considerations. Braverman's approach defines skill as technique, a combination of manual and mental

capacities for manipulating objects and tools. An alternative approach is one that acknowledges that skill contains a social dimension in addition to a technical one, sometimes called the "political" aspect of skill because it involves the element of power. Stephen Edgell, *The Sociology of Work: Continuity and Change in Paid and Unpaid Work*, 2nd ed. (London: Sage, 2012), 65–66. For critical evaluations, see Craig R. Littler, *The Development of the Labour Process in Capitalist Societies* (London: Heinemann Educational, 1982), 25–34; Peter Meiksins, "Labor and Monopoly Capital for the 1990s: A Review and Critique of the Labor Process Debate," *Monthly Review* 46, no. 6 (1994): 45–59; Chris Smith, "Rediscovery of the Labour Process," in *Sage Handbook of the Sociology of Work and Employment*, ed. Stephen Edgell, Heidi Gottfried, and Edward Granter (London: Sage, 2015), 205–24.

19. Andrew L. Friedman, *Industry and Labour: Class Struggle at Work and Monopoly Capitalism* (London: Macmillan, 1977), 78.

20. Ibid., 88.

21. Ibid., 101.

22. Ibid.

23. Ibid., 106.

24. Richard Edwards, *Contested Terrain: The Transformation of the Workplace in the Twentieth Century* (New York: Basic Books, 1979), 25.

25. Ibid., 34–36.

26. Ibid., 129.

27. Ibid., 159. Note that Edwards's three forms of control are ideal types of managerial control, which can be deployed as heuristic devices in studying particular cases without accepting his argument that each form of control produced worker resistance and was successively replaced.

28. Rose, *Industrial Behaviour*: 334–35.

29. Michael Burawoy, *Manufacturing Consent: Changes in the Labor Process under Monopoly Capitalism* (Chicago: University of Chicago Press, 1979), 27.

30. Michael Burawoy, *The Politics of Production: Factory Regimes under Capitalism and Socialism* (London: Verso, 1985).

31. Rose, *Industrial Behaviour*, 335.

32. Alan Fox, *Beyond Contract: Work, Power and Trust Relations* (London: Faber and Faber, 1974).

33. Kim Voss, *The Making of American Exceptionalism: The Knights of Labor and Class Formation in the Nineteenth Century* (Ithaca, NY: Cornell University Press, 1993), 2, 242.

34. Rose, *Industrial Behaviour*, 10–12, 336, 342.

35. Amitai Etzioni, *A Comparative Analysis of Complex Organizations*, revised and enl. ed. (New York: Free Press 1975).

36. Gideon Kunda, *Engineering Culture: Control and Commitment in a High-Tech Corporation* (Philadelphia, PA: Temple University Press, 1992), 11. Kunda gives this further explication: "Under normative control, members act in the best interest of the company not because they are physically coerced, nor purely from an instrumental concern with economic rewards and sanctions. It is not just their behaviors and activities that are specified, evaluated, and rewarded or punished. Rather, they are driven by internal commitment, strong identification with company goals, intrinsic satisfaction from work. These are elicited by a variety of managerial appeals, exhortations, and actions." Ibid., 11.

37. Erik O. Wright, "Working-Class Power, Capitalist-Class Interests, and Class Compromise," *American Journal of Sociology* 105, no. 4 (2000), 972.

38. Ibid.

39. Beverly J. Silver, *Forces of Labor: Workers' Movements and Globalization Since 1870* (New York: Cambridge University Press, 2003), 13.

40. Ibid.

41. Giovanni Arrighi and Beverly J. Silver, "Labor Movements and Capital Migration: The U.S. and Western Europe in World-Historical Perspective," in *Labor in the Capitalist World Economy*, ed. Charles Bergquist (Beverly Hills, CA: Sage, 1984), 193–95.

42. Smith, "Rediscovery of the Labour Process," 211.

43. Talcott Parsons, *The Social System* (Glencoe, IL: The Free Press, 1951); William H. Starbuck, "Organizational Growth and Development," in *Handbook of Organizations*, ed. James G. March (Chicago: Rand McNally, 1965), 451–583; Clark Kerr, John T. Dunlop, Frederick Harbinson, and Charles Meyers, *Industrialism and Industrial Man: The Problems of Labor and Management in Economic Growth* (Cambridge, MA: Harvard University Press, 1960).

44. Stephen A. Marglin, "What Do Bosses Do? The Origins and Functions of Hierarchy in Capitalist Production," *The Review of Radical Political Economics* 6, no. 2 (1974): 33–60; Michael Burawoy, "Towards a Marxist Theory of the Labor Process," *Politics and Society* 8, no. 3–4 (1978): 247–312; Burawoy, *Manufacturing Consent*; Ray E. Pahl, ed. *On Work: Historical, Comparative and Theoretical Approaches* (Oxford: Blackwell, 1988), 167–74; Edwards, *Contested Terrain*; David M. Gordon, Richard Edwards,

and Michael Reich, *Segmented Work, Divided Workers: The Historical Transformation of Labor in the United States* (New York: Cambridge University Press, 1982).

45. Sanford M. Jacoby, *Employing Bureaucracy: Managers, Unions, and the Transformation of Work in the 20th Century*, rev. ed. (Mahwah, NJ: Lawrence Erlbaum, 2004), 2.

46. Max Weber, *The Theory of Social and Economic Organization* (New York: Oxford University Press, 1947).

47. Reinhard Bendix, *Work and Authority in Industry: Ideologies of Management in the Course of Industrialization* (New York: Wiley, 1956), 251.

48. Robert K. Merton, *Social Theory and Social Structure*, 2nd enl. ed. (New York: Free Press, 1968), 252.

49. Daniel Bell, *The Coming of Post-Industrial Society* (New York: Basic Books, 1973).

50. Chester I. Barnard, *The Functions of the Executive* (Cambridge, MA: Harvard University Press, 1938).

51. Edwards, *Contested Terrain*, 148–52.

52. Rose, *Industrial Behaviour*, 333.

53. Jacoby, *Employing Bureaucracy*, 3.

54. Karl Polanyi, *The Great Transformation* (Boston: Beacon Press, 1957 [1944]), 132.

55. Robin Archer, *Why Is There No Labor Party in the United States?* (Princeton, NJ: Princeton University Press, 2007); Mel van Elteren, *Labor and the American Left: An Analytical History* (Jefferson, NC: McFarland, 2011), 36–72.

56. Jacoby, *Employing Bureaucracy*, 3–7.

Chapter 1

1. Marglin, "What Do Bosses Do?," 93–94.
2. Jacoby, *Employing Bureaucracy*, 10–11.
3. Friedman, *Industry and Labour*, 87.
4. Daniel Nelson, *Managers and Workers: Origins of the New Factory System in the United States, 1880–1920* (Madison: University of Wisconsin Press, 1975), 4.
5. Dan Clawson, *Bureaucracy and the Labor Process: The Transformation of U.S. Industry, 1860–1920* (New York: Monthly Review Press, 1980), 75–83; Nelson, *Managers and Workers*, 31, 38; Littler, *The Development of the Labour Process*, 167–69.
6. Clawson, *Bureaucracy and the Labor Process*, 130–166; David Montgomery, "Workers' Control of Machine Production in the Nineteenth Century," *Labor History* 17, no. 4 (1976): 488–89.

7. Clawson, *Bureaucracy and the Labor Process*, 126–30; Montgomery, "Workers' Control of Machine Production," 491.
8. Jacoby, *Employing Bureaucracy*, 12–13.
9. Littler, *The Development of the Labour Process*, 167–68.
10. Jacoby, *Employing Bureaucracy*, 18–22.
11. Littler, *The Development of the Labour Process*, 171.
12. Jacoby, *Employing Bureaucracy*, 23–24, 1, 15.
13. Ibid., 29.
14. Nelson Lichtenstein, *State of the Union: A Century of American Labor* (Princeton, NJ: Princeton University Press, 2002), 105.
15. Archer, *Why Is There No Labor Party in the United States?*, 142.
16. This tactic is named after the response developed by followers of the revolutionary Auguste Blanqui in French politics during the period 1864–1893. Patrick H. Hutton, *The Cult of the Revolutionary Tradition: The Blanquists in French Politics, 1864–1893* (Berkeley: University of California Press, 1981).
17. Patrick Renshaw, *The Wobblies* (Garden City, NJ: Doubleday, 1967), 119.
18. William Preston, Jr., *Aliens and Dissenters: Federal Suppression of Radicals, 1903–1933* (Urbana: University of Illinois Press, 1994), 39, 44–45; Seymour M. Lipset and Gary Marks, *It Didn't Happen Here: Why Socialism Failed in the United States* (New York: W.W. Norton, 2000), 239–41.
19. Archer, *Why Is There No Labor Party in the United States?*, 93–110.
20. Robert J. Goldstein, *Political Repression in Modern America*, 2nd ed. (Champaign: University of Illinois Press, 2001); Goldstein, "Labor History Symposium: Political Repression of the American Labor Movement During Its Formative Years—A Comparative Perspective," *Labor History* 51, no. 2 (2010): 271–93.
21. Michael Mann, *The Sources of Social Power, volume II: The Rise of Classes and Nation States, 1760–1914* (Cambridge: Cambridge University Press, 1993), 635.
22. Robert J. Goldstein, "Response in Labor History Symposium: Political Repression of the American Labor Movement During Its Formative Years—A Comparative Perspective," *Labor History* 51, no. 2 (2010): 31.
23. Shelton Stromquist, "United States of America," in *The Formation of Labor Movements 1870–1914*, ed. Marcel van der Linden and Jürgen Rojahn (Leiden: E.J. Brill, 1990), 561.
24. Michael Goldfield, "Worker Insurgency, Radical Organization, and New Deal Legisla-

tion," *American Political Science Review* 83, no. 4 (1989): 1258.

25. David M. Gordon, "Capitalist Development and the History of American Cities," in *Marxism and the Metropolis*, ed. William K. Tabb and Larry Sawers (New York: Oxford University Press, 1978), 37, 39.

26. Herbert G. Gutman, *Work, Culture, and Society in Industrializing America* (New York: Alfred A. Knopf 1976), 223–92; Bruce Laurie, *Artisans Into Workers: Labor in Nineteenth-Century America* (New York: Noonday Press, 1989).

27. Douglas C. North, Terry. L. Anderson, and Peter J. Hill, *Growth and Welfare in the American Past: A New Economic History*, 3rd ed. (Englewood Cliffs, NJ: Prentice-Hall, 1983), 145; John Walton, *Sociology and Critical Inquiry* (New York: Wadsworth, 1996), 102.

28. Carville Earle, *Geographical Inquiry and American Historical Problems* (Stanford, CA: Stanford University Press, 1992), 422–28.

29. Gordon, "Capitalist Development and the History of American Cities," 46–47.

30. Gordon, Edwards, and Reich, *Segmented Work, Divided Workers*, 138–39.

31. P.J. Ashton, "The Political Economy of Suburban Development," in *Marxism and the Metropolis*, ed. William K. Tabb and Larry Sawers (New York: Oxford University Press, 1978), 71. The Pullman strike was a nationwide railroad strike, which pitted the American Railway Union (ARU) against the Pullman Company, the main railroads, and the federal government. The conflict started in Pullman Chicago, on May 11, 1894, when nearly 4,000 factory employees of the Pullman Company began a wildcat strike in response to recent reductions in wages. Most factory workers who built Pullman cars lived in the company town of Pullman on the Southside of Chicago. When the Pullman company laid off workers and lowered wages, it did not reduce rents, and the workers called for a strike. The combined reasons for the strike were the absence of democracy within the town of Pullman and its politics, the rigid paternalistic control of the workers by the company, excessive water and gas rates, and a refusal by the company to let workers buy and own their own houses. They had not yet formed a union. Founded in 1893 by Eugene V. Debs, the ARU was an organization of unskilled railroad workers. Debs brought in ARU organizers to Pullman and signed up many disgruntled factory workers. When the Pullman Company refused recognition of the ARU or any negotiations, ARU called a strike against the factory, but it showed no sign of success. To win the strike, Debs decided to stop the movement of Pullman cars on railroads by calling a massive boycott against all trains that carried a Pullman car. At its peak it involved some 250,000 workers in 27 states. The federal government obtained an injunction against the union, Debs and the top leaders, ordering them to stop interfering with trains that carried mail cars. After the strikers refused, President Grover Cleveland ordered in the Army to stop the strikers from obstructing the trains. Violence broke out in many cities, and the strike collapsed. Debs was convicted of violating a court order and sentenced to prison, and the ARU dissolved. David R. Papke, *The Pullman Case: The Clash of Labor and Capital in Industrial America* (Lawrence: University Press of Kansas, 1999); Richard Schneirov, Shelton Stromquist, and Nick Salvatore, *The Pullman Strike and the Crisis of the 1890s: Essays on Labor and Politics* (Urbana: University of Illinois Press, 1999).

32. Gordon, "Capitalist Development and the History of American Cities," 48.

33. Ashton, "The Political Economy of Suburban Development," 71.

34. Edwards, *Contested Terrain*, 44–45.

35. Mansel G. Blackford, *The Rise of Modern Big Business in Great Britain, the United States, and Japan* (Chapel Hill: University of North Carolina Press, 1988), 55, 72; Eric Hobsbawm, *The Age of Empire: 1895–1914* (London: Weidenfeld & Nicholson, 1987), 43–44; Christopher J. Schmitz, *The Growth of Big Business in the United States and Western Europe, 1850–1939* (London: Macmillan, 1993), 46–48.

36. Gordon, "Capitalist Development and the History of American Cities," 50.

37. Edwards, *Contested Terrain*, 50.

38. David Montgomery, *Workers' Control in America: Studies in the History of Work, Technology, and Labor Struggles* (New York: Cambridge University Press, 1979), 26, 57–63; Daniel Nelson, *Managers and Workers: Origins of the Twentieth-Century Factory System in the United States, 1880–1920*, 2nd ed. (Madison: University of Wisconsin Press, 1995), 129–30.

39. Nelson, *Managers and Workers*, 2nd ed., 129.

40. As Marcel van der Linden has pointed out, important innovations in labor management originate outside the North Atlantic region, especially in the colonies, in attempts to control unfree workers. Some of these innovations date long before the Industrial Revolution, and the knowledge involved spread across continents, to various parts of the world. Prototypical examples are (1) permanent direct

supervision of the enslaved workforce (that is, the method of controlling labor directly through a gang system) on the Caribbean sugar plantations on seventeenth-century Barbados; and (2) the introduction of advanced management techniques with regard to Britain's "surplus" of prisoners in Australia, in particular Sydney in New South Wales. These innovations included: improved convict supervision to tighten the span of supervisor control; reducing negative and increasing positive reward systems to improve convict motivation; systematic matching of convict skills with convict employment; transforming work assessments into regular and detached weekly reports; and the construction of detailed job descriptions. Marcel van der Linden, "Re-constructing the Origins of Modern Labor Management," *Labor History* 51, no. 4 (2010): 509–22.

41. Daniel Jacoby, *Laboring for Freedom: A New Look at the History of Labor in America* (Armonk, NY: M.E. Sharpe, 1998), 79–80.

42. It must be remembered, though, that a number of non-corporate alternatives also emerged to challenge the dominance of the public corporation, including mutuals, co-ops, and municipally owned firms. Gerald F. Davis, "The Twilight of the Berle and Means Corporation," *Seattle University Law Review* 34 (2011): 1223; William G. Roy, *Socializing Capital: The Rise of the Large Industrial Corporation in America* (Princeton, NJ: Princeton University Press, 1997).

43. Jacoby, *Laboring for Freedom*, 80; Alfred D. Chandler, *The Visible Hand: The Managerial Revolution in American Business* (Cambridge, MA: Belknap Press, 1977), 62–78, 81–187.

44. Joseph A. Litterer, "Systematic Management: The Search for Order and Integration," *Business History Review* 35, no. 4 (1961): 461–76; "Systematic Management: Design for Organizational Recoupling in American Manufacturing Firms," *Business History Review* 37, no. 4 (1963); 369–91.

45. Hugh G. J. Aitken, *Taylorism at Watertown Arsenal: Scientific Management in Action, 1908–1915* (Cambridge, MA: Harvard University Press, 1960), 17–18.

46. Litterer, "Systematic Management: Design for Organizational Recoupling," 379.

47. Aitken, *Taylorism at Watertown Arsenal*, 18; Litterer, "Systematic Management: Design," 380–84.

48. Litterer, "Systematic Management: Design," 385–87.

49. Littler, *The Development of the Labour Process*, 174–75.

50. Chandler, *The Visible Hand*, 31–32.

51. Jefferson Cowie, *The Great Exception: The New Deal and the Limits of American Politics* (Princeton, NJ: Princeton University Press, 2016), 36.

52. Littler, *The Development of the Labour Process*, 162–63; Nelson, *Managers and Workers*, 4, 7–9; Davis, "The Twilight of the Berle and Means Corporation," 1209.

53. Littler, *The Development of the Labour Process*, 175–79.

54. David R. Roediger, *Working Toward Whiteness—How America's Immigrants Became White: The Strange Journey from Ellis Island to the Suburbs* (New York: Basic Books, 2005), 72–78.

55. Elizabeth Esch and David Roediger, "One Symptom of Originality: Race and the Management of Labour in the History of the United States," *Historical Materialism* 17, no. 4 (2009): 3–43; David R. Roediger and Elizabeth D. Esch, *The Production of Difference: Race and the Management of Labor in U.S. History* (New York: Oxford University Press, 2012).

56. Gordon, Edwards, and Reich, *Segmented Work, Divided Workers*, 141–43; David Montgomery, *The Fall of the House of Labor: The Workplace, the State, and American Labor Activism, 1865–1925* (New York: Cambridge University Press, 1987), 242–44.

Chapter 2

1. Frederick W. Taylor, "Why Manufacturers Dislike College Students," *Proceedings of the Society for the Promotion of Engineering Education* 18 (1909): 87.

2. Bryan Palmer, "Class Conception and Conflict: The Thrust for Efficiency, Managerial Views of Labor and the Working Class Rebellion," *Review of Radical Political Economics* 7, no. 2 (1975): 31–49.

3. This would be graphically depicted in Charlie Chaplin's 1936 comedy film *Modern Times*, which portrays him as a factory worker on an assembly line. There he is subjected to such indignities as being force-fed by a malfunctioning "feeding machine" and an accelerating assembly line, where he screws nuts at an ever-increasing rate onto pieces of equipment, and even gets caught up in the giant machine's wheels.

4. Frederick W. Taylor, "Shop Management" [1903], repr. in Frederick W. Taylor, *Scientific Management* (New York: Harper and Row, 1964), 35.

5. It comes as no surprise that the latter aspects of Taylor's original system did not materialize as he suggested. Even if management wanted to commit itself to scientifically determined production and pay, its efforts were undermined by the market. If every manufacturer adopted Taylor's methods—and assuming that Taylor's system really produced greater productivity—all workers would be more productive. Greater productivity would force firms to choose between laying off some workers or having excess production depress prices. Neither event boded well for maintaining Taylor's rates and bonuses. Firms that did so would find themselves at a competitive disadvantage. It was only a matter of time before scientific managers broke their own promises—which they did. In the steel industry, enormous productivity gains did not prevent managers from lowering the tonnage rates they paid their workers; by 1910, very few steelworkers earned more than the average wage in the manufacturing industry. An even more fundamental problem awaited scientific management, that is, Taylor's fervent belief that his methods brought the interests of labor and management together. This was certainly not the case, as his scheme made the labor contract a one-sided affair. Ultimately, scientific management operated based on the premise that management exercised its proper role when it unilaterally determined what constituted a "fair day's work for a fair day's pay." Jacoby, *Laboring for Freedom*, 81–82.

6. The following overview of the basic characteristics of Taylorism aims to provide a more accurate analysis than the one that Taylor himself gives in terms of the four general principles mentioned in Frederick W. Taylor, "The Principles of Scientific Management" [1911], repr. in Frederick W. Taylor, *Scientific Management* (New York: Harper and Row, 1964).

7. Littler, *The Development of the Labour Process*, 51–52.

8. Ibid., 52.

9. Stanley Aronowitz and William DiFazio, *The Jobless Future*, 2nd ed. (Minneapolis: University of Minneapolis Press, 2010), 26–27.

10. Littler, *The Development of the Labour Process*, 186.

11. When later studies of unskilled workers showed they habitually used their imagination and tacit skills, these findings were declared exceptional. Kenneth C. Kusterer, *Know-How On the Job: The Important Working Knowledge of "Unskilled" Workers* (Boulder, CO: Westview Press, 1978).

12. Philip Kraft, "To Control and Inspire: U.S. Management in the Age of Computer Information Systems and Global Production," in *Rethinking the Labor Process*, ed. Mark Wardell et al. (1999), 20.

13. Littler, *The Development of the Labour Process*, 52–54.

14. Ibid., 59–62.

15. Ibid., 55, 192–93.

16. Louis E. Davis, "The Design of Jobs," *Industrial Relations* 6, no. 1 (1966): 21–45.

17. Littler, *The Development of the Labour Process*, 55–56.

18. Huw Beynon, *Working for Ford* (London: Allen Lane, 1973), 19.

19. Littler, *The Development of the Labour Process*, 57. There are three interrelated meanings of the concept of Fordism. First and foremost, Fordism refers to a production system or labor process element characterized by mass production. The second meaning refers to an economic system or regime of accumulation characterized by mass consumption. Third, it refers to a sociopolitical system or mode of regulation that is supportive of mass production and mass consumption, which, among other things, ensures the supply of physically healthy workers and financially sound consumers. Edgell, *The Sociology of Work*, 90–91. In this book the focus will be primarily, but not exclusively (since all three dimensions are interrelated), on Fordism as an industrial production system.

20. Nicholas Abercrombie and Stephen Hill, "Paternalism and Patronage," *British Journal of Sociology* 27, no. 4 (1976): 413–29.

21. Palmer, "Class Conception and Conflict," 40.

22. Littler, *The Development of the Labour Process*, 57, 151–55.

23. Ibid., 58–59.

24. Daniel Nelson, *Frederick W. Taylor and the Rise of Scientific Management* (Madison: University of Wisconsin Press, 1980), 198–202; Littler, *The Development of the Labour Process*, 180–81.

25. Paul Thompson, *The Nature of Work: An Introduction to Debates On the Labour Process* (London: Macmillan, 1983), 14.

26. Edwards, *Contested Terrain*.

27. Friedman, *Industry and Labour*.

28. Donald Stable, *Prophets of Order: The Rise of the New Class, Technocracy and Socialism in America* (Boston: South End Press, 1984), 29–31.

29. Katherine Van Wezel Stone, "The Origins of Job Structures in the Steel Industry," in *Labor Market Segmentation*, ed. Richard C.

Edwards, Michael Reich, and David M. Gordon (Lexington, MA: D.C. Heath, 1975), 48–49; Littler, *The Development of the Labour Process*, 181–82.

30. David Montgomery, "The 'New Unionism' and the Transformation of Workers' Consciousness in America, 1909–22," *Journal of Social History* 7, no. 4 (1974): 52–53.

31. John P. Frey, "The Relationship of Scientific Management to Labor," *American Federationist* 20 (1913), qtd. in Littler, *The Development of the Labour Process*, 182.

32. Montgomery, *Workers' Control in America*.

33. When the United States entered World War I in 1917, the moral fervor of the American commitment, inspired by President Woodrow Wilson's call for a "war to end all wars," motivated a large number of prominent merchants, manufacturers, bankers, professional men, and others to enter the service of the government as executives in departments in which they were expert. For their service they accepted only a token salary of one dollar per year, plus their necessary expenses. Likewise "one-dollar-a year" men helped the government mobilize and manage American industry during World War II and the Korean War.

34. Sanford M. Jacoby, "Union-Management Cooperation in the United States: Lessons from the 1920s," *Industrial and Labor Relations Review* 37, no. 1 (1983): 18–26; Stanley Shapiro, "The Great War and Reform: Liberals and Labor 1917–1919," *Labor History* 12, no. 3 (1971): 323–44.

35. The fact that Taylor's followers were influenced by Progressive reform thought and activities was, perhaps, the major reason of the transformation. Samuel Haber, *Efficiency and Uplift: Scientific Management in the Progressive Era, 1890–1920* (Chicago: University of Chicago Press, 1964), 128–33.

36. In this 1921 book *Engineers and the Price System*, Veblen wrote that the AFL as a craft-based federation was doomed to marginalization; engineers were key persons to highly mechanized labor processes. He did not hold out much hope that engineers could be recruited into unions as long as capital was prepared to pay them well. At that time, engineers—in short supply—were just emerging from their tradition of self-employment to accept salaried positions. As large corporations of industrial production, such as General Electric, Westinghouse, General Motors, and U.S. Steel, actively recruited scientists and engineers, the main inducements they offered were economic. Stanley Aronowitz, *The Death and Life of American Labor: Toward a New Workers' Movement* (London: Verso, 2014), 122, 125; Thorstein Veblen, *The Engineers and the Price System* (New York: B.W. Huebsch, 1921).

37. Jacoby, "Union-Management Cooperation," 21, 23. During the 1930s, the Taylor Society became an important component of the political and economic network that put forward a Keynesian strategy based on the expansion of mass consumption via the intervention of the state. This strategy advocated an expanded and strong role for the state and unions in the political economy, along with macroeconomic policies that promoted social purchasing power and expanded mass consumption. Carlos E Pabon, "Regulating Capitalism: The Taylor Society and Political Economy in the Interwar Period." Doctoral dissertation, Graduate School of University of Massachusetts Amherst, 1992, http://www.scholarworks.umass.edu/dissertations/AAI9305877.

38. Littler, *The Development of the Labour Process*, 182–83.

39. Nelson, *Managers and Workers*, 2nd ed., 11.

40. Ibid., 11; Alan Trachtenberg, *The Incorporation of America: Culture and Society in the Gilded Age* (New York: Hill and Wang, 1982), 55–57.

41. Nelson, *Managers and Workers*, 2nd ed., 12, 15, 22–23.

42. Gordon, Edwards, and Reich, *Segmented Work, Divided Workers*, 139.

43. David Gartman, "The Historical Roots of the Division of Labor in the American Automobile Industry," in *The Labor Process and Control of Labor: The Changing Nature of Work Relations in the Late Twentieth Century*, ed. Berch Berberoglu (Westport, CT: Praeger, 1993), 21–43; Stephen Meyer, *The Five-Dollar Day: Labor Management and Social Control in the Ford Motor Company, 1908–1921* (Albany: State University of New York Press, 1981).

44. Gartman, "The Historical Roots," 33.

45. Interestingly, Fordism did not derive directly from Taylorism, however. It is likely that the production methods at Ford were developed independently in the period 1905–1915, and that any influence from Taylor's work was indirect at best. Charles E. Sorensen, a principal executive of the company during its first four years, credits the New England machine tool vendor Walter Flanders for the efficient floor-plan layout at Ford. It is unclear if Flanders had been exposed to the spirit of Taylorism elsewhere. David A. Hounshell, *From the American*

System to Mass Production, 1800–1932: The Development of Manufacturing Technology in the United States (Baltimore, MD: Johns Hopkins University Press, 1984), 249–53; Charles E. Sorensen, *My Forty Years with Ford* (New York: W.W. Norton, 1956), 41.

46. Hounshell, *From the American System to Mass Production.*

47. Meyer, *The Five-Dollar Day.*

48. Peter F. Drucker, *Concept of the Corporation* (New York: John Day, 1946), 176.

49. Stephen Meyer, "The Degradation of Work Revisited: Workers and Technology in the American Auto Industry, 1900–2000," 2004, http://www/autolife.umd.umich.edu.

50. David Gartman, *Auto Slavery: The Labor Process in the American Automobile Industry, 1897–1950* (New Brunswick, NJ: Rutgers University Press, 1986).

51. Alfred P. Sloan, *My Years With General Motors* (Garden City, NY: Doubleday, 1986 [1964]), 158.

52. Ibid., 438.

53. Meyer, *The Five-Dollar Day*, 82–83.

54. Meyer, "The Degradation of Work Revisited," 6.

55. Simon Head, *The New Ruthless Economy: Work and Power in the Digital Age* (New York: Oxford University Press, 2003), 35; Edgell, *The Sociology of Work*, 94–95.

56. Nona Y. Glazer, *Women's Paid and Unpaid Labor: The Work Transfer in Health Care and Retailing* (Philadelphia, PA: Temple University Press, 1993).

57. Paul Du Gay, *Consumption and Identity at Work* (London: Sage, 1996).

58. Edgell, *The Sociology of Work*, 122–24.

59. Braverman, *Labor and Monopoly Capital*, 371.

60. Ibid., 371–72.

61. As Zuboff explains the central goal: "Scientific management sought to reorient the office ... so that clerical jobs would no longer be able to absorb even vestigial elements of the executive process, with its requirements for action-centered skills in the service of interpersonal coordination. The application of scientific management to the office sought to redefine clerical work and to set clear boundaries on the downward diffusion of coordinative responsibility. The new concept of clerical work tried to eliminate the remaining elements of action-centered skill related to *acting-with* (that is interpersonal coordination and communication) in favor of tasks that were wholly devoted to *acting-on* (that is, direct action on materials and equipment)." Shoshana Zuboff, *In the Age of the Smart Machine: The Future of Work and Power* (New York: Basic Books, 1988), 119.

62. William H. Leffingwell, *Office Management, Principles and Practice* (Chicago: A. W. Shaw Company, 1925); Zuboff, *In the Age of the Smart Machine*, 117–18.

63. William H. Leffingwell, *Scientific Office Management* (Chicago: A.W. Shaw Company, 1917), 219–20.

64. William H. Leffingwell, *Textbook of Office Management*, 2nd ed. (New York: McGraw-Hill, 1932), 72.

65. Leffingwell, *Scientific Office Management*, 46, 48.

66. Ibid., 48.

67. Head, *The New Ruthless Economy*, 65–66.

68. Leffingwell, *Textbook of Office Management*, 367.

69. Daniel Bell, *The End of Ideology: On the Exhaustion of Political Ideas in the Fifties* (Cambridge, MA: Harvard University Press, 1962), 237.

70. International Labour Organization (ILO), "Effects of Mechanization and Automation in Offices: III," *International Labour Review* 81, no. 4 (1960), 351–52.

71. Zuboff, *In the Age of the Smart Machine*, 123.

Chapter 3

1. Bruno Ramirez, *When Workers Fight: The Politics of Industrial Relations in the Progressive Era, 1896–1916* (Westport, CT: Greenwood Press, 1978); Elaine Glovka-Spencer, *Management and Labor in Imperial Germany: Ruhr Industrialists as Employers, 1896–1914* (New Brunswick, NJ: Rutgers University Press, 1984); Eugene C. McCreary, "Social Welfare and Business: The Krupp Welfare Program, 1860–1914," *Business History Review* 42, no. 1 (1968): 24–49; Patrick Joyce, *Work, Society, and Politics: The Culture of the Factory in Late Victorian England* (New Brunswick, NJ: Rutgers University Press, 1980).

2. Sanford M. Jacoby, *Modern Manors: Welfare Capitalism Since the New Deal* (Princeton, NJ: Princeton University Press, 1997).

3. Ibid., 11; Jacoby, *Laboring for Freedom*, 92.

4. William E. Forbath, *Law and the Shaping of the American Labor Movement* (Cambridge, MA: Harvard University Press, 1991), 16.

5. Jacoby, *Modern Manors*, 11, 15; Sumner H. Schlichter, *The Turnover of Factory Labor*

(New York: D. Appleton, 1919); Alexander Keyssar, *Out of Work: The First Century of Unemployment in Massachusetts* (Cambridge: Cambridge University Press, 1986); David Brody, *Steelworkers in America: The Nonunion Era* (New York: Harper and Row, 1969); Walter Licht, *Working for the Railroad: The Organization of Work in the Nineteenth Century* (Princeton, NJ: Princeton University Press, 1983), 207–16.

6. Jacoby, *Employing Bureaucracy*, 2.

7. Ibid., 36–37; Christopher Lasch, *Haven in a Heartless World: The Family Besieged* (New York: W.W. Norton, 1977); Barbara Ehrenreich and John Ehrenreich, "The Professional-Managerial Class," in *Between Labor and Capital*, ed. Pat Walker (Boston: South End Press, 1979), 5–45.

8. James Leiby, *A History of Social Welfare and Social Work in the United States* (New York: Columbia University Press, 1978), 130.

9. Jacoby, *Employing Bureaucracy*, 37–40.

10. Ibid., 40; Margaret Crawford, *Building the Workingmen's Paradise: The Design of American Company Towns* (London: Verso, 1995); Kim McQuaid, *A Response to Industrialism: Liberal Businessmen and the Evolving Spectrum of Capitalist Reform, 1886–1960* (New York: Garland, 1986), 24–44; Stuart D. Brandes, *American Welfare Capitalism, 1880–1940* (Chicago: University of Chicago Press, 1976); Stanley Buder, *Pullman: An Experiment in Industrial Order and Community Planning, 1880–1930* (New York: Oxford University Press, 1967).

11. Jacoby, *Modern Manors*, 15.

12. Joanne B. Ciulla, *The Working Life: The Promise and Betrayal of Modern Work* (New York: Times Books, 2000), 97–98.

13. Jacoby, *Laboring for Freedom*, 93.

14. Jacoby, *Modern Manors*, 15, 21–23.

15. The AMA was the leading exponent of the SCC's conservative, decentralized model of personnel management which gave the foreman considerably more discretion and authority than he had under the wartime model of personnel management. The decentralization also slowed the pace of employment reform, making it more difficult to control foremen, set up internal promotion plans, and provide for employment security. But the personnel strategy promoted by the AMA and the SCC had some features that were intended to curb the worst features of the drive system. One such feature was foremen's training, designed to make foremen more effective and enlightened managers. Jacoby, *Employing Bureaucracy*, 138–39.

16. Jacoby, *Modern Manors*, 15.

17. Lizabeth Cohen, *Making a New Deal: Industrial workers in Chicago, 1919–1939* (New York: Cambridge University Press, 1990).

18. Ibid., 162–170.

19. Ibid., 171–173.

20. Ibid., 176–179.

21. Next to shared experiences in partaking in consumer culture, a series of immigration restrictions and quotas which culminated in the Johnson-Reed Immigration Act of 1924, was also a unifying factor in the culture. The Act contributed to greater ethnic and cultural homogeneity by restricting immigration to 2 percent of the total national population as of the 1890 census, which greatly favored Northwestern European peoples whose countrymen arrived before the "new immigration" from Southern and Eastern Europe. Cowie, *The Great Exception*, 79–80, 244n29.

22. Cohen, *Making a New Deal*, 206.

23. Ibid., 314.

24. Ibid., 315.

25. David Brody, "The Rise and Decline of Welfare Capitalism," in *Workers in Industrial America: Essays on the Twentieth-Century Struggle* (New York: Oxford University Press, 1980), 48–81.

26. Robert S. Lynd and Helen M. Lynd, *Middletown in Transition: A Study in Cultural Conflicts* (New York: Harcourt Brace Jovanovich, 1937), 41.

27. Cohen, *Making a New Deal*, 209, 246, 249.

28. The latter included Armour Company and U.S. Steel South Works (also laggards in the 1920s) and International Harvester, which began the 1920s as a vanguard but gradually lowered its standards, handing control of the shop floor to foremen again at Harvester's huge McCormick plant by the late 1920s. Jacoby, *Modern Manors*, 32.

29. Cohen, *Making a New Deal*, 206, 333; Jacoby, *Modern Manors*, 51–53.

30. Jacoby, *Modern Manors*, 33.

31. Ibid., 4–6, 13–14, 21–26, 31–32, 41.

32. Lynd and Lynd, *Middletown in Transition*, 74–101.

33. Jacoby, *Modern Manors*, 6.

34. Ibid., 41–42.

35. Ciulla, *The Working Life*, 99.

36. Qtd. in *ibid*.: 173, 438n46.

37. Ibid., 173–74.

38. Fritz J. Roethlisberger and William J. Dickson, *Management and the Worker* (Cambridge, MA: Harvard University Press, 1939).

39. Jacoby, *Modern Manors*, 40, 156.

40. Rose, *Industrial Behaviour*, 104–105.
41. Elton Mayo, *The Social Problems of an Industrial Civilization* (Boston: Graduate School of Business Administration, Harvard University, 1945); Harold I. Sheppard, "The Social and Historical Philosophy of Elton Mayo," *Antioch Review*, 10, no. 3 (1950), 398–400; William Graebner, *The Engineering of Consent: Democracy and Authority in Twentieth-Century America* (Madison: University of Wisconsin Press, 1987), 74–75.
42. Mary B. Gilson, "Review of F.J. Roethlisberger and William J. Dickson, *Management and the Worker*. Cambridge, Mass.: Harvard University Press, 1939," *American Journal of Sociology* 46, no. 1 (1940): 90–101.
43. *Ibid.*, 90–91.
44. Ciulla, *The Working Life*, 102–103.
45. George K. Bennett, "A New Era in Business and Industrial Psychology," *Personnel Psychology* 1, no. 4 (1948): 473–77; Ralph Canter, Jr., "Psychologists in Industry," *Personnel Psychology* 1, no. 2 (1948): 145–60; Joseph Tiffin, "How Psychologists Serve Industry," *Personnel Journal* 36, no. 7 (1958): 372–76 ; Loren Baritz, *The Servants of Power: A History of the Use of Social Science in American Industry* (Middletown, CT: Wesleyan University Press, 1960).
46. Sanford M. Jacoby, "Employee Attitude Testing at Sears, Roebuck and Company 1938–1960," *Business History Review* 60, no. 4 (1986): 602–32; Henry Eilbirt, "The Development of Personnel Management in the United States," *Business History Review* 33, no. 1 (1957): 345–64.
47. Jacoby, *Modern Manors*, 43–44; Jeanne L. Wilensky and Harold L. Wilensky, "Personnel Counseling: The Hawthorne Case," *American Journal of Sociology* 57, no. 3 (1951): 265–80; Clark Kerr and Lloyd H. Fisher, "Plant Sociology: The Elite and the Aborigines," in *Common Frontiers of the Social Sciences*, ed. Mirra Komarovsky (New York: Free Press, 1957), 281–309; Henry A. Landsberger, *Hawthorne Revisited: Management and the Worker: Its Critics, and Developments in Human Relations In Industry* (Ithaca, NY: Cornell University Press, 1958).
48. C. Wright Mills, "The Contribution of Sociology to Studies of Industrial Relations," in *Proceedings of the First Annual Conference of the Industrial Relations Research Association*, ed. Milton Derber (Urbana, IL: Industrial Relations Research Association, 1948), 199–222.
49. Daniel Bell, *Work and its Discontent* (New York: McGraw-Hill, 1956), 25–28.
50. Mills, "The Contribution of Sociology to Studies of Industrial Relations," 214.
51. *Ibid.*, 211.
52. Stanley Aronowitz, *Taking It Big: C. Wright Mills and the Making of Political Intellectuals* (New York: Columbia University Press, 2012), 94.
53. C. Wright Mills, *The New Men of Power: America's Labor Leaders* (New York: Harcourt, Brace, 1948), 6–7; *White Collar: The American Middle Classes* (New York: Oxford University Press, 1951), 318, 350–54, as qtd. in Lichtenstein, *State of the Union*, 157–58.
54. James C. Worthy, "Changing Concepts of the Personnel Function," AMA Personnel Series, no. 113 (New York, 1949), 7.
55. Jacoby, *Modern Manors*, 44.
56. Rose, *Industrial Behaviour*, 104–105.
57. Graebner, *The Engineering of Consent*, 70.
58. Jacoby, *Modern Manors*, 227.
59. Rose, *Industrial Behaviour*, 17.
60. Alfred J. Marrow, *The Practical Theorist: The Life and Work of Kurt Lewin* (New York: Basic Books, 1969). 146, 210–14. Lewin died unexpectedly in February, 1947. The Research Center for Group Dynamics that he had founded in 1944 at the Massachusetts Institute of Technology, collaborated on some of the Harwood studies. It moved in 1948 to the University of Michigan, where it merged with the Survey Research Center to form the Institute for Social Research. The Harwood studies findings formed the starting-point for a whole series of comparative studies, carried out on a grand scale at this institute. The outcomes of these studies were quite varied and not as clear as those of the Harwood studies. Starting with studies at the micro-level in organizations, more attention was gradually paid to organizational control issues at the meso-level, which made up a significant component of the work processes concerned. Rose, *Industrial Behaviour*, 173–75.
61. Warren G. Bennis, Kenneth D. Benne, and Robert Chin, *The Planning of Change*, 2nd ed. (New York: Holt, Rinehart, and Chin, 1969), Graebner, *The Engineering of Consent*, 75–78; Steve Heims, "Kurt Lewin and Social Change," *Journal of the History of the Behavioral Sciences* 14, no. 3 (1978): 238–41.
62. Rose, *Industrial Behaviour*, 175; Mel van Elteren, "Discontinuities in Kurt Lewin's Psychology of Work: Conceptual and Cultural Shifts Between His German and American Research," *Sociétés Contemporaines* 13, March (1993): 84–89. In this context, "manipulative" is used with its negative connotations, in the sense of a deliberate removal of freedom of

choice with regard to the subjects involved, and the exercise of power unknown to the manipulated.

63. Jacoby, *Modern Manors*, 227.

64. *Ibid.*, 205, 227; Wilensky and Wilensky, "Personnel Counseling: The Hawthorne Case"; Landsberger, *Hawthorne Revisited*.

65. Baritz, *The Servants of Power*, 197. Psychologists used the term "bias of the auspices" to refer to the fact that employees are less likely to speak truthfully to their employer or someone representing them than to an impartial observer. The fact that university-based researchers were often seen as a third party, unbeholden to management, was helpful in overcoming this bias. Jacoby, *Modern Manors*, 222.

66. William Graebner, "The Small Group and Democratic Social Engineering, 1900–1950," *Journal of Social Issues* 42, no. 1 (1986): 137.

67. Peter Miller and Ted O'Leary, "Hierarchies and American Ideals 1900–1940," *The Academy of Management Review* 14, no. 2 (1989): 250–65.

68. Within industrial sociology in the U.S. a similar tendency can be discerned from the 1920s onward. The parent discipline of sociology, at its inception, was to a considerable degree identical with the study of industrial organization and development; its political aim was the democratic self-regulation of industrial society, discussed under the label of "social control." The same applies to early industrial sociology, where this was interpreted as the extension of democratic participation in industrial organizations and in the communities in which they functioned. Steven Cohen describes similar movements of ideas in general sociology and industrial sociology, especially concerning the nature of social control and the debates over this issue between the Chicago School and Harvard sociologists. Steven R. Cohen, "From Industrial Democracy to Professional Adjustment: The Development of Industrial Sociology in the United States, 1900–1955," *Theory and Society*, 12, no. 1 (1983): 47–67.

69. Graebner, "The Small Group and Democratic Social Engineering," 139–41; Graebner, *The Engineering of Consent*, 78–87.

70. van Elteren, "Discontinuities in Kurt Lewin's Psychology of Work," 82–84.

71. Drucker, *Concept of the Corporation*, 157.

72. *Ibid.*, 134. Here Drucker implicitly refers to, and appears to underscore, the national ideology of "Americanism" revolving around the basic notions liberty, social egalitarianism, individualism and laissez-faire as identified by liberal consensus thinkers—at mid-century, Louis Hartz and Gunnar Myrdal in particular. They still followed a Tocquevillean approach to American political culture and basic institutions in their analysis of the country's distinctive features. Rogers M. Smith, "Beyond Tocqueville, Myrdal, and Hartz: The Multiple Traditions in America," *American Political Science Review* 87, no. 3 (1993): 549–66.

73. Ciulla, *The Working Life*, 107.

74. Adolf A. Berle and Gardiner C. Means, *The Modern Corporation and Private Property* (New York: Harcourt, Brace & World, 1968 [1932]); Morton Keller, "The Making of the Modern Corporation," *Wilson Quarterly* 21, no. 4 (1997): 58–69.

75. Ciulla, *The Working Life*, 107–08.

76. Aronowitz, *Taking It Big*, 133.

77. *Ibid.*, 134.

78. Mills, *White Collar*, 205.

79. *Ibid.*, 217–19.

80. Aronowitz, *Taking It Big*, 135–36.

81. Mills, *White Collar*, xi.

82. *Ibid.*, ix.

83. *Ibid.*, xi.

84. Ursula Huws, *The Making of a Cybertariat* (New York: Monthly Review Press, 2003), 156.

85. Qtd. in Braverman, *Labor and Monopoly Capital*, 296.

86. Mills, *White Collar*, 352–53.

87. *Ibid.*, 233.

88. Ciulla, *The Working Life*, 109–10.

89. Whyte's book was often mentioned in the same breath as the fictional best seller of the period, *The Main in the Gray Flannel Suit* (1955) by Sloan Wilson. However, in reality, this novel does not indict conformity in the corporate world as assumed. For Whyte, it was a novel that wanted to "have it both ways," suggesting that men could retain their moral integrity and still make it in the dog-eat-dog marketplace of the 1950s. Rampant materialism and spiritual life thus could be unified in a "self-ennobling hedonism"—a favorite phrase of the era used to describe the conflicted world of these mid-century office workers. William H. Whyte, *The Organization Man* (New York: Simon and Schuster, 1956), 251, 132; Nikil Saval, *Cubed: A Secret History of the Workplace* (New York: Anchor Books, 2014), 165–67.

90. Riesman described the book itself as "a study of the relation between political apathy and character structure" in a letter to cultural anthropologist Margaret Mead in July 1948. He and his assistants conducted in-depth inter-

views of college students, seeking to understand what they saw as the disengagement of the young generation from politics. This preoccupation was only touched upon briefly in *The Lonely Crowd* but figured prominently in the companion volume, *Faces in the Crowd.* Howard Brick, *Transcending Capitalism: Visions of a New Society in Modern American Thought* (Ithaca, NY: Cornell University Press, 2006), 175; David Riesman, with Nathan Glazer, *Faces in the Crowd: Individual Studies in Character and Politics* (New Haven, CT: Yale University Press, 1951).

91. David Riesman, *The Lonely Crowd: A Study of the Changing American Character* (New Haven, CT: Yale University Press, 1952), 34–35.

92. Ibid., 14–21.

93. Ibid., 285–306, 368–73; Brick, *Transcending Capitalism*, 179.

94. Riesman, *The Lonely Crowd*, 132; Daniel Geary, "C. Wright Mills and American Social Science," in *American Thought and Political Economy in the Twentieth Century*, ed. Nelson Lichtenstein (Philadelphia: University of Pennsylvania Press, 2006), 154.

95. Whyte, *The Organization Man*, 6–7.

96. Ibid., 80.

97. Ibid., 32.

98. Ibid., 51.

99. Ibid., 54.

100. Ciulla, *The Working Life*, 112.

Chapter 4

1. Head, *The New Ruthless Economy*, 35–36; Louis R. Eltscher and Edward M. Young, *Curtiss-Wright: Greatness and Decline* (New York: Prentice-Hall International, 1998), 103.

2. David F. Noble, *Forces of Production: A Social History of Industrial Automation* (New York: Alfred A. Knopf, 1984), 36–37.

3. Peter F. Drucker, *Post-Capitalist Society* (New York: HarperBusiness, 1993), 36.

4. Roger E. Bilstein, *The American Aerospace Industry: From Workshop to Global Enterprise* (New York: Twayne Publishers, 1996), 73–74, 77.

5. Noble, *Forces of Production*, 52–56, 240–41.

6. A servomechanism, sometimes shortened to servo, is an automatic device that uses error-sensing negative feedback to correct the performance of a mechanism and is defined by its function.

7. Noble, *Forces of Production*, 58–59.

8. Ibid., 66–67.

9. Nicholas Carr, *The Glass Cage: Where Automation Is Taking Us* (London: The Bodley Head, 2015), 34; James R. Bright, *Automation and Management* (Boston: Harvard University School Press, 1958), 4–5.

10. Carr, *The Glass Cage*, 37; Noble, *Forces of Production*, 67–71.

11. Noble, *Forces of Production*, 21–40.

12. As David Noble has shown in detail, the machines with numerically-controlled programming in its early stage (during the 1950s) were not as reliable as expected and programming was difficult and error-prone. As a result the quality of the product was erratic—and dependent primarily upon the cooperation and skills of the workforce—and machine downtime was excessive and costly. The workforce, moreover resented and actively resisted the way in which management was determined to introduce the new equipment, and viewed it as a direct threat to their skills, pay, jobs, and (in the case of unionized workers) hard-won rights. Ibid., 213, 230–78.

13. The Robot Hall of Fame, "Unimate" (2003), http://www.robothalloffame.org/inductees/03inductees/unimate.html.

14. Until 1988, control of large aircraft, whether manual or automatic, was carried out through hydraulic actuators. They moved when actuated by the autoflight systems or the pilots and thus provided visual and tactile feedback of flight control inputs. Throttles were electrically driven; they likewise moved when actuated by the pilots or the autothrust system. The 1988 Airbus A320 represented a departure from previous designs through its "fly-by-wire" system that was much more automated and gave less visual and tactile feedback to the pilots. These systems were later also introduced in the A330/340 and the Boeing 777, followed by more recent models, becoming standard in the aircraft industry. Charles E. Billings, *Human-Centered Automation: Principles and Guidelines* (Moffett Field, CA: NASA Ames Research Center, 1996), 15, 18, 22–24.

15. Thus universities shared with companies like IBM in their production of knowledge that led to the development of the personal computer in the 1980s.

16. Aronowitz, *The Death and Life of American Labor*, 125–26.

17. Bright, *Automation and Management*, 199–200.

18. Ibid., 205.

19. Braverman, *Labor and Monopoly Capital*, 231.

20. Robert Blauner, *Alienation and Freedom: The Factory Worker and His Industry* (Chicago: University of Chicago Press, 1964), 124.
21. Ibid., 147; Zuboff, *In the Age of the Smart Machine*, 51–52.
22. Blauner, *Alienation and Freedom*, 134.
23. Braverman, *Labor and Monopoly Capital*, 220.
24. Blauner, *Alienation and Freedom*, 182.
25. Ibid.
26. Braverman, *Labor and Monopoly Capital*, 225.
27. Zuboff, *In the Age of the Smart Machine*, 50.
28. For an excellent overview, see Edgell, *The Sociology of Work*, 62–72.
29. Joan M. Greenbaum, *Windows On the Workplace: Technology, Jobs, and the Organization of Office Work* (New York: Monthly Review Press, 2004), 69–71.
30. Kim Moody, *U.S. Labor in Trouble and Transition* (London: Verso, 2007), 28–29.
31. The computerized axial tomography (CAT) scan, is an X-ray procedure that combines many X-ray images with the aid of a computer to generate cross-sectional views and, if needed, three-dimensional images of the internal organs and structures of the body.
32. Aronowitz and DiFazio, *The Jobless Future*, 194–96.

Chapter 5

1. Philip Selznick, *Law, Society, and Industrial Justice* (New York: Russell Sage Foundation, 1969), 188–89; Richard B. Freeman and James L. Medoff, *What Do Unions Do?* (New York: Basic Books, 1984), 80, 128.
2. Jacoby, *Modern Manors*, 247.
3. Douglas McGregor, *The Human Side of Enterprise* (New York: McGraw-Hill, 1960); Ciulla, *The Working Life*, 115. On the other hand, the ethical question remained about how far an employer could involve his employees for the good of the company through sensitivity training that tended to invade their personal lives, ignoring privacy issues. Kurt W. Back, *Beyond Words: The Story of Sensitivity Training and the Encounter Movement* (Baltimore, MD: Penguin Books, 1973), 162, 168.
4. Jacoby, *Modern Manors*, 8–9, 238, 258.
5. Ibid., 9.
6. Gerry Hunnies, David Garson, and John Case, eds., *Workers' Control: A Reader on Labor and Social Change* (New York: Random House, 1973). Together with a group of leftist Social Democrats, these New Leftists hoped for a radical revitalization of the labor movement by workers rebelling against their alienating work situation. Peter B. Levy, *The New Left and Labor in the 1960s* (Urbana: University of Illinois Press, 1994), 122–27; Richard Sennett, *The Culture of the New Capitalism* (New Haven, CT: Yale University Press, 2006), 1. For a brief overview of New Left labor activism and the separate radical left-wing movement of black workers in the auto industry aimed at "workers' control" during the late 1960s and early 1970s, see van Elteren, *Labor and the American Left*, 118–20.
7. David Harvey, *A Brief History of Neoliberalism* (Oxford: Oxford University Press, 2005), 44.
8. Jefferson Cowie, *Stayin' Alive: The 1970s and the Last Days of the Working Class* (New York: New Press, 2010), 231–34.
9. Jacoby, *Modern Manors*, 258; Eileen Appelbaum and Rosemary Batt, *The New American Workplace: Transforming Work Systems in the United States* (Ithaca, NY: Cornell University Press, 1994).
10. Alan Fox, *Industrial Sociology and Industrial Relations* (London: HMSO, 1966), 3.
11. Jacoby, *Modern Manors*, 258–59.
12. Rose, *Industrial Behaviour*, 335.
13. Jacoby, *Modern Manors*, 259.
14. Andrew Ross, *No-Collar: The Humane Workplace and Its Hidden Costs* (New York: Basic Books, 2003), 5.
15. All previous quotes taken from United States Department of Health Education and Welfare, *Work in America: Report of a Special Task Force to the Secretary of Health, Education, and Welfare* (Cambridge, MA: MIT Press, 1973), as qtd. in Ross, *No-Collar*, 6.
16. James O'Toole, ed. *Work and the Quality of Life* (Cambridge, MA: MIT Press, 1974); Louis Davis and Albert Cherns, eds., *The Quality of Working Life* (New York: Free Press, 1975).
17. Ciulla, *The Working Life*, 119–22.
18. Lyman D. Ketchum and Eric Trist, *All Teams Are Not Treated Equal: How Employee Empowerment Really Works* (Thousand Oaks, CA: Sage, 1992), 20.
19. Ibid., 20–21.
20. One experiment backed by the UAW (specifically Irving Bluestone, a top official) which drew much attention from managers, academics, and union officials, occurred at Harman Automotive, a rearview mirror manufacturer in Bolivar, Tennessee. The Bolivar Project, which started in 1972, gave employees increased job security and an active role in deci-

sions concerning working conditions and training. The employees redesigned their jobs and made the production process run smoother. Labor relations improved so much that the company completed the 1975 contract with the UAW four months before the old one expired. But eventually the project failed for a variety of reasons, including the fact that even with an engaged workforce and company educational programs, work sometimes cannot compete with the lure of really free time, especially when people have job security. Harman Automotive also changed hands and the new owners were not interested in the worker-empowerment experiment. Ciulla, *The Working Life*, 119–21.

21. Jacoby, *Employing Bureaucracy*, 213.

22. Hans Van Beinum, "Playing Hide and Seek with QWL," *QWL Focus*, Ontario Ministry of Labour, 5, no. 1 (1986): 9.

23. D. Estok, "Old Wounds Still Fester," *The Financial Post*, Winter 1989, 42.

24. Rama Krishnan, "Democratic Participation in Decision Making by Employees in American Corporations," *Academy of Management Journal* 17, no. 2 (1974): 345.

25. Julia M. Christensen Hughes, "Organisational Empowerment: A Historical Perspective and Conceptual Framework," in *Ethics and Empowerment*, ed. John J. Quinn and Peter W.F. Davies (West Lafayette, IN: Ichor Business Books, 1999), 123.

26. Alfred D. Chandler, "The Emergence of Managerial Capitalism," *Business History Review* 58, no. 4 (1984): 473–504.

27. Jacoby, *Employing Bureaucracy*, 5–6.

28. Davis, "The Twilight of the Berle and Means Corporation," 1214–15.

29. Michael Useem, "Business Restructuring, Management Control, and Corporate Organization," *Theory and Society* 19, no. 6 (1990): 681–707.

30. Braverman, *Labor and Monopoly Capital*, 406–07; Chris Smith and Paul Thompson, "Reevaluating the Labor Process Debate," in *Rethinking the Labor Process*, ed. Mark Wardell, Thomas L. Steiger, and Peter Meiksins (Albany: State University of New York Press, 1999), 219–20.

31. Davis, "The Twilight of the Berle and Means Corporation," 1216.

32. Hedrick Smith, *Who Stole the American Dream?* (New York: Random House, 2012), 110–11.

33. Jacob S. Hacker, *The Great Risk Shift: The Assault on American Jobs, Families, Health Care, and Retirement and How You Can Fight Back* (New York: Oxford University Press, 2006).

34. Cass R. Sunstein, *Legal Reasoning and Political Conflict* (New York: Oxford University Press, 1996).

35. The M-form structure had been pioneered by DuPont, General Motors, and Jersey Standard in the 1920s, but was still rarely put in place in the 1930s and 1940s. It allowed corporate divisions to maintain their operating autonomy provided that they kept meeting targets set by company headquarters.

36. Jacoby, *Modern Manors*, 48, 260–62.

Chapter 6

1. Internationally, four different production systems emerged in response to Fordism during the last quarter of the 20th century: Swedish sociotechnical systems, Italian flexible specialization, German diversified quality production and Japanese lean production. The Swedish and German production models both operated at the higher end of the automobile market and were dependent on supporting social institutions such as government training policies, while Italian flexible specialization was best suited to small-scale production. These features inhibited their transferability and applicability to all segments of the global auto market, and more specifically the American one. Therefore only Japanese lean production in its relation to the American scene will be discussed here. Edgell, *The Sociology of Work*, 102; Appelbaum and Batt, *The New American Workplace*.

2. Michael J. Piore and Charles F. Sabel, *The Second Industrial Divide: Possibilities for Prosperity* (New York: Basic Books, 1984), 165–93, 205–08, 315.

3. James P. Womack, Daniel T. Jones, and Daniel Roos, *The Machine That Changed the World* (New York: Rawson Associates, 1990), 237.

4. Head, *The New Ruthless Economy*, 37–38.

5. E.g., Richard Schonberger, *Japanese Manufacturing Techniques: Nine Hidden Lessons in Simplicity* (New York: Free Press, 1982); Peter Wickens, *The Road to Nissan: Flexibility, Quality, Teamwork* (London: Macmillan, 1987).

6. E.g., Michael Cusumano, *The Japanese Automobile Industry: Technology and Management at Nissan and Toyota* (Cambridge, MA: Harvard University Press, 1985).

7. Taiichi Ohno, *Toyota Production System: Beyond Large-Scale Production* (Cambridge, MA: Productivity Press, 1988).

8. Womack, Jones, and Roos, *The Machine That Changed the World*, 13.

9. Ibid., 102.
10. Fred L. Block, *Postindustrial Possibilities: A Critique of Economic Discourse* (Berkeley: University of California Press, 1990), 103; Zuboff, *In the Age of the Smart Machine*, 57.
11. Block, *Postindustrial Possibilities*, 96.
12. Frank Webster, *Theories of the Information Society*, 4th ed. (London: Routledge, 2014), 98.
13. Larry Hirschhorn, *Beyond Mechanization: Work and Technology in a Postindustrial Age* (Cambridge, MA: MIT Press, 1984), 72-73.
14. Ibid., 40.
15. Webster, *Theories of the Information Society*, 99.
16. Zuboff, *In the Age of the Smart Machine*, 10.
17. Hirschhorn, *Beyond Mechanization*, 15.
18. Webster, *Theories of the Information Society*, 102-03; Gordon, Edwards, and Reich, *Segmented Work, Divided Workers*.
19. David Harvey, "Flexibility: Threat or Opportunity?," *Socialist Review* 21, no. 1 (1991): 73 (emphasis in original).
20. David E. Nye, *America's Assembly Line* (Cambridge, MA: MIT Press, 2013), 192.
21. Ibid., 193.
22. Christian Berggren, *Alternatives to Lean Production: Work Organization in the Swedish Auto Industry* (Ithaca, NY: ILR Press, 1993), 23-25.
23. Nye, *America's Assembly Line*, 193-94.
24. For the Dutch case, see Mel van Elteren, "Psychology and Sociology of Work within the Anglo-American Orbit" in *Dutch-American Relations 1945-1969: A Partnership. Illusions and Facts*, ed. Hans Loeber (Assen/Maastricht: van Gorcum, 1992), 153-78.
25. Nye, *America's Assembly Line*, 194-95.
26. Alfred Hornung, "Contribution to Debate on 'Transculturations: American Studies in a Globalizing World—the Globalizing World in American Studies'," *Amerikastudien/American Studies* 47, no. 1 (2002): 114.
27. Nye, *America's Assembly Line*, 195; William M. Tsutsui, "W. Edwards Deming and the Origins of Quality Control in Japan," *Journal of Japanese Studies* 22, no. 2 (1996): 318. The term "Total Quality Control" was coined by a General Electric consultant, Armand Feigenbaum, another outside expert to the Japanese business community.
28. Nye, *America's Assembly Line*, 196; Takahiro Fujimoto, *The Evolution of a Manufacturing System at Toyota* (New York: Oxford University Press, 1999), 61.
29. Nye, *America's Assembly Line*, 196-97; Fujimoto, *The Evolution of a Manufacturing System at Toyota*, 50, 59.
30. Berggren, *Alternatives to Lean Production*, 32; Eishi Fujita, *Labor Process and Labor Management: The Case of Toyota* (The Society of Social Sciences of Aichi Kyoiku University, 1988), 20.
31. Fujimoto, *The Evolution of a Manufacturing System at Toyota*, 71, 42, 44.
32. *The Birth of Lean: Conversations with Taiichi Ohno, Eiji Toyoda, and Other Figures Who Shaped Toyota Management*, ed. Koichi Shimokawa and Takahiro Fujimoto (Cambridge, MA: Lean Enterprise Institute, 2009), 9, xiv.
33. Ohno, *Toyota Production System*, xii.
34. Nye, *America's Assembly Line*, 199.
35. Cusumano, *The Japanese Automobile Industry*, 264-65.
36. Ohno, *Toyota Production System*, 26.
37. Cusumano, *The Japanese Automobile Industry*, 265.
38. Shigeo Shingo, *A Revolution in Manufacturing: The SMED System* (Stamford, CT: Productivity Press, 1985), 66, 14.
39. Womack, Jones, and Roos, *The Machine That Changed the World*, 53.
40. Shingo, *A Revolution in Manufacturing*, 116.
41. Schonberger, *Japanese Manufacturing Techniques*, 141.
42. Edgell, *The Sociology of Work*, 105.
43. Cusumano, *The Japanese Automobile Industry*, 320.
44. Ibid., 334.
45. Womack, Jones, and Roos, *The Machine That Changed the World*, 84, 102.
46. Berggren, *Alternatives to Lean Production*, 17.
47. Edgell, *The Sociology of Work*, 93.
48. Cusumano, *The Japanese Automobile Industry*, 272.
49. James W. Rinehart, Christopher V. Huxley, and David Robertson, *Just Another Car Factory?: Lean Production and Its Discontents* (Ithaca, NY: ILR Press, 1997).
50. Philip Garrahan and Paul Stewart, *The Nissan Empire: Flexibility at Work in a Local Economy* (London: Routledge, 1992).
51. McKinsey Global Institute, *Manufacturing Productivity* (Washington, D.C., 1993), Case Studies "Automobile Assembly," 1, 8, "Automobile Parts," 1.
52. The Magaziner Commission on the skills of the American workforce was headed by Bill Clinton's future healthcare czar, Ira Magaziner.
53. Head, *The New Ruthless Economy*, 55.

54. Ibid., 56.
55. McKinsey Global Institute, *Manufacturing Productivity*, "Synthesis," 8.
56. National Center on Education and the Economy, "America's Choice: High Skills or Low Wages!," In *Report of the Commission on the Skills of the American Workforce* (Rochester, NY, 1990), 24, http://www.eric.ed.gov/?id=ED323297.
57. McKinsey Global Institute, *Manufacturing Productivity*, "Synthesis," 8.
58. Head, *The New Ruthless Economy*, 57–58.
59. Mike Parker and Jane Slaughter, "Unions and Management by Stress," in *Lean Work: Empowerment and Exploitation in the Global Auto Industry*, ed. Steve Babson (Detroit: Wayne State University Press, 1995), 41–54.
60. Rinehart, Huxley, and Robertson, *Just Another Car Factory?*
61. A company in this vein also increased the communication between managers, salesmen, designers, engineers, and suppliers. Japanese manufacturers discovered the economic advantages of putting production engineers on teams designing new models with the goals of reducing the number of parts and of making them easier to assemble. Their example was followed by Ford in the late 1980s, when this company could reduce the number of parts in the front bumper of a Taurus model from more than 65 to 10, whereas the bumper of GM's Pontiac Grand still had 100 parts, due to its poor design. Nye, *America's Assembly Line*, 200.
62. Martin Kenney and Richard L. Florida, *Beyond Mass Production: The Japanese System and Its Transfer to the U.S.* (New York: Oxford University Press, 1993).
63. Laurie Graham, *On the Line at Subaru-Isuzu: The Japanese Model and the American Worker* (Ithaca, NY: ILR Press, 1995), 79.
64. Paul Adler, "Democratic Taylorism: The Toyota Production System at NUMMI," in *Lean Work: Empowerment and Exploitation in the Global Auto Industry*, 207–19.
65. Garrahan and Stewart, *The Nissan Empire*.
66. Parker and Slaughter, "Unions and Management By Stress."
67. John MacDuffie, "Workers' Role in Lean Production: The Implications for Workers Representation," in *Lean Work: Empowerment and Exploitation in the Global Auto Industry*, 57; see also Kenney and Florida, *Beyond Mass Production*, 279–80.
68. Rinehart, Huxley, and Robertson, *Just Another Car Factory?*, 223.
69. Graham, *On the Line at Subaru-Isuzu*.

70. Berggren, *Alternatives to Lean Production*, 39–40.
71. James Jacobs, "Lean production and Training: The Case of a Japanese Supplier Firm," in *Lean Work: Empowerment and Exploitation in the Global Auto Industry*, 311–25.
72. Rinehart, Huxley, and Robertson, *Just Another Car Factory?*
73. Their work organization was in contrast (at the time) to Volvo's main, more traditional, Gothenburg line plant.
74. Berggren, *Alternatives to Lean Production*, 7–8, 16, 19.
75. Mike Parker, "Industrial Relations Myth and Shop-floor Reality: The 'Team Concept' in the Auto Industry," in *Industrial Democracy in America: The Ambiguous Promise*, ed. Nelson Lichtenstein and Howell John Harris (New York: Cambridge University Press, 1993), 249–73; Parker and Slaughter, "Unions and Management By Stress." Parker and Slaughter's observations—and much of the controversy over worker participation at the time—focused on the New United Motoring Manufacturing, Inc. (NUMMI) plant in Fremont, California, a joint venture of Toyota and GM that made small cars and opened in 1984. NUMMI emphasized Japanese-style teamwork, guaranteed workers officially that there would be no layoffs in exchange for other concessions, and applied principles of lean production to all aspects of the manufacturing system. This led to a drastic reduction of the time needed to produce a car. Nye, *America's Assembly Line*, 201–02. Most of the workers had been employed by GM in the same plant before it was closed two years earlier. Unlike Toyota's Kentucky plant and the other fully Japanese-owned transplants, the workers at NUMMI were UAW members, which was due to its past relationship with GM, not Toyota. Ruth Milkman and Cydney Pullman, "Technological Change in an Auto Assembly Plant: The Impact on Workers' Tasks and Skills," *Work and Occupations* 18, no. 2 (1991): 144.
76. Christian Berggren, "'New Production Concepts' in Final Assembly—The Swedish Experience," in *The Transformation of Work?*, ed. Stephen Wood (London: Unwin Hyman, 1989), 171–203.
77. Ohno, *Toyota Production System*, 40.
78. Kenney and Florida, *Beyond Mass Production*, 121.
79. Shigeo Shingo, *Study of Toyota Production System: From Industrial Engineering Viewpoint* (Tokyo: Japan Management Association, 1981), 111 ff.

80. Dan Coffey, *The Myth of Japanese Efficiency: The World Car Industry in a Globalizing Age* (Cheltenham: Edgar Elgar, 2006).
81. Womack, Jones, and Roos, *The Machine That Changed the World*, 126.
82. Edgell, *The Sociology of Work*, 111–12.
83. "GM, Ford and Chrysler Strive to Become The Lean Three," *IndustryWeek*, November 15, 2009, http://www.industryweek.com/public-policy/gm-ford-and-chrysler-strive-become-lean-three?page=2.
84. Edgell, *The Sociology of Work*, 112.
85. *Ibid.*, 107, 116; Rinehart, Huxley, and Robertson, *Just Another Car Factory?*
86. Meyer, "The Degradation of Work Revisited."
87. Moody, *U.S. Labor in Trouble and Transition*, 33–34.
88. James P. Womack and Daniel T. Jones, *Lean Thinking: Banish Waste and Create Wealth in Your Corporation* (New York: Free Press, 2003).
89. Julia Hanna, "Bringing 'Lean' Principles to Service Industries, *HBS Working Knowledge*, October 22, 2007, http://hbswk.hbs.edu/item/5741/html.

Chapter 7

1. Moody, *U.S. Labor in Trouble and Transition*, 31–32.
2. Bennett Harrison, *Lean and Mean: The Changing Landscape of Corporate Power in the Age of Flexibility* (New York: Basic Books, 1994), 144–45.
3. Moody, *U.S. Labor in Trouble and Transition*, 32–33.
4. Jessica Bruder, "We're Watching You Work. Labor Is Fighting Employer's Techno-Utopian Dream of a Perfectly Efficient—and Totally Surveilled—Workforce," *The Nation* (June 15, 2015): 28–29.
5. *Ibid.*, 30.
6. Nelson Lichtenstein, "Wal-Mart and the New World Order: A Template for Twenty-First Century Capitalism?," *New Labor Forum* 14, no. 1 (2005): 25–30.
7. Nelson Lichtenstein, *The Retail Revolution: How Wal-Mart Created a Brave New World of Business* (New York: Metropolitan Books, 2009); Nelson Lichtenstein, "Wal-Mart's Authoritarian Culture," *New York Times*, June 21, 2011, http://www.nytimes.com/2011/06/22/opinion/22Lichtenstein.html.
8. These penalties include written reprimands in the form of Walmart's own "pink slips"; spoken reprimands in the form of "coachings"; then "decision-making days," when an employee must explain why s/he should not be fired; and eventually, dismissal itself. Simon Head, *Mindless: Why Smarter Machines are Making Dumber Humans* (New York: Basic Books, 2014), 31–33.
9. *Ibid.*, 36–37, 40–41.
10. Lichtenstein, *The Retail Revolution*, 216–22.
11. Moody, *U.S. Labor in Trouble and Transition*, 55–56.
12. Braverman, *Labor and Monopoly Capital*, 372.
13. Carl Gardner and Julie Sheppard, *Consuming Passion: The Rise of Retail Culture* (London: Unwin Hyman, 1989); Glazer, *Women's Paid and Unpaid Labor*.
14. Robin Leidner, *Fast Food, Fast Talk: Service Work and the Routinization of Everyday Life* (Berkeley: University of California Press, 1993).
15. Theodore Levitt, "The Production-Line Approach to Service," *Harvard Business Review* 50, no. 5 (1972): 41–52.
16. John F. Love, *McDonald's Behind the Arches*, revised ed. (New York: Bantam, 1995).
17. *Ibid.*, 14–15, 141.
18. George Ritzer, *The McDonaldization of Society: An Investigation into the Changing Character of Contemporary Social Life*, revised ed. (Thousand Oaks, CA: Pine Forge Press, 1996), 152.
19. Leidner, *Fast Food, Fast Talk*.
20. George Ritzer, *The McDonaldization Thesis: Explorations and Extensions* (Thousand Oaks, CA: Sage, 1998), 64.
21. Mills, *White Collar*.
22. Arlie Russell Hochschild, *The Managed Heart: Commercialization of Human Feeling* (Berkeley: University of California Press, 1983), 7.
23. Marek Korczynski, "The Mystery Customer: Continuing Absences in the Sociology of Service Work," *Sociology* 43, no. 5 (2009): 952–67.
24. Jackie Krasas Rogers, "Just a Temp: Experience and Structure of Alienation in Temporary Clerical Work," *Work and Occupations* 22, no. 2 (1995): 137–66.
25. J.C. Sarros, George A. Tanweski, Richard P. Winter, J.C. Santora, and I.L. Densten, "Work Alienation and Organizational Leadership," *British Journal of Management* 13, no. 4 (2002): 295–304.
26. Robin B. DiPietro and Abraham Pizam, "Employee Alienation in the Quick Service

Restaurant Industry," *Journal of Hospitality and Tourism Research* 32, no. 1 (2008): 22–39.

27. Edgell, *The Sociology of Work*, 51.

28. Chris Warhurst, Dennis Nickson, Anne Witz, and Anne Marie Cullen, "Aesthetic Labour in Interactive Service Work: Some Case Study Evidence from the 'New' Glasgow," *The Service Industries Journal* 20, no. 3 (2000), 4.

29. Leidner, *Fast Food, Fast Talk*, 128.

30. *Ibid.*, 133.

31. Linda Fuller and Vicki Smith, "Consumers' Reports: Management by Customers in a Changing Economy," *Work, Employment, and Society* 5, no. 1 (1991): 1–16.

32. Ritzer, *The McDonaldization Thesis*, 59.

33. Love, *McDonald's Behind the Arches*, 426.

34. Robin Leidner, "Rethinking Questions of Control: Lessons from McDonald's," in *Working in the Service Sector*, ed. Cameron Lynn MacDonald and Carmen Sirianni (Philadelphia, PA: Temple University Press, 1996), 33.

35. Tony Royle, *Working for McDonald's in Europe: The Unequal Struggle?* (London: Routledge, 2000), 122–23.

36. Eric Schlosser, *Fast Food Nation: The Dark Side of the All-American Meal* (New York: Perennial, 2002), 67.

37. Stephen Taylor, Sheena Smith, and Phil Lyon, "McDonaldization and Consumer Choice in the Future: An Illusion or the Next Marketing Revolution?," in *McDonaldization Revisited: Critical Essays on Consumer Culture*, ed. Mark Alfino, John S. Caputo, and Robin Wynyard (Westport, CT: Praeger, 1998), 109.

38. Edgell, *The Sociology of Work*, 133–34.

39. Four cities—Syracuse, Milwaukee, and Portland and SeaTac in Washington State—already enacted $15 in 2015. Four cities—Buffalo, Mountain View and Missoula, MT, and Seattle, WA—took steps toward $15 around New Year's day 2016. Aimee Picchi, "Will the U.S. Raise the Minimum Wage to $15?," *CBS News, Money Watch*, November 21, 2015, http://www.cbsnews.com/news/will-the-u-s-raise-the-minimum-wage-to-15/; National Employment Project, "14 Cities & States Approved $15 Minimum Wage in 2015," December 21, 2015, http://www.nelp.org/content/uploads/PR-Minimum-Wage-Year-End-15.pdf. The minimum wage was also a major issue during the 2016 presidential campaigns among the two candidates for the Democratic party's nomination. While Bernie Sanders was strongly supportive of a $15 federal minimum wage (and as U.S. Senator had introduced a bill in Congress to that effect), his rival Hillary Clinton seemed to favor gradually raising that wage, and whether that was to $12 or $15 remained unclear.

40. According to the U.S. Bureau of Economic Analysis's Regional Price Parity Indicator, which tracks the purchasing power across states and cities, in 2013 Hawaii had the highest prices of goods and services, followed by New York and New Jersey, California fourth, followed by Maryland, while D.C. was higher than any state. In Mississippi, where prices are lowest in the nation, workers would have to earn about $11.60 per hour to have the same purchasing power as a $15 hourly worker in California. There are, of course, also big price variations within states. In New York, for example, prices in metropolitan areas are as much as 24 percent higher than in non-metro areas. In California, prices in metro areas are about 16 percent higher than in non-metro areas. Prices may also vary dramatically among metropolitan areas in the same state. For example, in the San Francisco metro area $19.80 has the same purchasing power as $15 in El Centro. Niraj Chokshi, "California and New York Are Getting a $15 Minimum Wage. Here's How Much That Buys Everywhere Else," *The Washington Post*, April 4, 2016.

Chapter 8

1. Harrison, *Lean and Mean*. From the very outset, it was the fear of job loss itself that provided the primary driving force for American workers to accept the lean production system in places where it was introduced.

2. Silver, *Forces of Labor*, 67.

3. Moody, *U.S. Labor in Trouble and Transition*, 29–31.

4. Mike Parker and Jane Slaughter, *Working Smart: A Union Guide to Participation Programs and Reengineering* (Detroit: Labor Notes, 1994), 3.

5. Ciulla, *The Working Life*, 143–44.

6. Richard J. Pierce, *Leadership, Perspective, and Restructuring for Total Quality: An Essential Instrument to Improve Market Share and Productivity* (Milwaukee, WI: ASQC Quality Press, 1991), 11.

7. Ciulla, *The Working Life*, 144.

8. Randall S. Schuler and Drew L. Harris, *Managing Quality: The Primer for Middle Managers* (Reading, MA: Addison-Wesley, 1992), 160.

9. Pierce, *Leadership, Perspective, and Restructuring for Total Quality*, 13.

10. Kathleen Ryan and Daniel K. Oestreich,

Driving Fear Out of the Workplace: How to Overcome the Invisible Barriers to Quality, Productivity, and Innovation (San Francisco: Jossey-Bass Publishers, 1991), 31.

11. Ciulla, *The Working Life*, 146.

12. Office of Technology Assessment U.S. Congress, *Automation of American Offices* (Washington, D.C.: U.S. Government Printing Office, December 1985), 19.

13. Greenbaum, *Windows On the Workplace*, 77, 79–80.

14. Huws, *The Making of a Cybertariat*, 168–69.

15. Greenbaum, *Windows On the Workplace*, 87.

16. Ibid., 81.

17. Michael Hammer and James Champy, *Reengineering the Corporation: A Manifesto for Business Revolution* (New York: HarperBusiness, 1993), 65.

18. Ibid., 1–3.

19. Michael Hammer, "Reengineering Work: Don't Automate, Obliterate," *Harvard Business Review* 90, no. 4 (1990): 104–12.

20. Keith Grint, "Reengineering History: Social Resonances and Business Process Engineering," *Organization* 1, no. 1 (1994): 194 (emphases in original).

21. Michael Hammer, *Beyond Reengineering: How the Process-Centered Organization is Changing Our Work and Our Lives* (New York: HarperBusiness, 1996), 114.

22. Ciulla, *The Working Life*, 148.

23. Kunda, *Engineering Culture*; Philip Kraft, *Programmers and Managers: The Routinization of Computer Programming in the United States* (New York: Springer-Verlag, 1977).

24. B. Joseph Pine, *Mass Customization: The New Frontier in Business Competition* (Boston: Harvard Business School Press, 1993); Robert Simons, *Levers of Control: How Managers Use Innovative Control Systems to Drive Strategic Renewal* (Boston: Harvard Business School Press, 1995).

25. Peter F. Drucker, *Managing for Results: Economic Tasks and Risk-Taking Decisions* (New York: Harper & Row, 1964); George S. Odiorne, *Management by Objectives: A System of Management Leadership* (New York: Pitman Publishers Corp., 1965).

26. Kraft, "To Control and Inspire," 20–22, 34n16; James G. March and Herbert A. Simon, *Organizations* (New York: Wiley, 1958).

27. Mike Parker and Jane Slaughter, *Choosing Sides: Unions and the Team Concept* (Boston: South End Press, 1988).

28. Kraft, "To Control and Inspire," 23–24.

29. Ibid., 25; David Harvey, *The Condition of Postmodernity: An Enquiry into the Origins of Cultural Change* (Oxford: Blackwell, 1989).

30. Kraft, "To Control and Inspire," 24–25.

31. Wardell, "Labor Processes," 7.

32. Kraft, "To Control and Inspire," 26.

33. While it may initially appear that these new alternative models of organization rely less on rationalization and more on fostering creativity and intuition among employees to solve problems, in reality they continue to rely on rationalization as a form of control. Karen P. Nicholson, "The McDonaldization of Academic Libraries and the Values of Transformational Change," *College & Research Libraries* 67, no. 3 (2015): 330.

34. Kraft, "To Control and Inspire," 27.

35. March and Simon, *Organizations*.

36. Jointness was originally used in particular to describe the cooperation and integration of different branches of the U.S. military.

37. Kraft, "To Control and Inspire," 29.

38. James Gee, Glynda Hull, and Colin Lankshear, *The New Work Order: Behind the Language of the New Capitalism* (Boulder, CO: Westview Press, 1996), 44.

39. Kraft, "To Control and Inspire," 30.

40. Smith and Thompson, "Reevaluating the Labor Process Debate," 209; Patrick Dawson and Janette Webb, "New Production Arrangements: The Totally Flexible Cage?," *Work, Employment, and Society* 3, no. 2 (1989): 221–38; Deborah Kerfoot and David Knights, "Empowering the Quality Worker: The Managerial Evangelism of Total Quality in Financial Services," in *Making Quality Critical*, ed. Adrian Wilkinson and Hugh Willmott (London: Routledge, 1994), 219–39; Rolland Munro, "Governing the New Province of Quality: Autonomy, Accounting, and the Dissemination of Accountability," in *Making Quality Critical*, 127–55.

41. Head, *The New Ruthless Economy*, 58–59.

42. Ibid., 66–67.

43. Ibid., 68–70.

44. Of course, a much better way to trace this development would be to investigate in detail the actual implementations of reengineering initiatives in the workplace. Due to the dearth of such investigations, the following too relies on the published work of advocates of reengineering referred to here.

45. Head, *The New Ruthless Economy*, 72.

46. John Markoff, *Machines of Loving Grace: The Quest for Common Ground between Humans and Robots* (New York: Ecco, 2015), 127–28.

47. Huws, *The Making of a Cybertariat*, 179.
48. Hammer and Champy, *Reengineering the Corporation*, 3.
49. Thomas H. Davenport and James E. Short, "The New Industrial Engineering: Information Technology and Process Design," *MIT Sloan Management Review*, July 15, 1990, 15, http://sloanreview.mit.edu/article/the-new-industrial-engineering-information-technology-and-business-process-redesign/.
50. Head, *The New Ruthless Economy*, 73.
51. Thomas H. Davenport, *Process Innovation: Reengineering Work Through Information Technology* (Boston: Harvard Business School Press, 1993), 261.
52. Head, *The New Ruthless Economy*, 71.
53. Hammer and Champy, *Reengineering the Corporation*, 65.
54. Davenport, *Process Innovation*, 17, 257.
55. Head, *The New Ruthless Economy*, 74.
56. Zuboff, *In the Age of the Smart Machine*, 9–10.
57. Ibid., 170.
58. Greenbaum, *Windows On the Workplace*, 78–79.
59. Ibid., 72.
60. Ibid., 73.
61. Ibid., 76–77, 90.
62. Head, *The New Ruthless Economy*, 11–12.
63. Michael L. Dertouzos, *Made in America: Regaining the Productive Edge* (Cambridge, MA: MIT Press, 1989), 48.
64. National Center on Education and the Economy, "America's Choice: High Skills or Low Wages!," in *Report of the Commission on the Skills of the American Workforce* (Rochester, NY, 1990), http://www.eric.ed.gov/?id=ED 323297.
65. Head, *The New Ruthless Economy*, 12–13.
66. Hammer and Champy, *Reengineering the Corporation*, 207–08.
67. Head, *The New Ruthless Economy*, 77–78; Hammer, *Beyond Reengineering*, 29, 40–41, 50, 129, 144.
68. Greenbaum, *Windows On the Workplace*, 88.
69. Ibid., 90–91.
70. Ibid., 92–93.
71. Francis Fukuyma, *Trust: The Social Virtues and the Creation of Prosperity* (New York: Free Press, 1995), 27.
72. Ciulla, *The Working Life*, 153–55.
73. Lichtenstein, *State of the Union*, 128.
74. Ciulla, *The Working Life*, 161–62.
75. Ibid., 111–12.

76. Irving L. Janis, *Victims of Groupthink: A Psychological Study of Foreign-Policy Decisions and Fiascoes* (Boston: Houghton, 1972), 9. Groups affected by groupthink ignore alternatives and tend to take irrational actions that dehumanize other groups. A group is especially vulnerable to groupthink when its members are similar in background, when the group is insulated from outside opinions, and when there are no clear rules for decision making.
77. Ciulla, *The Working Life*, 113.

Chapter 9

1. Greenbaum, *Windows On the Workplace*, 93–94.
2. Rosabeth Moss Kanter, "Power Failure in Management Circuits," *Harvard Business Review* 57, no. 4 (1979): 65–75.
3. Andy Friedman, "Responsible Autonomy versus Direct Control over the Labour Process," *Capital and Class* 1, no. 1 (1977): 43–58.
4. Christensen Hughes, "Organisational Empowerment," 125.
5. Greenbaum, *Windows On the Workplace*, 95, 97.
6. Head, *The New Ruthless Economy*, 154.
7. Ibid., xv, 4–8.
8. Ibid., 155.
9. Ibid., 162.
10. Ibid., 163–164.
11. The closest approximations (circular and with a panoptic tower) are the buildings of the now-abandoned Presidio Modelo in Cuba (constructed 1926–28); the former Pavilhão de Segurança (1896)—now part of an Outsider Art and Science museum in Lisbon, Portugal; Autun penitentiary, France; penitentiaries ("dome prisons") in Breda and Arnhem (1884), and Haarlem (1901) in the Netherlands; and Stateville penitentiary (1919), Crest Hill, Illinois, USA. Ironically, the architectural design of Apple's future new headquarters in Cupertino, California—a gigantic ring-shaped building—has been compared to a space ship or even a silver donut, but it much more resembles a modern-day version of a Benthamite panopticon, a glass "dome prison," without the dome. Planned for the middle of the ring, will be a kind of inspection house in the shape of a round glass meeting hall; also made out of glass will be all inner and outer walls of the ring from top to bottom. The new campus is planned to house 13,000 employees in the super ring, one central four-stored circular building, and

will also have a café restaurant with 3,000 seats, a 1,000 seat auditorium, and a fitness center. Steve Jobs. co-founder of Apple who announced the design half a year prior to his death in October 2011, was a Bauhaus aficionado obsessed with transparency—in architecture therefore, he was crazy about glass. In 2006, he already had a complete glass cube built as entry of the new Apple Flagship Store. In order to attain optimal transparency, the architect used a new, specially designed glass so strong that it could also be used for supporting constructions. The glass walls of the new headquarters will be super transparent through specially designed glass panes, whose seams will be no thicker than 0.8 millimeters (a thickness of 3 millimeters is the standard for glass buildings). But Jobs—who was known as a "genius control freak"—did not want this optimally transparent building for esthetic reasons only; he also aimed to change the behavior of Apple employees. The round shape and the total transparency of this new panopticon were supposed to foster productive cooperation between workers; in reality, this new panopticon involves yet an another attempt at behavior modification through architectural design, albeit this time not of criminals, but of 'honest citizens,' combined with the digital panopticon of IT in the workplace. This project has also inspired author Dave Eggers in writing his novel *The Circle* (2013) about a (fictitious) powerful ICT company in San Francisco. Bernard Hulsman, "Het Alziende Oog van Steve Jobs," *NRC Handelsblad*, March 3, 2016, http://www.nrc.nl/next/2016/03/03/het-alziende-oog-van-steve-jobs-1594333.

12. Zuboff, *In the Age of the Smart Machine*, 320.

13. Michel Foucault, *Discipline and Punish: The Birth of the Prison* (New York: Vintage Books, 1975); Zuboff, *In the Age of the Smart Machine*, 321.

14. Head, *The New Ruthless Economy*, 166–67.

15. American Management Association, *Workplace Monitoring and Surveillance: Policies and Practices* (New York, 2001), http://www.amanet.org/research/pdf/ems/short.2001.pdf.

16. Ross, *No-Collar*, 12.

17. Edgell, *The Sociology of Work*, 224–25.

18. Simon Head acknowledges his indebtedness to other contrarian critiques of corporate CRM, such as the work of Erik Vinkhuyzen and Jack Whalen at Xerox PARC. Jack Whalen and Erik Vinkhuyzen, "Expert Systems in (Inter)Action: Diagnosing Document Machine Problems over the Telephone," in *Workplace Studies: Recovering Work Practice and Information Systems Design*, ed. Paul Luff, Jon Hindmarsh, and Christian Heath (Cambridge: Cambridge University Press, 2000), 92–140; Head, *Mindless*, 201n2.

19. Head, *The New Ruthless Economy*, 82–83.

20. *Ibid.*, 83–85.

21. *Ibid.*, 88–89.

22. *Ibid.*, 57.

23. Head, *Mindless*, 61.

24. Head, *The New Ruthless Economy*, 93–94.

25. *Ibid.*, 9–10.

26. Greenbaum, *Windows On the Workplace*, 120–21.

27. Head, *The New Ruthless Economy*, 98.

28. *Ibid.*, 98–99.

29. Communications Workers of American (CWA), "Offshoring American Call Centers: The Threat to Consumers, Communities, and National Security!," October 2012, http://www.cwa-union.org/pages/why_shipping_call_center_jobs_overseas_hurts_us_back_home.

30. The original 2013 bill died in the 113th, 2013–2015 Congress, and was reintroduced in this related bill in the 114th Congress in February 2016. Importantly, the bill does *not* target the quality of work and working conditions in call centers.

31. Edgell, *The Sociology of Work*, 226.

32. Phil Taylor and Peter Bain, "'An Assembly Line in the Head': Work and Employee Relations in the Call Center," *Industrial Relations Journal* 30, no. 2 (1999): 110–17.

33. Rosemary Batt and Lisa Monynihan, "Human Resource Practices, Service Quality, and Economic Performance in Call Centers," CAHRS Wk. Paper 04–16, http://www.ilr.cornell.edu/cahrs/2004.

34. Stephen J. Frenkel, Marek Korczynski, Karen A Shire, and May Tam. *On the Front Line: Organization of Work in the Information Economy* (Ithaca, NY: ILR Press, 1999); Edgell, *The Sociology of Work*, 226.

35. Edgell, *The Sociology of Work*, 227.

36. Erik Brynjolfsson and Andrew McAfee, *The Second Machine Age: Work, Progress, and Prosperity in a Time of Brilliant Technologies* (New York: W.W. Norton, 2014), 184.

37. Greenbaum, *Windows On the Workplace*, 76–77, 90.

Chapter 10

1. Jacoby, *Employing Bureaucracy*, 218; Richard Sennett, *The Corrosion of Character: The Personal Consequences of Work in the New Capitalism* (New York: W.W. Norton, 1998).
2. Robert B. Reich, *The Work of Nations: Preparing Ourselves For 21st-century Capitalism* (New York: Knopf, 1991).
3. Ross, *No-Collar*, 53.
4. Ibid., 44, 85.
5. Aronowitz and DiFazio, *The Jobless Future*, xvi.
6. Smith, *Who Stole the American Dream?*, 270.
7. Aronowitz and DiFazio, *The Jobless Future*, xii–xiii.
8. U.S. Bureau of Labor Statistics, Table 11, Household Annual Averages, 1995, 2000, http://www.bls.gov/cps/tables.htm.
9. Greenbaum, *Windows On the Workplace*, 103–04.
10. Joan M. Greenbaum, *In the Name of Efficiency: Management Theory and Shopfloor Practice in Data-Processing Work* (Philadelphia, PA: Temple University Press, 1979).
11. Greenbaum, *Windows On the Workplace*, 85, 133.
12. Ibid., 133.
13. Ibid., 122–23.
14. Huws, *The Making of a Cybertariat*, 179–80.
15. Aronowitz, *The Death and Life of American Labor*, 126.
16. In 2000, Microsoft hired about 3,000 temp employees as permanent employees with full benefits. It also adopted a policy favoring temp agencies that provided more generous benefits. In order to make sure that the temps it hired were not permanent employees, it required temp workers who stayed at Microsoft for 12 months to leave the company for at least 100 days. Steve Greenhouse, "Temp Workers At Microsoft Win Lawsuit," *New York Times*, December 13, 2000, http://www.nytimes.com/2000/12/13/business/technology-temp-workers-at-microsoft-win-lawsuit.html?pagewanted=print.
17. Greenbaum, *Windows On the Workplace*, 106–07.
18. Ibid., 107–08.
19. Sennett, *The Corrosion of Character*, 58.
20. Sennett studied a very specific group: young entrepreneurial people in the high-tech, global finance, and new professional service sectors during the 1990s. One of his protagonists, a high-tech venture capitalist, moved around the country four times in 12 years, leading Sennett to lament "the fugitive quality of friendship and local community" caused by new career patterns. Sanford Jacoby doubts whether Americans were overall more mobile at the time than in the 1950s, the heyday of the "Organization Man" and the classic bedroom suburb. He points out that cross-state geographic mobility rates actually were slightly lower in the 1990s than they were in the 1950s. Jacoby, *Employing Bureaucracy*, 219.
21. Sennett, *The Culture of the New Capitalism*, 7, 12, 26, 49, 127–28.
22. See also Sennett's book with an original perspective on craftsmanship and its close connection to work and ethical values. Richard Sennett, *The Craftsman* (New Haven, CT: Yale University Press, 2008). Craftsmanship once connected people to their work by conferring pride and meaning. It concerns a basic human impulse, the desire to do a job well for its own sake. The loss of craftsmanship—and of a society that values it—has impoverished people in ways they have long forgotten, which Sennett brings to light again. He argues that the craftsman's realm is much broader than skilled manual labor; it also encompasses a variety of skilled knowledge work, and extends to parenting and citizenship as well.
23. Here the key objective was creating new kinds of workers—highly flexible, empowered "portfolios" of skills and experiences ready to "throw themselves heart and soul into the work of the company in risky times." Gee, Hull, and Lankshear, *The New Work Order*, 19.
24. Sennett, *The Culture of the New Capitalism*, 115, 117.
25. Ross, *No-Collar*, 217.
26. Snigdha Srivastava and Nik Theodore, "A Long Jobless Recovery: Information Technology Markets After the Bursting of the High-Tech Bubble," *Working USA* 8, no. 3 (2005): 315–26.
27. Greenbaum, *Windows On the Workplace*, 107.
28. Ibid., 107–09.
29. Huws, *The Making of a Cybertariat*, 167.
30. U.S. Bureau of Labor Statistics, www.bls.gov; Aaron Bernstein, "One Giant Global Labor Pool?," *Business Week*, March 22, 2004, http://www.bloomberg.com/news/articles/2004-03-21/one-giant-global-labor-pool.
31. Greenbaum, *Windows On the Workplace*, 110–11; Pete Engardio, Aaron Bernstein, and Manjeet Kripalani, "Is Your Job Next?," *Business Week* (February 3, 2003): 50–60.
32. William Bridges, "The End of the Job,"

Fortune, September 19, 1994, http://www.archive.fortune.com/magazines/fortune/fortune_archive/1994/09/19/79751/index.htm.

33. Greenbaum, *Windows On the Workplace*, 112–13.

34. Henry A. Giroux, "Neoliberalism, Corporate Culture, and the Promise of Higher Education: The University as a Democratic Public Sphere," *Harvard Educational Review* 72, no. 4 (2002): 425–63. For the broader trend of McDonaldization of higher education in the United States and Britain, see Dennis Hayes and Robin Wynyard, eds., *The McDonaldization of Higher Education* (Westport, CT: Praeger, 2002). In relation to this, one can also witness the continued McDonaldization of academic libraries in North America: "Tiered reference service, self-check machines, and self-guided tours all represent ways in which libraries have sought to become more efficient. Just-in-time approaches to collection development—including a greater reliance on interlibrary loan and document delivery services, part of a larger trend toward access over ownership—and standardized approaches to information literacy instruction also provide greater efficiency. Calculability is represented in the focus on quantity, such as inputs (like financial resources, number of stacks, gate counts, number of volumes) and outputs (for instance, circulation stats, online transactions), as a surrogate for quality. McDonaldization is also apparent in the growing predictability of academic libraries' collections resulting from the use of approval plans and journal aggregator databases. Likewise ... most libraries offer the same suite of core services. Finally, in addition to their hierarchical structure and reliance on rules and regulations ... the increasing use of technology in libraries serves as a mechanism of rationalization of control." Nicholson, "The McDonaldization of Academic Libraries," 328.

35. John D. Curtis, "The Employment Status of Instructional Staff Members in Higher Education," April 2014, http://www.aaup.org/sites/default/files/files/AAUP-InstrStaff2011-April2014.pdf.

36. Democratic Staff House Committee on Education and the Work Force, United States House of Representatives, "The Just-In Time Professor: A Staff Report Summarizing eForum Responses on the Working Conditions of Contingent Faculty in Higher Education," January 2014, http://www.democrats.edworkforce.house.gov/sites/democrats.edworkforce.house.gov/files/documents/1.24.14-AdjunctEforumReport.pdf.

37. Greenbaum, *Windows On the Workplace*, 113–16.

38. *Ibid.*, 117.

39. This intervention of the British state in the management of academic research involved between the UK government at the top and the scholars at the base, the bureaucracies of the Higher Education Funding Council for England (HEFCE), the central university administrations, and the departments of the universities themselves. As this control regime was applied in British higher education, it not only made universities more like business in the way they conducted their affairs, but also gave business a greater role in the shaping of academic research. Simon Head vividly describes the dramatic changes the elaborate system of bureaucratic command and control brought about on the academic shop floor. Head, *Mindless*, 72–77.

40. Robert S. Kaplan and David P. Norton, "The Balanced Scorecard—Measures that Drive Performance," *Harvard Business Review* 70, no. 1 (1992): 71–85.

41. Head, *Mindless*, 73.

42. Robert S. Kaplan and David P. Norton, *Strategy Maps: Converting Intangible Assets Into Tangible Outcomes* (Boston: Harvard Business School Press, 2004).

43. Fahmi Fahdl Al-Hosaini and Saudah Sofian, "A Review of Balanced Scorecard Framework in Higher Education Institutions," *International Review of Management and Marketing* 5, no. 1 (2015): 26–35.

44. F. Azizi and Ahmad J. Afshari, "Which Perspectives in the Balanced Scorecard are Appropriate for the Universities?," *European Journal of Scientific Research* 74, no. 2 (2012): 164–75. Against this, a recent international review of the use of BSC in higher education institutions concludes with the suggestion that universities as non-profit organizations should apply other non-financial perspectives such as community participation, innovation, strategic partnerships and scientific research excellence. Al-Hosaini and Sofian, "A Review of Balanced Scorecard Framework," 33.

45. Kurt Schobel and Cam Scholey, "Balanced Scorecards in Education: Focusing on Financial Strategies," *Measuring Business Excellence* 16, no. 3 (2012): 17–28.

46. There is a less influential strain of organizational research of higher education institutions in the U.S., which began rethinking the Balanced Score Card framework in the late 1990s, looking for more appropriate measures to assess the quality of education and research.

Brent D. Ruben, "Toward a Balanced Scorecard for Higher Education: Rethinking the College and University Excellence Indicators Framework," *Higher Education Forum* (Fall 1999), http://www.qci.rutgers.edu.

47. This March 2013 petition, "Professionals Against Machine Scoring Of Student Essays In High-Stakes Assessment," is posted at http://www.humanreaders.org/petition/.

48. Martin Ford, *Rise of the Robots: Technology and the Threat of a Jobless Future* (New York: Basic Books, 2015), 130.

49. See list of research findings and references attached to the March 2013 petition mentioned earlier.

50. Carr, *The Glass Cage*, 206.

51. Ford, *Rise of the Robots*, 129–31.

52. "Resolution on Massive Open Online Courses and the Teaching of Writing," July 2013, posted by Arabella Lyon at http://www.ipetitions.com/petition/suny-cow.

53. Ford, *Rise of the Robots*, 132 (emphasis added).

54. Aronowitz and DiFazio, *The Jobless Future*, xxiii.

55. Head, *The New Ruthless Economy*, 117–18; Walter A. Zelman and Robert A. Berenson, *The Managed Care Blues and How to Cure Them* (Washington, D.C.: Georgetown University Press, 1998).

56. Smith, *Who Stole the American Dream?*, 84–85.

57. Head, *The New Ruthless Economy*, 118–19.

58. Zelman and Berenson, *The Managed Care Blues*, 25, 1; Head, *The New Ruthless Economy*, 119.

59. Smith, *Who Stole the American Dream?*, 85.

60. Laura Landro, "Costs, Politics of Health Care Will Dominate Debate on '03," *Wall Street Journal*, January 8, 2003.

61. Head, *The New Ruthless Economy*, 119–20.

62. Among others, Ernst and Young, and Andersen Consulting.

63. Head, *The New Ruthless Economy*, 124.

64. Donald Berwick and Chuck Kilo, "Idealized Design of Clinical Office Practice: An Interview with Donald Berwick and Chuck Kilo of the Institute for Health Improvement," *Managed Care Quarterly* 7, no. 3 (1999): 1–8.

65. J. D. Kleinke, *Bleeding Edge: The Business of Health Care in the New Century* (Gaithersburg, MD: Aspen Publishers, 1998), 173.

66. Head, *The New Ruthless Economy*, 124–25.

67. Ibid., 8–9.

68. Ibid., 129–30.

69. Rebecca Voelker, "Population Based Medicine Merges Clinical Care, Epidemiological Techniques," *JAMA* 27, no. 17 (1994): 1301–02.

70. Head, *The New Ruthless Economy*, 133.

71. "RAND Study Says Computerizing Medical Records Could Save $81 Billion Annually and Improve the Quality of Medical Care," RAND Corporate press release, September 14, 2005, http://www.rand.org/news/press/2005/09/14.html.

72. Arthur L. Kellermann and Spencer S. Jones, "What It Will Take to Achieve the As-Yet-Unfulfilled Promises of Health Information Technology," *Health Affairs* 32, no. 1 (2013): 63–68.

73. Carr, *The Glass Cage*, 93–95; Ashley D. Black, "The Impact of eHealth on the Quality and Safety of Health Care: A Systematic Overview," *PLOS Medicine* 8, no. 1 (2011), http://www.journals.plos.org/plosmedicine/article?id=10.1371/journal.pmed.1000387.

74. Carr, *The Glass Cage*, 114.

75. Aronowitz, *The Death and Life of American Labor*, 123–24, 183n9. The California Nurses Association is a notable exception. It has sponsored a research institute, that in response to the Affordable Care Act's invitation to providers to propose plans for patient-centered health care, issued several reports that reflect its perspective on qualitative aspects, thereby addressing autonomy concerns.

76. Carr, *The Glass Cage*, 100.

77. All previous quotes from Timothy Hoff, "Deskilling and Adaptation among Primary Care Physicians Using Two Work Innovations," *Health Care Management Review* 36, no. 4 (2011): 338–48.

78. Carr, *The Glass Cage*, 101–02.

79. Danielle Ofri, "The Doctor vs. the Computer," *New York Times*, December 30, 2010.

80. Beth Lown and Dayron Rodriguez, "Commentary: Lost in Translation? How Electronic Health Records Structure Communication, Relationships, and Meaning," *Academic Medicine* 87, no. 4 (2012): 392–94.

81. Emran Rouf, Jeff Whittle, Ma Lu, and Mark D. Schwartz, "Computers in the Exam Room: Differences in Physician-Patient Interaction May Be Due to Physician Experience," *Journal of General Internal Medicine* 22, no. 1 (2007): 43–48.

82. Carr, *The Glass Cage*, 104.

83. Lown and Rodriguez, "Commentary: Lost in Translation?"

84. Carlin Dowling, "Audit Support System Design and the Declarative Knowledge of Long-Term Users," *Journal of Emerging Technologies in Accounting* 5, no. 1 (2008): 99–108.
85. Carr, *The Glass Cage*, 76–77.
86. Richard G. Brody, "The Effect of a Computerized Decision Aid on the Development of Knowledge," *Journal of Business and Psychology* 18, no. 2 (2003): 157–74; Holli McCall, Vicky Arnold, and Steve G. Sutton, "Use of Knowledge Management Systems and the Impact on the Acquisition of Explicit Knowledge," *Journal of Information Systems* 22, no. 2 (2008): 77–101.
87. Carr, *The Glass Cage*, 166–67.
88. *Ibid.*, 77; Amar Bhidé, "The Judgment Deficit," *Harvard Business Review* 88, no. 9 (2010): 44–53.
89. Head, *Mindless*, 79.
90. For details about these Wall Street operations and the shenanigans of the human actors involved, see *ibid.*, 81–102. For a detailed discussion of how the (dismantled) regulatory regime allowed the financial machinery to turn bad, see Simon Johnson and James Kwak, *Thirteen Bankers* (New York: Pantheon, 2010).

Chapter 11

1. Carr, *The Glass Cage*, 67–70.
2. Sherry Turkle, *Simulation and Its Discontents* (Cambridge, MA: MIT Press, 2009), 55–56.
3. Raja Parasuraman and Dietrich H. Manzey, "Complacency and Bias in Human Uses of Automation: An Attentional Integration," *Human Factors* 52, no. 3 (2010): 381–410.
4. Andrey A. Povyakalo, Eugenio Alberdi, Lorenzo Strigini, and Peter Ayton, "How to Discriminate between Computer-Aided and Computer-Hindered Decisions: A Case Study in Mammography," *Medical Decision Making* 33, no. 1 (2013): 98–107.
5. Eugenio Alberdi, Lorenzo Strigini, Andrey A. Povyakalo, and Peter Ayton, "Why Are People's Decisions Sometimes Worse with Computer Support?," in *Proceedings of SAFECOMP 2009, the 28th International Conference on Computer Safety, Reliability, and Security*, ed. Bettina Buth, Gerd Rabe, and Till Seyfarth (Hamburg, Germany: Springer, 2009), 18–31.
6. Carr, *The Glass Cage*, 70–71.
7. Ford, *Rise of the Robots*, xv.
8. Wendell Wallach, Colin Allen, and Iva Smit, "Machine Morality: Bottom-up and Top-down Approaches for Modeling Human Moral Faculties," *AI and Society* 22, no. 4 (2008): 565–82.
9. Matthijs A. Pontier, Guy Widdershoven, and Johan F. Hoorn, "Moral Coppélia—Combining Ratio with Affect in Ethical Reasoning" in *Advances in Artificial Intelligence—IBERAMIA 2012. Proceedings of 13th Ibero-American Conference on AI, November 13–16, 2012, Cartagena de Indias, Colombia*, ed. Juan Pavón, Néstor D. Duque-Méndez, and Rubén Fuentes-Fernández (Berlin-Heidelberg: Springer, 2012), 442–51.
10. Carr, *The Glass Cage*, 49–63; Federal Aviation Administration (FAA), *Operational Use of Flight Path Management Systems. Final Report of the Performance-Based Operations Rulemaking Committee/Commercial Aviation Safety Team Flight Deck Automation Working Group* (Washington, D.C.: Federal Aviation Administration. September 5, 2013), https://www.faa.gov/about/office_org/headquarters_offices/avs/offices/afs/afs400/parc/parc_reco/media/2013/130908_PARC_FltDAWG_Final_Report_Recommendations.pdf.4.
11. For more on human-centered automation, see Billings, *Human-Centered Automation: Principles and Guidelines*; Raja Parasuraman, Thomas B. Sheridan, and Christopher D. Wickens, "A Model for Types and Levels of Human Interaction with Automation," *IEEE Transactions of Systems, Man, and Cybernetics* 30, no. 3 (2000): 286–97.
12. Carr, *The Glass Cage*, 158–59; David Meister, *The History of Human Factors and Ergonomics* (Mahwah, NJ: Lawrence Erlbaum Associates, 1999), 209, 359.
13. Carr, *The Glass Cage*, 164–65; Norman J. Slamecka and Peter Graf, "The Generation Effect: Delineation of a Phenomenon," *Journal of Experimental Psychology: Human Learning and Memory* 4, no. 6 (1978): 592–604.
14. Carr, *The Glass Cage*, 79–80. For a more elaborate, historically informed exposé on this issue, see Nicholas Carr, *The Shallows: What the Internet Is Doing to Our Brains* (New York: W.W. Norton, 2010).
15. Mihai Nadin, "Information and Semiotic Processes: The Semiotics of Computation," *Cybernetics and Human Knowing* 18, no. 1–2 (2011), 153–75.
16. Carr, *The Glass Cage*, 81.
17. *Ibid.*, 83.
18. *Ibid.*, 84.
19. *Ibid.*, 89–90.
20. Interview of Raja Parasuraman by Nicholas Carr, June 13, 2013, qtd. in *ibid.*, 166.
21. John D. Lee, "Human Factors and

Ergonomics in Automatic Design," in *Handbook of Human Factors and Ergonomics*, 3rd ed., ed. Gavriel Salvendy (Hoboken, NJ: Wiley, 2006), 1571.

22. Markoff, *Machines of Loving Grace*, 157–58, 164–65.

23. Robert J. Gordon, *The Rise and Fall of American Growth: The U.S. Standard of Living Since the Civil War* (Princeton, NJ: Princeton University Press, 2016), 444–47, 588–89.

24. Ford, *Rise of the Robots*, 256.

25. Ibid., 254–55.

26. DARPA also provided the initial financial backing for the development of Siri (now Apple's virtual assistant technology), and has underwritten the development of IBM's new SyNAPSE cognitive computing chips.

27. Ibid., 80–81.

28. Carr, *The Glass Cage*, 168–70.

29. The use of the term "neural network" may give the false impression that computers operate the way brains do (or vice versa). But the term should not be taken literally; it is a figure of speech. Since we do not yet know how brains operate, how thought and consciousness arise from the interplay of neurons, we are unable to build computers that function as brains do.

30. Carr, *The Glass Cage*, 113–14.

31. Ibid., 115.

32. Markoff, *Machines of Loving Grace*, 78.

33. Carr, *The Glass Cage*, 116–17.

34. Ibid., 118–19.

35. Ford, *Rise of the Robots*, 102; Brynjolfsson and McAfee, *The Second Machine Age*, 92–93.

36. Ford, *Rise of the Robots*, 103, 147–48.

37. Carr, *The Glass Cage*, 120.

38. Ford, *Rise of the Robots*, 104–06.

39. Gordon, *The Rise and Fall of American Growth*, 598.

40. Ford, *Rise of the Robots*, 102.

41. Carr, *The Glass Cage*, 123–24.

42. Ibid., 119.

43. Qtd. in Brynjolfsson and McAfee, *The Second Machine Age*, 255.

44. Ibid., 256.

45. Ibid., 191.

46. Ford, *Rise of the Robots*, 84–85; Brynjolfsson and McAfee, *The Second Machine Age*, 35.

47. In-depth studies of many examples of invention, innovation, and technological progress have shown that the way major steps forward in our knowledge and ability to accomplish things occur, is not by coming up with something big and new, but instead, by recombining things that already exist. This is called "recombinant innovation." Brynjolfsson and McAfee, *The Second Machine Age*, 78–81; W. Brian Arthur, *The Nature of Technology: What It is and How It Evolves* (New York: Simon & Schuster, 2009).

48. Brynjolfsson and McAfee, *The Second Machine Age*, 191–92.

49. Ford, *Rise of the Robots*, 110–11; John R. Koza, "Human-Competitive Results Produced by Genetic Programming," *Genetic Programming and Evolvable Machines* 11, no. 3 (2010): 251–84, http://www.genetic-programming.com/GPEM2010article.pdf.

50. Brynjolfsson and McAfee, *The Second Machine Age*, 193.

51. Ford, *Rise of the Robots*, 86–89.

Chapter 12

1. These systems originated in the needs of the military for battlefield control during World War II before they were applied to the needs of corporate businesses. Head, *Mindless*, 129–46.

2. Ibid., 4–5.

3. Ibid. 5.

4. Ibid., 6–7.

5. Ibid., 16–17.

6. Upannee Amnajmongkol et al., "Business Activity Monitoring with WebSphere Business Monitor V6.1," http://www.redbooks.ibm.com/redbooks/pdfs/sg247638.pdf.

7. Head, *Mindless*, 18.

8. Ibid., 19–20.

9. All quotes from IBM, "Executive Brief, Business Activity Management: Your Window of Opportunity for Better Business Operations," 2003, ftp://www.service.boulder.ibm.com/eserver/zseries/audio/pdgs/WBIMonitorbrief, 9, 16.

10. Head, *Mindless*, 21–22; IBM, "Frequently asked questions (FAQ) about IBM Business Monitor (formerly IBM WebSphere Business Monitor)," https://www.developer.ibm.com/answers/topics/monitor.html.

11. August-Wilhelm Scheer et al., eds., *Corporate Performance Management: ARIS in Practice* (Berlin: Spinger, 2005), pt. 1, ch. 2; Andreas Kronz, *Managing of Process Key Performance Indicators as Part of the ARIS Methodology* (Berlin: Springer, 2006), 36–39.

12. Philip Monson et al., "IBM Redbooks: Lotus Domino Domain Monitoring." (IBM International Technical Support Organization, 2005), http://www.redbooks.ibm.com/redpapers/pdfs/redp4089.pdf.

13. Head, *Mindless*, 22.
14. *Ibid.*, 23–24.
15. *Ibid.*, 25–26.
16. *Ibid.*, 27.
17. *Ibid.*, 28.
18. *Ibid.*, 165–194. On the other hand, Head signals the rise of a "concierge" economy for the very rich in the U.S. and the United Kingdom, side by side with the faulty service economy. In trying to escape mass-produced services, many wealthy people have turned to concierge-like doctors, bankers, and other skilled service workers with whom they can have more personal relationships. In the concierge economy, information systems are used to supplement rather than replace the skills of employees: "There are no digital scripts at the Goldman Sachs private bank." *Ibid.*, 122.
19. *Ibid.*, 68–69. In 2004, eighty-nine of the Fortune 100 companies used the Myers-Briggs test. The Wagner Enneagram Personality Style Scales (WEPPS) was used by, among others, AT&T, Boeing, DuPont, General Motors, Hewlett-Packard (HP), Proctor & Gamble, Motorola, Prudential Insurance, and Sony.
20. Carr, *The Glass Cage*, 117.
21. James J. Gross, "The Emerging Field of Emotion Regulation: An Integrative Review," *Review of General Psychology* 2, no. 3 (1998): 273–99.
22. Alicia A. Grandey, "Emotion Regulation in the Workplace: A New Way to Conceptualize Emotional Behavior," *Journal of Occupational Health Psychology* 5, no. 1 (2000): 95–110.
23. James J. Gross and Oliver P. John, "Mapping the Domain of Expressivity: Multimethod Evidence for a Hierarchical Model," *Journal of Personality and Social Psychology* 74, no. 1 (1998): 170–91.
24. Head, *Mindless*, 115.
25. *Ibid.*, 15.
26. Robert Skidelsky suggests that Head "would have done better in some cases to talk to the designers of these systems and ask them what they were really hoping to achieve, and to try to get a closer feel for life in automated distribution systems by working in one of them undercover, as Carole Cadwalladr did at Amazon." Robert Skidelsky, "The Programmed Prospect Before Us. Review of *Mindless: Why Smarter Machines Are Making Dumber Humans* by Simon Head. Basic Books, 2014," *New York Review of Books*, April 3, 2014, http://www.nybooks.com/articles/2014/04/03/programmed-prospect-us/; Carole Cadwalladr, "My Week as an Amazon Insider," *The Guardian*, November 30, 2013, https://www.theguardian.com/technology/2013/dec/01/week-amazon-insider-feature-treatment-employees-work. However, the first approach would still not directly trace the actual effects of CBSs on workers, and the latter experiential approach by a participant observer may be too limited to get a good overall grasp on the systems' ramifications in the workplace. Skidelsky overlooks the fact that Head makes use of participant observer accounts, reports by journalists and union officials, and a (German) television documentary in his chapter on work at Walmart and Amazon. Head points to the combination of old-fashioned, direct control practices and the newest information technology in these workplaces. He also describes the reception of Amazon fulfillment centers in Germany, where Amazon had to deal with work councils, a powerful services union, and high officials of the federal and state governments more closely aligned with labor than their counterparts in the U.S. and Britain. Head, *Mindless*, 29–46.
27. Head, *Mindless*, 191–92.
28. *Ibid.*, 193.
29. Cowie, *The Great Exception*, 30; Richard Hofstadter, *The Age of Reform: From Bryan to FDR* (New York: Vintage Books, 1955), 308.
30. Cowie, *The Great Exception*, 22–24, 30–31, 124–28, 172–73, 186.
31. Head saw a glimmer of hope in the bid of the self-avowed democratic socialist senator from Vermont, Bernie Sanders, for the 2016 Democratic presidential nomination. He called this a "quiet revolt" against the prevailing economy rigged in favor of the financial and economic elites, which brought together parts of the shrinking middle class, both white- and blue-collar, the working and non-working poor, as well as young, first time voters with large student-loan debts. Simon Head, "Bernie Sanders: The Quiet Revolt," *The New York Review of Books*, December 23, 2015, http://www.nybooks.com/daily/2015/12/23/bernie-sanders-quiet-revolt/. Sanders himself spoke about a "political revolution" brought about by the newly emerging people's movement, galvanized by his campaign. He drew large crowds at his political rallies and won a substantial number of primaries and caucuses, but ultimately lost to his rival Hillary Clinton. In his speeches, Sanders emphasized the massive job losses due to offshoring as a result of international free trade agreements, but did not explicitly mention the issue of work degradation, let alone unemployment due to automation. Yet this presumably served his broader political agenda that emphasized the dignity of labor

and workers' rights. At the time of this writing, Sanders and his supporters continue to push his progressive, populist economic agenda as the fractured Democratic Party seeks to rebuild now that Donald Trump won the White House and Republicans control Congress and a vast majority of statehouses. Sanders has set up the organization Our Revolution to recruit and support candidates for local, state and national office. The aim is to groom and empower the next generation of progressive leaders, working to capitalize on the gains Sanders made in 2016.

Chapter 13

1. Ford, *Rise of the Robots*, 93.
2. Ibid., xv–xvi.
3. John Maynard Keynes, "Economic Possibilities for Our Grandchildren," in *Essays in Persuasion* (New York: W.W. Norton, 1963 [1930]), 358–73.
4. Ford, *Rise of the Robots*, xvi; Head, *Mindless*, 59; Davis, "The Twilight of the Berle and Means Corporation," 1222.
5. Brynjolfsson and McAfee, *The Second Machine Age*, 181.
6. See https://en.wikipedia.org/wiki/Moravec's_paradox.
7. Hans P. Moravec, *Mind Children: The Future of Robot and Human Intelligence* (Cambridge, MA: Harvard University Press, 1988), 15.
8. Ibid., 15–16; Brynjolfsson and McAfee, *The Second Machine Age*, 140.
9. Brynjolfsson and McAfee, *The Second Machine Age*, 28–30.
10. Ford, *Rise of the Robots*, 5–6.
11. Ibid., 1–4; Markoff, *Machines of Loving Grace*, 241–44.
12. Daniel J. Levitin, "Book review of *The Glass Cage* by Nicholas Carr," *Wall Street Journal*, October 10, 2014.
13. Markoff, *Machines of Loving Grace*, 206; Ford, *Rise of the Robots*, 16–17.
14. Gordon, *The Rise and Fall of American Growth*, 596.
15. Ford, *Rise of the Robots*, 17.
16. Ibid., 20–21.
17. Brynjolfsson and McAfee, *The Second Machine Age*, 202; Tim Hornyak, "Towel-folding Robot Won't Do the Dishes," CNET, March 31, 2010, http://www.news.cnet.com/8301-17938_105-10471898-1.
18. A prototype is an early sample, model, or release of a product built to test a concept or process or to act as a thing to be replicated or learned from. The term is used in a variety of contexts, including semantics, design, electronics, and software programming.
19. Brynjolfsson and McAfee, *The Second Machine Age*, 135–37.
20. According to a 2013 study by Carl Benedikt Frey and Michael A. Osborne at the University of Oxford, UK, occupations amounting to about 47 percent of U.S. total employment may be vulnerable to automation within the next two decades. Carl Benedikt Frey and Michael A. Osborne. "The Future of Employment: How Susceptible Are Jobs to Computerisation?" (September 17, 2013): 38, http://www.oxfordmartin.ox.ac.uk/downloads/academic/The_Future_of_Employment.pdf. For a recent report on the global state of affairs, see McKinsey Global Institute, *A Future That Works: Automation, Employment, and Productivity*, January 2017, https://fredzimny.word press.com/2017/01/17/mckinsey-global-insti tute-a-future-that-works-automation-employ ment-and-productivity-job-jobs/.
21. Ford, *Rise of the Robots*, 41–43, 52–53, 59–60; Gordon, *The Rise and Fall of American Growth*, 615–16.
22. Smith, *Who Stole the American Dream?*, 273–89.

Chapter 14

1. Gerald F. Davis, *The Vanishing American Corporation: Navigating the Hazards of a New Economy* (Oakland, CA: Berrett-Koehler Publishers, 2016).
2. Berle and Means' analysis was based on four premises regarding the modern corporation. First, economic power, in terms of control over physical assets, is responding to a centripetal force, tending more and more to concentrate in the hands of a few corporate managements; second, "beneficial ownership is centrifugal, tending to divide and subdivide, to split into ever smaller units and to pass freely from hand to hand" (in other words, a tendency towards an increasing dispersal of ownership); third, large corporations typically make physical products, transport them, or provide infrastructure; fourth, corporations are long-lasting relative to the individuals whose destinies they control. Davis, "The Twilight of the Berle and Means Corporation," 1209–10. Importantly, Berle and Means were concerned about the separation of ownership from control in large U.S. corporations. They signaled a concentration of economic power brought on by the rise

of these corporations and the emergence of a powerful class of professional managers, insulated from the pressure not only of stockholders, but of the larger public as well. They warned that the ascendance of management (rather than owner) control and unchecked corporate power, had potentially serious consequences for the democratic character of the United States. Social scientists such as Daniel Bell, Ralf Dahrendorf, and Talcott Parsons, who drew on Berle and Means in subsequent decades, presented a far more benign interpretation of the rise of managerialism, however. For them, the separation of ownership from control actually led to an increased level of democratization in the society as a whole. Beginning in the late 1960s, sociologists and other scientists revived the debate over ownership and control, culminating in a series of rigorous empirical studies on the nature of corporate power in American society. By the late 1990s, however, sociologists had largely abandoned the topic, ceding it to finance economists, legal scholars, and corporate strategy researchers (a notable exception was G. William Domhoff who kept updating his 1967 analysis in *Who Rules America?*). Mark S. Mizruchi, "Berle and Means Revisited: The Governance and Power of Large Corporations," *Theory and Society* 33, no. 5 (2004): 579–617.

3. Davis, *The Vanishing American Corporation*, 15; Davis, "The Twilight of the Berle and Means Corporation," 1220.

4. For a detailed overview of how corporations reduced the portion of compensation paid with health insurance premiums, and shifted from defined benefit pensions to employee-funded defined contribution plans, see Smith, *Who Stole the American Dream?*, 84–85, 87, 158–59, 161–62, 177–79.

5. Davis, "The Twilight of the Berle and Means Corporation," 1213–15; Gerald F. Davis, "After the Corporation," *Politics and Society* 41, no. 2 (2013): 283–84, 289.

6. Berle and Means, *The Modern Corporation and Private Property*, 20–27.

7. Davis, *The Vanishing American Corporation*, 123.

8. Davis, "The Twilight of the Berle and Means Corporation," 1219.

9. *Ibid.*, 1219–20.

10. Davis, *The Vanishing American Corporation*, 52.

11. Nike, which is by far the world's largest athletic shoes and clothing company, with over $19 billion in revenues and a market capitalization of $42 billion, employed only 34,400 people globally in 2010. Davis, "The Twilight of the Berle and Means Corporation," 1218.

12. *Ibid.*, 1217–18; Davis, "After the Corporation," 284, 287.

13. Davis, After the Corporation," 292–93.

14. Apple (with 34,300 employees), Google (19,835), Intel (79,800), Cisco (65,550), Microsoft (93,000), and Amazon.com (24,300) combined had 316,785 workers, of whom 215,484 were employed in the United States in 2010. Compare this with grocery chain Kroger, with a U.S. workforce of 334,000 in the same year. Davis. "The Twilight of the Berle and Means Corporation," 1222. Companies that organize the production and distribution of online services need even fewer employees. In January 2013, Dropbox, the cloud-based storage site, had more than 100 million users and only 221 employees. Facebook with more than one billion users around the world, had only 4,619 employees. Davis, "After the Corporation." 294, 290. The numbers of employees of the best-known high-tech companies in 2015 were as follows: Facebook, 9,199 employees; Twitter, 3,638; Dropbox, 971; Zynga, 1,974; Zillow, 1,215; LinkedIn, 6,987; Uber, perhaps 2,000; Square, 1,000. Google—the paradigmatic corporation of the 21st century—was much bigger, with 53,600 employees around the world. But the combined global workforces of all of these companies together was still only 80,000. Davis, *The Vanishing American Corporation*, 92.

15. Davis, *The Vanishing American Corporation*, xiv, 81, 83.

16. *Ibid.*, 86–88.

17. *Ibid.*, 93–94.

18. Accounting tricks are used to make it appear that profits earned in the U.S. were generated in a tax haven. Profits are funneled through subsidiaries, often shell companies with few employees and little real business activity. Effectively, firms launder U.S. profits to avoid paying U.S. taxes. The Stop Tax Haven Abuse Act (S. 1533) bill has been introduced in Congress in 2013 and reintroduced in 2015 (now also including significant new provisions to curb so-called corporate inversions), which would close many of the loopholes concerned. Americans for Tax Fairness, "Offshore Corporate Tax Loopholes," 2014 Tax Fairness Briefing Booklet, http://www.americansfortaxfairness.org/files/ATF-Offshore-Corporate-Tax-Loopholes-Fact-Sheet.pdf; H.R. 297—Stop Tax Haven Abuse Act, 114th Congress (2015–2016), https://www.congress.gov/bill/114th-congress/house-bill/297.

19. Davis, *The Vanishing American Corporation*, 93–94.

20. See especially G. William Domhoff's most recent update of his 1967 analysis. G. William Domhoff, *Who Rules America?: The Triumph of the Corporate Rich*, 7th ed. (New York: McGraw-Hill, 2014). Cargill, Koch Industries, Bechtel, Publix, Pilot Corp., accounting firm Deloitte Touche Tohmatsu, Hearst Corporation, Cox Enterprises, S.C. Johnson, and Mars are among the largest privately held companies in the United States today.

21. Nicholas Confessore, Sarah Cohen and Karen Yourish, "Here Are 120 Million Monopoly Pieces, Roughly One for Every Household in the United States," *New York Times*, October 10, 2015, http://www.nytimes.com/interactive/2015/10/11/us/politics/2016-presidential-election-super-pac-donors.html?_r=0.

22. Super PACs may not make contributions to candidate campaigns or parties, but rather must do any political spending independently of the campaign. But unlike other PACs, there is no legal limit to the funds they can raise from individuals, corporations, unions and other groups, provided they are operated correctly. Super PACs were made possible by two judicial decisions. First, in January 2010 the U.S. Supreme Court held in *Citizens United v. Federal Election Commission* that government may not prohibit corporations and unions from making independent expenditures for political purposes. Two months later, in *SpeechNow.org v. FEC*, the Federal Court of Appeals for the D.C. Circuit held that contributions to groups that only make independent expenditures could not be limited in the size and source of contributions to the group.

23. Uber's "driver-partners" have no claim on employee benefits, overtime, unemployment, or even a minimum wage. Currently, Uber is under fire for classifying drivers as independent contractors rather than employees. In a recent $100 million settlement of a worker classification lawsuit in California and Massachusetts, Uber drivers remain independent contractors, while the original suit sought to have drivers re-classified as employees of the company, which would have added significant costs to Uber's bottom line. Some drivers in the lawsuit are not happy about this settlement, which, at the time of this writing, still needs to be approved by a federal judge. These drivers contend that the settlement figure is too low; several have filed objections with the court. Davey Alba and Issie Lapowsky, "Some Drivers Really Aren't Happy About the $100 M Uber Settlement," *Wired*, May 16, 2016, http://www.wired.com/2016/05/drivers-really-arent-happy-100m-uber-settlement/.

24. These are not jobs with Amazon. Amazon simply provides the platform for a market that matches those who need tasks being done with self-starters willing to carry them out. Amazon advertises MTurk as "a marketplace for work that requires human intelligence. The Mechanical Turk service gives businesses access to a diverse, on-demand, scalable workforce and gives workers a selection of thousands of tasks to complete whenever it's convenient." Mechanical Turk is an early instance of what came to be called "crowdsourcing," which has been defined as "an online, distributed problem-solving and production model." TaskRabbit is a well-known other instance of it. Brynjolfsson and McAfee, *The Second Machine Age*, 243.

25. The term "sharing economy" covers a wide range of digital platforms and offline activities, from financially successful companies (often with venture capitalist backers) like Airbnb, a peer-to-peer lodging service, to smaller initiatives (mostly non-profits) such as repair collectives, maker spaces, tool libraries, seed banks, time banks, and food swaps at the community level. Sharing economy activities fall into four broad categories: "recirculation of goods, increased utilization of durable assets, exchange of services, and sharing of productive assets." Juliet Schor, "Debating the Sharing Economy," October 2014, http://www.great transition.org/images/GTI_publications/Schor_Debating_the_Sharing_Economy.pdf.

26. Davis, *The Vanishing American Corporation*, 124, 144–45. But it is possible that corporate platforms will ultimately not prevail. Platforms do not necessarily add much value themselves, so that Uber could be replaced by user-governed and/or owned platforms (for instance, driver-owned taxi cooperatives), as Juliet Schor has pointed out. Schor, "Debating the Sharing Economy," 10–11. Uber and its kind might also lose out to open-source platform software, just like Microsoft arguably lost out to Linux, or AOL to a free Web. Davis, *The Vanishing American Corporation*, 155.

27. Kevin Roose, "The Sharing Economy Isn't About Trust, It's About Desperation," *New York Magazine*, April 24, 2014, http://www.nymag.com/daily/intelligencer/2014/04/sharing-economy-is-about-desperation.html.

28. Flip is an inexpensive camera that records onto flash memory and connects to a computer's USB port for easy editing and sharing of videos. It became a highly popular prod-

uct after it was launched in 2007. By 2009, the company had sold millions of units and dominated its category. In 2009, the company had only 100 employees, even though it had a roughly 20 percent share of the market for portable video cameras. That year Cisco bought the company for about $600 million. Production of the line of Flip video cameras ran until April 2011, when Cisco announced it was closing the Flip business. The Flip's function had been superseded by advances in cell phone technology leading to the smartphone that could do the same thing. Davis, "After the Corporation," 290.

29. Bureau of Labor Statistics, "Union Membership Summary," Jan. 28, 2016, http://www.bls.gov/news.release/union2.nr0.htm.

30. This concerned the American Recovery and Reinvestment Act of 2009, a stimulus package enacted by the 111th United States Congress in February 2009 and signed into law on February 17, 2009, by President Barack Obama.

31. Ford, *Rise of the Robots*, 257–64; Brynjolfsson and McAfee, *The Second Machine Age*, 232–39.

Conclusion

1. Barbara Baran, "Office Automation and Women's Work: The Technological Transformation of the Insurance Industry," in *On Work*, ed. R.E. Pahl (Oxford: Basil Blackwell, 1988), 684–706.

2. Hugh Willmott, "Strength is Ignorance: Slavery is Freedom: Managing Culture in Modern Organizations," *Journal of Management Studies* 30, no. 4 (1993): 512–52.

3. The latest addition to the repertoire of personnel surveillance techniques are so-called "quantified-self" gadgets and apps, which an increasing number of firms are using to monitor and track whether employees work appropriately and hard enough or live a healthy lifestyle. With the help of all kinds of sensors (including wearables), cameras and data-analysis software, these companies can monitor employees ever more accurately, within and outside working hours. Undoubtedly, the idea of Big Brother watching is becoming even more of a reality with this "quantified employee" software system that is being pushed by human resources consultants. Josh Bersin, "Quantified Self: Meet the Quantified Employee" *Forbes*, June 25, 2014, http://www.forbes.com/sites/joshbersin/2014/06/25/quantified-self-meet-the-quantified-employee/#5f0619bc216d; Lam Bourree, "The Quantified Workplace: Despite the Hype, Not All That Useful Yet," *The Atlantic*, March 17, 2015, http://www.theatlantic.com/business/archive/2015/03/the-quantified-workplace-despite-the-hype-not-all-that-helpful-yet/387853/.

4. There is an interesting new development at the frontier of AI. Recently a computer programmed with so-called deep-learning software defeated a human grandmaster (with a score of 4–1) at Go, an ancient board game that has long been viewed as one of the greatest challenges for artificial intelligence. (For AI researchers, it was as big of a moment as 1997, when Garry Kasparov lost a chess match to Deep Blue, a supercomputer built by IBM. It is much harder to program a computer to play Go than chess, because the sheer number of options in every move makes the kind of brute-force approach adopted by IBM unfeasible.) Google's London-based AI company, DeepMind, developed the program AlphaGo, which applied neural networking that mimics how the brain works—that is, connections between layers of simulated neurons are strengthened through examples and experience, aided by a technique known as reinforcement learning. According to DeepMind's co-founder, Demis Hassabis, similar techniques could be applied to other AI domains that require recognition of complex patterns, long-term planning and decision-making. Still, many challenges remain to DeepMind's goal of developing a generalized AI system. In particular, its programs cannot yet usefully transfer their learning about one system—such as Go—to new tasks, something that humans perform seamlessly. Elizabeth Gibney, "Google AI Algorithm Masters Ancient Game of Go," January 27, 2016, http://www.nature.com/news/google-ai-algorithm-masters-ancient-game-of-go-1.19234; Sebastian Anthony, "Score One For the Humans: Google AI Defeated at Go [Updated]," March 15, 2016, http://arstechnica.com/information-technology/2016/03/google-ai-begins-battle-with-humanitys-best-go-player-tonight/.

5. Alan Felstead and Nick Jewson, *In Work, At Home: Towards an Understanding of Homeworking* (London: Routledge, 2000); Christian Fuchs, *Digital Labour and Karl Marx* (New York: Routledge, 2014).

Bibliography

Abercrombie, Nicholas, and Stephen Hill. "Paternalism and Patronage." *British Journal of Sociology* 27, no. 4 (1976): 413–29.

Adler, Paul. "Democratic Taylorism: The Toyota Production System at NUMMI." In *Lean Work: Empowerment and Exploitation in the Global Auto Industry*, edited by Steve Babson, 207–19. Detroit: Wayne University Press, 1995.

Aitken, Hugh G. J. *Taylorism at Watertown Arsenal: Scientific Management in Action, 1908–1915*. Cambridge, MA: Harvard University Press, 1960.

Alba, Davey, and Issie Lapowsky. "Some Drivers Really Aren't Happy About the $100 M Uber Settlement." *Wired*, May 16, 2016, http://www.wired.com/2016/05/drivers-really-arent-happy-100m-uber-settlement/.

Alberdi, Eugenio, Lorenzo Strigini, Andrey A. Povyakalo, and Peter Ayton. "Why Are People's Decisions Sometimes Worse with Computer Support?" In *Proceedings of SAFECOMP 2009, the 28th International Conference on Computer Safety, Reliability, and Security*, edited by Bettina Buth, Gerd Rabe and Till Seyfarth, 18–31. Hamburg, Germany: Springer, 2009.

Al-Hosaini, Fahmi Fahdl, and Saudah Sofian. "A Review of Balanced Scorecard Framework in Higher Education Institutions." *International Review of Management and Marketing* 5, no. 1 (2015): 26–35.

American Management Association. *Workplace Monitoring and Surveillance: Policies and Practices* (New York, 2001), http://www.amanet.org/research/pdf/ems/short.2001.pdf.

Amnajmongkol, Upannee, Yi Che, Tom Fox, Alan Lim, and Martin Keen, "Business Activity Monitoring with Websphere Business Monitor V6.1, 2008, http://www.redbooks.ibm.com/redbooks/pdfs/sg247638.pdf.

Anthony, Sebastian. "Score One for the Humans: Google AI Defeated at Go [Updated]." March 15, 2016, http://arstechnica.com/information-technology/2016/03/google-ai-begins-battle-with-humanitys-best-go-player-tonight/.

Appelbaum, Eileen, and Rosemary Batt. *The New American Workplace: Transforming Work Systems in the United States*. Ithaca, NY: Cornell University Press, 1994.

Archer, Robin. *Why Is There No Labor Party in the United States?* Princeton, NJ: Princeton University Press, 2007.

Aronowitz, Stanley. *The Death and Life of American Labor: Toward a New Workers' Movement*. London: Verso, 2014.

———. *Taking It Big: C. Wright Mills and the Making of Political Intellectuals*. New York: Columbia University Press, 2012.

Aronowitz, Stanley, and William DiFazio. *The Jobless Future*. 2nd ed. Minneapolis: University of Minneapolis Press, 2010.

Arrighi, Giovanni, and Beverly J. Silver. "Labor Movements and Capital Migration: The U.S. and Western Europe in World-Historical Perspective." In *Labor in the Capitalist World Economy*, edited by Charles Bergquist, 183–216. Beverly Hills, CA: Sage, 1984.

Arthur, W. Brian. *The Nature of Technology: What It Is and How It Evolves*. New York: Simon & Schuster, 2009.

Ashton, P.J. "The Political Economy of Suburban Development." In *Marxism and the Metropolis*, edited by William K. Tabb and Larry Sawers, 64–89. New York: Oxford University Press, 1978.

Attewell, Paul. "The Clerk Deskilled: A Study in False Nostalgia." *Journal of Historical Sociology* 2, no. 4 (1989): 357–88.

Azizi, F., and Ahmad J. Afshari. "Which Perspectives in the Balanced Scorecard Are Appropriate for the Universities?" *European Journal of Scientific Research* 74, no. 2 (2012): 164–75.

Back, Kurt W. *Beyond Words: The Story of Sensitivity Training and the Encounter Movement.* Baltimore, MD: Penguin Books, 1973.

Baran, Barbara. "Office Automation and Women's Work: The Technological Transformation of the Insurance Industry." In *On Work*, edited by R.E. Pahl, 684–706. Oxford: Basil Blackwell, 1988.

Baritz, Loren. *The Servants of Power: A History of the Use of Social Science in American Industry.* Middletown, CT: Wesleyan University Press, 1960.

Barnard, Chester I. *The Functions of the Executive.* Cambridge, MA: Harvard University Press, 1938.

Batt, Rosemary, and Lisa Monynihan. "Human Resource Practices, Service Quality, and Economic Performance in Call Centers." *CAHRS Wk. Paper 04–16*, http://www.ilr.cornell.edu/cahrs/2004.

Bell, Daniel. *The Coming of Post-Industrial Society.* New York: Basic Books, 1973.

———. *The End of Ideology: On the Exhaustion of Political Ideas in the Fifties.* Cambridge, MA: Harvard University Press, 1962.

———. *Work and Its Discontent.* New York: McGraw-Hill, 1956.

Bendix, Reinhard. *Work and Authority in Industry: Ideologies of Management in the Course of Industrialization.* New York: Wiley, 1956.

Bennett, George K. "A New Era in Business and Industrial Psychology." *Personnel Psychology* 1, no. 4 (1948): 473–77.

Bennis, Warren G., Kenneth D. Benne, and Robert Chin. *The Planning of Change.* 2nd ed. New York: Holt, Rinehart, and Chin, 1969.

Berggren, Christian. *Alternatives to Lean Production: Work Organization in the Swedish Auto Industry.* Ithaca, NY: ILR Press, 1993.

———. "'New Production Concepts' in Final Assembly—The Swedish Experience." In *The Transformation of Work?*, edited by Stephen Wood, 171–203. London: Unwin Hyman, 1989.

Berle, Adolf A., and Gardiner C. Means. *The Modern Corporation and Private Property.* New York: Harcourt, Brace & World, 1968 [1932].

Bernstein, Aaron. "One Giant Global Labor Pool?" *Business Week*, March 21, 2004, http://www.bloomberg.com/news/articles/2004-03-21/one-giant-global-labor-pool.

Bersin, Josh. "Quantified Self: Meet the Quantified Employee." *Forbes*, June 25, 2014, http://www.forbes.com/sites/joshbersin/2014/06/25/quantified-self-meet-the-quantified-employee/#5f0619bc216d.

Berwick, Donald, and Chuck Kilo. "Idealized Design of Clinical Office Practice: An Interview with Donald Berwick and Chuck Kilo of the Institute for Health Improvement." *Managed Care Quarterly* 7, no. 3 (1999): 1–8.

Beynon, Huw. *Working for Ford.* London: Allen Lane, 1973.

Bhidé, Amar. "The Judgment Deficit." *Harvard Business Review* 88, no. 9 (2010): 44–53.

Billings, Charles E. *Human-Centered Automation: Principles and Guidelines.* Moffett Field, CA: NASA Ames Research Center, 1996.

Bilstein, Roger E. *The American Aerospace Industry: From Workshop to Global Enterprise.* New York: Twayne Publishers, 1996.

The Birth of Lean: Conversations with Taiichi Ohno, Eiji Toyoda, and Other Figures Who Shaped Toyota Management. Edited by Koichi Shimokawa and Takahiro Fujimoto. Cambridge, MA: Lean Enterprise Institute, 2009.

Black, Ashley D. "The Impact of Ehealth on the Quality and Safety of Health Care: A Systematic Overview." *PLOS Medicine*, 8, no. 1 (2011), http://www.journals.plos.org/plosmedicine/article?id=10.1371/journal.pmed.1000387.

Blackburn, Robin. *The American Crucible: Slavery, Emancipation and Human Rights.* London: Verso, 2011.

Blackford, Mansel G. *The Rise of Modern Big Business in Great Britain, the United States, and Japan.* Chapel Hill: University of North Carolina Press, 1988.

Blauner, Robert. *Alienation and Freedom: The Factory Worker and His Industry.* Chicago: University of Chicago Press, 1964.

Block, Fred L. *Postindustrial Possibilities: A Critique of Economic Discourse.* Berkeley: University of California Press, 1990.

Bourree, Lam. "The Quantified Workplace: Despite the Hype, Not All That Useful Yet." *The Atlantic*, March 17, 2015, http://www.theatlantic.com/business/archive/2015/03/the-quantified-workplace-despite-the-hype-not-all-that-helpful-yet/387853/.

Brandes, Stuart D. *American Welfare Capitalism, 1880–1940.* Chicago: University of Chicago Press, 1976.

Braverman, Harry. *Labor and Monopoly Capital: The Degradation of Work in the Twentieth Century*. New York: Monthly Review Press, 1974.

Brick, Howard. *Transcending Capitalism: Visions of a New Society in Modern American Thought*. Ithaca, NY: Cornell University Press, 2006.

Bridges, William. "The End of the Job." *Fortune* (September 19, 1994): 62–74, http://www.archive.fortune.com/magazines/fortune/fortune_archive/1994/09/19/79751/index.htm.

Bright, James R. *Automation and Management*. Boston: Harvard University School Press, 1958.

Brody, David. "The Rise and Decline of Welfare Capitalism." In *Workers in Industrial America: Essays on the Twentieth-Century Struggle*, 48–81. New York: Oxford University Press, 1980.

———. *Steelworkers in America: The Nonunion Era*. New York: Harper and Row, 1969.

Brody, Richard G. "The Effect of a Computerized Decision Aid on the Development of Knowledge." *Journal of Business and Psychology* 18, no. 2 (2003): 157–74.

Bruder, Jessica. "We're Watching You Work. Labor Is Fighting Employer's Techno-Utopian Dream of a Perfectly Efficient—And Totally Surveilled—Workforce." *The Nation* (June 15, 2015): 28–30.

Brynjolfsson, Erik, and Andrew McAfee. *The Second Machine Age: Work, Progress, and Prosperity in a Time of Brilliant Technologies*. New York: W.W. Norton, 2014.

Buder, Stanley. *Pullman: An Experiment in Industrial Order and Community Planning, 1880–1930*. New York: Oxford University Press, 1967.

Burawoy, Michael. *Manufacturing Consent: Changes in the Labor Process Under Monopoly Capitalism*. Chicago: University of Chicago Press, 1979.

———. *The Politics of Production: Factory Regimes Under Capitalism and Socialism*. London: Verso, 1985.

———. "Towards a Marxist Theory of the Labor Process." *Politics and Society* 8, no. 3–4 (1978): 247–312.

Cadwalladr, Carole. "My Week as an Amazon Insider." *The Guardian*, November 30, 2013, https://www.theguardian.com/technology/2013/dec/01/week-amazon-insider-feature-treatment-employees-work.

Canter, Ralph, Jr. "Psychologists in Industry." *Personnel Psychology* 1, no. 2 (1948): 145–61.

Carr, Nicholas. *The Glass Cage: Where Automation Is Taking Us*. London: The Bodley Head, 2015.

———. *The Shallows: What the Internet Is Doing to Our Brains*. New York: W.W. Norton, 2010.

Chandler, Alfred D. "The Emergence of Managerial Capitalism." *Business History Review* 58, no. 4 (1984): 473–504.

———. *The Visible Hand: The Managerial Revolution in American Business*. Cambridge, MA: Belknap Press, 1977.

Chokshi, Niraj. "California and New York Are Getting a $15 Minimum Wage. Here's How Much That Buys Everywhere Else." *The Washington Post*, April 4, 2016.

Christensen Hughes, Julia M. "Organisational Empowerment: A Historical Perspective and Conceptual Framework." In *Ethics and Empowerment*, edited by John J. Quinn and Peter W.F. Davies, 115–46. West Lafayette, IN: Ichor Business Books, 1999.

Ciulla, Joanne B. *The Working Life: The Promise and Betrayal of Modern Work*. New York: Times Books, 2000.

Clawson, Dan. *Bureaucracy and the Labor Process: The Transformation of U.S. Industry, 1860–1920*. New York: Monthly Review Press, 1980.

Coffey, Dan. *The Myth of Japanese Efficiency: The World Car Industry in a Globalizing Age*. Cheltenham: Edgar Elgar, 2006.

Cohen, Lizabeth. *Making a New Deal: Industrial Workers in Chicago, 1919–1939*. New York: Cambridge University Press, 1990.

Cohen, Steven R. "From Industrial Democracy to Professional Adjustment: The Development of Industrial Sociology in the United States, 1900–1955." *Theory and Society*, 12, no. 1 (1983): 47–67.

Communications Workers of America (CWA). "Offshoring American Call Centers: The Threat to Consumers, Communities, and National Security!" October 2012, http://www.cwa-union.org/pages/why_shipping_call_center_jobs_overseas_hurts_us_back_home.

Cowie, Jefferson. *The Great Exception: The New Deal and the Limits of American Politics*. Princeton, NJ: Princeton University Press, 2016.

———. *Stayin' Alive: The 1970s and the Last Days of the Working Class*. New York: New Press, 2010.

Crawford, Margaret. *Building the Workingmen's Paradise: The Design of American Company Towns*. London: Verso, 1995.

Curtis, John D. "The Employment Status of

Instructional Staff Members in Higher Education," April 2014, http://www.aaup.org/sites/default/files/files/AAUP-InstrStaff2011-April2014.pdf.

Cusumano, Michael. *The Japanese Automobile Industry: Technology and Management at Nissan and Toyota*. Cambridge, MA: Harvard University Press, 1985.

Davenport, Thomas H. *Process Innovation: Reengineering Work Through Information Technology*. Boston, MA: Harvard Business School Press, 1993.

Davenport, Thomas H., and James E. Short. "The New Industrial Engineering: Information Technology and Process Design." *MIT Sloan Management Review*, July 15, 1990, http://sloanreview.mit.edu/article/the-new-industrial-engineering-information-technology-and-business-process-redesign/.

Davis, David Brion. *Inhuman Bondage: The Rise and Fall of Slavery in the New World*. New York: Oxford University Press, 2006.

Davis, Gerald F. "After the Corporation." *Politics and Society* 41, no. 2 (2013): 283–308.

——. "The Twilight of the Berle and Means Corporation." *Seattle University Law Review* 34 (2011): 1207–24.

——. *The Vanishing American Corporation: Navigating the Hazards of a New Economy*. Oakland, CA: Berrett-Koehler Publishers, 2016.

Davis, Louis, and Albert Cherns, eds. *The Quality of Working Life*. New York: Free Press, 1975.

Davis, Louis E. "The Design of Jobs." *Industrial Relations* 6, no. 1 (1966): 21–45.

Dawson, Patrick, and Janette Webb. "New Production Arrangements: The Totally Flexible Cage?" *Work, Employment, and Society* 3, no. 2 (1989): 221–38.

Dertouzos, Michael L. *Made in America: Regaining the Productive Edge*. Cambridge, MA: MIT Press, 1989.

DiPietro, Robin B., and Abraham Pizam. "Employee Alienation in the Quick Service Restaurant Industry." *Journal of Hospitality and Tourism Research* 32, no. 1 (2008): 22–39.

Domhoff, G. William. *Who Rules America?: The Triumph of the Corporate Rich*. 7th ed. New York: McGraw-Hill, 2014.

Dowling, Carlin. "Audit Support System Design and the Declarative Knowledge of Long-Term Users." *Journal of Emerging Technologies in Accounting* 5, no. 1 (2008): 99–108.

Drucker, Peter F. *Concept of the Corporation*. New York: John Day, 1946.

——. *Managing for Results: Economic Tasks and Risk-Taking Decisions*. New York: Harper & Row, 1964.

——. *Post-Capitalist Society*. New York: HarperBusiness, 1993.

Du Gay, Paul. *Consumption and Identity at Work*. London: Sage, 1996.

Earle, Carville. *Geographical Inquiry and American Historical Problems*. Stanford, CA: Stanford University Press, 1992.

Edgell, Stephen. *The Sociology of Work: Continuity and Change in Paid and Unpaid Work*. 2nd ed. London: Sage, 2012.

Edwards, Richard. *Contested Terrain: The Transformation of the Workplace in the Twentieth Century*. New York: Basic Books, 1979.

Ehrenreich, Barbara, and John Ehrenreich. "The Professional-Managerial Class." In *Between Labor and Capital*, edited by Pat Walker, 5–45. Boston: South End Press, 1979.

Eilbirt, Henry. "The Development of Personnel Management in the United States." *Business History Review* 33, no. 1 (1957): 345–64.

Elteren see van Elteren

Eltscher, Louis R., and Edward M. Young. *Curtiss-Wright: Greatness and Decline*. New York: Prentice-Hall International, 1998.

Engardio, Pete, Aaron Bernstein, and Manjeet Kripalani, "Is Your Job Next?," *Business Week* (February 3, 2013): 50–60.

Esch, Elizabeth, and David Roediger. "One Symptom of Originality: Race and the Management of Labour in the History of the United States." *Historical Materialism* 17, no. 4 (2009): 3–43.

Etzioni, Amitai. *A Comparative Analysis of Complex Organizations*. revised and enl. ed. New York: Free Press 1975.

Federal Aviation Administration (FAA). *Operational Use of Flight Path Management Systems*. Final Report of the Performance-Based Operations Rulemaking Committee/Commercial Aviation Safety Team Flight Deck Automation Working Group (Washington, D.C.: Federal Aviation Administration, September 5, 2013, https://www.faa.gov/about/office_org/headquarters_offices/avs/offices/afs/afs400/parc/parc_reco/media/2013/130908_PARC_FltDAWG_Final_Report_Recommendations.pdf.

Felstead, Alan, and Nick Jewson. *In Work, at Home: Towards an Understanding of Homeworking*. London: Routledge, 2000.

Forbath, William E. *Law and the Shaping of the American Labor Movement*. Cambridge, MA: Harvard University Press, 1991.

Ford, Martin. *Rise of the Robots: Technology and*

the Threat of a Jobless Future. New York: Basic Books, 2015.
Foucault, Michel. *Discipline and Punish: The Birth of the Prison*. New York: Vintage Books, 1975.
Fox, Alan. *Beyond Contract: Work, Power and Trust Relations*. London: Faber and Faber, 1974.
———. *Industrial Sociology and Industrial Relations*. London: HMSO, 1966.
Freeman, Richard B., and James L. Medoff. *What Do Unions Do?* New York: Basic Books, 1984.
Frenkel, Stephen J., Marek Korczynski, Karen A Shire, and May Tam. *On the Front Line: Organization of Work in the Information Economy*. Ithaca, NY: ILR Press, 1999.
Frey, Carl Benedikt, and Michael A. Osborne. "The Future of Employment: How Susceptible Are Jobs to Computerisation?" September 17, 2013, http://www.oxfordmartin.ox.ac.uk/downloads/academic/The_Future_of_Employment.pdf.
Frey, John P. "The Relationship of Scientific Management to Labor." *American Federationist* 20 (1913): 296–302.
Friedman, Andrew L. *Industry and Labour: Class Struggle at Work and Monopoly Capitalism*. London: Macmillan, 1977.
Friedman, Andy. "Responsible Autonomy Versus Direct Control Over the Labour Process." *Capital and Class* 1, no. 1 (1977): 43–58.
Fuchs, Christian. *Digital Labour and Karl Marx*. New York: Routledge, 2014.
Fujimoto, Takahiro. *The Evolution of a Manufacturing System at Toyota*. New York: Oxford University Press, 1999.
Fujita, Eishi. "Labor Process and Labor Management: The Case of Toyota." The Society of Social Sciences of Aichi Kyoiku University, 1988.
Fukuyama, Francis. *Trust: The Social Virtues and the Creation of Prosperity*. New York: Free Press, 1995.
Fuller, Linda, and Vicki Smith. "Consumers' Reports: Management by Customers in a Changing Economy." *Work, Employment, and Society* 5, no. 1 (1991): 1–16.
Gardner, Carl, and Julie Sheppard. *Consuming Passion: The Rise of Retail Culture*. London: Unwin Hyman, 1989.
Garrahan, Philip, and Paul Stewart. *The Nissan Empire: Flexibility at Work in a Local Economy*. London: Routledge, 1992.
Gartman, David. *Auto Slavery: The Labor Process in the American Automobile Industry, 1897–1950*. New Brunswick, NJ: Rutgers University Press, 1986.

———. "The Historical Roots of the Division of Labor in the American Automobile Industry." In *The Labor Process and Control of Labor: The Changing Nature of Work Relations in the Late Twentieth Century*, edited by Berch Berberoglu, 21–43. Westport, CT: Praeger, 1993.
Geary, Daniel. "C. Wright Mills and American Social Science." In *American Thought and Political Economy in the Twentieth Century*, edited by Nelson Lichtenstein, 135–56. Philadelphia: University of Pennsylvania Press, 2006.
Gee, James, Glynda Hull, and Colin Lankshear. *The New Work Order: Behind the Language of the New Capitalism*. Boulder, CO: Westview Press, 1996.
Gibney, Elizabeth. "Google AI Algorithm Masters Ancient Game of Go." January 27, 2016, http://www.nature.com/news/google-ai-algorithm-masters-ancient-game-of-go-1.19234.
Gilson, Mary B. "Review of F.J. Roethlisberger and William J. Dickson, *Management and the Worker*. Cambridge, MA: Harvard University Press, 1939." *American Journal of Sociology* 46, no. 1 (1940): 90–101.
Giroux, Henry A. "Neoliberalism, Corporate Culture, and the Promise of Higher Education: The University as a Democratic Public Sphere." *Harvard Educational Review* 72, no. 4 (2002): 425–63.
Glazer, Nona Y. *Women's Paid and Unpaid Labor: The Work Transfer in Health Care and Retailing*. Philadelphia, PA: Temple University Press, 1993.
Glovka-Spencer, Elaine. *Management and Labor in Imperial Germany: Ruhr Industrialists as Employers, 1896–1914*. New Brunswick, NJ: Rutgers University Press, 1984.
Goldfield, Michael. "Worker Insurgency, Radical Organization, and New Deal Legislation." *American Political Science Review* 83, no. 4 (1989): 1257–82.
Goldstein, Robert J. "Labor History Symposium: Political Repression of the American Labor Movement During Its Formative Years—A Comparative Perspective." *Labor History* 51, no. 2 (2010): 271–93.
———. *Political Repression in Modern America*. 2nd ed. Champaign: University of Illinois Press, 2001.
———. "Response in Labor History Symposium: Political Repression of the American Labor Movement During Its Formative Years—A Comparative Perspective." *Labor History* 51, no. 2 (2010): 310–15.

Gordon, David M. "Capitalist Development and the History of American Cities." In *Marxism and the Metropolis*, edited by William K. Tabb and Larry Sawers, 25–63. New York: Oxford University Press, 1978.

Gordon, David M., Richard Edwards, and Michael Reich. *Segmented Work, Divided Workers: The Historical Transformation of Labor in the United States*. New York: Cambridge University Press, 1982.

Gordon, Robert J. *The Rise and Fall of American Growth: The U.S. Standard of Living Since the Civil War*. Princeton, NJ: Princeton University Press, 2016.

Graebner, William. *The Engineering of Consent: Democracy and Authority in Twentieth-Century America*. Madison: University of Wisconsin Press, 1987.

———. "The Small Group and Democratic Social Engineering, 1900–1950." *Journal of Social Issues* 42, no. 1 (1986): 137–54.

Graham, Laurie. *On the Line at Subaru-Isuzu: The Japanese Model and the American Worker*. Ithaca, NY: ILR Press, 1995.

Grandey, Alicia A. "Emotion Regulation in the Workplace: A New Way to Conceptualize Emotional Behavior." *Journal of Occupational Health Psychology* 5, no. 1 (2000): 95–110.

Greenbaum, Joan M. *In the Name of Efficiency: Management Theory and Shopfloor Practice in Data-Processing Work*. Philadelphia, PA: Temple University Press, 1979.

———. *Windows on the Workplace: Technology, Jobs, and the Organization of Office Work*. New York: Monthly Review Press, 2004.

Greenhouse, Steve. "Temp Workers at Microsoft Win Lawsuit." *New York Times*, December 13, 2000, http://www.nytimes.com/2000/12/13/business/technology-temp-workers-at-microsoft-win-lawsuit.html?pagewanted=print.

Grint, Keith. "Reengineering History: Social Resonances and Business Process Engineering." *Organization* 1, no. 1 (1994): 179–210.

Gross, James J. "The Emerging Field of Emotion Regulation: An Integrative Review." *Review of General Psychology* 2, no. 3 (1998): 273–99.

Gross, James J., and Oliver P. John. "Mapping the Domain of Expressivity: Multimethod Evidence for a Hierarchical Model." *Journal of Personality and Social Psychology* 74, no. 1 (1998): 170–91.

Gutman, Herbert G. *Work, Culture, and Society in Industrializing America*. New York: Alfred A. Knopf 1976.

Haber, Samuel. *Efficiency and Uplift: Scientific Management in the Progressive Era, 1890–1920*. Chicago: University of Chicago Press, 1964.

Hacker, Jacob S. *The Great Risk Shift: The Assault on American Jobs, Families, Health Care, and Retirement and How You Can Fight Back*. New York: Oxford University Press, 2006.

Hammer, Michael. *Beyond Reengineering: How the Process-Centered Organization Is Changing Our Work and Our Lives*. New York: HarperBusiness, 1996.

———. "Reengineering Work: Don't Automate, Obliterate." *Harvard Business Review* 90, no. 4 (1990): 104–12.

Hammer, Michael, and James Champy. *Reengineering the Corporation: A Manifesto for Business Revolution*. New York: HarperBusiness, 1993.

Harrison, Bennett. *Lean and Mean: The Changing Landscape of Corporate Power in the Age of Flexibility*. New York: Basic Books, 1994.

Harvey, David. *A Brief History of Neoliberalism*. Oxford: Oxford University Press, 2005.

———. *The Condition of Postmodernity: An Enquiry into the Origins of Cultural Change*. Oxford: Blackwell, 1989.

———. "Flexibility: Threat or Opportunity?" *Socialist Review* 21, no. 1 (1991): 65–78.

Hayes, Dennis, and Robin Wynyard, eds. *The McDonaldization of Higher Education*. Westport, CT: Praeger, 2002.

Head, Simon. "Bernie Sanders: The Quiet Revolt." *The New York Review of Books*, December 23, 2015, http://www.nybooks.com/daily/2015/12/23/bernie-sanders-quiet-revolt/.

———. *Mindless: Why Smarter Machines Are Making Dumber Humans*. New York: Basic Books, 2014.

———. *The New Ruthless Economy: Work and Power in the Digital Age*. New York: Oxford University Press, 2003.

Heims, Steve. "Kurt Lewin and Social Change." *Journal of the History of the Behavioral Sciences* 14, no. 3 (1978): 238–41.

Hirschhorn, Larry. *Beyond Mechanization: Work and Technology in a Postindustrial Age*. Cambridge, MA: MIT Press, 1984.

Hobsbawm, Eric. *The Age of Empire: 1895–1914*. London: Weidenfeld & Nicholson, 1987.

Hochschild, Arlie Russell. *The Managed Heart: Commercialization of Human Feeling*. Berkeley: University of California Press, 1983.

Hoff, Timothy. "Deskilling and Adaptation Among Primary Care Physicians Using Two Work Innovations." *Health Care Management Review* 36, no. 4 (2011): 338–48.

Hofstadter, Richard. *The Age of Reform: From Bryan to FDR*. New York: Vintage Books, 1955.

Hornung, Alfred. "Contribution to Debate on 'Transculturations: American Studies in a Globalizing World—The Globalizing World in American Studies.'" *Amerikastudien/American Studies* 47, no. 1 (2002): 110–14.

Hornyak, Tim. "Towel-Folding Robot Won't Do the Dishes." CNET, March 31, 2010, http://www.news.cnet.com/8301-17938_105-10471898-1.

Hounshell, David A. *From the American System to Mass Production, 1800–1932: The Development of Manufacturing Technology in the United States*. Baltimore, MD: Johns Hopkins University Press, 1984.

House Committee on Education and the Work Force, Democratic Staff, United States House of Representatives. "The Just-In Time Professor: A Staff Report Summarizing Eforum Responses on the Working Conditions of Contingent Faculty in Higher Education." January 2014, http://www.democrats.edworkforce.house.gov/sites/democrats.edworkforce.house.gov/files/documents/1.24.14-AdjunctEforumReport.pdf.

Hulsman, Bernard. "Het Alziende Oog Van Steve Jobs." *NRC Handelsblad*, March 3, 2016, http://www.nrc.nl/next/2016/03/03/het-alziende-oog-van-steve-jobs-1594333.

Hunnies, Gerry, David Garson, and John Case, eds. *Workers' Control: A Reader on Labor and Social Change*. New York: Random House, 1973.

Hutton, Patrick H. *The Cult of the Revolutionary Tradition: The Blanquists in French Politics, 1864–1893*, Berkeley: University of California Press, 1981.

Huws, Ursula. *The Making of a Cybertariat*. New York: Monthly Review Press, 2003.

International Labour Organization (ILO). "Effects of Mechanization and Automation in Offices: III." *International Labour Review* 81, no. 4 (1960): 350–69.

Jacobs, James. "Lean Production and Training: The Case of a Japanese Supplier Firm." In *Lean Work: Empowerment and Exploitation in the Global Auto Industry*, edited by Steve Babson, 311–25. Detroit: Wayne State University Press, 1995.

Jacoby, Daniel. *Laboring for Freedom: A New Look at the History of Labor in America*. Armonk, NY: M.E. Sharpe, 1998.

Jacoby, Sanford M. "Employee Attitude Testing at Sears, Roebuck and Company 1938–1960." *Business History Review* 60, no. 4 (1986): 602–32.

———. *Employing Bureaucracy: Managers, Unions, and the Transformation of Work in the 20th Century*. rev. ed. Mahwah, NJ: Lawrence Erlbaum, 2004.

———. *Modern Manors: Welfare Capitalism Since the New Deal*. Princeton, NJ: Princeton University Press, 1997.

———. "Union-Management Cooperation in the United States: Lessons from the 1920s." *Industrial and Labor Relations Review* 37, no. 1 (1983): 18–33.

Janis, Irving L. *Victims of Groupthink: A Psychological Study of Foreign-Policy Decisions and Fiascoes*. Boston: Houghton, 1972.

Johnson, Simon, and James Kwak. *Thirteen Bankers*. New York: Pantheon, 2010.

Joyce, Patrick. *Work, Society, and Politics: The Culture of the Factory in Late Victorian England*. New Brunswick, NJ: Rutgers University Press, 1980.

Kanter, Rosabeth Moss. "Power Failure in Management Circuits." *Harvard Business Review* 57, no. 4 (1979): 65–75.

Kaplan, Robert S., and David P. Norton. "The Balanced Scorecard—Measures That Drive Performance." *Harvard Business Review* 70, no. 1 (1992): 71–85.

———. *Strategy Maps: Converting Intangible Assets into Tangible Outcomes*. Boston, MA: Harvard Business School Press, 2004.

Keller, Morton. "The Making of the Modern Corporation." *Wilson Quarterly* 21, no. 4 (1997): 58–69.

Kellermann, Arthur L., and Spencer S. Jones. "What It Will Take to Achieve the As-Yet-Unfulfilled Promises of Health Information Technology." *Health Affairs* 32, no. 1 (2013): 63–68.

Kenney, Martin, and Richard L. Florida. *Beyond Mass Production: The Japanese System and Its Transfer to the U.S.* New York: Oxford University Press, 1993.

Kerfoot, Deborah, and David Knights. "Empowering the Quality Worker: The Managerial Evangelism of Total Quality in Financial Services." In *Making Quality Critical*, edited by Adrian Wilkinson and Hugh Willmott, 219–39. London: Routledge, 1994.

Kerr, Clark, John T. Dunlop, Frederick Harbison, and Charles Meyers. *Industrialism and Industrial Man: The Problems of Labor and Management in Economic Growth*. Cambridge, MA: Harvard University Press, 1960.

Kerr, Clark, and Lloyd H. Fisher. "Plant Sociology: The Elite and the Aborigines." In

Common Frontiers of the Social Sciences, edited by Mirra Komarovsky, 281–309. New York: Free Press, 1957.

Ketchum, Lyman D., and Eric Trist. *All Teams Are Not Treated Equal: How Employee Empowerment Really Works*. Thousand Oaks, CA: Sage, 1992.

Keynes, John Maynard. "Economic Possibilities for Our Grandchildren." In *Essays in Persuasion*, 358–73. New York: W.W. Norton, 1963 [1930].

Keyssar, Alexander. *Out of Work: The First Century of Unemployment in Massachusetts*. Cambridge: Cambridge University Press, 1986.

Kleinke, J. D. *Bleeding Edge: The Business of Health Care in the New Century*. Gaithersburg, MD: Aspen Publishers, 1998.

Korczynski, Marek. "The Mystery Customer: Continuing Absences in the Sociology of Service Work." *Sociology* 43, no. 5 (2009): 952–67.

Koza, John R. "Human-Competitive Results Produced by Genetic Programming." In *Genetic Programming and Evolvable Machines* 11, no. 3 (2010): 251–84, http://www.geneticprogramming.com/GPEM2010article.pdf.

Kraft, Philip. *Programmers and Managers: The Routinization of Computer Programming in the United States*. New York: Springer-Verlag, 1977.

———. "To Control and Inspire: U.S. Management in the Age of Computer Information Systems and Global Production." In *Rethinking the Labor Process*, edited by Mark Wardell, Thomas L. Steiger and Peter Meiksins, 17–36. Albany, NY: State University of New York Press, 1999.

Krishnan, Rama. "Democratic Participation in Decision Making by Employees in American Corporations." *Academy of Management Journal* 17, no. 2 (1974): 339–47.

Kronz, Andreas. *Managing of Process Key Performance Indicators as Part of the ARIS Methodology*. Berlin: Springer, 2006.

Kunda, Gideon. *Engineering Culture: Control and Commitment in a High-Tech Corporation*. Philadelphia, PA: Temple University Press, 1992.

Kusterer, Kenneth C. *Know-How on the Job: The Important Working Knowledge of "Unskilled" Workers*. Boulder, CO: Westview Press, 1978.

Landro, Laura. "Costs, Politics of Health Care Will Dominate Debate on '03." *Wall Street Journal*, January 8, 2003.

Landsberger, Henry A. *Hawthorne Revisited: Management and the Worker: Its Critics, and Developments in Human Relations in Industry*. Ithaca, NY: Cornell University Press, 1958.

Lasch, Christopher. *Haven in a Heartless World: The Family Besieged*. New York: W.W. Norton, 1977.

———. *The True and Only Heaven: Progress and Its Critics*. New York: W.W. Norton, 1991.

Laurie, Bruce. *Artisans into Workers: Labor in Nineteenth-Century America*. New York: Noonday Press, 1989.

Lee, John D. "Human Factors and Ergonomics in Automatic Design." In *Handbook of Human Factors and Ergonomics*, 3rd ed., edited by Gavriel Salvendy. Hoboken, NJ: Wiley, 2006.

Leffingwell, William H. *Office Management, Principles and Practice*. Chicago: A. W. Shaw Company, 1925.

———. *Scientific Office Management*. Chicago: A.W. Shaw Company, 1917.

———. *Textbook of Office Management*. 2nd ed. New York: McGraw-Hill, 1932.

Leiby, James. *a History of Social Welfare and Social Work in the United States*. New York: Columbia University Press, 1978.

Leidner, Robin. *Fast Food, Fast Talk: Service Work and the Routinization of Everyday Life*. Berkeley: University of California Press, 1993.

———. "Rethinking Questions of Control: Lessons from McDonald's." In *Working in the Service Sector*, edited by Cameron Lynn MacDonald and Carmen Sirianni, 29–49. Philadelphia, PA: Temple University Press, 1996.

Levitin, Daniel J. "Book Review of the *Glass Cage* by Nicholas Carr." *Wall Street Journal*, October 10, 2014.

Levitt, Theodore. "The Production-Line Approach to Service." *Harvard Business Review* 50, no. 5 (1972): 41–52.

Levy, Peter B. *The New Left and Labor in the 1960s*. Urbana: University of Illinois Press, 1994.

Licht, Walter. *Working for the Railroad: The Organization of Work in the Nineteenth Century*. Princeton, NJ: Princeton University Press, 1983.

Lichtenstein, Nelson. *The Retail Revolution: How Wal-Mart Created a Brave New World of Business*. New York: Metropolitan Books, 2009.

———. *State of the Union: A Century of American Labor*. Princeton, NJ: Princeton University Press, 2002.

———. "Wal-Mart and the New World Order: A Template for Twenty-First Century Capitalism?" *New Labor Forum* 14, no. 1 (2005): 21–25.

———. "Wal-Mart's Authoritarian Culture." *New York Times*, June 21, 2011, http://www.nytimes.com/2011/06/22/opinion/22Lichtenstein.html.

Lipset, Seymour M., and Gary Marks. *It Didn't Happen Here: Why Socialism Failed in the United States*. New York: W.W. Norton, 2000.

Litterer, Joseph A. "Systematic Management: Design for Organizational Recoupling in American Manufacturing Firms." *Business History Review* 37, no. 4 (1963): 369–91.

———. "Systematic Management: The Search for Order and Integration." *Business History Review* 35, no. 4 (1961): 461–76.

Littler, Craig R. *The Development of the Labour Process in Capitalist Societies*. London: Heinemann Educational, 1982.

Love, John F. *McDonald's Behind the Arches*. revised ed. New York: Bantam, 1995.

Lown, Beth, and Dayron Rodriguez. "Commentary: Lost in Translation? How Electronic Health Records Structure Communication, Relationships, and Meaning." *Academic Medicine* 87, no. 4 (2012): 392–94.

Lynd, Robert S., and Helen M. Lynd. *Middletown in Transition: A Study in Cultural Conflicts*. New York: Harcourt Brace Jovanovich, 1937.

MacDuffie, John. "Workers' Role in Lean Production: The Implications for Workers Representation." In *Lean Work: Empowerment and Exploitation in the Global Auto Industry*, edited by Steve Babson, 54–69. Detroit: Wayne State University, 1995.

Mann, Michael. *The Sources of Social Power, Volume II: The Rise of Classes and Nation States, 1760–1914*. Cambridge: Cambridge University Press, 1993.

March, James G., and Herbert A. Simon. *Organizations*. New York: Wiley, 1958.

Marglin, Stephen A. "What Do Bosses Do? The Origins and Functions of Hierarchy in Capitalist Production." *The Review of Radical Political Economics* 6, no. 2 (1974): 33–60.

Markoff, John. *Machines of Loving Grace: The Quest for Common Ground Between Humans and Robots*. New York: Ecco, 2015.

Marrow, Alfred J. *The Practical Theorist: The Life and Work of Kurt Lewin*. New York: Basic Books, 1969.

Mayo, Elton. *The Social Problems of an Industrial Civilization*. Boston, MA: Graduate School of Business Administration, Harvard University, 1945.

McCall, Holli, Vicky Arnold, and Steve G. Sutton. "Use of Knowledge Management Systems and the Impact on the Acquisition of Explicit Knowledge." *Journal of Information Systems* 22, no. 2 (2008): 77–101.

McCreary, Eugene C. "Social Welfare and Business: The Krupp Welfare Program, 1860–1914." *Business History Review* 42, no. 1 (1968): 24–49.

McGregor, Douglas. *The Human Side of Enterprise*. New York: McGraw-Hill, 1960.

McKinsey Global Institute. *A Future That Works: Automation, Employment, and Productivity*, January 2017, https://fredzimny.wordpress.com/2017/01/17/mckinsey-global-institute-a-future-that-works-automation-employment-and-productivity-job-jobs/.

———. *Manufacturing Productivity*. Washington, D.C., 1993.

McQuaid, Kim. *A Response to Industrialism: Liberal Businessmen and the Evolving Spectrum of Capitalist Reform, 1886–1960*. New York: Garland, 1986.

Meiksins, Peter. "Labor and Monopoly Capital for the 1990s: A Review and Critique of the Labor Process Debate." *Monthly Review* 46, no. 6 (1994): 45–59.

Meister, David. *The History of Human Factors and Ergonomics*. Mahwah, NJ: Lawrence Erlbaum Associates, 1999.

Merton, Robert K. *Social Theory and Social Structure*. 2nd enl. ed. New York: Free Press, 1968.

Meyer, Stephen. "The Degradation of Work Revisited: Workers and Technology in the American Auto Industry, 1900–2000." 2004, http://www/autolife.umd.umich.edu.

———. *The Five-Dollar Day: Labor Management and Social Control in the Ford Motor Company, 1908–1921*. Albany, NY: State University of New York Press, 1981.

Milkman, Ruth, and Cydney Pullman. "Technological Change in an Auto Assembly Plant: The Impact on Workers' Tasks and Skills." *Work and Occupations* 18, no. 2 (1991): 123–47.

Miller, Peter, and Ted O'Leary. "Hierarchies and American Ideals 1900–1940." *The Academy of Management Review* 14, no. 2 (1989): 250–65.

Mills, C. Wright. "The Contribution of Sociology to Studies of Industrial Relations," in *Proceedings of the First Annual Conference of the Industrial Relations Research Association*, edited by Milton Derber, 199–222. Urbana, IL: Industrial Relations Research Association, 1948.

———. *The New Men of Power: America's Labor Leaders*. New York: Harcourt, Brace, 1948.

———. *White Collar: The American Middle*

Classes. New York: Oxford University Press, 1951.
Mizruchi, Mark S. "Berle and Means Revisited: The Governance and Power of Large Corporations." *Theory and Society* 33, no. 5 (2004): 579–617.
Monson, Philip, Thomas Gumz, Frank Nostrame, and Leah Busque. "IBM Redbooks: Lotus Domino Domain Monitoring." IBM International Technical Support Organization, 2005, http://www.redbooks.ibm.com/redpapers/pdfs/redp4089.pdf.
Montgomery, David. *The Fall of the House of Labor: The Workplace, the State, and American Labor Activism, 1865–1925*. New York: Cambridge University Press, 1987.
———. "The 'New Unionism' and the Transformation of Workers' Consciousness in America, 1909–22." *Journal of Social History* 7, no. 4 (1974): 509–29.
———. *Workers' Control in America: Studies in the History of Work, Technology, and Labor Struggles*. New York: Cambridge University Press, 1979.
———. "Workers' Control of Machine Production in the Nineteenth Century." *Labor History* 17, no. 4 (1976): 488–91.
Moody, Kim. *U.S. Labor in Trouble and Transition*. London: Verso, 2007.
Moravec, Hans P. *Mind Children: The Future of Robot and Human Intelligence*. Cambridge, MA: Harvard University Press, 1988.
Munro, Rolland. "Governing the New Province of Quality: Autonomy, Accounting, and the Dissemination of Accountability." In *Making Quality Critical: Studies in Social Change*, edited by Adrian Wilkinson and Hugh Willmott, 127–55. London: Routledge, 1994.
Nadin, Mihai. "Information and Semiotic Processes: The Semiotics of Computation." *Cybernetics and Human Knowing* 18, no. 1–2 (2011): 153–75.
National Center on Education and the Economy. "America's Choice: High Skills or Low Wages!" In *Report of the Commission on the Skills of the American Workforce*. Rochester, NY, 1990, http://www.eric.ed.gov/?id=ED323297.
National Employment Project. "14 Cities & States Approved $15 Minimum Wage in 2015." December 21, 2015, http://www.nelp.org/content/uploads/PR-Minimum-Wage-Year-End-15.pdf.
Nelson, Daniel. *Frederick W. Taylor and the Rise of Scientific Management*. Madison: University of Wisconsin Press, 1980.

———. *Managers and Workers: Origins of the New Factory System in the United States, 1880–1920*. Madison: University of Wisconsin Press, 1975.
———. *Managers and Workers: Origins of the Twentieth-Century Factory System in the United States, 1880–1920*. 2nd ed. Madison: University of Wisconsin Press, 1995.
Nicholson, Karen P. "The McDonaldization of Academic Libraries and the Values of Transformational Change." *College & Research Libraries* 67, no. 3 (2015): 328–38.
Noble, David F. *Forces of Production: A Social History of Industrial Automation*. New York: Alfred A. Knopf, 1984.
North, Douglas C., Terry. L. Anderson, and Peter J. Hill. *Growth and Welfare in the American Past: A New Economic History*. 3rd ed. Englewood Cliffs, NJ: Prentice-Hall, 1983.
Nye, David E. *America's Assembly Line*. Cambridge, MA: MIT Press, 2013.
Odiorne, George S. *Management by Objectives: A System of Management Leadership*. New York: Pitman Publishers Corp., 1965.
Ofri, Danielle. "The Doctor Vs. the Computer." *New York Times*, December 30, 2010.
Ohno, Taiichi. *Toyota Production System: Beyond Large-Scale Production*. Cambridge, MA: Productivity Press, 1988.
O'Toole, James, ed. *Work and the Quality of Life*. Cambridge, MA: MIT Press, 1974.
Pabon, Carlos E. "Regulating Capitalism: The Taylor Society and Political Economy in the Interwar Period." Doctoral dissertation, Graduate School of University of Massachusetts Amherst, 1992, http://www.scholarworks.umass.edu/dissertations/AAI9305877.
Pahl, Ray E., ed. *On Work: Historical, Comparative and Theoretical Approaches*. Oxford: Blackwell, 1988.
Palmer, Bryan. "Class Conception and Conflict: The Thrust for Efficiency, Managerial Views of Labor and the Working Class Rebellion." *Review of Radical Political Economics* 7, no. 2 (1975): 31–49.
Papke, David R. *The Pullman Case: The Clash of Labor and Capital in Industrial America*. Lawrence: University Press of Kansas, 1999.
Parasuraman, Raja, and Dietrich H. Manzey. "Complacency and Bias in Human Uses of Automation: An Attentional Integration." *Human Factors* 52, no. 3 (2010): 381–410.
Parasuraman, Raja, Thomas B. Sheridan, and Christopher D. Wickens. "A Model for Types and Levels of Human Interaction with Automation." *IEEE Transactions of Systems,*

Man, and Cybernetics 30, no. 3 (2000): 286–97.

Parker, Mike. "Industrial Relations Myth and Shop-Floor Reality: The 'Team Concept' in the Auto Industry." In *Industrial Democracy in America: The Ambiguous Promise*, edited by Nelson Lichtenstein and Howell John Harris, 249–73 New York: Cambridge University Press, 1993.

Parker, Mike, and Jane Slaughter. *Choosing Sides: Unions and the Team Concept*. Boston, MA: South End Press, 1988.

———. "Unions and Management by Stress." In *Lean Work: Empowerment and Exploitation in the Global Auto Industry*, edited by Steve Babson, 41–54. Detroit: Wayne State University Press, 1995.

———. *Working Smart: A Union Guide to Participation Programs and Reengineering*. Detroit: Labor Notes, 1994.

Parsons, Talcott. *The Social System*. Glencoe, IL: The Free Press, 1951.

Picchi, Aimee. "Will the U.S. Raise the Minimum Wage to $15?" *CBS News, Money Watch*, November 21, 2015, http://www.cbsnews.com/news/will-the-u-s-raise-the-minimum-wage-to-15/.

Pierce, Richard J. *Leadership, Perspective, and Restructuring for Total Quality: An Essential Instrument to Improve Market Share and Productivity*. Milwaukee, WI: ASQC Quality Press, 1991.

Pine, B. Joseph. *Mass Customization: The New Frontier in Business Competition*. Boston, MA: Harvard Business School Press, 1993.

Piore, Michael J., and Charles F. Sabel. *The Second Industrial Divide: Possibilities for Prosperity*. New York: Basic Books, 1984.

Polanyi, Karl. *The Great Transformation*. Boston, MA: Beacon Press, 1957 [1944].

Pontier, Matthijs A., Guy Widdershoven, and Johan F. Hoorn. "Moral Coppélia—Combining Ratio with Affect in Ethical Reasoning " in *Advances in Artificial Intelligence—Iberamia 2012. Proceedings of 13th Ibero-American Conference on AI, November 13–16, 2012, Cartagena De Indias, Colombia*, Edited by Juan Pavón, Néstor D. Duque-Méndez and Rubén Fuentes-Fernández, 442–51. Berlin-Heidelberg: Springer, 2012.

Povyakalo, Andrey A., Eugenio Alberdi, Lorenzo Strigini, and Peter Ayton. "How to Discriminate Between Computer-Aided and Computer-Hindered Decisions: A Case Study in Mammography." *Medical Decision Making* 33, no. 1 (2013): 98–107.

Preston, William, Jr. *Aliens and Dissenters: Federal Suppression of Radicals, 1903–1933*. Urbana: University of Illinois Press, 1994.

Ramirez, Bruno. *When Workers Fight: The Politics of Industrial Relations in the Progressive Era, 1896–1916*. Westport, CT: Greenwood Press, 1978.

Reich, Robert B. *The Work of Nations: Preparing Ourselves for 21st-Century Capitalism*. New York: Knopf, 1991.

Renshaw, Patrick. *The Wobblies*. Garden City, NJ: Doubleday, 1967.

Riesman, David. *The Lonely Crowd: A Study of the Changing American Character*. New Haven, CT: Yale University Press, 1950.

Rinehart, James W., Christopher V. Huxley, and David Robertson. *Just Another Car Factory?: Lean Production and Its Discontents*. Ithaca, NY: ILR Press, 1997.

Ritzer, George. *The McDonaldization of Society: An Investigation into the Changing Character of Contemporary Social Life*. revised ed. Thousand Oaks, CA: Pine Forge Press, 1996.

———. *The McDonaldization Thesis: Explorations and Extensions*. Thousand Oaks, CA: Sage, 1998.

Roediger, David R. *Working Toward Whiteness—How America's Immigrants Became White: The Strange Journey from Ellis Island to the Suburbs*. New York: Basic Books, 2005.

Roediger, David R., and Elizabeth D. Esch. *The Production of Difference: Race and the Management of Labor in U.S. History*. New York: Oxford University Press, 2012.

Roethlisberger, Fritz J., and William J. Dickson. *Management and the Worker*. Cambridge, MA: Harvard University Press, 1939.

Rogers, Jackie Krasas. "Just a Temp: Experience and Structure of Alienation in Temporary Clerical Work." *Work and Occupations* 22, no. 2 (1995): 137–66.

Roose, Kevin. "The Sharing Economy Isn't About Trust, It's About Desperation." *New York Magazine*, April 24, 2014, http://www.nymag.com/daily/intelligencer/2014/04/sharing-economy-is-about-desperation.html.

Rose, Michael. *Industrial Behaviour: Research and Control*. 2nd ed. London: Penguin, 1988.

Ross, Andrew. *No-Collar: The Humane Workplace and Its Hidden Costs*. New York: Basic Books, 2003.

Rouf, Emran, Jeff Whittle, Ma Lu, and Mark D. Schwartz. "Computers in the Exam Room: Differences in Physician-Patient Interaction May Be Due to Physician Experience" *Jour-*

nal of General Internal Medicine 22, No. 1 (2007): 43–48.
Roy, William G. *Socializing Capital: The Rise of the Large Industrial Corporation in America*. Princeton, NJ: Princeton University Press, 1997.
Royle, Tony. *Working for McDonald's in Europe: The Unequal Struggle?* London: Routledge, 2000.
Ruben, Brent D. "Toward a Balanced Scorecard for Higher Education: Rethinking the College and University Excellence Indicators Framework." *Higher Education Forum* (Fall 1999), http://www.qci.rutgers.edu.
Ryan, Kathleen, and Daniel K. Oestreich. *Driving Fear Out of the Workplace: How to Overcome the Invisible Barriers to Quality, Productivity, and Innovation*. San Francisco: Jossey-Bass Publishers, 1991.
Sarros, J.C., George A.. Tanweski, Richard P. Winter, J.C. Santora, and I.L. Densten. "Work Alienation and Organizational Leadership." *British Journal of Management* 13, no. 4 (2002): 295–304.
Saval, Nikil. *Cubed: A Secret History of the Workplace*. New York: Anchor Books, 2014.
Scarborough, William K. *The Overseer: Plantation Management in the Old South*. Baton Rouge, LA: Louisiana State University Press, 1966.
Scheer, August-Wilhelm, Ferri Abolhassan, Wolfgang Joost, and Mathias Kirchner, eds. *Business Process Automation*. Berlin: Springer, 2004.
Scheer, August-Wilhelm, Jost Wolfram, Helge Hess, and Adrea Kronz, eds. *Corporate Performance Management: ARIS in Practice*. Berlin: Springer, 2005.
Schlichter, Sumner H. *The Turnover of Factory Labor*. New York: D. Appleton, 1919.
Schlosser, Eric. *Fast Food Nation: The Dark Side of the All-American Meal*. New York: Perennial, 2002.
Schmitz, Christopher J. *The Growth of Big Business in the United States and Western Europe, 1850–1939*. London: Macmillan, 1993.
Schneirov, Richard, Shelton Stromquist, and Nick Salvatore. *The Pullman Strike and the Crisis of the 1890s: Essays on Labor and Politics*. Urbana: University of Illinois Press, 1999.
Schobel, Kurt, and Cam Scholey. "Balanced Scorecards in Education: Focusing on Financial Strategies." *Measuring Business Excellence* 16, no. 3 (2012): 17–28.
Schonberger, Richard. *Japanese Manufacturing Techniques: Nine Hidden Lessons in Simplicity*. New York: Free Press, 1982.

Schor, Juliet. "Debating the Sharing Economy." October 2014, http://www.greattransition.org/images/GTI_publications/Schor_Debating_the_Sharing_Economy.pdf.
Schuler, Randall S., and Drew L. Harris. *Managing Quality: The Primer for Middle Managers*. Reading, MA: Addison-Wesley, 1992.
Selznick, Philip. *Law, Society, and Industrial Justice*. New York: Russell Sage Foundation, 1969.
Sennett, Richard. *The Corrosion of Character: The Personal Consequences of Work in the New Capitalism*. New York: W.W. Norton, 1998.
———. *The Craftsman*. New Haven, CT: Yale University Press, 2008.
———. *The Culture of the New Capitalism*. New Haven, CT: Yale University Press, 2006.
Shapiro, Stanley. "The Great War and Reform: Liberals and Labor 1917–1919." *Labor History* 12, no. 3 (1971): 323–44.
Sheppard, Harold I. "The Social and Historical Philosophy of Elton Mayo." *Antioch Review*, 10, no. 3 (1950): 396–406.
Shingo, Shigeo. *A Revolution in Manufacturing: The SMED System*. Stamford, CT: Productivity Press, 1985.
———. *Study of Toyota Production System: From Industrial Engineering Viewpoint*. Tokyo: Japan Management Association, 1981.
Silver, Beverly J. *Forces of Labor: Workers' Movements and Globalization Since 1870*. New York: Cambridge University Press, 2003.
Simons, Robert. *Levers of Control: How Managers Use Innovative Control Systems to Drive Strategic Renewal*. Boston, MA: Harvard Business School Press, 1995.
Skidelsky, Robert "The Programmed Prospect Before Us. Review of *Mindless: Why Smarter Machines Are Making Dumber Humans* by Simon Head. Basic Books, 2014." *New York Review of Books*, April 3, 2014, http://www.nybooks.com/articles/2014/04/03/programmed-prospect-us/.
Slamecka, Norman J., and Peter Graf. "The Generation Effect: Delineation of a Phenomenon." *Journal of Experimental Psychology: Human Learning and Memory* 4, no. 6 (1978): 592–604.
Sloan, Alfred P. *My Years with General Motors*. Garden City, NY: Doubleday, 1964.
Smith, Chris. "Rediscovery of the Labour Process." In *Sage Handbook of the Sociology of Work and Employment*, edited by Stephen Edgell, Heidi Gottfried and Edward Granter, 205–24. London: Sage, 2015.
Smith, Chris, and Paul Thompson. "Reevaluating the Labor Process Debate." In *Rethink-

ing the Labor Process, edited by Mark Wardell, Thomas L. Steiger and Peter Meiksins, 205–31. Albany, NY: State University of New York Press, 1999.
Smith, Hedrick. Who Stole the American Dream? New York: Random House, 2012.
Smith, Rogers M. "Beyond Tocqueville, Myrdal, and Hartz: The Multiple Traditions in America." American Political Science Review 87, no. 3 (1993): 549–66.
Sorensen, Charles E. My Forty Years with Ford. New York: W.W. Norton, 1956.
Srivastava, Snigdha, and Nik Theodore. "A Long Jobless Recovery: Information Technology Markets After the Bursting of the High-Tech Bubble." Working USA 8, no. 3 (2005): 315–26.
Stable, Donald. Prophets of Order: The Rise of the New Class, Technocracy and Socialism in America. Boston, MA: South End Press, 1984.
Stampp, Kenneth M. The Peculiar Institution: Slavery in the Ante-Bellum South. New York: Vintage Books, 1956.
Starbuck, William H. "Organizational Growth and Development " in Handbook of Organizations, Edited by James G. March, 451–83. Chicago: Rand McNally, 1965.
Stark, David. "Class Struggle and the Transformation of the Labor Process: A Relational Approach." Theory and Society 9, no. 1 (1980): 89–130.
Stone, Katherine Van Wezel. "The Origins of Job Structures in the Steel Industry." In Labor Market Segmentation, edited by Richard C. Edwards, Michael Reich and David M. Gordon, 27–84. Lexington, MA: D.C. Heath, 1975.
Stromquist, Shelton. "United States of America." In The Formation of Labor Movements 1870–1914, edited by Marcel van der Linden and Jürgen Rojahn, 543–77. Leiden: E.J. Brill, 1990.
Sunstein, Cass R. Legal Reasoning and Political Conflict. New York: Oxford University Press, 1996.
Taylor, Frederick W. "The Principles of Scientific Management" [1911], repr. In Frederick W. Taylor, Scientific Management. New York: Harper and Row, 1964.
———. "Shop Management" [1903], repr. In Frederick W. Taylor, Scientific Management. New York: Harper and Row, 1964.
———. "Why Manufacturers Dislike College Students." Proceedings of the Society for the Promotion of Engineering Education 18 (1909): 87.
Taylor, Phil, and Peter Bain. "'An Assembly Line in the Head': Work and Employee Relations in the Call Center." Industrial Relations Journal 30, no. 2 (1999): 110–17.
Taylor, Stephen, Sheena Smith, and Phil Lyon. "McDonaldization and Consumer Choice in the Future: An Illusion or the Next Marketing Revolution?" In McDonaldization Revisited: Critical Essays on Consumer Culture, edited by Mark Alfino, John S. Caputo and Robin Wynyard, 105–20. Westport, CT: Praeger, 1998.
Thompson, Paul. The Nature of Work: An Introduction to Debates on the Labour Process. London: Macmillan, 1983.
Tiffin, Joseph. "How Psychologists Serve Industry." Personnel Journal 36, no. 7 (1958): 372–76.
Trachtenberg, Alan. The Incorporation of America: Culture and Society in the Gilded Age. New York: Hill and Wang, 1982.
Tsutsui, William M. "W. Edwards Deming and the Origins of Quality Control in Japan." Journal of Japanese Studies 22, no. 2 (1996): 295–325.
Turkle, Sherry. Simulation and Its Discontents. Cambridge, MA: MIT Press, 2009.
U.S. Congress, Office of Technology Assessment. Automation of American Offices. Washington, D.C.: U.S. Government Printing Office, December 1985.
United States Department of Health Education and Welfare. Work in America: Report of a Special Task Force to the Secretary of Health, Education, and Welfare. Cambridge, MA: MIT Press, 1973.
Useem, Michael. "Business Restructuring, Management Control, and Corporate Organization." Theory and Society 19, no. 6 (1990): 681–707.
Van Beinum, Hans. "Playing Hide and Seek with QWL." QWL Focus, Ontario Ministry of Labour, 5, no. 1 (1986): 7.
van der Linden, Marcel. "Re-Constructing the Origins of Modern Labor Management." Labor History 51, no. 4 (2010): 509–22.
van Elteren, Mel. "Discontinuities in Kurt Lewin's Psychology of Work: Conceptual and Cultural Shifts Between His German and American Research." Sociétés Contemporaines 13, March (1993): 71–93.
———. Labor and the American Left: An Analytical History. Jefferson, NC: McFarland, 2011.
———. "Psychology and Sociology of Work Within the Anglo-American Orbit" in Dutch-American Relations 1945–1969: A Partnership. Illusions and Facts, Edited by Hans Loe-

ber, 153–78. Assen/Maastricht: Van Gorcum, 1992.

Veblen, Thorstein. *The Engineers and the Price System*. New York: B.W. Huebsch, 1921.

Voelker, Rebecca. "Population Based Medicine Merges Clinical Care, Epidemiological Techniques." *JAMA* 27, no. 17 (1994): 1301–02.

Voss, Kim. *The Making of American Exceptionalism: The Knights of Labor and Class Formation in the Nineteenth Century*. Ithaca, NY: Cornell University Press, 1993.

Wallach, Wendell, Colin Allen, and Iva Smit. "Machine Morality: Bottom-Up and Top-Down Approaches for Modeling Human Moral Faculties." *AI and Society* 22, no. 4 (2008): 565–82.

Walton, John. *Sociology and Critical Inquiry*. New York: Wadsworth, 1996.

Wardell, Mark. "Labor Processes: Moving Beyond Braverman and the Deskilling Debate." In *Rethinking the Labor Process*, edited by Mark Wardell, Thomas L. Steiger and Peter Meiksins, 1–15. Albany, NY: State University of New York Press, 1999.

Warhurst, Chris, Dennis Nickson, Anne Witz, and Anne Marie Cullen. "Aesthetic Labour in Interactive Service Work: Some Case Study Evidence from the 'New' Glasgow." *The Service Industries Journal* 20, no. 3 (2000): 1–18.

Weber, Max. *The Theory of Social and Economic Organization*. New York: Oxford University Press, 1947.

Webster, Frank. *Theories of the Information Society*. 4th ed. London: Routledge, 2014.

Whalen, Jack, and Erik Vinkhuyzen. "Expert Systems in (Inter)Action: Diagnosing Document Machine Problems Over the Telephone." In *Workplace Studies: Recovering Work Practice and Information Systems Design*, edited by Paul Luff, Jon Hindmarsh and Christian Heath, 92–140. Cambridge: Cambridge University Press, 2000.

Whyte, William H. *The Organization Man*. New York: Simon & Schuster, 1956.

Wickens, Peter. *The Road to Nissan: Flexibility, Quality, Teamwork*. London: Macmillan, 1987.

Wilensky, Jeanne L., and Harold L. Wilensky. "Personnel Counseling: The Hawthorne Case." *American Journal of Sociology* 57, no. 3 (1951): 265–80.

Willmott, Hugh. "Strength Is Ignorance: Slavery Is Freedom: Managing Culture in Modern Organizations." *Journal of Management Studies* 30, no. 4 (1993): 515–52.

Wilson, Sloan. *The Man in the Grey Flannel Suit*. New York: Simon & Schuster, 1955.

Womack, James P., and Daniel T. Jones. *Lean Thinking: Banish Waste and Create Wealth in Your Corporation*. New York: Free Press, 2003.

Womack, James P., Daniel T. Jones, and Daniel Roos. *The Machine That Changed the World*. New York: Rawson Associates, 1990.

Worthy, James C. "Changing Concepts of the Personnel Function." AMA Personnel Series no. 113. New York, 1949.

Wright, Erik O. "Working-Class Power, Capitalist-Class Interests, and Class Compromise." *American Journal of Sociology* 105, no. 4 (2000): 957–1002.

Zelman, Walter A., and Robert A. Berenson. *The Managed Care Blues and How to Cure Them*. Washington, D.C.: Georgetown University Press, 1998.

Zuboff, Shoshana. *In the Age of the Smart Machine: The Future of Work and Power*. New York: Basic Books, 1988.

Index

absenteeism 64, 104
academics 108, 183, 193–94, 196, 224–25, 279n20; *see also* higher education; university professors
Academy of Management Journal 104
Accenture 225
accounting firms 52, 207, 295n20
accounting methods 30
action research techniques 77
administrators 31, 194, 199, 202, 234
advertisers 183, 188
aesthetic labor 141
Aetna 199
Affordable Care Act 290n75
AFL *see* American Federation of Labor
AFL-CIO 187
African Americans 62–63; *see also* blacks
The Age of the Smart Machine (Zuboff) 162, 175
AIG 246
Airbnb.com 296n25
Airbus 92, 216; A320 and A330/340 plane models 278n14
aircraft industry: Japan 115; U.S. 88, 92, 216, 278n14
airline flight attendants 140–41
alert fatigue 206
algorithmic grading system 198
algorithms 179, 197–98, 202–03, 217–18, 220–21, 223, 236, 241–42, 253, 264; programming 179
alienation 5, 79–83, 93–95, 102–03, 123, 140–41, 232
AlphaGo (deep-learning software) 297n4
Amalgamated Association of Iron, Steel and Tin Workers 26
Amazon.com 135–36, 224, 234, 239–40, 250, 266, 293n26, 295n14, 296n24; fulfillment centers 136, 224, 293n26

American Association of University Professors (AAUP) 193
American Dream 82, 169
American Enterprise Institute 100
American Express and credit authorization 161
American Federation of Labor (AFL) 22–23, 26–27, 44–45, 58, 61–62, 187, 273n36
American Health Information Community 203
American industry, oligopolistic structure of 32
American Management Association (AMA) 62, 167, 176, 275n15
American Plan 61
American Railway Union (ARU) 270n31
American Recovery and Reinvestment Act (2009) 297n30
American Society of Mechanical Engineers (ASME) 35
American system of manufacturing 90, 253
American Telephone and Telegraph Company (AT&T) 62, 68, 70, 100, 245, 256, 293n19
Americanization and naturalization programs 62–63
Americanization in reverse 117
American-ness and Business Process Reengineering 149
analog computers 91
antecedent-focused emotion regulation 232
anthropology 73
anti-labor repression 26; *see also* repression
anti-laborism 57
anti-statism 57
anti-union consultants 100; *see also* union busting
anti-union employers/firms 22, 56, 99, 101, 137–38

313

A.O. Smith's Milwaukee automobile frame plant 90
Apple, Inc. 185, 237, 247, 286–87n11, 292n26, 295n14; new headquarters in Cupertino, California 286n11; *see also* panopticons
applied behavioral and social sciences 9, 72–73
apprenticeship system 23, 48, 54, 193, 267n1
Archer, Robin 26
architects 21, 264
Arkansas 136
armament production 88, 91
armed violence 26
armory 69
Armour Company 62, 65, 275n28
army 72, 270n31
Aronowitz, Stanley 75, 82, 185
art institutions 185
artificial intelligence (AI) 161, 197–98, 216–21, 230, 237, 242, 264, 297n4
Asda 137
Asia 184
assembled modules 133
assemblers 48, 50
assembly lines 6, 7, 11, 17, 22, 46–52, 54, 88–89, 91, 94–95, 113, 115, 118, 121–22, 124, 127, 129, 131, 136–40, 142, 144, 159, 173–74, 176, 180, 182, 186, 207, 226, 238, 254, 259, 271n3; labor divisions on 86; machine-paced work on 94; principles of 51; service provision assembly lines 51; techniques 254; U-shaped lines 122; virtual assembly lines on Wall Street 207; white-collar lines 159
associations, mutual 59–60
AT&T *see* American Telephone and Telegraph Company
Atlanta, Georgia 185
attitude surveys among employees 69, 73, 78, 101–02, 156–57
attorneys 217–18; *see also* lawyers
Austin, Texas 185
Australia 26, 33, 204, 271n40
authority 5–6, 12, 21–23, 29, 35, 38, 43, 61, 63–64, 66, 72, 74, 79, 87, 99, 101, 120, 127, 135, 158, 182, 242, 257–58, 261, 267n5, 275n15
auto industry 17, 46–47, 90–91, 111–12, 115, 117, 122, 125, 128, 130, 135, 227, 279n6
automaticity (proceduralization) 213
automation 16, 55, 89, 90–95, 111, 138, 147, 162, 176, 196, 203, 205–07, 209–16, 219, 230, 233, 236, 238–41, 251, 253, 259–60, 264–66, 293n31, 294n20; adaptive 214; capitalist logic and choices regarding type of 215–16; and deskilling 92–95; in distribution centers 239–40; of equipment 91, 93–94; of essay grading 196–97; information storage and retrieval vs. biological memory 212–13; inventory control 241; managerial control of workers as driving force 91; in medicine 203, 205–06; in the office 55, 158–166; of production of newspaper articles 221; in retail 138; regulation of high automation-related risks 216; side effects in medicine 205–06; and teaching part of professorial labor 196–97
automation bias 206, 209–10, 264
automation complacency 209–10, 264
Automation of America's Offices (U.S. Congress Office of Technology Assessment) 147
automatization 213
automobile engine plants 93
automobiles, planned obsolescence of 49
automotive production technology 47, 254
autonomy: relative 11, 38, 252; responsible 5, 6, 151, 157, 172; skill-based 114; technical 129; of workers 111, 129–30
autopilot, flying on 211
auto-supply industries 90

B-29 bomber 89
BA or MA in Computer Science 186
Babbage, Charles 37
Baker, Stephen 220
bakery 93
Balanced Scorecard (BSC) 194–95, 289n44, 289n46; statistical key performance indicators 194–95; Strategy Map 195–96
Baldwin Locomotive 58
Bank of America 100
banks 52, 60, 100, 207, 219, 244
barcode scanning system 137
Barnard, Chester 13
basic income guarantee 252
Baxter (humanoid manufacturing robot) 238–41
Bechtel 295n20
Bedaux system 43
Bell, Daniel 12, 74, 294ch14n2
Bell Telephone Laboratories 116
benchmark metrics 149
Bendix, Reinhard 12
Bentham, Jeremy 135, 175
Berggren, Christian 123–24, 128
Berle, Adolf A. 81, 244–45, 294ch14n2
Berwick, Donald 201
Bethel, Maine 77
Bethlehem, Pennsylvania, strike 24
Bethlehem Steel Company 53, 245
Better Office Management (Leffingwell) 52

Index

Beyond Mass Production (Kenney and Florida) 131
Beyond Reengineering (Hammer) 150
bias of the auspices 78, 277n65
Big Brother 86
big data 218, 220, 222–23, 225, 236, 242, 264; correlations vs. deep causal understanding 220, 222–23
big data analytics 242
biotechnology 107
blacklisting 26, 61
BlackRock 245
blacks 33, 63, 68; *see also* African Americans
Blanqui, Auguste 269n16
Blanquist response to repression 25
Blauner, Robert 93–95; definition of alienation 93; inverted U-shaped declining alienation curve 95
Block, Fred 112
blue-collar economy 226
blue-collar middle class 293n31
blue-collar workers 1, 67, 92, 95, 98, 103, 108
Bluestone, Irving 279n20
boards of directors *see* corporate governance
Boeing Corporation 89, 92, 216, 247, 293n19; B770 plane model 278n14
boilermakers 3
Bolivar Project 279n20
Bolshevism 65
bonuses 8, 36, 58–59, 63, 106, 188, 255, 272n5
Boston, Massachusetts 194, 238
bounded rationality 151, 155
Braverman, Harry 2–5, 44, 52, 92–95, 106, 112, 137–38, 200, 267n5, 267n18; degradation of work (or deskilling) thesis 2, 4, 95, 260; gender-blindness 267n18; romanticizing the pre-modern skilled manual worker 3; view on employment middle layers 106–07
Bright, James R. 93–95; inverted U-shaped curve of declining skill 95
British traditions and internal contract systems 21
broadbanding 167
Brody, David 66–67
brokerage firms 217
brokers 183–84
browser war, first 172–73
Bruder, Jessica 135
Brynjolfsson, Erik 221–22, 241–42
Buffalo, New York 284n39
Burawoy, Michael 8
bureaucratization: of managerial function 31; of structure of control 11, 42, 255; *see also* employment, bureaucratic
Bush, George W. 203

business culture, skill-biased reorganization in 242
business owners: sense of stewardship and paternal obligation 57
business power elite: enduring existence in U.S. 250
Business Process Management, IBM system 229
Business Process Reengineering (BPR) 147–49, 152–53, 155–57, 171, 207, 230, 261, 265; BPR and TQM combined in a multi-tiered control strategy 157–58; process assemblers 227–228, 230
Business Roundtable 100
business schools 150, 194
business services 107
business theorists 80
Business Week 200

cabinet makers 3
Cadbury 42, 56
California 127, 143, 185, 190, 194, 203, 282n75, 284n40, 286n11, 296n23
California Nurses Association 290n75
call center agents 176–178, 180, 224
call center work 176–79, 183; short-cycle routine tasks and software-driven conversations 176; knowledge management and data warehousing 177–79, 183; use of expert systems 178–179
call centers 132, 138, 148, 176–182, 191, 201; "digital assembly lines" 176, 180
Canada 26
Canadian Auto Workers (CAW) 104
cancers 201, 210
career ladders 6, 11, 42, 107, 166, 168, 245, 250; *see also* job ladders; promotion ladders
Cargill 295n20
Carnegie Steel Company 28
carpenters 19, 241
Carr, Nicholas 197, 209, 211–12, 214, 220, 233
carriage makers 47
case managers 160–61, 200, 225; in insurance industry 160–61; in managed care 200, 225
cashiers 51, 184
CAT scan 96, 279n31
catharsis 74, 86
CBSs *see* Computer Business Systems
Center for the Study of American Business 100
Centralized Traffic Control 134
Champy, James 149, 159, 161, 166
Chaplin, Charlie 271n3
checkout operator 51, 219

chemical engineers 32
chemical industry 22, 89, 93–95
Chemnitz machine-tool plant 234
Chevron 246
Chicago 8, 27, 62–65, 70, 270n31
Chicago Civic Federation 26
Chicago firms 63, 67
child care 251, 263
Children's Health Insurance Program (CHIP) 137
China 33, 137, 184, 218, 231, 237, 243, 265; Communist Party 231; state-owned enterprises 231
Chomsky, Noam 196
Chrysler Corporation 131, 245
CIA (Central Intelligence Agency) 219
CIO see Congress of Industrial Organizations
The Circle (Eggers) 287n11
Cisco 295n14, 296n28
Citigroup 219, 246–47
Citizens' Industrial Alliance 26
Citizens United v. Federal Election Commission 250, 296n22
citizenship instruction 57
Ciulla, Joanne B. 80, 146, 170
civics classes 63
civil engineering 222
civil engineers 96
Civil Rights Act 235
civil rights movement 235
Civil War, U.S. 20, 27, 30, 46, 90
clerical assembly line 54
clerical work 4, 11; professionalization of, vs. clericalization of professional work 163–64
clerical workers 11, 31, 38, 48, 52, 55, 83, 140, 160, 163–65, 254, 19th-century 4
Cleveland, Grover 270n31
Cleveland, Ohio 24, 27, 67, 79
Cleveland, Ohio, strike 24
Cleveland Clinic 219
Clinton, Bill (William Jefferson) 183, 281n52
Clinton, Hillary 284n39, 293n31
closed shop 23
clothing industry 21
the cloud 219, 241–42, 247, 264
CNC machines 91
coal industry 21; see also mining
cobblers 19
COBOL 186
codetermination and labor management in Germany 234
coercion 8, 13, 25, 258
Cohen, Lizabeth 62, 66–67
Cohen, Steven 277n68
Cold War 73, 75, 91–92, 169

collective actions 7, 44, 142, 187, 234
collective bargaining 8, 68, 74, 169, 256; see also unions
Columbus Iron Works 21
combination machine tools 90
command-and-control systems 69, 134, 151–53, 170, 196, 261, 265
command economy 8
Committee for Industrial Organizations see Congress of Industrial Organizations
commodification of feelings 139
commodified emotional labor 233
Communications Workers of America (CWA) 181, 187
company contests 57, 59
company housing 34, 57
company magazines 57, 59, 66
company outings 57
company picnics 59
company songs 59
company sports 57, 59, 65–66
company towns 28, 60, 77, 270n31; as form of social control 60
company unions 9, 61–62, 64, 68, 116, 119, 256
company welfarism 24, 42, 56–60, 67, 251; creating sense of family life within firm 59; see also welfare capitalism
Computer Business Systems (CBSs) 207, 224–26, 228–33, 237, 261, 293n26; caveat regarding relation to actual practices 233; and electronic representations of human beings 226; product manuals of 225–30, 233; top-down workplace control 225
computer models for moral decision making 211
computer programming 185–86, 265
computer programs 96, 186, 216
computer science 186
computer scientists 92, 213, 218, 220, 222
computer telephony integration (CIT) 177
computer-aided design (CAD) 91
computer-aided design and drafting (CADD) 96
computer-aided detection 210, 230
computer-aided diagnosis 96, 202, 264
computer-aided manufacturing (CAM) 91
computerized semi-automatic checkout systems 52
computing services: centralized "cloud" 242
The Concept of the Corporation (Drucker) 80
conceptual workers 38; see also designers
concierge economy 234, 292n18
Congress of Industrial Organizations (CIO) 24, 45, 67
consent 8, 68, 73
consultants 32–33, 45, 72, 100–01, 108, 115–

Index

16, 118, 145, 157, 163, 183, 188, 193–95, 201, 02, 209, 219, 263, 297n3; self-employed 193
consulting firms 32, 100, 145, 194, 219, 225, 231, 290n62
consumer electronics industries 125, 237
consumer goods logistics 240
containerization in sea transport 134
Contested Terrain (Edwards) 6
contingent work 132, 192–93, 262
continuous flow production 47; in steel manufacturing 22
continuous improvement (CI) 120, 124, 126, 142, 145, 152, 157; *see also* Japanese lean production (JLP)
continuous-process industry 89–90, 93–95
contract systems 21, 30, 43
contractors 20–23
control: bureaucratic { 6, 7, 13; ideological 6, 10, 40, 172; indirect 38, 151, 154; normative 9–12, 40, 68, 154, 156, 182, 256, 261, 268n36; numerical 89, 91, 134,278n12; technical 6, 7, 13, 48; technical-organizational 11, 46, 153, 233
control regime *see* Business Process Management system, Corporate Panoptics, monitoring, surveillance
conveyor belts 47, 118, 160, 239, 259
Cooke, Morris L. 44–45
cooks 241
cooperative banks 60
coordinators 150, 183
coppersmiths 3
corporate audits 207
corporate citizens 81
corporate cultures 10, 67, 100–01, 145, 149–50, 156, 251, 261
corporate delayering 166
corporate governance 106–07, 246, 248, 262
Corporate Panoptics 230–31; *see also* panopticons
corporate paternalism 24, 40–42, 48, 56, 58–59, 65, 68, 77, 255, 270n31
Corporate Performance Management (Scheer) 228
corporate process assemblers 227–28, 230
corporate welfarism 57, 251; *see also* welfare capitalism
corporations' accounting tricks 249, 295n18
corporations, public 18, 29, 105, 107, 235, 244–49, 251, 265–66, 271n42; requirements for accountability and transparency 248
corporations' tax "deferral" 249
correlations in data vs. causal explanation 220, 222–23
The Corrosion of Character (Sennett) 189

cost-accounting 30–31
Costco 248
counseling 49, 70, 73–74, 183, 256
counselors 74
court injunctions 26
court repression 26
Cowie, Jefferson 234–35
Cox Enterprises 295n20
craft knowledge 3, 38
craft-like methods of production 111
craft skills 20, 22, 36, 85, 125
craft tradition of German industry 125
craft work 3–4
craft workshops 3, 19
craftsmanship 1, 82, 190, 267n5, 288n22; standards of 5; erosion of 190
The Craftsman (Sennett) 288n22
craftsmen/craft workers 2–5, 8, 19, 22–23, 31, 38, 60, 82, 146, 194; bargaining power of 22; their craft ethic 146; their ethos of manly defiance against foremen's attempts to undermine traditional shop rules; their moral code about output quotas 21
creative workers 150–152, 155, 157, 184, 236, 242
CRM *see* customer relations management
cross-function teams 159
cross-state geographic mobility 288n20
crowdfunding 249
crowdsourcing 296n24
culture of unity, Depression-based 67
Cummins Engines 102
Cupertino, California 286n11
Curtis Publishing Company 53
Curtiss-Wright plant in Lockland, Ohio 88
customer relations management (CRM) 173–74, 178–79, 224, 287n18
Cusumano, Michael 122, 124
cybernetics 89, 212
cycle time analysis 149

Dahrendorf, Ralf 294ch14n2
DARPA *see* Defense Advanced Research Projects Agency
data marts 225
data warehouses 225
database administrators 185
database management 186
Davenport, Thomas H. 159, 161
Davis, Gerald F. 244, 246–47, 249–51
Dayton, Ohio 79
deal structurers in credit loan sector 160–62
Death of a Salesman (Miller) 83
Debs, Eugene V. 270n31
decision-support systems 180, 207, 209–10, 214, 216, 264; *see also* expert systems
decline, in learning 207

deep learning 214, 297n4
DeepMind 297n4
Defense Advanced Research Projects Agency (DARPA) 216
defense industries 88, 116
deferred compensation 58–59
defined benefit (pension) plans 106, 295n4
defined contribution (pension) plans 263, 295n4
degeneration effect 213
degradation of work 2, 4, 92, 234, 260, 293n31; *see also* deskilling
Dell Corporation 185
Deloitte Touch Tohmatsu 295n20
Deming, W. Edwards 116–18, 145–46
Deming Prize 119
Democratic Party 67, 284n39, 293n31
democratic social engineering 16, 76–79, 99, 257; mixture of social control and democracy 77
Denmark 234
Denney, Reuel 84
dentists 241
department stores 51
depression of 1930s *see* Great Depression
design jobs, routine 96
design philosophy 233
designers (or design workers) 38, 126, 150–51, 153–54, 183, 188, 195, 211–12, 215, 220–21, 225, 231, 237, 254, 264, 282n61, 293n26; *see also* conceptual workers
deskilling 2–5, 37–41, 45, 51, 92, 95–96, 112, 138–39, 187, 205, 211, 261, 265; *see also* degradation of work
Detroit 28
devaluation of programming skill 186
The Development of the Labour Process in Capitalist Society (Littler) 36
Dewey, John 73; principles of democratic participation 77
dexterity, physical 92, 94, 128, 239–40
dialectics of control over the labor process 10
Dickson, William J. 71, 74
die castings 91
DiFazio, William 185
Digital Equipment 102, 108
digital managerialism 226
digital mapping tools 210
digital platforms 250–52, 266, 296n24, 296n25, 296n26
direct control 5, 6, 29, 38, 129, 152, 154, 172, 293n26
direct labor/workers 2, 124, 153, 155–56
direct patient care 96
direct sensory feedback on automated system's performance 214

direct supervision 2, 5–6, 47–48, 61, 69, 254, 270–71n40
disciplinary procedures 20
Discipline and Punish: The Birth of the Prison (Foucault) 175
discipline of workers: craftsmen's/skilled workers' self-discipline 5, 48; factory-like form in retail work 136; industrial-like form in service work 141, 180, 202, 225; JLP teamwork and collective "self-discipline" 110; *see also* disciplining workers; social discipline; work discipline
disciplining workers: assembly line 47–48, 226; consumer service reports 141; direct supervision by first-line management/foremen 7, 14, 23, 64; reengineered business "process" 173–75, 180, 198, 202, 225, 227–28, 231; rigors of scientific management 53–54, 158, 160, 226
discretion in work 9, 11–13, 20, 23, 38, 124, 138, 150, 153, 182, 260, 275
disintermediation 184
dismissal restraint 58
dismissals *see* layoffs
Disney World 141
division of labor 4, 10, 12, 19, 23, 30–31, 36–37, 40, 42, 45, 71, 83, 88, 101, 162, 214, 234, 260
divorce of direct and indirect labor 37
doctors 96, 161, 194, 199–201, 203–06, 210, 222, 262, 293n18; *see also* physicians
document discovery in law offices 217
"dollar-a year" men 44, 273n33
domestic industry 19
domestic science 58
domestic servants 3
dot-com bubble 188, 190
Dow Jones Industrial Index of 1930, 1987 and 2009, firms in 246
downsizing 107, 152, 162, 166–69, 184, 189
drive system 24, 58, 62, 68, 75, 130, 255, 275n15
Drucker, Peter F. 47, 80, 89, 277n72
DuPont 61, 68, 256, 280n35, 293n19
durable-goods companies 67

e-mail 164, 176–77, 180, 193, 209, 228
early industrial shops 29
Earned Income Tax Credit (EITC) 137, 252
Easly, Ralph 26
East Asia 246
East Chicago 24
Eastman Kodak 68, 92, 101, 108, 251, 256
Economic and Philosophical Manuscripts (Marx) 82

"Economic Possibilities for Our Grandchildren" (Keynes) 236
economic security 16; *see also* job security
economic stimulus package 252, 297*n*30
economists 67, 73, 107, 183–84, 241, 295*n*2
Edgar v. MITE decision 105
Edgell, Stephen 131
e-discovery software 217
education 1, 3, 7, 13, 54, 79, 98, 102, 128, 168, 184–86, 191, 193–98, 205, 219, 224–25, 251, 279*n*20, 289*n*34, 289*n*39, 289*n*44, 289*n*46; *see also* higher education
Edwards, Richard 6, 7, 8, 13, 268*n*27
edX 198
efficiency 2, 10, 11, 15, 24, 33, 36, 43, 47, 55, 63, 71, 101, 105, 108, 118, 120–22, 126, 135, 138–39, 142, 169–70, 181, 190, 196, 201, 204–05, 223, 228, 232–33, 239, 253, 289*n*34; experts 36, 43; management 29; *see also* systematic management movement
effort bargain 9
Eggers, Dave 287*n*11
Egypt 181
1890 census 275*n*21
eight-hour day 26
electric fork-lift trucks 118
electric machinery industry 22
electrical engineers 32
electrical power industry 198
electrical-parts manufacturer 93
electricians 3
electromechanical special-purpose production machinery 90
electronic medical records (EMR) systems 203–05
emotion management theories 232
emotion regulation theory 232–33
emotional labor 139–40, 177, 232–33, 259
employee loyalty 5, 24, 57, 59–62, 65, 69, 73, 81, 86, 95, 101, 146, 150, 167–68, 177, 179, 190, 255, 257
employee participation in software design 234
employee performance 3, 12, 30, 36, 39, 42, 45, 54, 77, 81, 101, 106, 119, 126–28, 136, 145–49, 149, 157, 159, 160, 163, 175–76, 180–81, 194–96, 210, 214, 223, 225, 227–30, 236–37, 256–57, 259, 261, 263
employee representation 9, 13, 61, 64–65, 70, 78, 102
employee savings into mutual funds 106
employee stock ownership plans 65
employees' lives outside the workplace 57
employer hostility toward organized labor 25–27
Employers' Association of Detroit 28

employers' associations 28, 61
employer's prerogative 80
employment-based social welfare system 251
employment, bureaucratic 11–16, 25, 109, 245, 255; methods of coordination and control 6, 7, 13, 24; impersonal rules and procedures 7, 12
employment relations 9, 14, 36, 40–42
employment security 6, 41–42, 106, 144, 275*n*15; *see also* job security
employment stability 101, 108, 162; employer stabilization technique 108, 262
empowerment 110–11, 123, 155–56, 158, 172, 261, 280*n*20; employees' view as "virtual slavery" 172; as management tool 172; "organizational empowerment," contradiction in terms 172; of workers 110–11, 115–16, 280*n*20
encounter groups 99; *see also* sensitivity training
energy industry 107
engineering design philosophy 233
engineering profession 32
engineers 4, 22, 24, 30, 32–33, 38, 43, 48, 74, 82, 86, 89, 91–92, 95–96, 116–18, 121, 126, 150–51, 153, 158–60, 162–63, 165–66, 173–74, 180, 183, 185, 187, 201–02, 209, 212, 215, 222, 227, 231, 238–39, 254, 263–64, 273*n*36, 282*n*61; *see also* reengineers
England 210, 289*n*39; *see also* Great Britain; United Kingdom
enhanced top-down management systems 144–66
Enterprise Resource Planning (ERP) 165, 173–5, 224, 261; basic vs. extended ERP 173–74
entrepreneurial firm 6, 59
environments, turbulent 10
equity markets 16
"era of good feeling" 26
ergonomics 212
Ericsson 247
ERP *see* Enterprise Resource Planning
espionage 26
esprit de corps 66; *see also* morale; team spirit
ethics, choices in automated system designs 215
ethnicity 66, 167; conflicts 24; divisions 27, 33–34, 62; ethnic mutual benefit society 65, *see also* mutual associations; ethnic building and loan associations 65; ethnic solidarity 63
Etzioni, Amitai 9
Europe 25–26, 33, 56, 59, 92, 111, 116–17, 125, 128, 190, 192, 235, 255; northwestern

59, 255, 275n21; southern 59, 235, 255, 275n2; western 26, 116–17, 190
event-driven process chains (EPCs) 226, 228–29
evidence-based medicine 204; and treatment options 219
exception principle 53–54, 161, 254
exchange-traded funds (ETFs) 245
expert systems 161–62, 178, 182, 201, 207, 209, 211, 214–15, 217, 225, 230–31, 234, 261, 263; sophisticated versions 182, 263; *see also* decision-support systems
explicit (or declarative) knowledge 213
extraverted intuitive thinking judges (ENTJs) 170
Exxon 245–46

Facebook 237, 295n14
Faces in the Crowd (Riesman) 277n90
face-to-face interactive service work 138–41
factory and shop floor: geography of 6, 45; spatial organization of 45–46; technical organization of 45–46
factory designs 46
factory system, rise of 19–22
"failure of socialism" 25
"a fair day's pay for a fair day's work" 36, 39, 272n5
Fair Deal 235
"false collectivization" 86
farm-laborers 3
farriers 3
fast-food restaurants 138–39, 142, 258; principles of 139; *see also* McDonald's restaurants
fast-food workers 139, 142–43, 259
fatigue 55, 63, 132, 206; tests 63
FDR administration *see* Roosevelt administration
fear, of job loss 24, 169, 284n1
Federal Aviation Administration (FAA) 211, 216
Federal Express (FedEx) 102, 135; computerized package scanner 135
Federal Quality Institute 145
federal troops 25
Feigenbaum, Armand V. 145, 281n27
fertilizers industry 89
Fidelity 245
finance capitalism 32, 245
financial crisis (2008) 207
financial deregulation 16, 208
financial incentives 5, 8, 48, 58, 59, 65, 203, 256
financial risk, shift to employees 107, 192
firms, nonunionized 13, 67, 69, 73, 78, 98, 101–02, 104, 108, 111, 127, 256, 259, 280

first-line supplier firms 133–34
Flanders, Walter 273n45
Flex Force (Hewlett-Packard) 108
flexible accumulation 110, 114, 153; *see also* flexible manufacturing, flexible specialization
flexible manufacturing 114, 125, 133, 142; *see also* flexible mass production; flexible specialization
flexible mass production 16, 49–50, 111, 260; *see also* flexible manufacturing, flexible specialization
flexible specialization 49, 110–14, 121, 125, 133, 260, 280n1; in "Third Italy" 110–11
flexi-time used as form of social control 189
flexi-workers 132
flight automation in aviation 211
flight decks of airplanes 210, 264
Flip video camera 251, 296n28
flow, state of 214
Fluid, Inc. 219
fly-by-wire system, digital 211, 216, 278n14
Forbes 221
Ford, Henry 41, 46–47, 49, 52, 88, 162–63, 174
Ford, Martin 197, 211, 215, 220–21, 236
Ford Motor Company 32, 41, 48–50, 52, 67, 88–91, 111, 115, 117–18, 131, 174–75, 185, 226, 245–46, 254; English School 48–49; Five Dollar Day program 41–42, 48; Focus car 131; profit-sharing plan 49; progressive layout system of shop floor 46–47; Sociological Department 41, 48; sociological investigators 49; Taurus car 282n61
Fordism 41–42, 46–47, 110, 119–20, 123–24, 130–32, 137, 154, 177, 260, 272n19, 273n45, 280n1; key features 124
foremen 7, 9, 14–15, 20–24, 30–31, 38–39, 43–44, 48, 54, 58, 61, 63, 65, 70, 76, 79, 119, 129, 136, 176, 254, 275n15, 275n28; anti-union 21; degree of control 22; drive system 24; foremen training 63, 70, 275n15; functional foremen 44, 119, 136, 176; moral code 21–22; restriction of authority 64; rule-of-thumb methods 43
Foremen's Clubs movement 79
forges, rural 20
formal organization theorists 30
Fortune 100 companies 293n19
Foucault, Michel 175
foundries 20–22
401(k) pension plans 106
Foxconn 237
fragmentation, of labor/jobs/tasks 30–31, 37–39, 41, 47, 123–24, 129, 151, 155, 157
France 286n11

freelancers 148, 191, 193; academics 193; professionals 191
Fremont, California 282n75
French, John 77
Frey, John P. 44
Friedman, Andrew L. (Andy) 5, 6, 8, 172
Friendly Societies 59; see also mutual associations
frontline workers 121–22, 178
Fukuyama, Francis 168
functional organization, principle of 38
The Functions of the Executive (Barnard) 13

gang boss 38
Gap, Inc. 240
gardeners 241
Gartner Corporation 25
Gary, Indiana 28
gas stations 51
Geer/Allied 8
gender 51, 83, 166–67, 267; gender-blindness 83, 267n18
General Dynamics 247
General Electric (GE) 28, 62, 185, 245–46, 273n36, 281n27
General Mills 102
General Motors (GM) 47, 49–50, 61, 80, 91, 98, 111, 115, 131, 185, 199, 245, 260, 273n36; Cadillac car 49; Chevrolet car 49; Lordstown assembly line in Ohio 103; Pontiac Grand 282n61; recalls 131
general-purpose machinery 50, 90
general-purpose robots 238
general-purpose technology 237
generation effect 212–13
generic manufacturers 247
geographical isolation, of industries 60
Germany 42, 126, 225, 234, 293n26
Gilson, Mary B. 71–72, 74
glad handers 85
glass industry 21–22
Glazer, Nathan 84
globalization 133, 136, 150, 192, 243
GM-Suzuki joint venture in Canada 124
Golden Age Clubs 79
golden parachutes 106
Gompers, Samuel 26
Goodyear Tire and Rubber Company 61–62
Google 197, 213, 237, 240, 295n14; online language translation 197; robotics division 240
Gordon Personal Profile 170
GPS (Global Positioning System) 134, 210, 250
Graebner, William 78–79
Great Britain 4, 42, 112, 125, 129, 131, 137, 204, 234, 271n40, 289n34, 293n26; see also England; United Kingdom
Great Depression 15, 66–68, 235, 256
Great Society 235
Greenbaum, Joan 147, 164
Gross, James J. 232
group life insurance plans 65
group medical practices 96
group piecework of the 1920 127
group problem solving 77
groupthink 170
guaranteed income *see* basic income guarantee
guns 21

Hammer, Michael 149–50, 159, 161, 166
hard power (coercion) 69
Harder, Del 90
Harman Automotive 279n20
Harrison, Bennett 134
Hartz, Louis 277n72
Harvard Business School 70, 112, 194
Harvard University 198
Harvey, David 114, 153
Harwood Manufacturing Corporation 77
Harwood studies 76–77, 79, 276n60
Hawaii 284n40
Hawthorne effect 70
Hawthorne experiments 73
Hawthorne plant 116
Hawthorne studies 71–72, 80
Hawthorne Works (a Western Electric plant) 66, 70, 73–74
Head, Simon 125, 159, 161, 165, 173, 176–81, 224–26, 231–34, 289n39, 292n18, 293n26, 293n31
health care 132, 177, 185, 194, 198–201, 203–05, 224–26, 230, 263, 290n75
Health Information Technology Adoption initiative 203
health insurance 59, 107, 137, 198–200, 245, 251, 266, 295n4; fee-for-service system 198, 99; see also manager care; medical care
health judges 211
health maintenance organization (HMO) 199, 225, 227
Hearst Corporation 295n20
hedge fund activism 249
help desk technicians 185
"helping professions" 58
Heritage Foundation 100
Hewlett-Packard 107–08, 185, 293n19
higher education 185, 191, 193–96, 224–25, 289n34, 289n39, 289n44, 289n46; adjunct professors and other non-tenured faculty 193; contingent instructors 193;

corporatization of 193–96; graduate students' teaching as apprenticeship 193; massive open online courses (MOOCs) 198; tenured university jobs and changes in quality of work 193–94; *see also* university professors
Higher Education Funding Council for England (HEFCE) 289*n*39
Highland Park plant 47–48, 50, 52, 119, 174
high-level reasoning 237
high-risk situations 210, 264
high-skilled knowledge work 16
high-speed cutting tools 88
high tech, shift toward 184
high-technology industries 102
Hirschhorn, Larry 113
Hochschild, Arlie Russell 139–41, 232–33
Hoff, Timothy 205
Hofstadter, Richard 235
home-care workers 140, 143
Home Depot 245
home health aides 241
home ownership plans 59–60
Homestead Steelworks 28
homo sapiens 222
Honda 125–26, 131; Accord 131
Honduras 181
Hoover, Herbert 33
Hoover Institute 100
hospitals 96–97, 160, 184, 199–204, 226; administrators 199; attendants 184
hostile takeovers 105–06, 245–46
hotel workers 140
Hotpoint 117
Hoxie Report (1915) 44
human relations 10, 40, 42, 56, 68–70, 72–78, 80, 84, 101–02, 123, 151, 155, 256–57, 260; criticisms of 74–76; neglect of power issues 76
human resource management (HRM) 224–25, 227, 230–32
human resources (HR): consultants 297*n*3; departments 101; expert 165; managers 157; officers 73, 227; process recombinator's role 231
The Human Side of Enterprise (McGregor) 99
Humana 199
human-centered automation 211–12, 216, 233; designs 211; government intervention into private sector 216
human-centered engineering 219
human-factor experts 211
humanoid robots 238, 240–41
Hungary, communist 8
Huws, Ursula 83, 148

hydraulic special-purpose machinery 90
hyper-reengineering 173

IBM 68, 92, 102, 108, 187, 218–20, 225–29, 237, 247, 256, 264, 278*n*15, 292*n*26, 297*n*4; Domino Administrator 8, 228; employees' legal actions over loss of secure pension benefits 187; Websphere Business Monitor VI 226, 229
ICTs *see* information and communication technologies 11
Idealized Design of Clinical Office Practices (ID-COP) 201
ideation 221
ideology 5–6, 9, 10, 14, 30, 32, 40, 42–43, 45, 66, 74, 77, 82, 100–01, 156, 172, 277*n*72; "empowerment" 156, 172; *see also* managerial rhetoric
Illinois Central Railroad 44
ILO *see* International Labour Organization
immigrants 24, 31, 33–34, 45, 59, 62, 68, 79, 235, 255; Eastern European 59, 63, 235, 255, 275*n*21; first and second generation "new immigrants" 68, 235; Southern European 59, 63, 235, 255, 275*n*21
immigration 31, 60, 265, 275*n*21; restriction and quotas 63, 275*n*21
Immigration Act of 1924 *see* Johnson-Reed immigration Act
imprisonment 20
incentive payments 6, 8, 36, 58, 63; systems 36, 39, 58, 63–64, 242, 255
indentured service 267*n*1
India 181, 193, 243, 265
Indian IT companies 132
indirect labor/workers 37, 50, 124, 154
individual abilities vs. equal treatment for all 99
individual pay determination and merit 98
individualization of employee-employer relations 64
indulgency pattern 101
industrial capitalism 4, 9, 15, 27–28, 45–46, 75, 79
industrial control rooms 210, 264
industrial democracy 62, 64
industrial dualism in Japan 116
industrial engineering 24, 32, 254
industrial engineers 24, 32, 48, 91, 129, 151
industrial paternalism *see* corporate paternalism
Industrial Perception, Inc. 239–40; box-moving robot 239
industrial psychology/psychologists 100
industrial relations 1, 62–63, 70, 74–76; *see also* unions
Industrial Revolution 4, 71, 162

industrial robots 91, 237, 239
industrial sociology 277n68
industrial suburbs 27–28
industrial workers 14, 25, 27–28, 66, 80, 93, 257
Industrial Workers of the World (IWW) 25, 45
informal organization 71, 77, 251
information and communication technologies (ICTs) 11, 39, 112, 155, 247, 261; see also information technologies
information technologies (ITs) 18, 107, 113–14, 132, 149, 158, 160, 162–63, 165, 177, 179, 184, 186, 190, 202–04, 207, 216, 219, 224, 232, 235–37, 241, 244, 263, 293n26; its powers as to measurement, monitoring, and control of office work 160
initial public offerings (IPOs) 188
inner-directed social type 85
innovation work 265
innovations: in labor management outside North Atlantic region 270n40; recombinant 221, 292n47; in robotics/robots 219, 238, 240; technological 4, 6, 48–50, 58, 88–89, 115, 126, 142, 255, 292n47
in-person services 184
insourcing 187
inspectors 9, 38, 48, 120, 122
Institute for Social Research at University of Michigan 78, 276n60
insurance companies 52, 160
integrity groups 99
Intel 102, 185, 295n14
intellectual slack time 150
interactive service work 137–41, 259; workers 118, 140–41
interactive voice-response systems 182
interchangeable parts manufacture 47, 90
internal contractors 21, 31
internal labor markets 7–8, 166
internal promotion 63, 275n15
International Brotherhood of Electrical Workers (IBEW) 181
International Harvester 28, 58, 61–62, 275n28
International Labour Organization (ILO) 55
International Motor Vehicle Program of MIT 112
Internet 171–74, 176–178, 180, 184–85, 188–89, 190, 192, 194, 198, 202, 216, 218–19, 225, 237, 265
Internet Explorer 172
interstate commerce clause 105
intervention practices, psychosocial 9, 78
investment banking firms 217
iron and steel industry 20–22
Italy 110–11

IT system, overriding (or bypassing) 180
ITs see information technologies
IWW see Industrial Workers of the World

Jacoby, Sanford 14, 57, 70, 75, 77, 99–100, 288n20
Janis, Irving 170
janitors 184, 241
Japan: appropriation of American methods 115; appropriation of German manufacturing practices 115; corporate paternalism 40, 42; engineering and electronics industries 121; labor unions 116; productivity missions to U.S 117; transplants in auto industry within U.S. 111, 127, 129; see also Japanese Lean Production
Japan Productivity Council 117
Japanese-American joint ventures in car manufacturing 111, 127–28, 282n75
Japanese Lean Production (JLP) 111–12, 115, 120, 123–28, 130–31, 141–42, 144, 177, 260, 280n1; and alternative work schedules 132; analysis in terms of Fordism 124–132; an extended form of 134; "lean and mean" vs. "lean and dual" model 144; life-time employment in original JLP model for core labor force 120, 144; its neo–Fordist features 131; as participative form of Taylorism 126; peer pressure 127–28; a post–Fordist interpretation 131; retaking drive system of early 20th century 130; small batch-manufacturing with highest possible cumulative product volume 130–31; and teamwork 110, 120, 123, 127–29, 145–46, 182, 261, 282n75; waste elimination 119–20, 130, 158, 169, 201; as white-collar Taylorism 55, 159; worker opposition to 2, 6, 43–45, 130, 262
Japanese Union of Science and Engineering (JUSE) 116–17
Jeopardy! 218–20
Jersey Standard see Standard Oil of New Jersey
Jim Crow South 235
job analysis 30, 36
job design 1, 36
job enrichment 103, 110, 124
job fragmentation 38, 134
job hopping 189
job jurisdiction 23
job ladders 10, 64, 149, 166–67, 250–51; from job ladder to job to task 250–51; see also career ladders; promotion ladders
job mobility 31
job performance 128, 256; see also employee performance

job retention 64
job rotation 124–25, 131, 182
job security 7, 9, 64, 66, 108, 120, 144, 183, 187, 190, 263, 279–80n20; *see also* employment security
job segregation: by gender 167; by race/ethnicity 167
job transfers 58, 62, 255
"jobless recovery" 190
Jobs, Steve 286n11
John Lewis Partnership in Britain 234
Johnson & Johnson 107
Johnson-Reed Immigration Act (1924) 275n21
joint management/employee task forces 105
Jones, David T. 112, 123, 131
J.P. Morgan 32
Juran, Joseph 118, 145
just-in-case practice 120
just-in-time (JIT) practices 11, 18, 114–15, 120, 133–36, 149, 153, 192–93; delivery 11, 136, 149; inventory 153; office work 192–93; production 114–15, 120, 133–34, 142, 192; service providing 18, 193; supply 120; techniques in retail 135–36
juvenile justice reform 58

kaban (or tag) 120
kaizen concept and activities 120, 122, 128
Kalmar, Sweden 128
kanban system 118, 149, 152, 157
Kaplan, Robert 194–95
Kentucky, USA 129
Key Performance Indicators (KPIs) 194–95, 227–28
Keynes, John Maynard 236
keypunch operators 167
Kilo, Chuck 201
Kinect 236, 241
Kiva robots 239–40
Kiva Systems 239
Knights of Labor 23
knowledge economy 185
knowledge engineering 161
knowledge generation 212–13
knowledge, tacit (or implicit) 153–56, 182, 207, 297, 213
knowledge work 149, 192, 288n22
knowledge workers 1, 138, 182, 185
Knudsen, William S. 49–50, 88
Koch brothers (Charles and David) 248
Koch industries 248, 295n20
Korczynski, Marek 140
Korean War 273n33
Koreans 184
Koza, John 222

Kraft, Philip 153–54, 157
Kroc, Ray 139
Kroger 240, 245, 295n14
Krupp, Germany 42, 56
Kunda, Gideon 268n36

L3C (low-profit LLC) 249
Labor and Monopoly Capital (Braverman) 2
labor economists 69, 73
labor force: dividsion by race and national origins 33; participation rate 242; preindustrial capitalist 3
labor immigration, virtual 265
labor market conditions: in Japan 116, 124, 129; in Sweden 129; in U.S. 7–8, 10–11, 14–16, 33, 98, 116, 166, 169, 189, 191, 250, 266
labor militancy 28, 64–65, 69, 254
labor party, in U.S. 14
labor power: associational and structural forms 10
labor process theory 5, 8; and five dimensions of control 9
labor-saving technology 237
labor spies 61
labor substitutability, concept of 41
labor unions *see* unions
labor unrest 24, 28, 56–57, 59, 255, 295
Lafayette, Indiana 127
language barriers 24, 62
language processing, natural 217–19
Latin America 25
lawyers 82, 168, 217; *see also* attorneys
layoffs 65, 67–68, 101, 108–09, 130, 132, 162, 169, 184, 190, 263
leaderless groups, experiment on 85
leadership training 77–78, 257
lean thinking in non-manufacturing sectors 132
Le Creusot 56
Lee, John 214–15
Leffingwell, William Henry 52–55, 158–62, 180, 254, 259; simplification concept of office management 52
left-wing agitation 61
legal software firms 218
Leidner, Robin 138–39
leveraged buyouts 106
Levitt, Theodore 138–39
Lewin, Kurt 76–79, 256, 276n60; his associates and disciples 76–79, 257
Lewinian applied (social) psychology 76–78, 257
Lex Machina 218
Lichtenstein, Nelson 136
limited liability company (LLC) 247
Lincoln Electric 234

Littler, Craig 36, 42
loading and unloading machine tools 91
Local Area Networks (LANs) 96, 171
Lockheed Martin 247
locomotive drivers 3
locomotives 21
logistics 133–36, 173, 239, 290
Loman, Willy 83
The Lonely Crowd (Riesman) 84, 277n90
longshoremen 239
Lordstown strike 103
Love, John F. 138
lower-level work 11
low-income service workers 140
low-level sensorimotor skills 237
low-skilled manual jobs 242
lumbering 34, 60
lumpers 239
Lynd, Robert, and Helen 67, 267n5

MacDuffie, John 127
Machine Ethics 211
machine intelligence *see* artificial intelligence
machine learning 197, 217, 241; *see also* deep learning
Machine Morality 211
machine operators 4, 47–48, 50–51, 88, 94–96, 137, 161–62, 167, 212, 214–16, 227, 232, 260, 61
machine shops 8, 22, 50, 53, 88, 121, 163
machine tending industry 93
The Machine That Changed the World (Womack, Jones and Roos) 111, 121, 131
machine tools industry 125
machinery fitters 3
machinists 39, 47, 121, 166, 178; at Midvale Steel Company in 1880, 121, 166, 178
Magaziner, Ira 165, 281n52
Magaziner Commission 125, 165, 281n52
mail-order houses 52–53, 159
maintenance workers 4, 34
Malcolm Baldrige National Quality Award 145
mammograms 210
The Man in the Gray Flannel Suit (Wilson) 277n89
managed care 198–204, 263; implications for relations between physicians, their coworkers and patients 202; managed care organizations (MCOs) 199–203; *see also* health maintenance organization (HMO); preferred provider organization (PPO)
The Managed Heart: Commercialization of Human Feeling (Hochschild) 139, 232
Management and the Worker (Roethlisberger and Dickson) 70–71, 74

management by objectives (MBO) 151–52
"management by stress" 127, 135, 152
management cybernetics 89
management innovations 110, 119, 149
management literature 80, 172
management of emotional labor in HR management 232–33
management theories 200, 232
management theorists 13, 37, 89, 99, 169–70
managerial practices to control and inspire "creative" workers 151, 154–55, 184; motivational seminars and appeals to professionalism 154
managerial prerogatives 64, 66, 104, 142, 158, 261
managerial rhetoric 64, 69, 119, 123–24, 128, 130, 146, 149–50, 158, 162, 167, 172, 182, 261; corporate relationships as *Gemeinschaft* 69; discrepancy between unitary concept and practice of employee participation 182; "empowerment" 158, 172, 261; "enhancing human resources" 164; the "new workplace" 162; trust, commitment, loyalty and "corporate responsibility" 146–47, 167–70
Manual of Standard Time Data for the Office 55
Manufacturing Consent (Burawoy) 8
Manufacturing Productivity (McKinsey Global Institute) 125
March, James G. 151, 155
marketers 126, 183
marketing *see* call centers, customer relations management (CRM)
market-oriented employment system 14
marketplace bargaining power 10–11
Mars 295n20
Marshall Aid, Technical Assistance Program in Western Europe 117
Marx, Karl 2, 12, 82, 140; his view on alienated labor 82–83, 140
Marxism 3, 5, 8, 11
Marxist theorists of bureaucracy and bureaucratic employment 11–14
Maryland 284n40
masons 3
mass production special machine-based industry 88
Massachusetts 44
Massachusetts Institute of Technology (MIT) 112, 198, 225, 276n60
mass-distribution industries 31
mass-production 31
material-handling and conveyance functions 90
Mayo, Elton 70–74, 76–78, 80, 257

326 Index

Mayoites/Mayo school 74, 78; "authoritarian Mayoism" 70
MBA in Information Technology 186
MBA students 150
McAfee, Andrew 221–22, 241–42
McCormick 28, 275n28
McDonald brothers 138
McDonaldization 139, 258, 289n34; commonalities with Fordist industrialization of work 139; neo–Weberian perspective on 139
McDonald's restaurants 138–142, 258; their equivalent of JLP teamwork and quality circles 141–42; their system of mass production 139–41; their version of just-in-time production "Made for You" 142; *see also* fast-food restaurants
McDonnell Douglas 92
McGregor, Douglas 99
"McJobs" 141
McKees Rocks strike 24
McKinsey Global Institute 125
MCOs *see* managed care organizations
MD Anderson Cancer Center 219
Mead, Margaret 277n90
Means, Gardiner C. 81, 244–45, 294ch14n2
meatpacking 47, 62–63; plant 62
mechanical engineering 32
mechanical engineers 30, 32, 96
Mechanical Turk (MTurk) 250, 266, 296n24
mechanization 3–5, 17, 55, 64, 82, 92, 94, 96, 215, 254
Medicaid 137
medical administrators 202
medical care 57, 107; *see also* health care, managed care
medical diagnoses 91, 161, 201–06, 210, 219, 222, 263–64
medical ethicists 211
medical insurance *see* health insurance
medical reengineering 198–204
medical school 201
Medicare 137
Medline 202
merger waves (1895–1904 and 1919–1929) 28, 31–32
Merton, Robert K. 11
Metal Workers' Union in Sweden 129
metallurgical engineers/metallurgists 22, 32
metalworking industries 21, 52, 58, 89–90, 255
Methods, Timing, Measurement Association 55
Mexican Americans 68
Mexicans 63
Mexico 181

M-form structure (multi-divisional form) of corporation 108, 280n35
Microsoft 179, 185–88, 288n16, 295n14, 296n26; its call center in Canadian Maritimes 179; permatemps and class-action lawsuit against Microsoft 187–88
mid–Atlantic states, traditional industrial areas in 21
middle-class: professionals 15; reformers 14
middle-level managers 108, 262
middle-skilled routine jobs 242
Midwest 28, 67
militant labor 69
military contractors 247
military equipment 91
military-industrial complex 73
military Keynesianism 73
militias 24, 69
Miller, Arthur 83
Mills, C. Wright 74–76, 81–84, 86–87, 140, 257–58, 267n5
Milwaukee 90, 284n39
Mindless: Why Smarter Machines Are Making Dumber Humans (Head) 224
mines 33
minimum wage 142–43, 250, 284n39, 296n23; collective actions to raise 142–43
mining 33–34, 60; *see also* coal industry
mining engineers 32–33
Mississippi 284n40
Missoula, Montana 284n39
MIT *see* Massachusetts Institute of Technology
MIT Commission on Industrial Productivity 165
Mobil Oil 102
Model T production *see* Ford Motor Company
The Modern Corporation and Private Property (Berle and Means) 81, 244
modern organization theory 12
modern sociologists' view of bureaucracy 12–13
Modern Times (1936 comedy film) 271n3
modular production 114, 133, 246–47, 260
mom-and-pop store owners 82
Mondragon cooperatives in Basque region of Spain 234
monitoring 7, 39, 93, 126, 136, 160, 162–63, 165, 172,, 174–77, 179–80, 195–96, 203, 224, 30, 261–62; all-pervasive forms of 39, 126, 135, 174, 179, 228, 261; and control 126, 160, 162, 172, 174, 176, 195, 226, 227–28, 230; embedded in Computer Business Systems 227; software 176, 179, 224, 228, 230; technology 136, 180; *see also* surveillance

Montgomery Ward 53
Moore's Law 215
"moral capitalism," workers' belief in 66–67, 255
moral hazard concept 107
morale 15, 73, 76–78, 84, 105, 123, 256–57
morality 84
Moravec, Hans 237, 241
Moravec's paradox 237–38
motivation: of convicts 271n40; of employers 24, 101; of workers 43–41, 69, 80, 84, 110, 256
motor vehicle industry *see* auto industry
Mountain View, Montana 284n39
multi-division industries 29
multi-skilling 111, 122, 125, 131
multifunctional teams 155
Muncie, Indiana 67
muscular fatigue 55
mutual funds 106, 245
Myers-Briggs test 170, 231, 293n19
Myrdal, Gunnar 277n72

Nadin, Mihai 213
Narrative Science, Inc. 221
National Association of Manufacturers (NAM) 26, 100
National Bureau of Economic Research (NBER) 100
National Civic Federation (NCF) 26, 57
National Health Service legislation, defeat of 198
National Labor Relations Act 27, 69, 235
National Science Foundation 216
National Training Laboratories 77, 86, 99
natural gas industry 89
"natural soldiering" 35
Navy contracts 89
NEC 116
negative income tax 252
neo–Fordism 131
neoliberalism 100, 193
neo–Taylorism 132
Netherlands 211, 286n11
Netscape Navigator 172
neural networks, artificial 217, 292n29; *see also* deep learning
neurobiologists 212
New Deal era 24, 45, 234–35, 255
New Deal order 16, 235, 256
New Deal policies and social legislation 67–68, 235, 256
New Deal–style collective action 235
New England: textile industry 19; traditional industrial areas in 21
New Jersey 62, 68, 91, 284n40
New Left 100, 279n6

"new little men" 83
The New Men of Power (Mills) 75
"new nonunion model" 101–02, 108, 260, 262
New United Motor Manufacturing Inc. (NUMMI) 127, 282n75
New York City 27, 183, 185, 190
New York State 143, 205, 284n40
New Zealand 26
Nike Corporation 246, 295n11
Nikefication 18, 246–47, 251, 266
1984 (Orwell) 86
1970 census 83
1960 census 83
Nissan 111, 115, 119, 123, 125–26, 127, 129
Nixon, Richard 103
Nixon administration 103
Noble, David 278n12
no-collar workers 184, 188–91
no-layoff policies 109, 234, 282n75
Northeast, U.S. 28
Northwestern Europe 59, 255, 275n21
Northrop Grumman 247
Norton, David 194–95
Norway 234
NSA (National Security Agency) 219
nurses 97, 140, 199, 203–04, 218, 290n75
nurses' aides 97
nursing home aides 184
Nye, David 118, 120, 126

Obama, Barack 203, 252, 297n30
off-the-shelf software 186
The Office 55
Office Control and Management 55
Office Economist 55
Office Equipment Digest 55
Office Management: Principles and Practice (Leffingwell) 52
Office Management (periodical) 55
office work 3, 16–18, 53, 55, 83, 95, 147, 158, 167, 172, 176, 187, 192, 210, 254, 264; in cubicles 164, 176, 180; proliferation of fax machines, voice mail, databases and spreadsheets 164; reengineering and enhanced industrialization of 158–167
office workers 18, 167, 176, 187, 210; back office workers 165–66; front office workers 164, 176–77, 180; individual bargaining as corporate employees 187
offshore tax havens 249
offshoring 16, 181, 190, 192, 243, 247, 251, 265, 293n31; electronic form of 243; *see also* outsourcing
Ohno, Taiichi 118, 122, 124–25, 130, 201
oil industry 31, 89, 198

on-the-job-training 54
open shop drive 28
open shop movement 26
open shop policy 61
open-source platform software 296n26
operations management 89
operations research (OR) 89, 134, 151
Oracle Corporation 225–26, 237
order fulfillment, business process of 53, 159, 173; *see also* mail-order industry
The Organization Man (Whyte) 84, 257
organizational innovations 16, 47, 88, 104–05, 115, 126, 142
Orwell, George 86
other-directed social type 85–86
outsourcing 16, 133–34, 136, 152, 173, 187, 190, 231, 246, 253, 265–66; *see also* offshoring
overseers, of textile mills 19–20, 22
overtime 127, 132

paid vacations 65
pan–Slavic "hunky" jobs 34
panoptic power 175–76; *see also* monitoring, surveillance, panopticons
panopticons 135, 175, 228, 261; digital 135, 228, 261, 287n11; Jeremy Bentham's architectural plan of panoptic prison 135, 175; modern, high-security prison as high-tech panopticon 175; monitoring regime 227; panopticon-like buildings resembling Bentham's design 286–87n11
paper replica of production 30
Paperwork Simplification 55
paralegals 217
Parasuraman, Raja 214
Parker, Mike 127, 130, 282n75
Parsons, Talcott 294ch14n2
participative work groups 78, 99–100, 126, 257
participatory management 99
part-time work 132, 189
part-time workers 51
patent lawsuits 218
pattern recognition 217, 237, 241
payroll processing software 241
peer pressure on employees 36, 64, 127–28, 154, 182
pensions 9, 58–59, 65, 106–07, 187–88, 198, 245, 251, 263, 295
people analytics software 231
Perlman, Selig 67
personal biological sensors and health-monitoring apps 204, 297n3
personality tests 86, 170, 231, 258; automated versions of 231; *see also* psychological tests

personnel departments 15, 25, 41, 63, 84, 87, 105, 128; differences between personnel department and production division 15, 105
personnel management 14–15; *see also* human resource management (HRM)
pet food 247
pharmaceutical companies 204, 207
pharmaceuticals 247
Philippines 181
physicians 82, 96–97, 198–200, 202–06, 218–19, 222, 224–25, 227, 263; *see also* doctors
physiologists 212
piece rates 36, 43, 255
piece work 8, 39
piecemeal remuneration 63
piece-rate schemes/systems 36, 43, 63, 127
Pierce, Richard J. 146–47
Piggly Wiggly stores 16
Pilot Corp. 295n20
Piore, Michael 110–11, 125
Pizza Hut 141
plagiarism detection 197
plant superintendents 14
platform capitalism 250
platforms, online *see* digital platforms
plating plants 93
plumbers 241
pneumatic special-purpose production 90
Polanyi, Karl 14; his "double movement" of two great organizing principles in society 14, 16
police 24, 25, 27, 42, 156; private 25–26
political and capitalist-industrial conditions in U.S. 234, 266
politics 16, 215, 221, 234–35, 250, 252, 269n16, 270n31, 277n90; and automated system designs 215; hegemonic production politics 8; Northern European–style politics 235; "social democratic tinge" of post–World War II U.S. politics 235
The Politics of Production (Burawoy) 8
post–Fordism 131
postindustrial economy 184, 188
postindustrial society 12
potters 19
pottery industry 21–22
power, legitimate 12
practical nurses 97
precariat 251
precision casting 89
predictive algorithms 204, 217, 220; pre-digital office technologies 159
preferential shop *see* closed shop
Preferred Provider Organization (PPO) 199
prerogatives of craft/skilled workers 8, 102

The Principles of Scientific Management (Taylor) 32
printing industry 93
private ownership, of companies 248
privatization 16
process chain, virtual 226
process improvement metrics 226
process innovation 37
process specialization 30
Procter & Gamble 68, 102, 256, 293n19
producerism 3; vs. managerialist view of labor 35
product specialization 30
production control clerks 31
production control systems 30
production division 15
production-engineering specialists 6
production lines 7; *see also* assembly lines
production managers 8, 14–15, 22, 102, 105
production output: quotas 21, 23, 36, 40, 127, 129; restriction 2, 24, 40, 43; target 8
professional and administrative middle class 224
Professional Employees Department of AFL-CIO 187
professional work 163–64, 217–18, 265
professional workers 11, 187, 194
profit-sharing programs 49, 57, 59, 73, 251
programmable technologies 113
programming languages: object-oriented, general-purpose 186; procedural 186
Progressive education 79
Progressive Era 58
Progressive reform movement 15, 44, 79, 257, 273n35
project management 186
promotion ladders 58, 255; *see also* career ladders; job ladders
Protestant work ethic 169
proto-industry *see* putting-out system
prototyping 242, 294n18
Proudhon, Pierre-Joseph 3
psychiatry 73
psychological tests 170; *see also* personality tests
psychologists 72, 76, 86, 100, 145, 170, 212, 232, 258, 277n65
psychology 73, 77–78; industrial 73, 76, 79, 256
public safety net 137
public service organizations 42
Publix 295n20
puddlers (in iron and steel industry) 21
Pullman Company 28, 270n31; strike (1894, 28, 270n31
putting-out system 19–20, 148, 265

quality circles (or quality control circles) 102, 110, 123, 126, 142, 144–45, 182
quality control 22, 118–20, 122, 134, 145, 152–53, 169, 239
quality inspector 38
Quality of Working Life (QWL) movement 102–04, 258
"quantified self" gadgets and apps 297n3
Quill 221

race 33–34, 166–67
racial communities 63, 65
racial divisions 33–34, 169
"racial knowledge" and organization of production 33
rag trade 114
rail mills 20
railroads 28–32, 44, 46, 58, 134, 270n31; elimination of brakemen, rear flagmen, and on-board maintenance crews 134; expansion of system 20; workers' strikes 11, 28, 270n31
RAND Corporation 203–04
rationalization 4, 10–11, 17, 35, 44, 53, 83, 95, 105–07, 112, 116, 119, 128, 137, 139, 151, 153, 164, 176, 224, 235, 252–54, 285n33, 289n34; industrial 11, 17, 112, 137, 224, 235, 252, 254; of interactive service work 137–39; of layers of management and intermediate technical labor 106
rational-legal authority 12
Raytheon 247
Reagan, Ronald 104, 105, 245
real-time information, about employee performance 159, 225
receptionists 140, 167
recession: of 1990–9 148; of 2001 and ensuing "jobless recovery" 190
recognition, visual 240–41
recruitment 26, 41, 63, 89, 124, 128, 148, 273n36
reduced "observability" in large, complex organization (pre-digital era) 39
Reengineering the Corporation: A Manifesto for Business Revolution (Hammer and Champy) 149, 159, 161
reengineers 153, 158–60, 162–63, 165–66, 173–74, 180, 201–02, 263–64
refinery 93
"reflexivity" and the "informating" process 113
Reich, Robert 183–84
religious services, compulsory 57
Remote Control Operation (RCO) 134
repair boss 38
repairmen 241
repetitive strain injuries (RSI) 165

repression, political 25–27
Republicans 294n31
Research Assessment Exercise (RAE) in United Kingdom 194, 289n39
Research Center for Group Dynamics at MIT 276n60
restaurant workers 140
retail 3, 50–52, 133, 135–38, 219, 224, 234, 239–40, 245, 248, 254, 258, 264; food trading 52; large companies 17, 239–40, 245, 248, 264; online 239; warehouses 135–36, 239–40; workers in 3, 16, 51, 137
Rethink Robotics 238
retirement security *see* pensions
A Revolution in Manufacturing: The SMED System (Shingo) 121
Riesman, David 84–85, 277n90
Rise of the Robots (Ford) 197, 236
Ritzer, George 139, 258
River Rouge plant 32, 47, 52, 117–18, 174, 246
road transportation and delivery: technologies to track and control workers in 134–35
robotics 237–238, 240; *see also* automation; robots
robots 91, 141, 219, 221, 237–42, 264; with machine vision capability 237; towel-folding robot 241; *see also* automation
Rockefeller, John D. 32
Roethlisberger, Fritz J. 71–72, 74
Rogers, Jackie Krasas 140
rollers (in iron and steel industry) 21
Roos, Daniel 112, 123, 131
Roosevelt, Franklin Delano 67, 80, 88, 235; "arsenal of democracy" 88
Roosevelt administration 235
Rose, Michael 8–9
Ross, Andrew 176, 184, 190
rote information processing 242
Royle, Tony 142

Saarbrücken, Germany 225
Sabel, Charles 110–11, 125
safety alert 216
safety belt 134
safety checks of cars 131
safety, in work 29, 62, 122, 124, 126, 142, 239
safety rules 29
Saito, Shoichi 117
salary: for employees 56, 58; for professional managers 105
sales and marketing *see* call centers, customer relations management (CRM)
sales attendants 184
Samsung 248

San Francisco 284n40, 287n11
Sanders, Bernie 284n39, 293n31
SAP Corporation 173, 176, 225
S.C. Johnson 102, 295n20
Scheer AG 225, 228
Schlosser, Eric 142
schools 54, 60, 79, 122, 185, 197, 257
Schor, Juliet 296n26
scientific management 2–5, 32–33, 43–45, 49–50, 52–53, 55, 57, 69, 76, 89, 111, 122, 125–26, 139, 145, 153, 156, 158–60, 162, 165, 174, 180, 231, 253–56, 259, 265, 272n5; its principles 36–42, 274n61; *see also* Taylorism
screw machines 90
Sears Roebuck 68, 73, 78, 101, 155, 245, 256; personnel research department 73
Seattle, Washington 187
The Second Industrial Divide (Piore and Sabel) 110
secondary education 224
secretaries 89, 140
security guards 61, 167, 184; male 167
segmented labor 114, 169
SEIU *see* Service Employees International Union
self-driving cars 222
self-employment: contract work 132; freelancers 148, 193
self-improvement, individual 84
self-service: customers 51; retailing 50–52, 254
semiconductors 237
semiskilled workers 24, 31, 47, 62, 75, 201, 253–54, 265
senior executives 195, 224, 230–31; decisive role in setting rules of CBSs 234–35; preferences for CBS process settings 227
seniority-based layoff system 23
seniority rules 58, 255
Sennett, Richard 189–90, 288n20, 288n22
sensitivity training 77, 99, 102, 150, 279n3
sequence-control mechanisms 90
service economy 159, 184, 224, 226, 230, 234, 292n18
Service Employees International Union (SEIU) 143, 205
service industries 52, 55, 100, 102, 158, 174, 198–99, 259
servo system 89
servomechanisms 91, 278n6
setting-up boss 38
settlements: houses 79, 257, schools 79, 25; work 58, 79, 257; *see also* social workers
setup men 50, 88
setup operations 121
setup times 121

Index

shareholder-type system of capitalism 183
shareholders 105, 107, 245, 249, 262; bedrock for managers of new public corporations 107; shareholder sovereignty vs. stakeholder orientation 16; shareholder value movement 105–06, 245, 265; *see also* stockholders
sharing economy 250, 296n25
shelf-stocking 51–52, 240, 251
Shingo, Shigeo 121, 125, 130
shoe factories 20
shop floor games 8
Shop Management (Taylor) 32
shop management movement 30
sickness pay 65
Silicon Alley 183, 185, 190
Silicon Valley 165, 183, 185, 189–90, 265
Silver, Beverly 10
Simon, Herbert A. 151, 155
simple control 6, 13
single-purpose machines 47, 50, 138–39, 254, 259
Skidelsky, Robert 293n26
skilled workers 5, 21–22, 31, 35–36, 44, 46, 50–51, 58–60, 95, 102, 114, 184, 220, 253, 255, 264; prerogatives 102; shop culture 21; steelworkers 22; tradesmen 19
Slaughter, Jane 127, 130, 282n75
slave labor 267n1
slave plantations 29, 271n40
Sloan, Alfred P. 47, 80, 89
Sloanism 49, 111, 260
slowdowns 24
small batch production runs 112
small batches of nonstandardized product, craft-based 20, 88
small-scale merchants 82
SMED (Single Minute Exchange of Die) system 121
Smith, Adam 162
social activism: targeting public corporations 248–49
social change, planned 77
social classes preindustrial 27
"social control," debate about 277n68
social discipline 48; *see also* discipline of workers; work discipline
social engineering 16, 49, 74, 76–79, 99, 257
social engineers 74, 86
social ethic: legitimizing pressure of society against individual 86, 257, 257
social psychologists 78, 170
social psychology 16, 73, 76, 79, 150, 257
social reformers 14
social responsibilities in local community: corporations assuming 62
Social Security 68, 186, 198, 235, 256

Social Security number 186
social theorists of bureaucratic employment 11–13
social welfare functions of U.S. corporations 16
social workers 15, 58–59, 201
socialists 3, 15, 31, 293n31
socio-drama 77
sociologists 12, 73–74, 86, 116, 212, 258, 277n68, 295n2
sociology 74, 76, 79, 120, 150; of work 120
sociometry 69
sociotechnical principles and practices 101, 156, 260, 280n1; used as form of control 136; *see also* teamwork in auto industry
soft power (persuasion) 68
Sony Corporation 247–48, 293n19
Sorensen, Charles E. 273n45
South Africa 32
Southeast Asia 237
Southern Europe 59, 235, 255, 275n21
Soviet of Technicians (Veblen) 45
Special Conference Committee (SCC) 60–62, 275n15
special (or single)-purpose machines 50, 88, 90, 254
specialist service workers 138
SpeechNow.org v. FEC 296n22
speech recognition 182
speed boss 38
speed-ups 55, 58, 126–27, 130, 134, 152, 155, 164, 166, 177, 181, 186, 201, 207, 220, 224, 255, 259, 263
spell checker 209
Sperry Gyroscope Company 92
Spock, Benjamin 79
SPORH (Stops Per On-Road Hour) 135
staff departments, central 31
stakeholders 107, 147, 195–96, 262; businesses' orientation toward 16
standard job time 39
Standard Oil (Exxon) 245, 256
Standard Oil of New Jersey 62, 68, 280n35
Stanford University 218, 232
Staples 240
state laws: limiting hostile takeovers of domestic corporations 105
state troops 25
statistical process control 116–17, 145, 153; vs. traditional quality control 153
stealing time/"time theft" 135–36
steam-powered machinery 20
steel industry 20–22, 24, 31, 34, 43, 62–63, 125, 128, 198, 230, 272n5
stereotypes: ignorant immigrant 57, 59; lazy, greedy, untrustworthy worker 14, 57, 59; woman as empathetic and nurturing 59

stints 24
stock bonuses 58
stock market *see* shareholders
stockholders 81, 106, 294; *see also* shareholders
stopwatch, use of 36, 44, 47
straw bosses 48
strike insurance 63
strikes 7, 11, 24–25, 28, 43–45, 57, 59–60, 62, 64, 75, 103, 142, 255, 270n31; strikebreakers 24, 27, 61, 69
structure of control over task performance 36–39, 42, 45
structured programming 186
subcontractors 133, 139, 193
suggestion programs 105, 182
Sun Systems 185
Sunstein, Cass R. 108
SUNY University at Albany School of Public Health 205
Super PACs (Political Action Committees) 250, 296n22
Supervalu 245
supervision system 9
supervisors 39, 43, 62–63, 69–70, 74, 77, 94, 101, 104, 126–27, 134–36, 146, 149, 154, 156, 159–60, 162, 166, 175, 177, 180, 182, 256, 271n40; positions 3, 95; training 43, 73
supervisory management 77
Supplemental Nutritional Assistance Program (SNAP) 137
supply chain management (SCM) 173–75, 246
surplus value 8, 83
surveillance 20, 135, 156, 175–78, 204, 261, 297n3; personal surveillance techniques 297n3; *see also* monitoring
Survey Research Center at the University of Michigan 276n60
sweating *see* speed-up
Sweden 128–29
Swedish sociotechnical systems 280n1; *see also* teamwork, Swedish model in auto industry
Swift 62, 65
"symbolic analysts" 183–84
SyNAPSE 292n26
Syracuse 284n39
systematic management 29–32, 35, 37, 45, 253; *see also* scientific management
"systematic soldiering" 2, 36, 40
systems analysts 185–86

tacit (or procedural) knowledge 153–56, 182, 207, 213, 272n11
Taiwanese companies in China 237

takt system 115
Target 245
task performance 3, 36, 39, 45; *see also* employee performance
TaskRabbit 296n24
Taylor, Frederick Winslow 2, 32, 35–45, 52–55, 88–89, 99, 119, 121, 125, 151–52, 154, 162, 166, 173, 176, 178, 231, 253–54, 272n5, 273n35, 273n45
Taylor Society 44–45, 273n37
Taylorism 2, 3, 4, 5, 29, 32–33, 35–45, 47, 50, 52–56, 58, 75–76, 81, 88–89, 100, 119, 121, 124–26, 130–32, 135–37, 139, 151–55, 157–59, 162, 166, 171, 173, 176, 178, 204, 231, 253–55, 258, 260, 263, 272n5, 272n6, 273n45; divorce of planning and doing 37; inadequacy to manage "creative" workers 151; maximum work/job fragmentation, principle of 37; minimum interaction model of employment relations 40–42; planning department 37–39; planning staff 54, 63; and "racialization" of labor systems 33–34; reluctance of managers, supervisors and foremen to embrace Taylorism 43; separation of conception from execution of production process 2–3, 41, 47; as set of managerial practices 36–42; task control, principle of 37–38; Taylor-Barth slide rule 162; technocratic theme 45; wage/effort exchange system 39–40; work study 40; *see also* scientific management
team spirit 5, 168; *see also* esprit de corps; morale
teamwork 87, 100–01, 110, 120, 123–24, 127–29, 141–42, 145, 147, 150, 182, 258, 261, 282n75; Swedish vs. Japanese model in auto industry 128–30; *see also* Japanese Lean Production
technical intelligentsia 45
technological change, skill-biased 241–42
technological determinism 113
technological unemployment 236
technology-first automation 211, 233, 264
technology-first design of expert systems 211
telecommuters 148
telematics 134
telephone operators 167
telephone triage system 201
temp agencies 188, 288n16
temporary workers 132, 148, 187–88
Texas Instruments 102
Textbook of Office Management (Leffingwell) 52
textile firms of Lancashire, UK 48, 56
textile industry 19–20, 22, 56, 60, 76, 93
Thatcher, Margaret 194

thatchers 3
theory of skill-biased technological change 241–42
Theory X vs. Theory Y management 99
"Third Italy" 110–11
Thompson Products 67, 102
Thompson-Ramo-Wooldridge (TRW) 78, 102
3M Corporation 108
thrift clubs 57
time-and-motion studies 2, 10, 36–37, 39, 55, 62, 124, 135–36
"to informate" (or "informating") 113, 162–63, 174, 215, 263
Tokyo 116
Toro 107
Toshiba call center 179
Total Quality Control (TQC) 118, 120, 122, 134, 152
Total Quality Management (TQM) 145–48, 152–53, 155–58, 168–69, 261; its core values and basic features 145–46; TQM combined with BPR, and tendency toward transforming all workers into "design workers" 155
toy makers 114
Toyoda, Eiji 117
Toyota company 111, 115, 117–19, 121–22, 124–31, 135, 137, 201, 282n75; Corolla car 130–31; first-line management's strengthened role in production system 119, 129; personnel selection system 128; recalls 119, 131
Toyota-GM joint venture see New United Motor Manufacturing Inc. (NUMMI)
Toyota-style clinic 201, 203
Toys "R" Us 240
trade unions see unions
tradition-directed social type 84–85
training 3, 9, 10, 12, 40–41, 43, 51, 54, 57, 63, 70, 73, 77–78, 93, 95, 101–02, 108, 113, 122, 137, 145, 147, 167, 222, 242, 251, 254, 257, 262, 264, 279n20, 280n1
training groups (T-groups) 99
transfer devices 47
transfer lines 90
transfer machines 90
transportation industry 198
truck drivers 134
Trump, Donald 293n31
trust relationship 9, 11, 77, 146, 162, 167–68, 182, 189–90; culture of mistrust 228; diminished trust and commitment among younger generation of workers in high tech, finance, and media 189–90; high-trust work situations 182; historically low-trust, low-discretion system in American

industry 9; shareholder-type capitalism and low trust 183
Trust (Fukuyma) 168
TRW *see* Thompson-Ramo-Wooldridge
turnkey manufacturers and distributors 247
turnover, of labor 24, 41–42, 57, 64, 124, 137, 181, 245–46
typists 52, 159

Uber 250–51, 266, 295n14, 296n23, 296n26
Uberization 251
Uddevalla, Sweden 128
unemployment 11, 23–24, 41, 107–08, 128, 184, 236, 252, 262, 293n31, 296n23
Unimate 91
union avoidance activities 73, 101, 103–04; *see also* union busting
union busting 61, 100, 181, 262; *see also* union avoidance activities
union density 22, 252
Union Pacific Railroad 44
unionism 14, 22, 34, 56, 61, 69, 71, 99, 102, 130; *see also* unions
unionization 14, 23, 68, 187, 191; obstacles to neo craft-based unionization 191; *see also* unions
unionized firms 8, 17, 73, 98, 101–02, 111, 116, 169, 259
unions 5, 7–10, 13–16, 22–24, 26–27, 44–45, 57–62, 64, 66–69, 71–76, 78, 83, 91, 98, 99, 102, 04, 116, 119, 126, 129, 142–43, 156, 181, 187, 191, 198, 204–05, 252–56, 262, 270n31, 273n36, 273n37, 279n20, 293n26, 296n22; countervailing power against foremen and employer 23; exclusive craft unions 23, 26; inclusive industrial unions 26; leaders 44, 57, 75, 103, 270n71; organizers 60; organizing drives 101; organizing of professional and high-skilled technical workers 187; resistance to behavioral science in 1950s and 1960, 99; union stewards 91; unionized doctors and other professionals 204–05, 262
unitary team concept 127
unitary (single-status) employment systems 101–02, 260
United Auto Workers (UAW) 103–04, 126, 279n20, 282n75
United Kingdom 127, 194, 292n18; *see also* Great Britain
United Nations 55
U.S. Bureau of Labor Statistics 15, 191
U.S. Call Center Worker and Consumer Protection Act (2016) 181, 287n30
U.S. Chamber of Commerce 100

U.S. Congress Office of Technology Assessment 147
U.S. Department of Commerce 145, 185
U.S. Department of Defense 116, 171
U.S. Department of Health and Human Services 203
U.S. Department of Health, Education, and Welfare 102
U.S. Department of Justice 105
U.S. Department of Labor 72
U.S. House of Representatives 44
U.S. Steel 26, 28, 58, 61–62, 65, 67, 100, 185, 245, 273n36, 275n28
U.S. Supreme Court 105, 250, 296n22
United Technologies 247
University of Akron College of Education 197
University of California at San Diego 194
University of Texas 219
university professors 193–97, 205, 218, 227; reengineering of their work 193–97; see also higher education
unskilled workers 21, 23–24, 31, 37, 45, 47–50, 52, 60, 75, 83, 88–89, 124, 201, 239, 253–54, 257, 265, 270n31, 272n11
UPS (United Parcel Service) 134–35, 245
upskilling 4, 51, 112, 114, 164; of retail customers 51
utilities 29

value-added activities, higher vs. lower 246
value-adding workers 151, 154–55, 184
van der Linden, Marcel 270n40
The Vanishing American Corporation (Davis) 246
Vauxhall (General Motors UK) Astra 131
Veblen, Thorstein 45, 273n36
venture-capital firms 217
Verizon 245
Veterans Administration clinic 206
Vinkhuyzen, Erik 287n18
violence, to resist or repress labor 25, 27, 44, 69, 235, 255, 270n31
virtual organizations 154
virtualization of industries 247; factories 265
Vizio 248
voice-response systems 182
voice-to-voice interactive service work 138; see also call centers
Volvo plants in Sweden 128
Voting Rights Act 235

wage bargaining 78
wage determination 23
wage formulas 2
wage incentives/incentive plans 63–65
wage scales 23, 39

Wagner Enneagram Personality Style Scales (WEPPS) 231, 293n19
waiters 184
Walgreens 240, 245
Wall Street 29, 52, 153, 207, 217, 246, 291n90; crash (1929, 52; crash (2008, 207
Walmart (or Wal-Mart) 135–37, 143, 192, 224, 234, 245–46, 283n8, 293n26; associates 136, 224; "managerial authoritarianism" 136; Supercenters 246; system of penalties 136, 283n8; Task Manager 136
Warren, Nancy 145
Washington, D.C. 284n40
Washington Alliance of Technology Workers 187
Washington State 187, 284n39
Watertown Arsenal, Massachusetts 44
Watson (IBM super computer system) 218–20, 222, 264; repurposed as diagnostic tool 218; vs. human diagnosticians 222; WatsonPaths 220
Weber, Max 12, 169; concept of bureaucracy 12, 42; general view of power relations or "domination" 12
Weberian theorists of bureaucratic employment 11–12
welders 89
welfare capitalism 16–17, 56–61, 66–69, 77, 98, 100–02, 155, 254–56, 259–60, 263; activities aimed at creating productive middle-class citizens 59; in distress 107, 08; its modern form 57, 68–69, 98, 100–02, 260; "modern manors" 57, 68; and Quaker businessmen 56; and raised expectations among workers 66; silent transformation into its modern variant 68; and Social Gospel influence 56
welfare capitalist firms 8, 10, 69, 108–09, 256, 260, 262; and anti-union strategies 99; dualist policies to preserve career jobs 108; vanguard and laggard employers 67–68, 275n28; and view of "industrial community" 10; welfare provisions 2, 10, 42, 48, 56–57, 59–60, 62–63, 65, 67–68, 251, 263; welfare services outside the workplace 42, 58, 255
welfare work 24, 56, 58–59, 77, 255; see also welfare capitalism; welfare capitalist firms
welfare workers 59; see also social workers
Western Electric Company 62–63, 65–66, 70–73, 116; intensive interviewing of employees 70; personnel counseling section 70
Western Europe 26, 116–17, 190
Westinghouse Electric Company 245, 273n36

Index

Whalen, Jack 287n18
White Collar (Mills) 75, 81, 257
white-collar economy 226
white-collar middle class 187, 293n31
white-collar sector 193
white-collar workers 1, 11, 81–84, 87, 98, 103, 172, 187, 194, 224, 231, 257
white-collar workplaces 176, 226
wholesale 136, 224
Whyte, William H., Jr. 84, 86–87, 169–70, 257–58, 277n89
Willard, F.W. 70
Wilson, Sloan 277n89
Wilson, Woodrow 273n33
Wired Area Networks (WANs) 171
Womack, James P. 112, 123, 131
women 20, 45, 49, 51, 59, 62–63, 65, 68, 72, 75, 83, 98, 132, 138, 166–67, 169, 255, 259
word processing 164, 209, 241
work: nonstandard 132, 189; routinization of 11, 38, 41
Work and Authority in Industry (Bendix) 12
work design 42, 151
work discipline 48–49; *see also* discipline of workers, disciplining workers
work effort, normative basis of 39
work ethic 57, 84, 103, 167, 257
work groups 33, 40–41, 64, 66, 71, 78, 110, 122, 127, 154, 157–58, 256
Work in America (U.S. Department of Health, Education, and Welfare) 102, 258
The Work of Nations (Reich) 183
work organization 1, 9, 21, 31, 40, 42, 94, 100–01, 163–64, 182, 244–45, 252–53
work redesign 105
work rules 2, 6, 21
work stoppages 11

work teams 40, 43, 103, 117, 123, 129, 158, 230; decision-making prerogatives 129; *see also* teamwork; work groups
worker empowerment 280n20
workers' bargaining power 10–11
workers' collective efforts at self-improvement 59
workers' control 2, 46, 100, 114, 134, 141, 266; as envisioned by New Left labor activists 100, 279n6
workers' councils 61
workers' rights 72, 252, 293n31
working hours 23, 122, 124, 146, 189, 194, 297n3
workplace bargaining power 10–11
workplace control 204, 252, 262; medical professionals' calls for 204, 262
World War I 15, 22, 24–25, 27, 44, 47, 53, 57, 61, 254, 273n33
World War II 17, 72, 80–81, 88–89, 92, 99, 105, 115–16, 118, 194, 212, 216, 235, 251, 273n33, 292n1
Wright, Erik Olin 10

Xerox 231, 234; employee-friendly expert systems 234; PARC 287n18
x-rays 210, 279n31

yellow-dog contracts 26
yeoman democracy, dream of revival of 111
Yerkes-Dodson law 214
YMCA (Young Men's Christian Association) 79, 257
Youngstown Sheet & Tube 61

Zuboff, Shoshana 112–13, 162–63, 174–75, 215, 263, 274n61

www.ingramcontent.com/pod-product-compliance
Lightning Source LLC
Chambersburg PA
CBHW051207300426
44116CB00006B/463